THE PRESS

THE PRESS

A·J·LIEBLING

WITH AN INTRODUCTION BY JEAN STAFFORD

PANTHEON BOOKS: NEW YORK

Library of Congress Cataloging in Publication Data

Liebling, Abbott Joseph, 1904-1963.
  The press.

Reprint of the 1975 ed. published by Ballantine books, New York.
Includes index.
1. Press—United States—Addresses, essays, lectures. 2. Newspaper
publishing—United States—Addresses, essays, lectures. I. Title.
[PN4867.L48 1981]   071′.3   80-8924
ISBN 0-394-74849-2   AACR1

Manufactured in the United States of America

First Pantheon Books Edition 1981

Contents

Note. A Dateline following the title of an article refers to the *New Yorker* issue in which that article first appeared.

Introduction

Soon after my husband, A. J. Liebling, died on December 28, 1963, William Shawn, editor of *The New Yorker,* wrote, "Liebling joined the staff of *The New Yorker* as a reporter in 1935, and in the next twenty-eight years he wrote a prodigious number of articles—in the hundreds—for this magazine. As time went on, he wrote with greater and greater elegance, and the journalism he was ostensibly doing somehow turned into the kind of writing that endures." In 1947, Liebling collected some of his articles and published them in a book entitled *The Wayward Pressman* and, in 1949, he brought out another book, *Mink and Red Herring, the Wayward Pressman's Casebook.* These were followed by *The Press,* in 1961, and a revised edition of the same book in 1964. In putting together this new edition, I have added a good deal of material that did not appear in any of the earlier books, and I have made some changes in the order of the contents. But I have put in no explanatory footnotes, because, with Mr. Shawn, I agree that this is writing that endures and stands on its own without exegesis.

Besides the added articles on the press, I have included, as well, a tribute Joe wrote to Harold Ross, the founder of *The New Yorker,* without whose magazine this book would not exist. Something similar to it might, but I doubt that any other magazine of the past, the present or the future could have offered the latitude and the hospitality necessary for the fruition of Liebling's idiosyncratic talents.

Ross had been a newspaper man and he remained a newspaper buff. Comment on and criticism of the press began in the second issue of *The New Yorker,* February 28, 1925. The heading for the department was "Behind the News." It was changed several times: "The Current Press," "In the Press," "Reviewing the News," "The Press in Review." On December 24, 1927, it became "The Wayward Press," and the first article, "Fruits for a Dull Monday," was signed by Guy Fawkes, the pseudonym Robert Benchley chose for reasons I wish I knew. Between then and January, 24, 1939, he wrote more than ninety "Wayward Press" pieces on subjects ranging from Einstein's theory of relativity (1929) to the abdication of Edward VIII in 1936. Before and during the Guy Fawkes days, other contributors coolly viewed the news; among them were Horace Greeley, Jr., St. Clair McKelway, Wolcott Gibbs, and John Lardner.

A. J. Liebling became the principal Wayward Press-man with a piece in the issue of May 19, 1945; his last piece, the eighty-second, was run on April 13, 1963. During those years, except for one contribution by John Lardner, one by John Hersey, one by Faubion Bowers, one by Joseph Alsop, and ten by E. J. Kahn, the Wayard Press pieces were all Liebling's. The department was discontinued after his death.

To many readers, and especially to the young, dozens, probably hundreds of the names in the following pages will be unfamiliar. It seems impossible that Colonel Robert Rutherford McCormick, xenophobic overlord of the Chicago *Daily Tribune,* or that Westbrook Pegler, whose tempestuous syndicated column showed up all over the nation for decades, can have been forgotten—can, indeed, have never heretofore been heard of. But some reputations attract enshrouding cobwebs with astonishing speed; having once beguiled or outraged, they can, dusted off, do so again and a tour of galleries of old rogues, demigods, and heroes can divert and instruct. Just as a lot of the names will be strange, so a lot of the events Liebling analyzes will sound quaint to the reader. Yet they, too, have their relevance, however oblique. Discussing the Long Island Railroad Strike of 1960, Liebling wrote, "The cost of each of my transitions from country to city is normally $9.67. This is divided into $2 for the taxi from my house to the East Hampton station . . . ; $7.52 for railroad fare, including parlor-car seat; and a fifteen-cent subway token for the ride between Pennsylvania Station and Times Square, which

is a block and a half away from my office. The fare
by day coach is $4.85, but since the journey lasts just
under three hours, I indulge myself." One day after
the trains had stopped, he had an engagement in the
city which he could not break, and he went in by taxi
for $45. A couple of weeks later "I . . . I had to go in
to town again, and this time I flew, incurring an expense of $3.50, instead of $2 for the initial taxi (the
airport is five miles farther from my house than the
railroad station; of $18, instead of $7.52 for the main
leg of the trip; and of $4.35 including tip, for the taxi
from La Guardia Marine Terminal to my office, instead
of the fifteen cents that gets me there by subway when
the Long Island is running." The only fares that have
not risen phenomenally in these past fifteen years are
those of the railroad and of the local taxi to the station and to the airport: I pay $2.50 taxi fare to the
train depot and I can travel by coach for $5.50 or
by parlor car for $11. If I fly, it costs me $4.50 to get
to the airfield; on a scheduled flight, I pay $40, and
if I charter I am set back $95. The planes no longer
land at the Marine Terminal but in a no man's land
in Flushing and the taxi from there to mid-Manhattan
comes, with tip, to about $12.50—more if traffic is
dense or if the driver has a poor sense of direction and
a frail command of the language. By hired car, instead of $45, we now pay $95. And the subway token
now costs thirty-five instead of fifteen cents.

Today half the population (my estimate is modest)
has gone or is going crazy in public, spree murder at
high noon on Main Street is endemic, and Uncle Sam's
diary reads like the Book of Job. The scandal on
which Joe's story "V-Day in Court" was based kept
tabloid-readers titivated for weeks in the early fifties,
and, while it is still richly rancid, now it would have
to travel more labyrinthine ways to enthrall as it did
then—and in the dark alleys and cul-de-sacs, in order
to play to a full house, there would have to lurk prominent political figures of seven continents, and there
would have to be heard *sotto voce* (or clarion, depending on the editorial complexion of the newspa-

per) innuendoes implicating the IRS and the CIA, the Red Guard and the KGB.

One Saturday last month, Russell Baker began his column, "The Observer," thus, "The news that the entire United States Senate has undergone sex-change surgery has apparently shocked no one. Few persons seem even mildly interested." He goes on to list other phenomena that so far have not taken place but may very well have done so by the time this book is on the stands: Nelson Rockefeller leaves Washington to accept an invitation to become the Emperor of Japan; China falls; President Ford has "Ronald Reagan crated in a box and shipped to Senator Goldwater as a birthday present." It is not that there isn't any news, says Mr. Baker, but that there is too much. You can't see the woods for the trees, and you can't hear the screams of aged widows being raped and orphans being pistol-whipped for the sirens of the squad cars on their way to City Hall, where terrorists are chucking hand grenades through the windows. Nothing can rouse us from our ennui.

So much has happened and happened so preposterously and villainously and with such criminal stupidity and improbable impropriety in the twelve years Joe has been dead that once in a while I wonder if prescience contributed to his final illness; maybe he felt in his bones that he couldn't do justice to every act in the twelve-ring circus and cover the side shows as well. But I can't maintain this hypothesis for more than a couple of seconds. Like the rest of us, he would have been awed by Watergate and he would have scrutinized the handling of it by the press with the acuity of an eagle. In "Spotlight on the Jury," writing in 1949 about the first of the two Alger Hiss trials, he said, "Nixon, however, was never of more than almost-importance, since he was running too fast to leave footprints on the sands of time. He just skimmed them, like a coot taking off." Would he not have shuddered at the bird's later flights and marveled to see it molting as it roosts in San Clemente!

Before the Great Newspaper Strike that began on December 8, 1962, and ended on March 31, 1963, a heap of papers lay each morning outside the door of our New York City apartment: The New York *Times*, the *Herald Tribune*, the *Daily News*, the *Daily Mirror*, and the *Wall Street Journal*. Joe always got up at nine and he began to read as he ate his grapefruit. When he had finished breakfast, he removed the cat from his favorite chair and went on reading steadily until noon or a little later. (When he got to his office at *The New Yorker*, he would find waiting for him the New York *Post*, the *World-Telegram & Sun* and the *Journal-American*.) From time to time he laughed, now in amusement and now in disbelief; often, wrathful, he used rude language. Occasionally he would stare into space for a long time and, his arm hanging limply at his side, allow the cat to box his thumb. By the time he got up and went to shower and shave and dress, the environs of his chair were a mess of ripped pages from broadsheets and wads of tabloid matter—the kind you put in teacups when you're packing china. It was Joe's habit as he read to tear off small pieces of paper and roll them between the thumb and fore-finger of his right hand as if he were making spitballs. Once, I asked him why he so mauled the raw material that was in a large part the source of his livelihood, and, as he put on his derby preparatory to leaving the domestic quarters and going to work, he answered, "Each man kills the thing he loves." He was fond of using mildewed clichés, particularly if they were poeti-cal. An editorial in the New York *Times* on December 30, 1963, concluded, "He was, by his own description, 'a chronic, incurable, recidivist reporter,' and his ad-miration for skill in reporting was boundless. His death stills a pen that could inspire as well as wound. The press will be duller for the loss of his barbs."

Joe did love the press. He harried it, ridiculed it, anatomized it, sternly brought it to book, punched it in the nose, and gave it the hotfoot, but he loved it. It was his wayward concubine.

                                        Jean Stafford

East Hampton, N.Y.
May 1, 1975

Acknowledgments

I am more grateful than I can say to Kenneth Robbins for helping me with the emendation of this book. And I owe thanks, as well, to William Shawn, Joseph Mitchell, Mary Painter, Milton Greenstein, and Katherine S. White. Gloria Hammond, of Ballantine Books, has been so tireless and patient, so sagacious and sympathetic and winningly funny that if I were a university, I would give her an honorary degree.

—J.S.

THE PRESS

Prologue: The End
of Free Lunch

In Great Britain, the Government, whether of Right
or Left, considers the state of the press a matter of
public concern. When, early this past winter, Lord
Rothermere, owner of the morning *Daily Mail* and
the *Evening News* in London, bought the *News-
Chronicle* (morning) and the *Star* (evening) and scuttled them, thus making life easier for his own papers,
there were questions in Parliament. When, a month or
two later, Cecil King and Roy Thomson, each the proprietor of a press empire, made rival bids for Odhams
Press, which publishes the *Daily Herald* and the Sunday newspaper *People,* a storm broke that compelled
the Prime Minister to appoint a Royal Commission to
investigate the state of the press. Doing so, he said, in
part: "The recent developments are widely taken to
suggest that conditions . . . are such as to lead inevitably toward concentration of ownership and a reduction in—to quote the words of the Royal Commission
of 1949—the number and variety of the voices speaking to the public through the press." The 1949 Royal
Commission was appointed by a Labor Government.
Here the Tory Prime Minister, like his predecessors,
acknowledged that the more voices, and the more
various they that spoke, the better for the public.

In the United States, the American Newspaper Publishers' Association would treat such a pronouncement
as heresy and interference in their own damned business, not to mention an infringement of the freedom
of the press and a partisan pronouncement—since the
press being almost exclusively Republican, any criticism is implicitly Democratic.

Yet the United States is much farther advanced toward a monovocal, monopolistic, monocular press
than Britain. With the decline in the "number and

1

variety" of voices there is a decline in the number and variety of reporting eyes, which is at least as malign.

Editor & Publisher, a trade publication, recently stated that of 1,461 American cities with daily newspapers, all but 61 were one-ownership towns—that is, monopolies. In Great Britain, where the London papers circulate everywhere, the regional journals cannot dent the London hold on news and opinion. The typical American monopoly is local rather than national. The big-city papers, since they do not arrive, cannot dent the *local* monopoly. Sixty or seventy years ago, the founders of great newspaper chains, like E. W. Scripps and William (the Real Article) Randolph Hearst, would fight for 20 cities simultaneously with 20 newspapers, taking on three or four enemy newspapers in each city. They would win in one place, lose in another, struggle on without profit for anybody in a third. It was a costly and wasteful process.

The industry's ideal now is absolute control in a moderate number of cities, or even one. These become one-ownership towns, and as the publisher turns monopolist, his troubles end. He is in the position of a feudal lord after the period of wars in the Middle Ages ended. He has his goods, but he need no longer fight for it. He is a *rentier.*

Such properties fall into only three classes: good, better, and bestest. There are no poor ones, since the proprietor can impose his own terms; he gets all the advertising, all the circulation, and he can give, in return, exactly as much or little newspaper as his heart tells him. Newspaper proprietors are not distinguished as a class for large or talkative hearts.

As the number of cities in the United States with only a single newspaper ownership increases, news becomes increasingly nonessential to the newspaper. In the mind of the average publisher, it is a costly and uneconomic frill, like the free lunch that saloons used to furnish to induce customers to buy beer. If the quality of the free lunch fell off, the customers would go next door.

When New York State created its Alcohol Board of

Control after the repeal of the prohibition amendment, the A.B.C. abolished the handout. With no free lunch to be had anywhere, the customers continued to buy beer, and the saloonkeepers raised the price and pocketed the difference. In a monopoly situation, the paper can cut out news as the saloons cut out free lunch. There is no longer a place next door for the customers to go to. They will continue to buy the paper to read the advertisements. The advertisers will continue to buy space in order that they be read.

Under present conditions, frightened still by old superstitions about what newspapers are for, the publisher, out of force of habit and because he does not wish to be called a piker, usually provides for the customer a smattering of press association scraps and syndicated features. The saloonkeeper, in the same moral position, puts out a few stale pretzels and moldy salted peanuts.

Each publicly blames his own soft heart for his display of generosity. It comes under the head of public service, and the newspaper owner probably will make a speech about it at the next convention of the American Newspaper Publishers' Association. He will then suggest that the Associated Press, a burden on all of them, ought to cut down on excessive foreign coverage; he often sees a dispatch almost a hundred words long. But such vestigia offer little to rely on for the future. Like the immigrant orthodox Jew, who learns to dispense first with his sidecurls, then his beard, and at length his skullcap, the publisher will progressively shed his scruples.

With the years, the quantity of news in newspapers is bound to diminish from its present low. The proprietor, as Chairman of the Board, will increasingly often say that he would *like* to spend 75 cents now and then on news coverage but that he must be fair to his shareholders.

This, of course, is the current excuse for every instance of ignobility. A drug company, controlling 95 percent of its own shares, says it would *like* to hold the profit on its pet pill down to 1,500 percent, but it has to protect the minority shareholders, all widows of F.B.I. men strangled by juvenile delinquents. The president of a motor company says he would *like* to build cars that would last at least a year, but he could do it only at the expense of his shareowners, who are entitled to maximum profit and are without exception paraplegics. He then whips around backstage and exercises his option on the three shares that he has let his uncle hold during the annual meeting. And so it goes, even in novels. The popular hero-victim is the thief-in-spite-of-himself, the fundamentally decent corporation executive who has to steal for the stockholders. He is a Robin Hood misunderstood, since the stockholders are a cross-section of the American Public, and the American Public is not rich. There will, almost inevitably, be proxy fights within newspaper corporations, as there are within railroads, in which potty widows with two shares will arise to denounce management for extravagance. They will say that a telephone-answering service for murderers who want to turn themselves in and a subscription to *Time* should be enough of a news side.

Many proprietors, moreover, have a prejudice against news—they never feel at home with it. In this they resemble racing owners who are nervous around horses.

The corrective for the deterioration of a newspaper is provided, in nineteenth-century theory, by competition, which is governed equally by nature's abhorrence of a vacuum and Heaven will protect the working girl. Theoretically, a newspaper that does not give news, or is corrupt, or fails to stand up for the underdog attracts the attention of a virtuous newspaper looking for a home, just as the tarantula, in the Caribbees, attracts the blue hornet. Good and bad paper will wrestle, to continue our insect parallel. Virtue will triumph, and the good paper will place its sting in the bad paper's belly and yell, "*Sic semper* Newhouse management!" or something of the sort. Then it will eat the advertising content of the bad paper's breadbasket.

This no longer occurs. Money is not made by competition among newspapers, but by avoiding it. The wars are over, and newspaper owners are content to buy their enemies off, or just to buy them. The object of diplomacy is to obtain an unassailable local position, like a robber-castle, in New Orleans or Elizabeth or Des Moines, and then levy tribute on the helpless peasantry, who will have no other means of discovering what is playing at the Nugget.

To cite an example of the new strategy of noncombat: the Hearst people, who have a paper in Albany, buy the second paper and thus make a monopoly. They sell the Detroit *Times* and skedaddle from that city, leaving the purchaser, the Detroit *News,* with an evening monopoly there. This substitutes two monopolies for two competitive situations. All the respective owners need by way of a staff is a cash register.

The old system was abandoned even before the historically recent deaths of the last specimens of the Giant Primordial Gobblers. William (the Genuine) Randolph Hearst, Joseph Medill Patterson and Col. Robert Rutherford McCormick, when they went into a city, tried to make its inhabitants obey them as well as pay tribute. Their personalities howled, and they displayed their photographs constantly on their meal-tickets. The men of the new order do not meddle with the locals as long as they come up with the tithe. They are, for the public, faceless, and their coups are often inside jobs. Hearst tried to take cities by storm, but the new men prefer a rendezvous at the back gate.

Mr. Samuel I. Newhouse, the archetype, specializes in disgruntling heritors, or profiting by their disgruntlement. A family feud is grist to his mill, but if he can't get a paper that way he will talk beautifully of the satisfactions of cash, rapidly quoting sections of the capital-gains law as he accepts his hat. If the owner shows him the door, he exhibits no resentment.

"I regret that you do not feel you can sell me the overcoat now, Madame," he says as he backs down the porch steps, "but if your husband dies and you should reconsider, I do hope you'll give me the first chance to make you an offer." (Mr. Roy Thomson, the Canadian who has taken to buying newspapers in Britain, is the same sort.) Newhouse and Thomson,

quizzed about their politics, are evasive. They have no
political ideas; just economic convictions.

The function of the press in society is to inform,
but its role is to make money. The monopoly publisher's reaction, on being told that he ought to spend
money on reporting distant events, is therefore exactly that of the proprietor of a large, fat cow, who
is told that he ought to enter her in a horse race.

To concretize the dichotomy, as I might write if I
were a popular sociologist, last summer I made a talk
before a small group of fellowship winners that got reported in *Newsweek*. In it I said that the Washington
Star, a disgustingly rich newspaper with an unassailable position, spent millions on promotional activities
while it maintained only one foreign correspondent.
In the *Star*'s opinion this ill-merited a reproach, because there are even richer, if that is remotely conceivable, papers, that have no foreign correspondents
at all. I got an indignant letter, day and date with the
magazine, from a Mr. Newbold Noyes, Jr., vice-president of the *Star,* saying it spent only $375,000 a year
on promotion. This of course would run into millions
pretty fast, but I accept the correction, if it is one. He
did not say that the *Star* had more than one foreign
correspondent, though, so I assume it hasn't. They
may, indeed, have fired that one.

Newspapers were not the first to discover the superiority of noncompetition. Corporations, instead of
exhorting their executives to get out there and fight for
dear old Westinghouse, or for dear old General Electric, have now taken to telling them to get out and
not-fight unless threatened with an injunction. "I'd
rather go to jail than subscribe to the theory of a competitive economy," has become one of the new slogans
of the individual-enterprise system.

Despite this universal trend, however, there are
still, in the newspaper field, a few locales that are, at
least until the conclusion of negotiations, competitive.

One of these provisionally competitive zones, the
top quarter of the New York market for morning papers, provides, at my rough guess, two-thirds of the
foreign news reaching the United States that is of any

service to a reader who gives a damn. This proceeds from the foreign staffs of the New York *Times* and the *Herald Tribune,* who have about a million readers between them, split 650,000 *Times* and 350,000 *Trib.* The New York *Daily News* and the *New York Daily Mirror,* battling for the low three-quarters of morning circulation, split *three* million readers, in a 2-to-1 ratio, but foreign coverage plays no part in their war, which is conducted with comic strips, cheesecake, nudging headlines, and between-us-fellers editorials as weapons. Here rules the classic trichotomy—blood, money, and the female organ of sex—that made good papyrus in Cleopatra's time. It is a kind of journalism that has not changed much since.

The *Times*-versus-*Trib* battleground and the other are more widely separated than San Diego and Long Island. It is impossible that either embattled duo draw a reader from the other's field. The prizes at stake are therefore *two* monopolies. Whoever wins up top, *Times* or *Trib,* will get all the middle-to-high-price advertising and whoever triumphs downstairs will get all the low-to-middle. At this point I take leave of the *News* and *Mirror,* like a big eel and a small eel in a tank. Whenever I look again I expect to see that the big eel has swallowed the small eel, but it hasn't happened yet.

The *Times* has a big lead over the *Trib,* but the *Trib* knows that if it packs in its foreign staff it is through. Consequently it continues to compete, like a down cock hitting back at the bird on top, and not only New York readers benefit. Both papers syndicate their services, each to about 50 clients, out of 1,763 American dailies. The clients include a number of big papers, so that the effect on the total amount of foreign news available to American readers is greater than the discouraging figure would suggest.

How long this situation lasts depends on how long the New York department stores find it economic to let it continue. If they clamp down on advertising in the *Trib,* as they did on the poor old *Evening Sun* in 1950, they can put it down instantly, unless its proprietor, John Hay Whitney, consents to carry it purely as a tax-free expenditure on public relations for airlines and railroads. This is hardly likely. The disappearance of the *Trib* would be followed, I would bet confidently, by a heavy cut in the amount of foreign news provided by the *Times*. (Free lunch, principle of.) The country's present supply of foreign news, therefore, depends largely on how best a number of drygoods merchants in New York think they can sell underwear.

Since competition can no longer be relied upon to produce newspapers that provide news, the mind turns to regulation. In the case of a public monopoly, for example, water supply, there is always a governmental agency to maintain standards of limpidity and taste and its freedom from excess of harmful beasts. But analogies, as Ibn Khaldun, the Tunisian historian, has said, are not to be too far trusted. Public regulation would conflict with the principle of the freedom of the press, which has nothing to do with freedom from impurities or distortion, and still less with clarity or taste. Men of politics cannot be trusted to regulate the press, because the press deals with politics. *Pravda* is even duller than the *Times*.

I abandoned myself long ago to hope, and, so far, luck has always prevented the absolute worst. When I got my first newspaper job in 1925, the drift toward profitable stagnation was already apparent. Frank Munsey, a mass murderer of newspapers, had just burked and buried four New York papers, reducing the number of morning dailies from nine to seven and of evenings from seven to five. We are down to four mornings and three evenings, yet I do not believe that New York will be a one-ownership or even a two-ownership city in my lifetime.

Something will turn up. I remind myself often of the plight of Byzantium at the end of the fifteenth century. The Empire of the East was cooked. The Emperor wore paste crown jewels because the real ice was in hock to the Venetians. The Turks, on a winning streak that had lasted for three centuries, were about to gobble the imperial capital, and there was nothing the Greeks could do about it. Then along came Timur the Lame out of Central Asia. He hated the Greeks, and he hated the Turks, but the Turks were nearer, so he pulverized them and put the Sultan in a cage in 1402, and then died before he got to Constantinople to do in the Greeks. It saved the empire until 1453, and although the Turks eventually took the Greeks, they were not, for the most part, the same Greeks who worried uselessly in 1402.

It was so in the recent election campaign. The almost monolithic press had Kennedy well screened from public gaze, and was about to misrepresent him as a callow gossoon, hiding a low IQ under his father's thumb. Then television, a crude Timur with a grudge based on the press's ribbing of television payola, came to Kennedy's rescue and exhibited Nixon. He was not in a cage, but exposure to the eye proved sufficient. In performing this kind action, the networks were motivated no kindlier toward the public than Timur toward the Greeks. They just wanted to get even with the newspapers.

Now there is a temporary rift in the clouds. In the next four years the President should be able to do enough favors for individual publishers to set up a small circle of Copperheads in their ranks. These will allow dispatches in their papers to differ from dispatches in other papers until they themselves despair of being named ambassadors. By such small accidents dissidence survives. Unanimity is delayed, doom postponed, and by 1964 public information may by some other accident again escape extinction.

The Republican Party handles publishers much better. It wastes no time trying to make friends with reporters, knowing they can do nothing their bosses won't let them. Mr. Nixon, after the last campaign, charged that reporters were telling the truth behind their bosses' backs, but this was so inherently improbable that nobody took him seriously. As for the A.N.P.A. (without a school for whose members, a wise American once wrote, no school of journalism can have meaning), Republicans treat it fine. (As for the School, it will remain a fantasy, because *a.* the potential students are sure they know everything already, and *b.* there are no entrance examinations they could all pass. The ones who couldn't, though, are precisely those who need the school most.)

The relations between the Grand Old Party and the newspaper owners remind me of a man I saw come into a fine old barroom on a snowy Sunday with a boy about three years old, done up in a snowsuit. Clearly he had told his wife he was taking the kid for a romp. He ordered a sour-mash bourbon, sat the boy on the end of the bar and told the bartender to give him a maraschino cherry. The father pronounced it "Marciano," but that is only an interesting detail. There the two stayed all afternoon, perfectly happy. It was evidently a routine arrangement between the men in the family. Every time the old man took a shot, the boy got a cherry. The boy seemed to feel this was an equitable arrangement. He was so small.

In the same way, while the big Republicans, during a favorable administration, sell themselves national resources, block flood-control because it implies public power projects, take the ceilings off natural-gas rates, perpetuate contracts for the manufacture of obsolete war material (*vide,* General James M. Gavin's book explaining his resignation), give the States (which means their own agents at one remove) tidal oil lands, and resell to the Government, at unlimited profit, in the form of machines, patents developed in Government laboratories, their Administration buys the publishers cherries. These take the form of exempting newsboys from the provisions of the minimum-wage law, making ex-publishers ambassadors to small countries dependent on American goodwill, giving newspapers licenses for local television stations, appointing practicing publishers' wives ambassadors to rather larger countries, permitting newspaper owners to call on the President for five minutes when they want to impress particularly important advertisers, and furnishing the President's *hajib,* or Guardian of Access, with a list of the first names of such publishers, so he can tip off the President when they appear and the President will know whether to say "Roy" or "Bill."

The *hajiba,* or Office of the Doorkeeper, or Guardian of Access, incidentally, reached the highest importance in the last Administration that it had attained since the reign of Abu Bakr, the twelfth Sultan of the Hafsid dynasty in Ifrikiyah (Tunis) from 1318 to 1346 A.D. Of the Hafsid system of government Ibn Khaldun, the immortal of Tunisian history, wrote: "The Ruler stayed in seclusion, and the doorkeeper [*hajib*] became the *liaison* officer between the people and all the officials." Naturally, politicians and rich merchants desirous of access or the furtherance of their affairs subjected the *hajib* to temptation in the form of magnificent entertainment at caravanserais and gifts of slave girls rolled in Oriental carpets. No instance is known of the last Republican *hajib,* Llewellyn Sherman Adams, having accepted a slave girl.

Ibn Khaldun is the kind of acquaintance you meet on a street corner when you are hurrying to an appointment, but from whom you find it difficult to break off once he has hooked you in conversation. So I must add here: "Afterwards his [Abu Bakr's] grandson, Sultan Abul'Abbâs, regained control of his affairs. He removed the vestiges of seclusion and outside control by abolishing the office of *hajib,* which had been the stepping-stone toward control of the government. He handled all his affairs himself without asking anybody else for help." Ibn Khaldun does not state whether this was an improvement.

—A. J. L.

1
Toward
a
One-Paper
Town

Here is how I summarized the basic situation, as I thought it existed then, for the *Dartmouth Alumni Magazine* in 1947. There was a symposium. Two other alumni, an editor and an Associated Press man, also took part. As one would expect, they were completely wrong about everything.

A Free Press?

I think almost everybody will grant that if candidates for the United States Senate were required to possess ten million dollars, and for the House one million, the year-in-year-out level of conservation of those two bodies might be expected to rise sharply. We could still be said to have a freely elected Congress: anybody with ten million dollars (or one, if he tailored his ambition to fit his means) would be free to try to get himself nominated, and the rest of us would be free to vote for our favorite millionaires or even to abstain from voting. (This last right would mark our continued superiority over states where people are compelled to vote for the government slate.)

In the same sense, we have a free press today. (I am thinking of big-city and middling-city publishers as members of an upper and lower house of American opinion.) Anybody in the ten-million-dollar category is free to buy or found a paper in a great city like New York or Chicago, and anybody with around a million (plus a lot of sporting blood) is free to try it in a place of mediocre size like Worcester, Mass. As to us, we are free to buy a paper or not, as we wish.[1]

---

[1] *A Free and Responsible Press*, the published report of a committee headed by Robert Maynard Hutchins in 1947, says, "Although there is no such thing as a going price for a great city newspaper, it is safe to assume that it would cost somewhere between five and ten million dollars to build a new

In a highly interesting book, *The First Freedom,*
Morris Ernst has told the story of the increasing concentration of news outlets in the hands of a few people. There are less newspapers today than in 1909, and
less owners in relation to the total number of papers.

---

metropolitan daily to success. The investment required for a
new newspaper in a medium-sized city is estimated at three-
quarters of a million to several million." Prices have gone up
very considerably since this was written. The rise underlines
my thesis.

Earl L. Vance, in an article in the *Virginia Quarterly Review*
(summer 1945) cited in "Survival of a Free, Competitive
Press," a publication of the Senate Committee on Small Businesses, says, "Even small-newspaper publishing is big business.
Time magazine recently reported sale of the Massillon, Ohio,
Independent (circulation 11,858) for 'around $400,000,' the
Spartanburg, S.C., *Herald* (17,351) and *Journal* (8,678) for
$750,000—all smaller dailies. In contrast, William Allen White
paid only $3,000 for the Emporia *Gazette* in 1892. A metro-
politan daily now represents an investment of many millions.
Scripps-Howard in 1923 paid $6,000,000 for the same newspa-
per that had been offered in 1892 for $51,000; the Philadel-
phia *Inquirer* sold for $18,000,000 in 1930; the Kansas City
Star for $11,000,000 in 1926."

I hadn't seen either of these publications before I wrote my
alumni magazine article; I cite them here to show I wasn't
dreaming my figures. The only recent instance I know of a man
buying a newspaper for under five figures and making it go occurred in Las Vegas, Nevada. There in 1950, the typographical
unions struck the only paper. It was a long, stubborn strike,
and the unions started a small paper of their own, which lost
so much money, for such a small strike, that they agreed to
sell it to a young publicity man for gambling halls named
Hank Greenspun for $1,000. Hank bought it and then found a
bank account with $2,500 in it among the cash assets. He thus
made an immediate profit of $1,500, which must be a record.
Within three years Greenspun built it into a rough, spectacularly aggressive and quickly profitable newspaper, the *Sun,* and
it is, or should be, a mighty moneymaker today. This was,
however, possible only because Las Vegas, in a decade, has
quadrupled or quintupled its population, and the older paper
remains without interest, a small-town sheet. There was therefore created an instantaneous vacuum, and the *Sun* filled it.
The same thing could happen in another boom town, as it used
to in the Gold Rush days, but there has been only one Las
Vegas in a half-century.

In 1909 there were 2,600; today 1,750.[2] Ernst refrains from any reflection on the quality of the ownership; he says merely that it is dangerous that so much power should be held by so few individuals. I will go one timid step further than Ernst and suggest that these individuals, because of their economic position, form an atypical group and share an atypical outlook.

The newspaper owner is a rather large employer of labor. I don't want to bore you with statistics, but one figure that I remember unhappily is 2,867, the number of us who lost jobs when the Pulitzers sold the *World* for salvage in 1931. He is nowadays forced to deal with unions in all departments of his enterprise, and is as unlikely as any other employer to be on their side. As owner of a large and profitable business, he is opposed to government intervention in his affairs beyond the maintenance of the subsidy extended to all newspapers through second-class-mail rates. As an owner of valuable real estate, he is more interested in keeping the tax rate down than in any other local issue. (Newspaper crusades for municipal "reform" are almost invariably tax-paring expeditions.) A planned economy is abhorrent to him, and since every other nation in the world has now gone in for some form of economic planning, the publisher has become our number-one xenophobe. His "preference" for Socialist Britain over Communist Russia is only an inverse expression of relative dislike.[3] Because of publishers' wealth, they do not have to be slugged over the head by "anti-democratic organizations" to force them into using their properties to form public opinion the N.A.M. approves. The gesture would be as redundant as twisting a nymphomaniac's arm to get her into bed.[4]

---

[2] Now 1,763 but the number of ownerships has decreased.

[3] He likes Conservative Britain rather better, except for its Socialized Medicine.

[4] *A Free and Responsible Press,* that result of the collaboration of thirteen bigwigs, which I again cite lest you think I am flippant, says:

"The agencies of mass communication are big business, and their owners are big businessmen. . . . The press is a large employer of labor. . . . The newspapers alone have more than

I am delighted that I do not have to insinuate that they consciously allow their output to be shaped by their personal interests. Psychoanalytical after-dinner talk has furnished us with a lovely word for what they do: they rationalize. And once a man has convinced himself that what is good for him is good for the herd of his inferiors, he enjoys the best of two worlds simultaneously, and can shake hands with Bertie McCormick, the owner of the Chicago *Tribune*.[5]

The profit system, while it insures the predominant conservative coloration of our press, also guarantees that there will always be a certain amount of dissidence. The American press has never been monolithic, like that of an authoritarian state. One reason is that there is always important money to be made in journalism by standing up for the underdog (demagogically or honestly, so long as the technique is good). The underdog is numerous and prolific—another name for him is circulation. His wife buys girdles and baking powder and Literary Guild selections, and the advertiser has to reach her. Newspapers, as they become successful and more to the right, leave room for newcomers to the left. Marshall Field's Chicago *Sun,* for

---

150,000 employees. The press is connected with other big businesses through the advertising of these businesses, upon which it depends for the major part of its revenue. The owners of the press, like the owners of other big businesses, are bank directors, bank borrowers, and heavy taxpayers in the upper brackets.

"As William Allen White put it: 'Too often the publisher of an American newspaper has made his money in some other calling than journalism. He is a rich man seeking power and prestige. . . . And they all get the unconscious arrogance of conscious wealth.'

"Another highly respected editor, Erwin D. Canham of the *Christian Science Monitor,* thinks upper-bracket ownership and its big-business character important enough to stand at the head of his list of the 'shortcomings of today's American newspapers.' "

A Free and Responsible Press was published after the appearance of my article.

[5] McCormick died in 1955. If he is not in Heaven he is eternally astonished.

example, has acquired 400,000 readers in five years, simply because the *Tribune,* formerly alone in the Chicago morning field, had gone so far to the right.[6] The fact that the *Tribune*'s circulation has not been much affected indicates that the 400,000 had previous to 1941 been availing themselves of their freedom not to buy a newspaper. (Field himself illustrates another, less dependable, but nevertheless appreciable, factor in the history of the American press—the occasional occurrence of that economic sport, the maverick millionaire.) E. W. Scripps was the outstanding practitioner of the trade of founding newspapers to stand up for the common man. He made a tremendous success of it, owning about twenty of them when he died. The first, James Gordon Bennett's *Herald* and Joseph Pulitzer's *World,* in the eighties and nineties, to say nothing of the Scripps-Howard *World-Telegram* in 1927, won their niche in New York as left-of-center newspapers and then bogged down in profits.

Another factor favorable to freedom of the press, in a minor way, is the circumstance that publishers sometimes allow a certain latitude to employees in departments in which they have no direct interest—movies, for instance, if the publisher is not keeping a movie actress; or horse shows, if his wife does not own a horse. Musical and theatrical criticism is less rigorously controlled than it is in Russia.[7]

The process by which the American press is pretty steadily revivified, and as steadily dies (newspapers are like cells in the body, some dying as others develop), was well described in 1911 by a young man named Joseph Medill Patterson, then an officer of the Chicago *Tribune,* who was destined himself to found an enormously successful paper, the *Daily News* of

[6] The *Sun-Times,* having become almost equally prosperous, has by now, 1961, gone almost equally as far. Poor Mr. Field is dead and his son is a Republican. Mavericks seldom breed true.

[7] There is, however, no theater to write about, except in New York, and provincial critics of music lean over backward to be kind, because it is hard enough to get people to subscribe for concerts without underlining their deficiencies.

New York, and then within his own lifetime pilot it over the course he had foreshadowed. The quotation is from a play, *The Fourth Estate,* which Patterson wrote in his young discontent.

"Newspapers start when their owners are poor, and take the part of the people, and so they build up a large circulation, and, as a result, advertising. That makes them rich, and they begin most naturally, to associate with other rich men—they play golf with one, and drink whisky with another, and their son marries the daughter of a third. They forget all about the people, and then their circulation dries up, then their advertising, and then their paper becomes decadent."

Patterson was not "poor" when he came to New York eight years later to start the *News;* he had the McCormick-Patterson *Tribune* fortune behind him, and at this side Max Annenberg, a high-priced journalist condottiere who had already helped the *Tribune* win a pitched battle with Hearst in its own territory. But he was starting his paper from scratch, and he did it in the old dependable way, by taking up for the Common Man—and sticking with him until 1942, by which time the successful-man contagion got him and he threw his arms around unregenerated Cousin Bertie's neck. The *Tribune* in Chicago and the *News* in New York have formed a solid front ever since. Patterson was uninfluenced by golf, whiskey, or social ambitions (he was a parsimonious, unsociable man who cherished an illusion that he had already hit the social peak). I think it is rather the complex of age, great wealth, a swelled head, and the necessity to believe in the Heaven-decreed righteousness of a system which has permitted one to possess such power that turns a publisher's head. The whiskey, weddings, yachts, horse shows, and the rest (golf no longer sounds so imposing as it did in 1911) [8] are symptoms rather than causes.

Unfortunately, circulations do not "dry up" quickly,

---

[8] There has been a revival since the first Eisenhower inaugural. I attribute it to the invention of the electric go-cart, in which, I am informed, the golfers now circulate, obviating ambulation. It sounds like the most fun since the goat-wagon.

nor advertising fall away overnight. Reading a newspaper is a habit which holds on for a considerable
time. So the erstwhile for-the-people newspaper continues to make money for a while after it changes its
course. With the New York *Herald* this phase lasted
half a century. It would, moreover, be difficult to fix
the exact hour or day at which the change takes place:
it is usually gradual, and perceptible to those working
on the paper before it becomes apparent to the outside public. At any given moment there are more
profitable newspapers in being than new ones trying
to come up, so the general tone of the press is predominantly, and I fear increasingly, reactionary. The
difference between newspaper publishers' opinions and
those of the public is so frequently expressed at the
polls that it is unnecessary to insist on it here.

Don't get me wrong, though. I don't think that the
battle is futile. I remember when I was a freshman, in
1920, listening to a lecture by Professor Mecklin in a
survey course called, I think, Citizenship, in which he
told how most of the newspapers had misrepresented
the great steel strike of 1919. The only one that had
told the truth, he said, as I remember it, was the old
World. (I have heard since that the St. Louis *Post-
Dispatch* was good, too, but he didn't mention it.) It
was the first time that I really believed that newspapers lied about that sort of thing. I had heard of
Upton Sinclair's book *The Brass Check,* but I hadn't
wanted to read it because I had heard he was a "Bolshevik." I came up to college when I was just under
sixteen, and the family environment was not exactly
radical. But my reaction was that I wanted someday
to work for the *World,* or for some other paper that
would tell the truth. The *World* did a damned good
job, on the strikes and on the Ku Klux Klan and on
prohibition and prison camps (in Florida, not Silesia),
and even though the second-generation Pulitzers let it
grow namby-pamby and then dropped it in terror
when they had had a losing year and were down to
their last sixteen million, it had not lived in vain.

I think that anybody who talks often with people
about newspapers nowadays must be impressed by the

growing distrust of the information they contain. There is less a disposition to accept what they say than to try to estimate the probable truth on the basis of what they say, like aiming a rifle that you know has a deviation to the right. Even a report in a Hearst newspaper can be of considerable aid in arriving at a deduction if you know enough about (a) Hearst policy and (b) the degree of abjectness of the correspondent signing the report.[9]

Every now and then I write a piece for *The New Yorker* under the heading of "The Wayward Press" (a title for the department invented by the late Robert Benchley when he started it early in *The New Yorker*'s history). In this I concern myself not with big general thoughts about Trends (my boss wouldn't stand for such), but with the treatment of specific stories by the daily (chiefly New York) press. I am a damned sight kinder about newspapers than Wolcott Gibbs [10] is

---

[9] Albert Camus, the brilliant and versatile young French novelist, playwright, and critic, who was also editor of *Combat*, a Paris daily, once had an idea for establishing a "control newspaper" that would come out one hour after the others with estimates of the percentage of truth in each of their stories, and with interpretations of how the stories were slanted. The way he explained it, it sounded possible. He said, "We'd have complete dossiers on the interests, policies, and idiosyncrasies of the owners. Then we'd have a dossier on every journalist in the world. The interest, prejudices, and quirks of the owner would equal Z. The prejudices, quirks, and private interests of the journalist, Y. Z times Y would give you X, the probable amount of truth in the story." He was going to make up dossiers on reporters by getting journalists he trusted to appraise men they had worked with. "I would have a card-index system," he said. "Very simple. We would keep the dossiers up to date as best we could, of course. But do people really want to know how much truth there is in what they read? Would they buy the control paper? That's the most difficult problem." Camus died without ever learning the answer to this question. His energies were dissipated in creative writing and we lost a great journalist.

[10] Gibbs is dead too. Shortly after his funeral I got a letter from a *New Yorker* reader in Hico, Texas, previously unknown to me, that began: "Well, Gibbs is dead and soon the whole damn lot of you will be."

about the theater, but while nobody accuses him of
sedition when he raps a play, I get letters calling me
a little pal of Stalin when I sneer at the New York
Sun. This reflects a pitch that newspaper publishers
make to the effect that they are part of the great American heritage with a right to travel wrapped in the
folds of the flag like a boll weevil in a cotton boll.
Neither theatrical producers nor book publishers, apparently, partake of this sacred character. I get a lot
more letters from people who are under the delusion
that I can Do Something About It All. These reflect a
general malaise on the part of the newspaper-reading
public, which I do think will have some effect, though
not, God knows, through me.

I believe that labor unions, citizens' organizations,
and possibly political parties yet unborn are going to
back daily papers. These will represent definite, un-
disguised points of view, and will serve as controls on
the large profit-making papers expressing definite, ill-
disguised points of view. The Labor Party's *Daily
Herald,* in England, has been of inestimable value in
checking the blather of the Beaverbrook-Kemsley-
Rothermere newspapers of huge circulation. When one
cannot get the truth from any one paper (and I do not
say that it is an easy thing, even with the best will in
the world, for any one paper to tell all the truth), it is
valuable to read two with opposite policies to get an
idea of what is really happening. I cannot believe that
labor leaders are so stupid they will let the other side
monopolize the press indefinitely.[11]

I also hope that we will live to see the endowed
newspaper, devoted to the pursuit of daily truth as
Dartmouth is to that of knowledge. I do not suppose
that any reader of the *Magazine* believes that the test
of a college is the ability to earn a profit on operations
(with the corollary that making the profit would soon
become the chief preoccupation of its officers). I think
that a good newspaper is as truly an educational institution as a college, so I don't see why it should have

---

[11] To reread this paragraph makes me glum. Mergerism has
hit Britain with a sudden rush; the *News-Chronicle* is gone and
the *Herald* looks to be for it.

to stake its survival on attracting advertisers of ball-point pens and tickets to Hollywood peep shows. And I think that private endowment would offer greater possibilities for a free press than state ownership (this is based on the chauvinistic idea that a place like Dartmouth can do a better job than a state university under the thumb of a Huey Long or Gene Talmadge). The hardest trick, of course, would be getting the chief donor of the endowment (perhaps a repentant tabloid publisher) to (a) croak, or (b) sign a legally binding agreement never to stick his face in the editorial rooms. The best kind of an endowment for a newspaper would be one made up of several large and many small or medium-sized gifts (the Dartmouth pattern again. Personally, I would rather leave my money for a newspaper than for a cathedral, a gymnasium, or even a home for streetwalkers with fallen arches, but I have seldom been able to assemble more than $4.17 at one time.[12]

---

[12] Professor Michael E. Choukas, of the Dartmouth faculty, summing up after the last article of the Public Opinion in a Democracy series, commented: "Mr. Liebling's 'endowed newspaper' would probably be free from direct pressure, but it would be unable to avoid the indirect efforts of the propagandists." I think that Professor Choukas, a sociologist who has specialized in the study of propaganda, has developed an exaggerated respect for the opposition. Albert Camus's plan for the "control newspaper," which I have briefly described in another footnote, is an example of the ingenuity a good newspaperman can bring to bear, and men like Vic Bernstein, Paul Sifton, and Edmund Taylor in this country (to cite only a few—there are hundreds of others) would certainly bring into the ring with them more perspicacity than anybody the national Association of Manufacturers could hire. A man who thinks he can fool other men is always a little a fool himself. His assumption that he can do it presupposes a foolish vanity—like that of the recidivist con man who spends most of his life in jail. His contempt for the truth marks him as a bit subhuman. Professor Choukas did not mention my hopes for strong labor papers.

The professor's own remedy for the dilemma, however, is worthy of citation. I hope somebody makes a good hard try at it.

"I frankly do not believe that any indirect assault would have much effect as a check against those who deliberately set out to

The above piece, written 14 years ago, was in manner laboriously offhand, but represented my serious thought. I erred badly on the side of optimism. The postwar euphoria that lingered in the air like fallout must have trapped me. There has been no new competition in any large American city since the piece was written, and now if seems infinitely less likely that there ever will be.

The period between the two wars, while it marked a great diminution in the number of newspapers in New York, had brought at least one tremendously successful newcomer, the *Daily News,* which changed the whole physiognomy of Metropolitan journalism. When I wrote in 1947, the two Marshall Field entries, *PM* in New York and the *Sun* (the *Sun-Times* to be) in Chicago, were both still in there battling. *PM,* which was destined to fail, had been founded in 1940, and the *Sun,* fated to succeed financially, had begun in 1942. It did not seem to me, therefore, that the times already precluded new starts, although, as I noted, they were harder than before.

The suggestions I made about where new papers might find sponsors now sound infantile, but at the time I thought, wrongly, that labor retained some of the intelligence and coherence of the Roosevelt days, and it seemed to me not inconceivable that some finan-

---

mislead us," he wrote. "A direct attack could be launched against them by a privately endowed, independent agency whose main task would consist of compiling a list of all the propaganda groups in the country, analyzing their techniques, discovering their goals, and releasing the available information to government officials, to men responsible for our channels of communication, to men who measure public opinion, to colleges and universities, and to those pathetically few groups in the country who have undertaken to fight the battle of Democracy in a positive manner.

"This I feel should be done before our crisis reaches climactic proportions—before the next depression."

cial Megabelodon might fancy a good newspaper as a
more distinctive memorial than the habitual foundation
for research into some disease that had annoyed the
testator during life. (These bequests always seem to
me to mark a vengeful nature, and the viruses they are
aimed at profit by them almost as much as the doctors.
They eat tons of cultures, play with white rats, and
develop resistance by constant practice, as slum children learn to get out of the way of automobiles.)
Megabelodon, however, although a huge creature, had
a brain cavity about as big as the dime slot on a telephone coin box, and most men who could afford to
endow a newspaper seem to be rigged the same way.

Silliest of all, as I read back now, is the line about
the profit system guaranteeing a certain amount of
dissidence. This shows, on my part, an incurable weak-
ness for judging the future by the past, like the French
generals who so charmed me in 1939. I still believe
that "there is always important money to be made by
standing up for the underdog," but the profit system
implies a pursuit of *maximum* profit—for the shareholders' sake, distasteful though it may be. That it is
theoretically possible to make money by competition
in the newspaper field is therefore immaterial, since
there is a great deal more money to be made by (a)
selling out and pocketing a capital gain, and (b) buying the other fellow out and then sweating the serfs.

The *Guild Reporter,* organ of the American Newspaper Guild, C.I.O., which includes all editorial workers, recently announced that the guild had achieved a
record membership despite "a contracting industry"—
a reference that will be clarified by the next item, from
The Wayward Press.

Do You Belong
in Journalism?

MAY 14, 1960

My bed-table book for some months past has been a volume called *Do You Belong in Journalism?* (Appleton-Century-Crofts). "Eighteen Editors Tell How You Can Explore Career Opportunities in Newspaper Work," the subtitle says, but none of them tell how you can manage to have your own paper, like William Randolph Hearst, Jr., or Mrs. Dorothy Schiff, or Marshall Field, Jr., or even John Hay Whitney. All of them warn the aspirant that he won't get rich (nine of the editors are still in shirtsleeves, according to the illustrations), but they offer other compensations, among them a dangerous life. Robert M. White, II, co-editor and co-publisher of the Mexico, Missouri, *Evening Ledger,* for example, is portrayed accompanying a raid of Missouri state troopers on a brick house that harbors an undisclosed peril. The troopers, with fowling pieces at the ready, are preceding him, and the photographer must be standing in the back yard, right in the line of fire if any desperado is lurking behind the window that the lead trooper is sneaking up on. (It pays to take risks. A footnote states, "On August 3, 1959, Mr. White became Editor and President of the New York *Herald Tribune.*" [1]) And Frank H. Bartholomew, president of United Press International, is shown in flying clothes, ready to be assisted into a Navy plane on the flight deck of a carrier, and no more daunted than he would be by the news that a bureau chief had squandered a dollar and a half.

"Other advantages," J. M. McClelland, Jr., editor and publisher of the Longview, Washington, *Daily News* (circulation 17,147), says, "include employment in a remarkably stable industry. The income of news-

---

[1] He was handed his hat later in 1960.

papers is generally quite even, and the danger of losing one's job due to sudden and perhaps temporary slumps is remote." When Mr. McClelland wrote that, he must have been thinking of a job on the only newspaper in town—which, in fact, the Longview *Daily News* is. If a journalist is working in a town where there are two ownerships, he is even money to become unemployed any minute, and if there are three, he has two chances out of three of being in the public-relations business before his children get through school. The loss of the job will be due not to a sudden slump but a merger; the effect on the fellow who thought he belonged in journalism will be the same.

American cities with competing newspapers will soon be as rare as those with two telephone systems. I had occasion to regret this not long ago during a visit to New Orleans, where the Times-Picayune Company now owns the only morning and the only evening newspaper, having bought out the *Item,* sole channel of occasionally dissenting opinion. The resulting daily complacency is hard to take. The recent annual convention of the American Newspaper Publishers' Association in New York brought the trend even more poignantly to mind. The convention reaches here at the same season as the Ringling Brothers and Barnum & Bailey Circus. (Circuses were hit by mergers even earlier than newspapers.) Like the Big Show, the convention always bears a certain basic resemblance to its predecessors. The New York publishers, through their editorial-page hirelings, welcome their country cousins, usually referred to as "the newspaper clan" or "the press family," and acclaim them as uniformly astute fellows, with their ears to the grass roots beneath every paved street from San Diego, California, to Bangor, Maine, and their fingers on the pulse of the nation. Reporters then go out and ask the fingermen what the pulse says, and the publishers predict a year of unexampled prosperity, accompanied by high costs that preclude a rise in wages. If a national election is coming up, they say that the Republicans will win, and after denouncing the current Administration (of no matter which party) for withholding information from the press they go off to a series of closed meetings and later dole out releases to reporters, who wait respectfully in the hall between the door and the men's room. From the meetings the publishers go to banquets offered by syndicates that sell them services, and are there entertained by "glamorous stars," who appear gratis. The invitation to appear at such a function conveys an implied threat that the host organization's columnists will be less than kind to the performer if he refuses, while they may hand him an extra dollop of publicity if he accepts. It is a form of payola that, as of this writing, has had small space in the press. Performers resent it.

But beneath this superficial uniformity change goes on, though it is clearly discernible only at considerable intervals, like the advance of a glacier. I last commented on New York newspaper coverage of the A.N.P.A. in 1953—a memorable year for the publishers, because most of them (84 percent, by their own proclamation) were celebrating their first winner in a national presidential election since 1928 and Mr. Hoover. They were exhilarated but still incredulous, like a man who has been kissing his wife every morning for 24 years and has finally got kissed back. One of their chief concerns appeared to be the charge that the newspapers as a whole had been unfair to Adlai Stevenson and the Democrats in the campaign just concluded. Mr. Stevenson, borrowing a phrase from Richard Strout, of the *Christian Science Monitor,* had called it a "one-party press in a two-party country." The *World-Telegram* ran the headline ONE-PARTY PRESS CHARGE DENIED over a story quoting the then president of the A.N.P.A., a Mr. Charles F. McCahill, general manager of the afternoon Cleveland *News,* who, "denied charges by some followers of Adlai E. Stevenson, the Democratic candidate, that the press was too lop-sided in its support of President Eisenhower." Just lopsided enough, he must have meant. What impressed me when I reread the 1953 story the other day was that the Cleveland *News* is no more, although I hope Mr. McCahill is still around to differentiate degrees of lopsidedness. Another potentate I

quoted then was McHenry Browne, general manager of
the Boston *Post,* which had the largest circulation
(302,000) of any standard-size newspaper then in
Boston. The *Post*—which had an unforgettable habit
of running a front page of headlines in assorted type
sizes, none under an inch high, and then leaving you
to burrow inside the paper for the stories—is as dead
as yesterday's *News.* The Washington *Times-Herald,*
with the largest circulation in the capital, is another
goner of the interim, and so are the Los Angeles *News,*
the aforementioned New Orleans *Item,* and either the
Call Bulletin or the *News* of San Francisco. (They are
jointly survived by something called the *News-Call
Bulletin,* and I cannot tell from the *Editor & Publisher
International Year Book* which swallowed the other.)
The Taft family newspaper in Cincinnati, the *Times-
Star,* is gone, and so is the Columbus *Ohio State Journal.* That is quite a lot of nationally famous newspapers to go out in the space of seven years that have
been far from lean.[2] The list does not pretend to be a
complete catalogue of decedents; come to think of it,
the Brooklyn *Eagle* still breathed in 1953, although
feebly, and there probably are at least a score of less
illustrious cadavers. Each of these shipwrecks tossed a
hundred or a few hundred people who thought they
belonged in journalism out onto the stormy seas of
pressagentry or ghostwriting. Mortality among newspapers has been high from the twenties on, but the last
years have brought a quickening of decimation. The
worst of it is that each newspaper disappearing below
the horizon carries with it, if not a point of view, at
least a potential emplacement for one. A city with one
newspaper, or with a morning and an evening paper
under one ownership, is like a man with one eye, and
often the eye is glass.

For once, there was a realistic allusion to this phe-

---

[2] The Detroit *Times,* with a circulation of around 300,000,
went under late in 1960. The blow fell, as usual, without warning—the theory being that employees, if they knew a paper is
to be scuttled, will slack off in their work. Members of the
Times staff, coming to work in the morning, found locks on
the office doors.

nomenon at the A.N.P.A. meeting. Usually, the publishers either have pretended that it wasn't happening or have pointed to it as proof of ruthless competition, assuring survival of the fittest, which they, as survivors, had to be. (Incidentally, they often added, it also proved that newspapermen were lucky to have jobs at all, and consequently should accustom their families to cheap cuts of meat. There was one such speech at this session, by a man named Richard Amberg, publisher of the St. Louis *Globe-Democrat,* but it sounded as démodé as "Silver Threads Among the Gold" played by a silver-cornet band. Often when a publisher talks like this, he is preparing to sell.) As a New York *Times* story by Russell Porter had it, D. Tennant Bryan, of the Richmond, Virginia, *Times-Dispatch* and *News Leader,* who was the outgoing president of the A.N.P.A., "noted that 1,755 daily newspapers in the United States produced and sold 58,000,000 copies every day. 'There may be some other industry that does better, but offhand, I can't think what it might be,' he said." (This was frankness that may cost publishers dear at the bargaining table.) Mr. Bryan denied that newspaper mergers were a sign of debilitation in the industry, as some critics have contended. He said that mergers represented nothing more than the natural workings of economics to effect operating economies through joint production plants. " 'This has nothing to do with the demand for newspapers as such, which today is at an all-time peak, and continues to grow at a steady pace,' he asserted."

The point is, of course, that even when two, or several, competing newspapers in a town are both, or all, making money, it is vastly to the advantage of one to buy out the others, establish a monopoly in selling advertising, and benefit from the "operating economies" of one plant, one staff, and exactly as much news coverage as the publisher chooses to give. The advertisers must have him anyway, and the readers have no other pabulum. He will get all the income for a fraction of the outlay, so he can afford to pay a price for his competitor paper far beyond what it might be worth to a buyer from outside, who would continue to operate it competitively. Almost as frequently as not, the "weak" ownership in a town buys out the "strong" ownership. Whoever buys, at almost whatever price, is bound to get his money back fast. The temptation to the seller is the large, beautiful lump of cash he gets by virtue of the limitation of the capital-gains tax to 25 percent. If his paper earned the same amount in its regular operations—which would be highly unlikely as long as the field remained competitive—he would have to pay out a much higher percentage in the graduated income tax. The best thing Congress could do to keep more newspapers going would be to raise the capital-gains tax to the level of the income tax. (Freedom of the press is guaranteed only to those who own one.) There are irresistible reasons for a businessman either to buy or to sell, and anybody who owns the price of a newspaper nowadays must be a businessman.

What you have in a one-paper town is a privately owned public utility that is constitutionally exempt from public regulation, which would be a violation of freedom of the press. As to the freedom of the individual journalist in such a town, it corresponds exactly with what the publisher will allow him. He can't go over to the opposition, because there isn't any. If he leaves, he ends his usefulness to the town, and probably to the state and region in which it is situated, because he takes with him the story that caused his difference with the management, and in a distant place it will have no value. Under the conditions, there is no point in being quixotic.

Frankly, this galloping contraction of the press worries me more than it does Mr. Bryan, who, according to Mr. Porter in the *Times* story, "denied that there was danger of a growing monopoly of news outlets in the growth of single-ownership newspaper cities." (Mr. Bryan's company, with morning and evening papers, is the only ownership in Richmond.) "This danger is minimized," he said, "by the fact that most Americans today have within easy reach not only their hometown papers, but papers published elsewhere, news magazines, and news broadcasts." In any American city that

I know of, to pick up a paper published elsewhere means that you have to go to an out-of-town newsstand, unless you are in a small city that is directly within the circulation zone of a larger one. Even in New York, the out-of-town newsstands are few and hard to find. The papers are, naturally, late; they cost more; and most people would use up a sizable part of every day just traveling to get one. In smaller cities, such stands are even fewer—I know of only one in New Orleans—and in really small places they don't exist. The news magazines—without going into their quality, which would explode me—carry little news, in the course of a year, of any one particular state or city, and what they do carry is usually furnished by a stringer who works on the local paper. News broadcasts offer even less, because often the newspaper owns the radio station, and because television and radio have been pulling steadily out of the news field and regressing toward the animated penny dreadful.

Diversity—and the competition that it causes—does not insure good news coverage or a fair champion for every point of view, but it increases the chances. To make things even stickier, there has been a constriction of the already narrow pipeline through which nearly all the American press receives its foreign and national news. Until a couple of years ago, there were three news services—Associated Press, United Press and International News Service. International was the weakest of the three, and the least trustworthy, being pure Hearst. Nevertheless, good men sometimes worked for it, and every once in a while it had a story that the others didn't. Now it is gone, merged with the U.P. like a canary with a cat. The Washington *Times-Herald* and the Boston *Post* were wretched publications—straight McCarthy-on-the-rocks, with a sprig of David Lawrence—but while they existed it was always possible that by chance or spite one of them might turn up a good story. The same is true of every paper, good or bad, that perishes in an age of no replacements. That there are some competent newspapers in monopoly cities changes nothing. It is not right that a citizen's access to news should be completely aleatory, depending on the character of the monopoly publisher in the city where he happens to live.

There are still a number of cities, usually very big ones, that are not newspaper monopolies, but everywhere the trend is the same. Chicago, for example, had four newspapers—two morning and two evening— seven years ago. It still has, but instead of four ownerships there are now only two, each with one morning paper and one evening paper. That's also the way it is in Los Angeles, now minus the *News,* and Philadelphia has three ownerships and only three papers. (In 1876, Philadelphia had fifteen dailies in English, and Chicago eight.) Here in New York, we still have seven, as we had in 1953—the *Times, Herald Tribune, Mirror,* and *News* in the morning, and the *Post, World-Telegram & Sun,* and *Journal-American* in the afternoon. But in the early twenties, when we were young and gay, there were fourteen dailies of general circulation in Manhattan—the *Times, World, Sun, Herald, Tribune, American,* and *News* in the morning, and the *Evening Sun, Evening World, Post, Mail, Globe, Journal,* and *Telegram* in the afternoon—besides five or six in Brooklyn and the Bronx. So the rate of attrition here is as fast as in the two-paper towns that have dropped to one paper. London, for purposes of comparison, has twelve,[3] not counting a cluster of independent Sunday newspapers—a genre that has never caught on here. The fan of opinion is consequently much wider, including Communist, Socialist, Liberal, and all shades of Conservative, each anxious to catch the others out. The range here is from conservative to reactionary, with the *Post* occasionally making a bolt as far left as Nelson Rockefeller. The spectrum provides little fun, and as the process of blurring goes on, it will provide less.

The rest of the A.N.P.A. meeting here was just about normal. Murray Davis, of the *World-Telegram,* a Scripps-Howard newspaper, interviewed a number of Southern publishers, including W. H. Metz, of the

---

[3] Now ten. The *News-Chronicle,* a morning, and the *Star,* an evening paper, have been sunk. Both were Liberal in politics. The "fan of opinion" is narrower by that much.

Birmingham *Post-Herald,* a Scripps-Howard newspaper, about trouble that they told him they weren't having with the colored people, although they predicted bloodshed if it didn't stop. Mr. Metz said, "The problem won't be solved overnight." The Newspaperboy Committee, a philanthropic cell of the association, "warned that new efforts have been made in Congress to remove the exemption covering newspaper delivery boys from the Wage-Hour Law"—a move that would compel publishers to pay the boys a dollar an hour. "Noting that newspaper delivery boys seldom are involved in youth crime," the *World-Telegram* reported, "the committee observed that 'those concentrating on destruction of newspaperboy work might well direct their energy toward the problem of juvenile delinquency.' " If they got a dollar an hour, the boys might buy narcotics. Finally, the moguls elected a new president to succeed Mr. Bryan—a matter as cut-and-dried as Mr. Nixon's nomination, since the A.N.P.A. vice-president always succeeds to the presidency. The new president, a Mr. Mark Ferree, of the Scripps-Howard newspapers, "has done about everything there is to do on a newspaper except set type," again according to the *World-Telegram,* our Scripps-Howard authority. "He was a reporter, copy reader, editor, advertising salesman, and business executive." His last immersion in editorial ink, according to *Who's Who in America,* was as Sunday editor of the Miami *Herald* in 1927; he has been on the side of the house where they keep the money ever since. This is the side of journalism that it pays best to be on. In fact, it is the lop side.

When I put together *The Wayward Pressman* (1947), the first collection of the Wayward Press pieces I do now and then for *The New Yorker,* I dedicated it, "To the Foundation of a School for Publishers, failing which, no School of Journalism can have meaning."

Nobody has responded to that appeal, either. My

advice apparently has no weight with Megabelodons.
But I read last year in the New York *Times* that Mr.
Newhouse, the journalist chiffonier I have already had
occasion to mention, has set aside $26,000,000 to be
used, after his death, for the foundation of a School of
Communications. The change in title from the old-
fashioned school of journalism underlines the decreas-
ing role of newspapers in the future as envisaged by
a busy paper-jobber. The institution will not be called
a School of Information, either, I noted without astonishment, or a School of News. Communication means
simply getting any idea across and has no intrinsic
relation to truth. It is neutral. It can be a peddler's tool,
or the weapon of a political knave, or the medium of a
new religion. "Journalism" has a reference to what
happens, day by day, but "communication" can deal,
just as well, with what has not happened, what the
communicator wants to happen, or what he wants the
dupe on the other end to think. Its general and increasing substitution, in the schoolmen's jargon, for harm-
less old Journalism disturbs me, as the next little piece
indicated.

Q—What do you do for a living?
A—I am a communicator.
Q—What do you communicate? Scarlet fever? Ap-
prehension?

The Big Decision

OCTOBER 29, 1960

Newspapers write about other newspapers with cir-
cumspection. The two surviving press associations,
whose customers are newspapers, write about newspapers with deference. Newspapers write about themselves with awe, and only after mature reflection.
They know and revere their awful power; like a prizefighter in a bar full of nonprizefighters, they are loath
to loose it. That is why they wait until late in a presi-

dential campaign to let the public know which man they support. The public is not supposed to be able to guess. The newspaper of even moderate self-esteem thinks that if it stated at the beginning of a campaign which candidate it favored, the other fellow might cancel his speaking engagements and quit. To avert this contretemps, the newspaper holds its right cocked as long as possible, or until the unsuspecting fellow it is going to hit has got so far along with his campaign that he will be ashamed to pull out. The paper bites its editorial lip—or, more accurately, the publisher bites the editor's lip. On 80 percent of American newspapers, he makes the editor restrain himself until he can see the whites of the Democrats' eyes. On a dwindling 20 percent, he makes him wait for the whites of the Republicans' eyes. (Headline over a story in the *World-Telegram* on October 18: U.S. DAILY NEWSPAPERS SUPPORT NIXON 4 TO 1, SURVEY SHOWS.) According to legend, though, the decision is unpremeditated. The editorialist, impartial, observes the conflict until, revolted by the gross idiocy of one party or the other, he can contain his wrath no longer. Indignation mounts within his breast, and the bursting point is reached. This happens on all papers at about the same stage of the campaign. They begin to pop all over, and the press associations carry the pops, gravely and without comment. The preponderance of pops is supposed to show the general trend of reasonable thought throughout the country—vox pop, as it were.

Thus, on Sunday, October 16, I was electrified by a box on the first page of the *Herald Tribune* that said, "The *Herald Tribune* has now chosen sides in the Presidential election campaign. In the lead editorial today this newspaper discusses the reasons why it believes one slate of candidates is superior to the other. See page one, Section 2." I turned as directed to see whether the *Tribune* had now chosen to side with Senators Kennedy and Johnson, since I had had the impression that up until then it hadn't. Whom it had chosen to side with were Nixon and Lodge. When I read its reasons, I wondered how it could have taken

so long to make up its mind: "The Nixon-Lodge
ticket presents an unparalleled combination of demonstrated leadership to the American voter, whether he
is accustomed to voting for the *man,* the *party,* or the
principles." The *Times* of the same day dutifully recorded the decision at which the *Tribune* had arrived:
NIXON CHOICE URGED BY HERALD TRIBUNE. The *Times*
quoted a couple of paragraphs, and then some sabo-
teur added, "The *Herald Tribune* is a continuation of
the *Tribune,* which absorbed the *Herald* in 1924. The
Tribune was established in 1841 by Horace Greeley,
who became one of the founders of the Republican
Party in 1854." In this I discerned a discreet attempt
to hint that the *Trib's* decision was hardly unexpected.
It smacked of interpretive reporting—a dangerous
practice—and also indirectly promoted the idea that
the *Tribune* had never supported a Democratic candidate anyway. This is not true. The *Tribune* supported Greeley himself when he ran for President with
Democratic endorsement in 1872, and under similar
circumstances it would be likely to switch again.

Two days earlier, the *Times* had printed, without
comment, an Associated Press dispatch to the effect
that the Scripps-Howard papers had at length made
up *their* minds for Nixon and Lodge: "The nineteen
member papers describe themselves as politically independent. Scripps-Howard backed President Eisenhower in 1952 and 1956." The dispatch, I was happy
to see, did not say that eighteen of the nineteen papers
independently arrived at an identically worded decision every four years (in Memphis there are two
Scripps-Howard papers, so a little rewording is required in one of them), or that the last time they
endorsed a non-Republican for President was in 1936.
(In 1924, they were for Robert M. LaFollette, Sr.,
but they have quieted down mightily since then.) In
the same week, the Hearst papers, which last backed
a Democrat in 1932, reached a conclusion in favor of
the Republican candidates. The A.P. and the U.P.I.
reported the decision deadpan, and the *Times* published it that way. The *News,* on October 13, "having
carefully considered the merits and demerits of the

candidates," made the same decision it had made every presidential year since its late publisher, Joseph Patterson, split with Franklin Delano Roosevelt over the Second World War. The *Times* treated its announcement just as solemnly.

If I cite the *Times* here, it is only because it sets a pattern for newspapers in this country. It did not originate—although it helps perpetuate—the custom of treating a foregone conclusion as news in order to butter up a fellow-publisher. If Thomas E. Dewey announced in the third month of the campaign that he was supporting Mr. Nixon, or if Senator Mike Mansfield said that he was for Mr. Kennedy, their declarations would not be considered hot news, and the newspaper "decisions" quoted above are no more astonishing. If one employs the old man-bites-dog standard of news value, the only newspapers whose decisions make news are those that change from their alignment in the last election, like the New Bedford (Massachusetts) *Standard-Times,* which, according to an A.P. dispatch in the *Times* on October 15, endorsed the two senators and "noted that this was the first time it had supported Democrats in a Presidential election." The dispatch added, "In 1952, its publisher, Basil Brewer, was campaign manager in Massachusetts for Senator Robert A. Taft, of Ohio, when Mr. Taft sought the Republican Presidential nomination." But such defections grow more rare each year, and, like the *Standard-Times*'s, usually reflect an eccentric situation. (Mr. Brewer's complaint against the Republican candidates is apparently that they are not Republican enough.)

The decisions of papers that have changed sides at least once since the Second World War may also be worth reporting, since there is a possibility that the positions of such papers are not permanently fixed. The Chicago *Sun-Times,* for example, which announced its support for Nixon and Lodge two weeks ago, supported President Eisenhower in 1952 and 1956 but was for Truman in 1948, while the St. Louis *Post-Dispatch*, which has announced for Kennedy and Johnson, supported Dewey in that year. But if such decisions are worth reporting, they should be given a bit of illuminative background, such as that when the *Sun-Times* supported Truman its proprietor was a Democrat, who has since died, and that his son and successor is a Republican. The paper is as regularly Republican now as its arch-rival in the advertising field, the Chicago *Tribune*. And instead of recording briefly and without comment the *Post*'s endorsement of Kennedy and Johnson on October 17, the *Times*, if it had considered reader interest, would have noted that in 1958 the *Post* editorially endorsed Averell Harriman for Governor of New York but that Mrs. Dorothy Schiff, the publisher, canceled the endorsement sixteen hours before the election, much as she might have returned a dress to a department store. This time, both Mrs. Schiff and James A. Wechsler, the *Post*'s editor, signed the declaration of choice, but it is hardly likely that the signatures are legally binding.

The *Times* itself, as I write, has not signified which ticket it *will* endorse in the election, and here, at least, there is considerable reader curiosity about whether it will defect, or redefect, from the nearly one-party press that is one of the oddest phenomena of national politics. (The *Times* used to call itself "independent-Democrat.") It would be a hopeful portent for the press as a whole—the first in a great many years.[1] For a situation in which 80 percent of the press consistently takes a position in which it is followed by only about 50 percent of the people must be an unhealthy one for an industry that in this campaign is meeting its greatest challenge as the medium through which the public gets its political information. The television confrontations of the two candidates, whether you choose to call them debates or quiz shows, have admittedly done more than any one other feature of the campaign to form the public's impression of the two men. The meetings have proved so popular that they will be hard for future candidates to avoid, or for the networks to play down. They serve as controls on mis-

---

[1] The *Times* endorsed Kennedy, and it was a good portent. Never sell hope short.

representation of the candidates' qualifications and ideas by a press that in many regions is a partisan monopoly. To regain public confidence, newspapers from now on will have to work up some difference of opinion among themselves.

There are many objections to the visual presentation of candidates as a principal method of deciding issues; it would be unfair to a homely genius or to a hero who stuttered, and the first procedures adopted for the joint appearances of Mr. Nixon and Mr. Kennedy were frequently silly. Still, they *were* the first. There was about them some of the ungainliness that must have afflicted early baseball, but they are dangerously (from the newspaper point of view) susceptible of improvement. The disappearance of newspapers, accelerating the obsolescence of the written word, would be a misfortune for a lot of us. I myself was recently frightened by the receipt of a letter from the Ohio State University School of Journalism enclosing a questionnaire about my "experience in communications." One of the questions was "How do you rate the importance of the following skills in your present job? WRITING? Essential? Important? Useful? Occasionally useful? Of little value? . . ." I would hate to have to answer "No value at all. Now looking for a job mugging electronically."

I was at this point about to quit, temporarily at least, the gloomy theme of newspaper mortality, when my eye fell upon the following passage in *The Wayward Pressman,* a book now completely out of print, and thought it too good to spare the reader. It refers to a tragedy of 1931:

The pattern of a newspaperman's life is like the plot of *Black Beauty.* Sometimes he finds a kind master who gives him a dry stall and an occasional bran mash in the form of a Christmas bonus, sometimes he falls into the hands of a mean owner who drives him in spite of spavins and expects him to live on potato peelings. The *Sunday World* was a dry-stall interlude in my wanderings (without bran mash), but I was soon to be put between the shafts of the ragman's cart.[2]

So personal a memory of the end of the *World* newspapers may seem as limited as an account by the ship's cat of the sinking of the Titanic. But there were nearly three thousand employees (2,867 was the official count), and each lost his illusions about the validity of the kind-master concept in the newspaper world as abruptly as I did. The total effect, when nearly three thousand workers in a limited field are thrown on the street simultaneously, is much worse than three thousand times one. One newspaper worker out of a job, even in slack times, always has some chance of catching on again. So he has hope. There just aren't enough newspaper jobs in the country to take care of three thousand. So each one knows that the odds are all against him. This three thousand included printers and circulation and advertising personnel, as well as editorial workers. The printers, who were already well organized, did better than the others. They got a couple of days' work a week in the chapels of other newspapers, in accordance with union share-the-work plans, to tide them over until, one by one, full-time jobs opened up. For editorial workers it was a free-for-all scramble, in which we young men had an advantage over the more experienced and less adaptable seniors, with the higher salaries that they had painfully achieved. A high salary, in a time of newspaper disaster, operates like too much rank in the Army. It would be indelicate to offer a general officer a company or battalion, so superfluous general officers get nothing to do. In the same way, city editors do not like to offer a high-priced man a low salary, because he will be discontented.

---

[2] Scripps-Howard.

So scores of skilled journalists like my old preceptors Max Fischel and Lindsay Denison of the *Evening World* were out of jobs and stayed out to the end of their lives. They got nice funerals and long obits in the papers that hadn't hired them after the *World* went down. Not that there is any harm in good funerals or obits. The friends who attended the former and wrote the latter had no power to do anything more.

I had never before been so glad that I had no dependents.

The end of the *World* marked the beginning of realism in the relation of American newspaper employees to their employers. The employers had been realistic for a long time.

It took the abandonment of an "institution" like the *World* to drive the lesson home.

There are two good books describing the scuttling while under way of the *World,* which had been the greatest and was still one of the leading newspapers in America. I can vouch for their excellence since I have just reread them after a lapse of sixteen years. Few events in history have been more vigorously reported.

One is called *The End of the World* (Harper's, 1931), subtitled "A Post-Mortem by its intangible assets," in which 27 members of the staff cover each aspect of their common disaster. The other is Jim Barrett's *The World, the Flesh and Messrs. Pulitzer* (Vanguard, 1931), in which the city editor, who led a great impromptu anti-scuttle movement, reviewed the events leading up to the tragedy. Both must be required reading in schools of journalism if the schools are any good.

So there is no need for me to describe in detail here the legally sanctioned desertion by Joseph Pulitzer's heirs of the papers he had forbidden them ever to sell. The heirs had, Barrett points out, taken out $25,000,000 in profits from the papers subsequent to the founder's

death. They had plowed back nothing into the property—the same story as the New England textile men,
except that newspaper publishers like to advertise
themselves as more idealistic than mere bag-spinners.
The papers had lost $3,000,000 in their last three years,
according to the heirs, who wished to make the deficit
sound as impressive as possible. They therefore decided to quit—$22,000,000 for them, plus the sale
price, and a kick in the pants for the three thousand
employees, some of whom had helped the big Pulitzer
make the papers.

The Pulitzer heirs, without any warning of their intention, made public on Tuesday, February 24, their desire
to sell the newspapers immediately to Roy Howard for
a sum of $5,000,000, to be paid in installments by a
plan that made the receipt of the last two millions decidedly aleatory. Howard declared his intent to suppress the papers, except "in spirit," combining the
name *World* and some features from the *World* papers
with his *Evening Telegram,* a punch-drunk enterprise
which had already cost him $8,000,000 in four years.

Each of the 2,867 regular employees of the *World*
got two weeks' pay, and Herbert Pulitzer for the trus-
tees promised that the first $500,000 received from
Howard would be distributed among the ex-Worldings.
I do not know whether this sum was to be in addition
to the two weeks' pay or to include it: if distributed
equally among the former employees, it would have
amounted to $174.43 a head.

Back of the city editor's desk on the twelfth floor of
the World Building was a bronze tablet subscribed for
by members of the *World* staff. It is significant that the
tablet was paid for by members of the staff, not their
bosses. The legend read:

In memory of
George T. Humes
reporter on the World
mortally injured in the Stamford Railroad wreck
he thought first of his paper

and with indomitable courage
sent the news of the disaster
Born April 12, 1878
Died June 13, 1913.

Poor Humes should go down in history as a founding member of the American Newspaper Guild. The contrast of his loyalty to that of his employers had an influence on the mind of every man who had ever worked on the *World*.

The abandonment of the *World* and *Evening World* seemed to me then a unique enormity. Two more New York newspapers disappeared during the Depression years, the *Daily Graphic* and the *American*, but they were small loss. The advent of *PM* in 1940 marked the first increase in the roster in nearly twenty years. We greeted it with the delight that bird-watchers manifest when the Department of the Interior reports the birth of a new whooping crane, Alas, it had no morrow. By 1949, when I had the grim duty of writing the following obituary notice, I had a sickly feeling that I was in the presence of an Irreversible Trend. (A Mr. Carl E. Lindstrom, for many a year executive editor of the Hartford *Times* and subsequently a professor at the University of Michigan School of Journalism, last fall published a book entitled *The Fading American Newspaper*.)

Toward a
One-Paper Town

FEBRUARY 18, 1949

"I wouldn't weep about a shoe factory or a branch-line railroad shutting down," Heywood Broun wrote in the newly named *World-Telegram* after the *World* and *Evening World* expired, nearly eighteen years ago. "But newspapers are different."

Little of the emotional writing that followed the

passing of the *World* was evident in the recent news stories on the disappearance of the *Star*, the short-lived epilogue to *PM,* which ran out of money on Thursday, January 27. The Pulitzer papers were glorious has-beens in 1931, and could have made a comeback, I still think. Poor *PM* and its continuation, the *Star,* never quite got there. The *World* story was bigger in a physical sense, too. The shutdown in 1931 put twenty-eight hundred men and women on the street, while the *Star*'s end threw out only four hundred and eight. Still, to the people on the *Star* it was tragic, especially because they had tried to put out a memorable newspaper.

The *Star* didn't carry any real news story of its end at all; merely stated the fact in a bleak, page-one announcement, phrased like an office memorandum and signed by Bartley C. Crum, the publisher, and Joseph Barnes, the editor. An old-time newspaperman called this to my attention a little sadly. "When you looked at the last copy of the *World,* you saw a detailed story of the final disposition of the paper all over the right-hand side of the first page," he said. "But *PM* and the *Star* were never strong on reporting." The end result, of course, was the same. It seems more and more to be the rule that the Democrats lose the newspapers and the Republicans the elections.

The *Herald Tribune* was the only New York newspaper to give a full story of the *Star*'s death front-page play. The story was a column and a quarter long and unobtrusively sympathetic. The reporter, Don Ross, had evidently been at the meeting of *Star* editorial employees on the afternoon of January 27, when Crum announced his bad news. "Mr. Crum, who looked drawn and pale, hoisted himself to a desk and said that today's three editions would be the last the *Star* would publish," Ross wrote. "Mr. Barnes, looking equally fatigued, also attended the meeting. The staff was stunned. They had heard reports that the paper needed money, but most of them apparently believed that Mr. Crum and Mr. Barnes would pull them through." Ross might have added that people on *PM* had got used to such scares, having experienced recurrent ones almost since the founding of the paper, in the summer of 1940, when it soon became touch and go whether Marshall Field would take over from his fellow-investors in the original scheme, who had no more to invest.

The *Times,* second only to the *Tribune* in the amount of space devoted to the story, gave it a full column on the first page of the second edition. Five of the six other surviving New York dailies of general circulation apparently took a calm view of the disappearance of their contemporary. The exception was the *Journal-American,* to which I shall refer later. The *News* and *Mirror,* in fact, polished off the *Star* with a well-buried paragraph apiece on the morning after the *Star* suspended publication. The *Mirror,* to be sure, did get word of the occurrence onto its front page a couple of days later, in the form of an announcement that it had taken over the *Star*'s comic strip "Barnaby," and that, beginning Monday, January 31, former *Star* readers would be able to follow their favorite cartoon characters in the pages of the *Mirror.* The *Post* and *Sun* stories, on the day of suspension, were brief but decent. The *World-Telegram* story said that the announcement "brought to an end today a weird and costly chapter in the history of contemporary journalism in which a Chicago millionaire, who inherited a vast department store and real-estate fortune, attempted to establish himself as a New York publisher." Over the weekend, the *Times, Herald Tribune,* and *Post* followed up with kindly editorials.

None of the obituary articles mentioned the fact that *PM,* of which the *Star* was a sequel, was the only new daily started in New York since 1924, a vintage year that produced the *Mirror* and the *Evening Graphic.* Five papers have gone out of business since: the *World* and *Evening World,* in February, 1931; the *Graphic* in July, 1932 (even *PM,* under its own name, lasted a couple of months longer); Mr. Hearst's pet, the *American* ("A Paper for People Who Think"), in June, 1937; and finally *PM* and the *Star,* which I here count as one. This leaves the city with three fewer papers than it had 24 years ago, although the population has increased by at least two million, and indicates how quickly the consolidation of control over the sale of news has advanced. I think this was the most important aspect of the *Star* story. The record does not indicate that only papers that try to be liberal or literate, or both, are doomed in New York. The *Graphic* was an atrocious job and the *American* was beneath contempt, but they died just as dead as if they had been meritorious. Someday, a towering genius of the publishing business will get Lil' Abner and Steve Canyon and Dick Tracy and Moon Mullins *and* Barnaby under one tent with Walter Winchell and the Harvest Moon Dance Festival, and some other towering genius—or maybe the same one, using a different corporate name—will get Walter Lippmann and Arthur Krock and the Fresh Air Fund and the Hundred Neediest Cases under the same management, and the number of morning papers will be halved. It is so hard to tell the *World-Telegram* and the *Sun* apart now, except typographically, that a merger would be hardly noticeable. If the trend continues, New York will be a one- or two-paper town by 1975.

One of the good things about *PM* was that it was different from any other New York paper, and the differences were irreconcilable. You couldn't imagine it, or the *Star,* merging with any other paper. Also, it was pure in heart. It sometimes seemed to me to make virtue unnecessarily repulsive by publishing pictures of buck-toothed ballad singers and knobby-kneed rhythmic dancers and interior shots of neglected mental wards in distant states, and it occasionally occurred to me that the space thus employed could have been used for news stories. The injustices it whacked away at were genuine enough, but an awful lot of whacks seemed to fall on the same injustices. A girl to whom I gave a subscription to *PM* in 1946 asked me after a time, "Doesn't *anybody* have any trouble except the Jews and the colored people?" When you read it steadily for a while, you got the impression that you were reading the publication of some such large order as the Lonely Hearts or the American Treehound Association, whose members shared a lot of interests that you didn't. Two articles of *PM*'s faith seemed to be salvation through psychotherapy[1] and damnation through a frivolous approach to amusements. Still, while other papers were inventing anecdotes to discredit price control or lamenting the hard lot of large corporations, *PM* kept the facts of the case available to anybody who would bother to read them.

PM's editors were not humorous men, but they realized that the paper lacked gaiety, and every now and then they brought in professional funnymen to run columns. It never did any good. The humorists took to reading Max Lerner and became ashamed of themselves. They reminded me of the cocker spaniels belonging to the father of Henri Cartier-Bresson, the photographer. "My father was a great fancier of cockers," Cartier-Bresson *fils* once told me. (He pronounced cocker in the French fashion, "co-kare.") "He had a dear friend in Paris who was the director of the morgue. The morgue is a large place quite near the Gare de Montparnasse, where my father would arrive from the country with his dogs when he was

---

[1] The *Post* has picked up this approach and learned to make it pay. It permits a longer, droolier, treatment of sex and crime stories, with more specific details, than the old tabloid method, which was comparatively reticent, being based on hints of the too-awful-to-mention and headlines hard to comprehend: ORGY, MAD, HORROR, FIEND. If you work up on a story of prostitution or murder from an enlightened direction you can say *what kind* of orgy, madness, fiendishness. The reader gets his drool and is at the same time filled with a sense of superiority because he is participating in the progress of science. The call girl feels a need of approval, the murderer has been caught masturbating by his pa. Nobody does anything for the hell of it. In the frivolous department, though, the *Post* has *not* followed the *PM* formula. It runs endless wordage on movie stars, whom it habitually calls by their first names, and on some days reads like a cross between the *Psychoanalytical Journal* and *Silver Screen,* all clotted around an intelligent editorial page, a couple of superior Washington columns, Herblock's frequently inspired cartoons, and a number of soliloquists with overflowing hearts. The total effect is that of a daily visit to the first act of a play by Clifford Odets.

going to exhibit them at the National Dog Show. Rather than put them in a boarding kennel, he would keep them in the morgue until the show opened, thus saving expense. But the atmosphere depressed the dogs so much that they never won any prizes."

One trouble with *PM* in its early years, I have heard (I did not see it regularly then), was that it was completely unpredictable, with the result that the reader who had got to like it one week would find it quite different the next. By 1945, when I did begin to see it every day, it had fallen into the antithesis of this difficulty; it always seemed the same. Also, it had gathered about a hundred thousand readers, who loved it exactly as it was. One hundred thousand was an awkward number, because it was half of what *PM* needed to pay its way. It was too many to throw away but not enough to make the paper go. *PM* couldn't get the second hundred thousand unless it changed; it couldn't change without losing a substantial number of the first hundred thousand. Once, in a gesture toward popular appeal, the sports department picked an all-scholastic Greater New York football team. The paper received a flock of letters from old readers reproaching it for exalting brutality and asking why it didn't pick an all-scholastic *scholastic* team.

I think the *Star* was making progress toward a successful changeover, although the process resembled changing clothes under water. The *Star* could—and, tactically, should—have claimed credit for bringing down the price of milk in New York City. Probably the price would have come down eventually without the investigation that the *Star* fostered, but it would have taken a longer time doing it. It seemed to me that a young *Star* cartoonist named Walt Kelly,[2] who used to be a Walt Disney draftsman, did a wonderful job during the presidential campaign. The only bit of caricature that I remember from that period is Kelly's mechanized Mr. Dewey, with a torso that might have been either a cash register or a slot machine. Kelly had an advantage enjoyed by few of his competitors

---

[2] Mr. Pogo-to-be.

in that he was turned loose on Mr. Dewey. The *Star* took the winning political line, although it shocked half its old customers when it did it; the circulation manager grew melancholy when he heard the paper was going to come out against Wallace. The new management got the circulation up by thirty-five thousand before the *Star* folded, and that meant it must have gained at least fifty thousand new readers, for during the campaign it surely lost many of the old ones to the *Post,* which, as far as I could see, made Zionism the chief issue of the election. The *Post* supported Dewey and Wallace, in equal portions.

I shall always be saddened by the thought that I saw Mr. Crum miss a signal that, had he heeded it, might have sent the *Star*'s circulation up to a quarter of a million almost overnight. I am not in a position to blame him, because I missed it, too. I was in the Biltmore bar with a couple of *Star* men on the evening of the Thursday before the election, when President Truman was making his last campaign tour of the city. The President, of course, was staying at the Biltmore, which houses Democratic National Headquarters. Crum came down from the presidential suite and said, "The old boy is crazy. He thinks he's going to win. He's standing there under the shower telling everybody that he'll sweep the country." I laughed with the others. If, guided by some mystic light, Crum had believed and ordered the *Star* to headline the flat, unique prediction that the President would win, he would have sold more, rather than fewer, papers during the days remaining before election. And after Election Day the *Star* would have been famous from coast to coast. Crum was rooting for Truman. But he didn't believe the feedbox tip. It's a wonderful example of how you get to believe what you read in the opposition newspapers.

The *Journal-American* began its story about the end of the *Star* in this manner: "The New York *Star* wrote its own obituary today, ceasing publication seven months after it succeeded the newspaper *PM,* from which it inherited its leftist line. . . . Demise of the *Star* threw 408 employees out of jobs. Most of

them consistently followed the leftist line." This comes
under the head of shooting at lifeboats. "The *Star* was
the only New York paper to support President Truman, but it also subtly backed Henry Wallace. It also
supported pro-Communist Representative Vito Mar-
cantonio and leftist former Rep. Leo Isaacson of the
Bronx in his losing bid for reelection. Left-wingers
and the Moscow-line faithful said they expected some
of the *Star*'s circulation will be picked up by the Communist *Daily Worker*."

Twenty-four hours later, the *Mirror*, which is the
Journal-American's sister-in-Hearst, was soliciting circulation from among *Star* readers who liked Barnaby,
without insisting upon a loyalty test for anybody possessed of three cents.

The follow-up on this performance was a column
in the Monday *Journal-American* by Frank Conniff,
one of a large squad of apprentice Peglers. (Pegler
himself, as I write this, has not yet got around to the
subject of the *Star*'s finish. I presume he is waiting for
it to get dead enough for him to light into, like most
of the objects of his spleen.) "Many and varied will
be the reasons for its demise," Conniff wrote, in part,
"but all autopsies must agree on one salient point. The
deceased was never a good newspaper. The *Star* consumed its energies poking derision at its betters without bothering to observe the fundamentals of our
craft. . . . [Readers] want lively news, intelligent features, good pictures, comics, and departments. And it
was in just these categories that the *Star* lagged behind
the newspapers it sought to deride."

Eager to observe the fundamentals of Mr. Conniff's
craft, I looked through the copy of the *Journal-American* in which his little gem appeared. Not counting
the sports and financial pages, it carried eighteen columns of what might be called news—ALI TO SUE WIFE
TODAY, EX-COP AND WOMAN DIE IN AUTO CRASH, RED
TRIAL POLICE SCAN SPECTATORS, and DOWDY GALS
BACK UP DAPPER REDS AT TRIAL are sample headlines.
Eight columns—two on the first page and six on the
second—were consecrated to the memoirs of Robert
Stripling, recently resigned investigator for the House

Un-American Activities Committee. ("I want to tell in detail the price that men must pay for the dubious privilege of being reviled in print and on the air. I want to tell how remarkably difficult it is to direct the people's attention to a sleepless conspiracy being waged against them.") There were also 34 columns of space occupied by the output of 26 columnists, including Bob Hope, Major General David P. Barrows (retired president of the University of California), Cholly Knickerbocker (who suggested that the Republicans run Tyrone Power for President, because "President Tyrone Power could do just as well as President Truman"), Mary Haworth, Betty Betz Bets (The Teen Set); Dorothy Kilgallen, Louella Parsons, Paul Gallico, Louis Sobol (*"perdrix aux choux,* that's matzoh balls with a French accent"), Bob Considine, and Conniff himself. Considine, by the way, appeared to be the busiest man in the paper. He was listed as the editor of Mr. Stripling's autobiography as well as the author of his own column, which means that he filled six columns, or a third as much as the paper's total of straight news. In addition to all this writing, he posed for a picture on page 2, in which he was shown receiving the Golden Book Award of the Catholic Writers' Guild for being the author of a biography of Babe Ruth.

In this copy of the *Journal-American,* I was particularly impressed by a lively bit of news headed, FAITH IN AMERICA SHATTERED ABROAD, by Karl H. Von Wiegand, billed by the paper as Dean of Foreign Correspondents. Without Mr. Conniff's guidance, I might have suspected the swatch of rhetoric that followed of having some editorial content. "Germany, Austria, Italy, and Japan, which for a long time have held back expansion of Soviet Russia and its communism in Europe and Asia, were utterly destroyed and their leaders hanged," Dean Von Wiegand had written regretfully. ". . . While trying to 'sell' or impose 'Americanism' in Europe, America imported far greater 'Europeanism' and its socialism, as reflected in the election of Truman and the State of the Union message to Congress."

The most "intelligent feature" in that day's *Journal-American,* I thought, was an Office Orchid contest, in which one girl in each of a number of office buildings is being selected as prettiest by the elevator starter. Elimination beauty contests are being held between the building winners, and there is to be a ten-girl semifinal at the Stork Club, where the contestants will meet Harry M. Popkin, producer of the gay celluloid comedy *My Dear Secretary.* Then there will be a five-girl final, to be decided during a week of voting at the theater where *My Dear Secretary* is playing, and where all the voters will have to pay their way in. I thought right up until I came on the name of the picture that it would be "For Whom the Elevator Bell Tolls." The layout and the story take up slightly less than a half page, and the two Office Orchids *du jour* look even prettier than Mr. Considine.

Looking back over this piece, I don't think I've done justice to what the loss of the *Star* did to the town. The *Star,* as I have explained perhaps too fully, had never been a really good newspaper, but as long as it existed there was always a chance it would become one, because it was trying. At least five of the eight survivors are content with being successful bad newspapers, and the *Post,* reaching out for columnists in all directions at once, seems to be trying to be a successful bad-good-and-indifferent newspaper, depending on which page you turn to. Without the New York *Times* and *Herald Tribune,* New York would have to depend on the air-mail editions of *The Times* of London for world news. And neither of these two tolerable journals of information expresses the political or economic thought of the majority of Americans. Viewed from this side of the Atlantic, the gamut of London newspapers, the Labour Party's *Daily Herald,* the Liberal *News-Chronicle,* the reasonably Conservative *Times* and the unreasonably Conservative *Daily Telegraph,* with the big circulation *Mail, Express* and tabloids making up the pack, looks almost too good to be true, with the *News of the World* on Sunday (7,500,000 circulation) obviously the champion newspaper of the world by Hearst-McCormick standards. The final floundering of the Star, moreover, will probably have a deterrent effect on other millionaires who might be talked into backing a paper. There is a much readier market for baseball clubs. What we need here, I believe more firmly than ever, is a large, rambunctious, American equivalent of the *Daily Herald* to balance our all-out Tory press. Once that was established I think we would find the *Times* and *Herald Trib* coming over toward a true center, or maybe a little left of it. At present they can afford thoroughly stodgy editorial policies, because no matter what they do their readers can't desert them for the *News* and *Mirror*.

Just about a year later, I preached at another newspaper funeral. My eulogy was headed as follows.

Dismally

JANUARY 28, 1950

The first quarter of the year is the most perilous for newspapers. The lift of holiday advertising, which keeps an ailing paper going through Christmas, has disappeared; the optimism of spring has not yet begun to affect the hard-pressed publisher or anybody he might borrow money from. So he does it in. The *Sun* disappeared below the horizon early this month, offering evidence that a conservative policy is no guarantee of immortality. The *World-Telegram* bought the *Sun*'s good name and whatever goodwill came with it, and appeared on January 5 as the New York *World-Telegram and the Sun.* Like the vitamins we are assured are added to bread, the *Sun* was visible only on the label.

Thomas W. Dewart, president and publisher of the

Sun, wrote in his valedictory statement, on January 4:
"Recently advertising revenues of the *Sun* and the
World-Telegram have not kept pace with mounting
production costs. . . . Between them they have divided
approximately 650,000 circulation—enough to assure
the economic stability of one newspaper, but not
enough for two in this metropolitan area." (The
World-Telegram's circulation was 365,000, Monday
through Friday, and the *Sun's* 277,000; averaging in
Saturday sales, always much lower, the figures were,
respectively, 335,000 and 231,000.) Mr. Dewart pref-
aced this statement of essentials with a denunciation
of labor unions, by way of a last shot before his guns
flooded out. Roy Howard, editor and president of the
World-Telegram, wrote: "Tomorrow the New York
Sun will cease publication, and its journalistic functions in the New York newspaper field will be assumed by the *World-Telegram.*" In 1931, Mr.
Howard, in a statement of similar tone, had as blithely
assumed for his paper the functions of the Democratic
and liberal *World.* The 1950 assumption seemed better
founded; I could recall offhand few of the *Sun's* functions that the *World-Telegram* had not already assumed. The *Post,* which, with the *Journal-American,*
now constitutes the survivor's only afternoon competition, commented editorially: "It might be said that
the *World-Telegram's* hardening conservatism destroyed the *Sun's* last reasons for existence. . . . The
conservative publishing field was hopelessly overpopu-
lated." The *Post,* which had the members of its own
staff worried last year, was obviously feeling its beans.

I could not help wondering, however, whether Mr.
Howard would succeed in assuming the *Sun's* readers
as easily as its functions. In 1931, I remembered, he
had merged the *World* and the *Evening World* with
what was then the *Telegram,* thus "acquiring" a combined circulation of 800,000. But the resultant *World-
Telegram* enjoyed a circulation of more than a half
million only momentarily and had dropped to a six-
day average of 413,000 by September 30 of the same
year, whence it slowly but steadily declined to a five-
day 365,000, and a six-day 335,000. Where the other

readers went is a subject for speculation; they apparently did not consider themselves part of the property. [Note: The *World-Telly and Sun's* six-day average now is not 556,000, the combined average of 1950, but about 400,000. Again there have been fugitives— if this continues, publishers will ask for a Dred Scott runaway-reader decision.]

The first issue of the New York *World-Telegram and the Sun* did not at first glance seem to have assumed any new functions. Far inside it, however, I found the "Word Game," a feature I had long considered the warmest spot in the *Sun's* slowly chilling mass. In the "Word Game," you form as many four-letter-or-better words as you can from the letters of an eight- or ten-letter word proposed by the department's anonymous editor. A median and an optimum score are given, and there is a small gridiron in which the reader may write down all the words he can think of before reaching his suburban destination. A time limit, usually 20 or 30 minutes, is set, but in practice the duration of the game is likely to be decided by the New York Central or the New Haven timetable. The word on the first day of the new venture was "dismally."

The *Sun's* dramatic and movie critics, Ward Morehouse and Eileen Creelman, had also moved over to the N.Y. *W.-T and the S.,* I noted, but apparently not to take the place of William Hawkins and Alton Cook (Hawkins and Cook reviewed the new show and movie that afternoon, while the émigrés did chitchat columns), and so had H. I. Phillips, the *Sun's* officially comical columnist, who found himself among such younger japes as Frederick Othman and Robert Ruark. Also, the N.Y. *World-Telegram etc.,* had become the only New York paper in my memory with two columns on contract bridge, one by Charles Goren, ex-*Sun* bridge editor, the other by William McKenney, ex-*World-Telegram* bridge editor. None of these innovations, except the "Word Game," appeared basic. Rather, it seemed to me, it was the *Journal-American* that, in rescuing George Sokolsky, had preserved from the wreckage of the *Sun* a hunk so big that it might well be considered a function. His column should complement Westbrook Pegler's magnificently in commenting on the disintegration of the American Republic, which will now be able to disintegrate all in one paper.

One of the *Sun*'s functions that *nobody* assumed was the publication of the solution of the *Sun*'s last crossword puzzle, which appeared in the January 4 issue with the usual accompanying line, "Tomorrow the Solution." This presumably left thousands of puzzlers in a state of eternal uncertainty about a three-letter word meaning "candlenut tree."

The decision that either the *Sun* or the *World-Telegram* had to disappear from the metropolitan scene was made neither by their proprietors nor by their readers but by the advertising departments of a number of New York retail stores. When a liberal paper fails, one frequently hears the charge that politically antagonistic advertisers discriminated against it. No such suspicion was attached to the departure of the *Sun*, which indicates that conformity may contain its own peril. What had happened was made clear by *Editor & Publisher*, a trade weekly that keeps sentimentality and factual research in separate, airtight compartments. "A highly-placed *Sun* man said: 'This would not have happened if the department stores hadn't kicked us in the pants,'" *Editor & Publisher* reported. "A million and a half lines at a contract rate of about 85 cents tells the story. Department store losses are especially significant. Of the 1,561,634 lines lost by the *Sun* between 1948 and 1949, fully 1,466,-296 was in the retail classification, and more than two-thirds of that figure—1,000,000 lines—was in the department-store field. Figures for the *World-Telegram* show a similar trend, though not nearly as sharp a one. . . . The *World-Telegram*'s loss in total linage between 1948 and 1949 was about 6%, virtually all of it (some 700,000 lines) in the department-store field." By cutting down more on their advertising in the *Sun* than in the *World-Telegram*, the department stores rendered their decision.

The fullest editorial comment I saw upon the *Sun*'s

businesslike exit appeared in the Chicago *Daily News,* over the signature of its proprietor, John S. Knight, who also publishes the Detroit *Free Press* and papers in Akron and Miami. Mr. Knight writes a Saturday editorial called "The Editor's Notebook" for all his papers and does not stint himself on space. The heading on the January 7 "Notebook" read: "New York *Sun* Extinguished by High Costs and Low Spirit." After paying his respects to the *Sun*'s golden days under Charles A. Dana, who died in 1897, Mr. Knight turned chill. 'The *Sun* became just another good newspaper with dull, factual reporting and complete market coverage," he wrote, "but wholly lacking a sparkle, imagination and impact. . . . More than anything else, the setting of the *Sun* is a graphic illustration of what can happen to any newspaper when it lives with a cash register in the place where its editorial heart belongs."

This summed up the event, I thought, except for the references to a "good newspaper," which the *Sun* had never been in my personal, post-Dana memory, and to "factual reporting," which the *Sun*'s wasn't always, particularly during the 1947–48 preelection buildup of phony spy stories. But the *Sun* had its good spots during its last, coverlet-picking days, such as the series on waterfront rackets by Malcolm Johnson, which illustrated the advantages of union hiring halls, forbidden by the *Sun*'s cherished Taft-Hartley Act, and the book reviews by William McFee.

The *Herald Tribune*'s pip-pip here was more tactful. "For decades the name of the *Sun* symbolized a type of journalism which was a precious part of our national heritage," it stated. "Through the editorship of Charles A. Dana and Edward P. Mitchell [publisher 1909–11] the human touch in news reporting became the American way of reporting. It is to these old days of warmth and wit and straightforward writing that memories will turn with regret as the death of the *Sun* appears in the headlines."

The number of people in the United States, or even on the editorial staff of the *Herald Tribune,* whose memories go as far back as newspaper writing before the Spanish-American War is limited, and that, I think, was a basic cause of the *Sun*'s failure. "The *Sun* stood by its convictions to the end," the *Herald Tribune* said. It might have added that the *Sun*'s convictions were not essentially different from those of the successful New York *Daily News*. The trouble with the *Sun* was that it never changed its manner, and its stories often produced the effect of bebop played by the Society for Ancient Instruments. Its public, like that for red flannel underwear, was hard to renew. The *Sun* news story most frequently recalled in its obituaries was the one known as the Moon Hoax, a stunt perpetrated by its founder, Benjamin Day, in 1835; the most famous bit of *Sun* writing anybody could remember was the Christmas editorial, written by a man named Francis P. Church in the vintage year of 1897, that began, "Yes, Virginia, there is a Santa Claus."

The end-of-a-newspaper story has become one of the commonplaces of our time, and schools of journalism are probably giving courses in how to write one: the gloom-fraught city room, the typewriters hopelessly tapping out stories for the last edition, the members of the staff cleaning out their desks and wondering where the hell they are going to go. The technique involves a certain amount of reference to earlier disasters of the same sort, as does a story about a hotel fire or the sinking of a submarine. One measure of such events is called in headlines the "Toll"; the folding of the *World* put twenty-eight hundred employees on the street, of the *Star* four hundred, of the *Sun* twelve hundred. Another is the age of the decedent. The *Sun* was in its hundred-and-seventeenth year; the *Star,* founded as *PM,* in only its ninth. So the end of the *Sun* filled a great deal more space in the surviving newspapers than that of the *Star* had. Dozens of columns were devoted to its history alone.

Mr. Howard's paper, naturally enough, went for this story enthusiastically, and illustrated it with a half-page layout that included portraits of E. W. Scripps, founder of the Scripps-Howard chain; Charles A. Dana; Joseph Pulitzer the elder, of the *World*s; and the James Gordon Bennetts. THREE

GREAT TRADITIONS OF AMERICAN JOURNALISM ARE
UNITED, an eight-column streamer above this gallery
announced. "In those three names in the new paper's
masthead, *'World,' 'Telegram,'* and *'Sun,'* three of the
greatest traditions in American journalism are joined,"
the accompanying story said. "Behind those words
are the spirits of three of the fightingest liberals who
ever ran newspapers, Joseph Pulitzer, E. W. Scripps,
and Charles A. Dana." No claim was filed on the tradition of the Bennetts, who apparently were brought
into the display because the estate of the younger Bennett, who founded a paper called the *Telegram* as an
evening adjunct to the *Herald,* which was founded by
his father, peddled both papers to Frank A. Munsey,
who, after having sold the *Herald* to the Reid family,
left the *Telegram* to the Metropolitan Museum of Art,
which sold it to William Dewart, father of the *Sun*'s
last proprietor, who sold it to Scripps-Howard in
1927. Scripps had died in 1926. The way Joseph
Pulitzer's spirit got into the paper was that he died in
1911 and left the *World* to his sons, who sold it in
1931. You already know about Dana.

The man who wrote the *Times*'s retrospective story
offered the ritual genuflection to Dana but noted that
the old boy "turned . . . from a liberal of rather extreme views (for his day) into a stalwart conservative,
opposed to labor movements and income taxes"—a
circumstance that should make his spirit feel at home
in its present repository. Then, after finishing off Dana
and "Yes, Virginia," in seven-eighths of a column, the
Times man got onto a more relevant phase of journalistic history: the operations of Frank A. Munsey, the
chain-store grocer who bought the *Sun* on June 30,
1916. Munsey, according to the *Times,* "acquired
seventeen papers [nine of them were in New York],
merged and consolidated them on business lines, and
at his death owned only two papers." These were the
Evening Telegram and the *Sun,* which have now come
to their resting place, on Barclay Street. The *Times*
told of Munsey's purchase and extinction of, one after
another, the *Press,* the *Globe,* the *Herald,* and the
Evening Mail, and of his conversion of the *Evening*

Sun into the *Sun*. (The ante-Munsey *Sun,* which Munsey merged with the *Herald,* was a morning paper that had an affiliate called the *Evening Sun.*) After making the *Telegram* swallow the *Mail,* in 1924, Munsey said: "The New York evening newspaper field is now in good shape through the elimination of an oversupply of evening newspapers." There were five evening newspapers then: the *Sun,* the *Telegram,* the *Evening World,* the *Post,* and the *Journal.*

Another story in the same issue of the *Times* set me straight on a matter about which I had long been curious: how much money Munsey wound up with after his career of barratry, and what happened to it. The gross value of his estate, the *Times* said, turned out to be about $20,000,000, including the two newspapers, a chain of grocery stores, and a lot of real estate here and on Long Island. All this went to the Metropolitan Museum, which sold the newspapers and the stores to the elder Dewart but had to stay in the real-estate business for nearly twenty years before it could cash in completely. The net residue of the estate, after debts and taxes, was appraised at $13,618,648, and the Museum finally realized $10,000,000 on it, of which, the *Times* man ingeniously and convincingly calculated, less than $3,500,000 represented the price of the *Telegram* and the *Sun.* Both stories, I thought, showed the *Times* at its careful and inclusive best.

The other aspect of the disaster, the city room with its hopelessly tapping typewriters and all the rest, received full justice, as one might have expected, from almost every writer assigned to it. For one thing, it has become increasingly easy for any newspaperman to identify himself with the casualties of such an event. Even if he hasn't lived through one, he tells himself he very well may do so. Once there was a time—it continued long after Dana's death and I can remember it myself—when newspapermen exchanged stories about papers they had been bounced from. Now they yarn about the ones that have sunk under them.

In each of these précis of catastrophes, strung out over 20 years. I tried to isolate individual reasons for failures that would make a special case: in that of the *World* papers, a particularly pusillanimous ownership; in *PM*'s, a paper that never found its groove; in the *Sun*'s, a paper that couldn't get out of it. But the disturbing common factor was that nobody came to the rescue, and that nothing grew in the place of the dead trees. The Wayward Press piece called "Do You Belong in Journalism?" carried the story through the fifties.

On the morning of November 8, 1960—Election Day —newspaper readers in Detroit learned from the *Free Press,* its only morning paper, that there would thereafter be only one evening paper. The Detroit *News* had bought and instantly put down the Detroit *Times.* This was a clean suppression, without pretense. the *News* did not even bother to call itself the *News-Times,* but added, like a scalplock, to its masthead "including best features from the Detroit *Times*"—"18 extra comic strips."

The *Free Press,* which could afford to be sympathetic, carried a first-page editorial that began: "The death of a newspaper is to its readers like the passing of a close friend."

The story of the bucking was headed TIMES ENDS PUBLICATION—IT'S BOUGHT BY NEWS, and was written by a fellow named Tom Nicholson, who did a good job.

The Detroit *Times* died at the age of 60 Monday without even a chance to write its own obituary.

First official word of the Hearst paper's long-rumored sale to the Detroit *News* was contained in telegrams sent to the *Times*' 1,400 employes, most of them arriving after 3 A.M. Monday (when they would be beginning to go to work).

"It is with deep regret that the management of

the Detroit *Times* must inform you of termination of your services as of the opening of business on Nov. 7, 1960," the terse telegrams began.

"It is not necessary for you to report for further duty."

Reportedly, the *News* paid 10 million dollars for the *Times*. Both are afternoon papers.

Imminence of the sale of the *Times* was known only to one of the paper's 1,400 staff members—General Manager William H. Mills.

Last Friday, he received a telephone call from Hearst Newspapers General Manager H. G. Kern, who negotiated the sale to the *News.*

Kern said only to inform the employes early Monday that the paper was folding, Mills said.

"I was not involved in the sale negotiations, and I don't know the specific reasons," Mills said. He had been with the paper for 24 years.

Mills said he had no idea what the *News* should do with the *Times* plant. He also said he had no idea why the paper's end was handled in such a cold, curt fashion.

"I've just had my horse shot out from under me," he said sadly. "I have no plans."

Mills said the 390–400 members of the American Newspaper Guild would be given full severance pay under the paper's contract with the union.

The contract provides two weeks' pay for each year of service with a maximum of 60 weeks' pay.

In addition, each Guild member will receive two weeks' pay in lieu of notice and accumulated vacation pay. Other employes will receive two weeks' pay, plus accumulated vacation money.

The payments will be made by the Hearst organization.

The Guild and other unions representing workers at the *Times* immediately set up placement bureaus to aid in finding jobs.

When *Times* employes went to the building Monday to pick up their belongings, they found the elevators barred by private policemen.

They were allowed to go to their upstairs offices and clean out their desks only if accompanied by a private police escort.

Mills said he had no idea how many of the *Times'* employes might be absorbed by the *News-Times* operation.

"The *Times* has been beset by the same basic problems confronting so many other metropolitan newspapers. Publishing costs, including labor, newsprint, equipment and supplies of every nature, have risen far more rapidly than have revenues.

"This is especially true in a multi-paper city and has naturally resulted in a decrease in the number of newspapers in many such cities."

C. Arthur Weis, general manager of the *News,* said the posting of guards at the *Times'* building was "normal procedure in an operation of this type."

He said it was uncertain how many of the *Times'* staff might be needed in the combined operation.

"We are reviewing our manpower requirements now," he said.

Weis declined to say how the *News* would utilize the *Times* plant.

In an earlier formal statement, *News* Publisher Warren S. Booth said:

"No one in the newspaper business likes to see a newspaper die.

"But in recent years, production costs have risen astronomically, with the unfortunate results that in a number of American cities a newspaper has been forced to close down."

The *Times* was first published on Oct. 1, 1900, as *Detroit Today.* It was bought in 1921 at a receiver's sale by William Randolph Hearst. At that time, it had a circulation of 26,000.

The story is like that of the end of the *World,* with one or two differences in detail. The first is that the American Newspaper Guild, called into being by the

World disaster, guarantees the Detroit survivors severance pay, up to 60 weeks, in addition to the usual two weeks' notice. The *World* men and women got only the two weeks. (Even 60 weeks' pay is not much reward for a man who has worked on one paper for 30 years. His chances of getting a job on another paper at the age he must be are almost nil. But it is a great deal better than nothing.) The other is that $10,000,000 is a great price to give—or to get—for a losing paper "forced by rising costs to shut down." The Hearst newspaper-holding corporation reported, at the end of its fiscal year, a net *profit* of $3,660,000 on the sale over the price paid in 1901, and after deducting the severance pay to the employees, and the cost of the physical plant. The *News* was buying, in fact, not a paper at all, but a monopoly in the afternoon field in the fifth largest city in the United States.

And John S. Knight, proprietor of the *Free Press,* mourning the passing of his old friend, the *Times,* had not long ago sold his fine, strong, prosperous, historic Chicago paper, the Chicago *Daily News,* to Marshall Field, Jr., owner of the *Sun-Times,* for what must have been a whopping consideration. The two papers give Field a clock-around operation with all sorts of happy possibilities for a combined advertising rate and the elimination of duplicate plant and personnel. The sale of the Chicago *Daily News* is an outstanding example of the new strategy. Far from being a loser, crushed by rising costs, it was a winner, with an unassailable position in the Chicago evening field.

The small campaign of *condottieri* almost accidentally under our gaze in these random notes may be summarized thus, then: Hearst Corporation abandons battle in Detroit in return for *douceur* of 10 million, part of which serves to buy off sole competition in smaller, but prosperous Albany. Gives up fight, gets 10 million and unassailable position with many times that in years to come. Detroit *News* acquires unassailable position in Detroit evening field *moyennant* 10 million, will get the 10 million back rapidly and then sit pretty. Knight newspapers retire from profitable position in Chicago while it is still profitable, and fall back on sure things in Detroit, Akron, Miami.

Young Field, who was locked in battle with the *Tribune* in the morning field, gets the strong evening paper. The *Tribune* had recently acquired from Hearst the *American,* the perilously weak other evening paper. The new Field combination has strength around the clock, the superiority of the *News* over the *American* in the afternoon balancing the *Tribune*'s edge on the *Sun-Times* in the morning. By pulling the two papers into one plant and gradually eviscerating the *News* staff—beginning with the business and typographical departments—he can produce two papers for the cost of one-and-a-fraction. Many an advertiser who would give the *Tribune* an edge over the *Sun-Times* in the morning will prefer a combination of the *Sun-Times* and *News* to one of the *Tribune* and *American.* Field, with inestimable family resources behind him, is thus sure to get his investment back and more, infinitely more, through the years.

The only losers, in all three cities, are the readers. Instead of four editorial points of view in Chicago, there will now be two, and instead of four competing reporters on a story, two. In Detroit the reduction will be from three to two, and in Albany from two to one.

To this Mr. Field would answer, if he bothered about it, that the *Sun-Times* and *Daily News* retain completely independent identities, which nobody believes. (The late Gen. Patton carried two revolvers, one with a pearl handle, one without. But no matter which one you got shot with, it was always Gen. Patton who shot you.) The two survivors in Detroit both proclaimed that they were going to furnish even *more* news than they did before the disappearance of their competitor, which is like a saloon-keeper saying he was doubling the free lunch now that he had bought out the joint next door. It's against human nature.

In Albany, readers will have to like Westbrook Pegler and Cholly Knickerbocker, or move to Schenectady.

I have traced, in very slight detail, the above triple

switch, as one would exhibit one cartouche of a general carpet pattern, as an illustration.

There are one-ownership newspaper cities like Providence, as I have acknowledged, where the readers, like subjects of a benevolent despot, are a bit better off for news than those of other cities, like Boston, where a low-grade competition persists. There are also cities, like New Orleans, where the over-power in silly hands has led to large-scale disaster. There the *Times-Picayune* company, which owned the only morning paper and the *States,* one of the two evenings, bought the *Item,* the other evening paper, "forcing to the wall" the competing publisher by pressing $3,500,000 against his navel.

With the *Item* out, and its name tied to the *States*'s tail (*States-Item*), the *Picayune* people brushing aside two Southern "moderates" of great courage, Earl Long and DeLesseps Morrison, insisted on the election of a State Administration pledged to white supremacy, "interposition" of the State against the Federal Government in civil rights cases, disestablishment of the schools, and a whole rout of measures doomed in advance to be thrown out of court. Encouraged by the election of this Government, the least savory elements of the New Orleans population took to the streets to demonstrate against the admission of four colored children to white schools. They succeeded, within a few months, in reducing Louisiana's reputation as the most tolerant of Deep South states, to a level with those of Mississippi and Alabama. The contorted faces of the women of the New Orleans mobs have replaced, in the consciousness of readers all over the world, the old images of sophistication and Creole grace that the name of the city used to evoke.

The heaviest responsibility for the degrading change lies, not upon the racists, who are idiots anyway, but upon the publishers, who were erroneously supposed to have known better.

It is inconceivable that the *Item,* if it had continued to exist, would have gone along with the Times-Picayunion of papers in its aberration, if only because the *Item*'s raison d'être was opposition. Its mere existence might have exerted a restraining influence on the Times-Picayunion of papers, and certainly would have afforded a voice for the many civilized minds within the state.

My point here is not only that there are evil, or potty, or capricious, as well as benevolent, despots, but that it is evil that men anywhere be forced to depend, for the information on which they must govern their lives, on the caprice of anybody at all. There should be a great, free, living stream of information, and equal access to it for all. Our present news situation, in the United States, is breaking down to something like the system of water distribution in a casbah, where peddlers wander about with goatskins of water on small donkeys, and the inhabitants send down an oil tin and a couple of pennies when they feel thirst.

In almost all my stories on the downhill march of the American press during the last 30 years, I have paused at some point to genuflect gratefully in the direction of Britain, where a wider gamut of points of view survived, each embodied in at least one powerful national newspaper. It was this independence and strength of her newspapers that, I wrote from London at the time of the Suez crisis, had pulled the Tory Government back with one foot over the brink of terminal disaster. After the last such salute to Britain, contained in "Do You Belong in Journalism?" I had a note from Mr. Malcolm Muggeridge warning me that things had changed for the worse over there, but I disregarded it, with the reflection that I had always heard Mr. Muggeridge was a gloomy fellow.

But late last October the narrowing of the British spectrum began, with what Mollie Panter-Downes, in *The New Yorker's* "London Letter," described as

the abrupt poleaxing, by the economics of increasingly hard times and tough competition in the newspaper world, of the immensely respected old Liberal morning newspaper the *News Chronicle* and its evening satellite, the *Star*. Though there have been gloomy rumors over the last few years that the *News Chronicle* was feeling the draft, its end was totally unexpected and seemed barbarously without dignity. . . . On Oct. 17, it carried on the front page of what few people knew was its final issue a paragraph saying that a statement about its future, "which has been the subject of many ill-informed rumours," would be made shortly—no further off than that very evening, in fact, when startled television viewers saw a newscaster hold up a copy of the *News Chronicle* and heard his brief announcement that on the following day its Liberal identity would be merged with, of all things, the popular and true-blue Conservative *Daily Mail,* one of the Rothermere group, which would also swallow the *Star* into its *Evening News.*

Apart from the two papers' redundant employees [they included practically all the *News Chronicle*'s] the people who felt the worst shock were, of course, the *News Chronicle*'s redundant readers—over a million of them, who, without a word of editorial farewell from the paper of their choice, found themselves plumped overnight on the Tory doorstep of the *Daily Mail.* The secrecy of the transaction was explained as having been insisted on by the Rothermere press so that *News Chronicle* readers could take a look at the newly furbished *Mail* and decide that they might as well go along with it. . . .

The whole affair has pointed up the newspaper position here, which seems gloomy. . . . The dead *News Chronicle,* monopoly's latest meal, was in its way a truly unique paper—dowdily honest in spite of recent and fatal attempts to slick it up here and there, always courageous (it violently attacked the Government over Suez, for instance, even though it must have known that it would, as it indeed did, drop many thousand readers overboard for doing so), and strongly idealistic.

The *News Chronicle* employees got severance pay at the rate of one week for each year served after the age of 21.

The aftermath in Fleet Street has been no happier than it was on Park Row after the *World* scuttle thirty years ago, or in Detroit last November; and Francis Williams, in his Fleet Street column in the *New Statesman* wrote:

> Meanwhile the more one learns about the actual method of close-down on the *News Chronicle,* the more squalid it becomes. At no stage—even when the final decision was made—did Mr. Laurence Cadbury or any other member of the management meet the staff as a whole to explain matters and express regret. Nor did the editor call the staff together as a whole. Nor did anyone even have the courtesy to send them personal notices of dismissal. All they received were copies of a duplicated circular from the secretary of the company, beginning "Dear Sir or Madame." . . . And up to the last, members of the staff were being assured that all rumours were quite unfounded— by men who already knew they were true.
>
> I have spent nearly 40 years in journalism. I did not believe until now that, even in the jungle of a world that is Fleet Street, any group of men could behave as those at the top of the *News Chronicle* have shown themselves capable of doing both in large matters and small.

(It is evident that Mr. Williams has never operated in *our* league.)

The death of the *News Chronicle* brought $4,200,000 to its proprietor, a cloyingly rich chocolate manufacturer. Mr. Williams wrote: "The main burden of keeping alive the radical tradition in British daily journalism in the face of greater and greater concentration in a few mainly Conservative hands is now bound to fall on the *Daily Herald* and the *Guardian,* with the *Mirror* helping, intermittently no doubt, with its usual technical brilliance as and when its imagination is stirred or its readers are judged to be in the mood for a dose of radical fervour."

The *Daily Herald* is the semi-official standard-size Labour newspaper, and the *Mirror* a loud, effective, rambunctious, Labour-oriented tabloid, to an American disquietingly reminiscent of the New York *Daily News* in its phase of being for the common man.

The current furor in London, the one that inspired the Royal Commission of Inquiry into the state of the press, was set off by the successive offers to take over Odhams Press, which publishes the *Herald,* by the Canadian Thomson and by Cecil King, proprietor of the *Mirror.* King got it. He does not look like a promising foster-parent for the *Herald,* since he is the proprietor of a paper that is the *Herald*'s rival for Labour readership.

With its disappearance the British press would become almost, although not quite, as lopsided politically as the American.

2
The
Great
Strike

Dressed in
Dynamite

The long stoppage of the New York newspapers—
four-sevenths strike against the *Times, News, World-
Telegram,* and *Journal-American,* and three-sevenths
sulks by the *Herald Tribune, Post,* and *Mirror,* which
declined to publish while the printers struck their
colleagues—has enabled me to catch up on news in
Las Vegas, Nevada, which is livelier than it is around
here, even when all seven papers are publishing. When
all the seven papers stopped (so did two dormitory-
borough dailies, the *Long Island Star-Journal* and the
Long Island Press, which Manhattanites seldom see),
their customary readers were thrown back upon whatever unstopped publications they chanced to subscribe
to. My list was short, consisting principally of the
Wall Street Journal, five days a week, and the airmail
edition of the London *Observer,* which appears only
on Sundays. This is not a completely inadequate combination.

The *Observer,* which reaches me Monday, does me
almost too well for foreign news, including the sort of
speculation and meaning-musing that fills so large a
portion of the *Times* and *Tribune* when they are with
me every day. It also keeps me posted on British
racing and intellectual knife-throwing. The *Wall Street
Journal* carries a column of predigested general news
on the front page every day (it always has, for the
benefit of readers who have small time to spare from
the market report), and so I know that if anything
really big happens between arrivals of the *Observer*—
if Russia declares war on China, or Adlai Stevenson
elopes with Ayn Rand—the *Journal* will carry at least
a paragraph. It has, besides, its great daily humorous
column, "Pepper . . . and Salt," which keeps me in un-

failing good humor and occasionally positive stitches. "Some folks who flee from temptation have been known to move a lot faster on other occasions," a joke said in it the other day, and there are frequently others just as good, but of course nothing risqué. There was one in the same issue about a bear hunter who was asked to have a drink, but "stated firmly," "I don't want to get too brave!" Some of the items in "Business Bulletin" give me a lot to think about, too, as, for example: "R. J. Reynolds (Camels), which last month moved to acquire Pacific Hawaiian Products Co., a maker of cake mixes, fruit beverages, and shoeshine kits, is on the lookout for other non-tobacco acquisitions. . . ." What is the interrelevancy of these products?

What I principally missed, then, during the early days of the strike, was ordinary, run-of-the-mill newspaper news, mostly crime and shenanigans. But by good fortune I have for the past eight years been on the subscription list of the Las Vegas *Sun,* "Southern Nevada's Only Home-Owned Daily Newspaper" (circulation 22,000). My justification is that I want to know what odds the professionals out there are laying on future political events and prizefights. My true reason, though, is that the *Sun* offers a grand escape when I weary of the graying world around me. Opening its pages is like buying a small stack of chips at the Sands or Tropicana: the pleasure does not last long, but you get a change. Between these vicarious fugues there are weeks when the *Sun* just piles up on top of my "in" basket, successfully hiding all bills, and all the telephone messages that I do not wish to answer. Several days of the stoppage elapsed before I remembered that the newer deposits on this mountain of newsprint might, like the slag heaps by the old workings in Virginia City, also Nevada, contain retrievable ore.

The first number I looked at with these new eyes, the December 15 one, after one newspaperless week in the metropolis, carried a press-association story about cold weather on the Atlantic Coast, which I already knew about, being here, and one headed GUN-

MEN KILL TWO OFFICERS IN BANK HEIST—in Montreal. (Unfavorable Eastern weather and gunmen anywhere are always sure of a good play in Las Vegas.) There are also bits about the Chinese in India and the fall of a Brazilian airliner that made me feel I had lost little by not reading the papers that weren't published. Airliners fall so casually now that I don't notice them unless I have to duck. But it was when I reached Walter Winchell, on page 4, that I realized why my days without the *Mirror,* which carries him here, had seemed so flat. (Winchell's version is that he carries the *Mirror,* but it has not for many years been carried in the style to which it once was accustomed.) Winchell had had to send the essential news of New York clean out to Las Vegas via his syndicate to get it back to me via the *Sun!* Without his "Memos of a Midnighter" I would never have known who was "Frank Sinatra's new No. 1 Favorite Flame"—I have since forgotten, but maybe Sinatra has, too. Nor would I have learned that "When the newspaper strike ends one of the eve'g blatts expects a shake-up of execs"— a tip that bowled me over, because shake-ups on evening newspapers are as rare as hiccups in Glasgow. And without "The Broadway Lights," another Winchell department, I wouldn't have known that James Stewart, the cinemillionaire, had been at the Tower Suite, or Ginger Rogers, full of vintage "shelectricity," at the Forum of the XII Caesars.

After that I kept au courant with life around me by reading my rediscovered pal. An eight-column headline announced VEGAS 'MARRYING SAM' RACKET DRAWS BLAST, in two-inch red type over the front page of the *Sun* in which I found Winchell. Hank Greenspun, the *Sun*'s publisher, threw away all headline type less than very big when he bought the paper, for $1,000 in 1950. (He found $2,500 in the till.) It was like stripping a poker deck of the low cards.

A Marrying Sam, it appears from the story, is a parson who performs only marriages, like a barber who does only haircuts. Las Vegas is great territory for impulsive marriages; the wedding chapels, like the casinos, are open twenty-four hours a day, because

single people who stay up all night gambling feel
lonely when they have to go to bed. A minister out
there gets a license, valid indefinitely, to perform marriages, whenever he can convince a district judge that
he *is* a minister. The test question is whether he has a
congregation and a place to sit it down. Having got
the license, he can shuck the congregation and put in
full time marrying, which pays a high rate per minute
and provides high ancillary profits, since the wedding
chapels advertise—in neon lights—packaged weddings
that include a choir, bridesmaids, and (if required)
refreshments. The marrier usually owns at least a piece
of all these concessions.

The Clark County (which includes Las Vegas)
Ministerial Association, the *Sun* said, was accordingly
petitioning the state legislature to put marriers on a
yearly-license basis, so that a soi-disant pastor would
have to prove annually that he still has a flock. A Dr.
Roger Sawyer, appearing as a witness before the Clark
County delegation to the legislature, which meets at
Carson City, said, as quoted by the *Sun,* that many a
Marrying Sam had left his flock in the bulrushes. This,
he implied, worked prejudice to those who had to ex-
pend time in preparing sermons, preaching, burying
and visiting with parishioners, as well as just splicing.
He felt this was a horse on the regulars. "He cited an
amusing incident," the *Sun* said, "in which a would-be
minister, not yet a resident, attempted to obtain a cer-
tificate to perform marriages to finance his own divorce
six weeks later." (Six weeks' residence is mandatory
for a divorce there, but you have to stay six months
for a license to shoot sage hen.) "Also on the amusing
side," the *Sun* went on, "was the instance of a 'semi-
nary on wheels' in Las Vegas, with the self-styled
'theologian' selling 'ministerial degrees' from his station wagon. Another practice related to the legislators
was that in which the 'minister' certified to his own or-
dination in order to be able to get in on the lucrative
Las Vegas marriage business. Dr. Sawyer continued to
cite examples of the racket among itinerant men of the
cloth, by telling of the parson whose only congregation was his own family, and another who assembled

the required 'congregation' by serving free meals."
Asked if the association could rally support behind
legislation from ministerial groups elsewhere in Nevada, Dr. Sawyer said that "it is favored throughout
the state, and that some are in favor of even stronger
regulations."

This, I felt sure, was cheerier than most of the
church news I would not have read anyway in the
Times and the six others, and the Las Vegas crime
story of the day, BOWDEN'S FATE DELIBERATED BY LAS
VEGAS JURY, introduced me to a procedure in trial reporting that I had never encountered in less enterpris-
ing papers anywhere. "As the jury of nine men and
three women commenced its deliberation at 3:40 yesterday afternoon on whether to send Edward J. Bowden to the gas chamber for the murder of his wife,"
the *Sun* began, in boldface (the usual body type for
the top half of the paper), "alternate jurors, dismissed
after hearing the trial since Monday morning, agreed
the defendant was guilty." Interviewing the two alternates, who are excused before the others even begin
to argue, provides a sneak preview, or cross-section
poll, of what the effective jury will decide. It expedites
the process of communication and serves the public,
whose anxiety over the official verdict is thus shortened. As at the race track, the apparent winner's number goes up, but it does not become official until it is
confirmed by the judges. In the meantime, bettors are
warned not to tear up their tickets.

The account continued:

One [alternate juror] felt inclined toward the extreme penalty, the determining factor being the non-introduction
into evidence of proof of accidents the defendant claimed
he was in that produced headaches and blackouts. [Appar-
ently the other fellow didn't favor the gas room.]

Highlight of yesterday's session was the dramatic power-
packed plea noted for its brevity and quiet, serious appeal
to reason delivered by defense counsel Albert Stewart,
which commenced with "A man's life will be placed in
your hands." Stewart ended his summation in a whisper
as he asked the jury: "Do not return to this courtroom

with a doubt that will haunt you forever—'Did I send an innocent man to his death?' " District Attorney John Mendoza . . . retorted . . . by shouting: "Was he (pointing to Bowden) guided by God when he killed her? Who is this man to judge his wife's life?" The defense had relied on sworn testimony of witnesses that Bowden was drunk the afternoon and night of Sept. 9, when he pumped five shots at his estranged wife, Louella Mae Kendall Bowden, as she tended bar at Honest John's in midtown Las Vegas.

This sounded as if he had pumped the first shot, at least, in the afternoon and the last at night, but I took it that he had been less deliberate. (The regular jurors, kinder than the cited alternate, decided not to be haunted forever by a doubt. They found Bowden guilty in the first degree, but recommended life.)

In this corner of the effete East, the judge, when dismissing the alternates, tells them not to talk to anybody about the case, and interviewing them for quotation might, even the *News* has always assumed, lead to a charge of contempt of court. I telephoned Las Vegas and got the city editor of the *Sun,* a Mr. Dave Bradley. He said he had always thought it was the same out there until the reporter covering the Bowden trial had tried it out—just a case of individual enterprise. "This is a very informal part of the country," Bradley added. He said there had been no reactions from the Bench. It is an innovation that, if it became standard procedure, would add a lot to the fun of a murder trial. In the event that the regular jurors reversed the alternates, the losing lawyer would at least have credit for a split decision, which might help him get a return match for his man.

The next day's *Sun* topped my first sample—and, in fact, topped just about any crime thriller I have recently read—with a local story headed: DYNAMITE-CLAD ROBBERY SUSPECT NABBED IN VEGAS (By Gene Tuttle, Sun Staff Writer). That is the kind of headline that makes you look twice to be sure. But it was no fake; "dynamite-clad" the man had been. The lead said (starting in boldface, of course):

A woman's intuition led local F.B.I. agents to the capture of a human bomb late Friday night at Alamo Airways. He arrived in a chartered plane carrying loot from a bank robbery committed earlier in the day.

Allen Ray Lisenbury, 27, was arrested as he stepped into the main office of Alamo Airways after arriving in Las Vegas. He was highly wired with dynamite electric blasting caps and six sticks of dynamite fastened within his attaché case which also contained $20,000 in $10 and $20 bills plus a cashier's check for $9,890 taken from the Security First National Bank, 102 Pine Avenue, Long Beach [the California one].

A touch of his fingers to the attaché case could have caused a tremendous explosion and possibly killed a great number of persons. . . . Lisenbury didn't seem to care about himself, though he had taken many safety precautions.

Special agent in charge, Dean W. Elson of the Las Vegas office of the F.B.I., led his agents to Alamo Airways and captured the wanted criminal after a telephone call from Fullerton, Calif., F.B.I. office warning them that Lisenbury was flying to Las Vegas.

Lisenbury had robbed the bank at 4:15 p.m. Friday. He spent about 75 minutes in the bank with the bank manager, brandishing a snub-nosed revolver and threatening to blow up the bank with his bomb device that he had concealed in his attaché case. He demanded $29,890 from the bank manager in small bills. [Why that precise amount, I wonder.] The manager gave the cash and check to Lisenbury and he left.

Several hours later, Mrs. Bette Pastor, who with her husband operates the Sunset Beach Charter Service, received a call from a man who claimed he was a writer and wanted to fly to Las Vegas to obtain background for a story.

This last touch is the kind of detail that I do not think would have survived in any wire story that reached New York. The wire services, keen to save money by sending as few words as possible, would almost surely have eliminated it. Yet it constitutes social commentary; criminals and pilots' wives alike,

basing their notions about the literary life on films
they have seen, think of writers as persons of afflu-
ence. A *writer's* wife, had she received a call from a
man posing as a writer who was prepared to spend
more than 50 cents, would have immediately recognized him as an imposter and called the cops. Lisenbury's choice of a story and Mrs. Pastor's response to
it place them both in the world that gets its *Anschau-
ung* from the media of romance—whodunits, television, and the flicks.

Mrs. Pastor [without summoning the cops] told him her
husband was on a flight, but would return shortly.

Lisenbury arrived at the airport, and Mrs. Pastor furnished coffee and they talked. She noticed a large bulge
under his coat and was a little suspicious. [She probably
decided, though, that he was carrying a built-in muse, or
—like many of the current crop of interviewers—a recording device.] After Lisenbury and Pastor took off for Las
Vegas, Mrs. Pastor picked up a late edition of the newspaper [had it been lying, just arrived and neatly folded,
on her table as she talked to Lisenbury?] and read of the
robbery and the $10 and $20 bills. She checked the cash
Lisenbury had paid and it was new $10 and $20, so she
called the F.B.I. immediately, fearful of her husband's life.

F.B.I. agents reported at Alamo Airways to Pat Stanley,
night manager, who then contacted the McCarran Field
tower for the plane to land at Alamo where the F.B.I.
agents would wait.

But did they yet know how Lisenbury was rigged?
They had part of the truth if Fullerton had relayed the
bank manager's story of the robber's threats. But how
much? The flight of the two men would make a wry
sequence in the movie that someday must be made
from Tuttle's text, with Lisenbury wondering whether
he had been identified after the takeoff, Pastor at first
pleased to get the unexpected charter and then, perhaps, puzzled by his odd passenger. Or had Pastor received a message over the earphones, and had it included the dynamite bit? There is no evidence in the
story that he had. The stranger must have held on to

his case all the way, huddled against Pastor in the front seat.

Lighting troubles caused by fuses kept the lights going on and off at Alamo during the long wait. Morton Cutler, flight line service attendant at Alamo, waited and met the incoming plane with Lisenbury and Pastor and guided them to the pumps by the building.

As Lisenbury alighted, the lights went on and he started to leave, but Cutler offered to get him a taxi, and as they started toward the office, the lights went off. Lisenbury became suspicious, but Cutler said:

"Bosses here can't pay their light bills—so we have to work in the dark."

This for me was one of the high moments; would the small joke reassure the human bomb, or would he touch his fingers to the attaché case and blow up the air terminal? And I wondered whether, as Lisenbury got out of the plane, Cutler had offered to carry the case or whether he had feared that this would give the game away. And how did he plan to get Lisenbury within reach of the F.B.I. men undetonated? It surprised me that an F.B.I. man had not substituted for the airport worker. But the joke worked: "This took Lisenbury off guard as he chuckled." Reading, I was as relieved as the airport man must have been. And now: "He paused as they started through the doorway into the office, but Cutler gave him a shove with his flashlight and he fell forward into the waiting grasp of the F.B.I. agents who quickly pinned him to the floor."

I especially liked this part of the story, because Mr. Tuttle had not given away Cutler's plan until he acted. I was as much surprised as Lisenbury must have been, walking gingerly because of his explosive condition, and perhaps, because of that, paying insufficient attention to the joker's movements; to refuse to go first into the office as Cutler opened the door would have seemed unnatural, in any case, and Lisenbury had wanted above all things to avoid attention.

Lisenbury had his left arm wrapped with surgical tape

with wires running down from his shoulder to his wrist. He had electric blasting caps on his fingertips which were metal covered and he wore a specially constructed rubber insulated glove. He also wore heavy rubber insulated shoes. The moment he made contact with the case which held the six sticks of dynamite, it could have blown up an area of 50 feet or more.

Chief of Detectives William J. O'Reilly, Clark County Sheriff's office, was with the F.B.I. agents and quickly deactivated Lisenbury. O'Reilly is an expert in handling explosives. [I wondered, though, how he felt as he worked: had he been a booby-trap man in the war?] The agents quickly stripped Lisenbury. They found many dynamite caps upon his person and in his hip pocket was a good supply of bullets for his revolver, which was fully loaded.

There the prize was, landed, and now there was a touch of banality that the robber, not the narrator, introduced: " 'Well, it took five of yuh to get me,' he snarled at the officers. 'If I'd been arrested a little earlier, I'd a blown yuh all to hell.' "

These do not sound like the words of an arch-criminal impersonating a literary man, but perhaps Lisenbury had abandoned his role. It is possible also that he was misquoted by the arresting officers, for cops often make criminals sound the way cops think they should. I take it that Tuttle was not there.

"Being careful not to cause an explosion," the story continued, adding an extra touch of science and modernity, "the F.B.I. agents took Lisenbury to Nellis Air Force Base to complete deactivating; then he was booked in the Clark County jail on $50,000 bail. During the trip to Nellis, all law-enforcement agencies were requested not to transmit over the air for fear of static in the air which could cause an explosion."

This is a point that I don't understand, being a complete electronic square, but that entranced me as much as the rest. Why couldn't *any* emanations—the "Late Late Show," for example—set the guy off as readily as law-enforcement transmissions? Did the officers call for nationwide radio silence?

There was a coda: "Officers yesterday were trying

to determine why Lisenbury selected Las Vegas as his destination."

Several possible answers occur. Perhaps he wanted to change those new tens and twenties into chips, and the chips into assorted money, which would be harder to identify. This can be done fast in a gambling town, without attracting any attention, if each transaction is held down to several hundred dollars. And I think a cashier's check could be negotiated there with less formality than almost anywhere else—after banking hours, especially, since the big gambling houses keep masses of cash around and are eager to oblige prospective customers. A cashier's check cannot bounce, unless it is a phony, and so inspires confidence.

Or he may have felt he had an infallible system for beating roulette, for which he had to have a minimum starting stake—the amount he brought to Las Vegas with him. The odd sum suggests that. Perhaps he had planned, after winning all the money in Las Vegas, to repay the bank and then go on to Monte Carlo. He may even have planned the most spectacular grab in history: to seize the million dollars in cash that used to be displayed in the window of a gambling place there after threatening to blow the joint up if the guards interfered. I can see him backing, a lone Untouchable, his arms loaded with ten-thousand-dollar bills, through the crowd of players toward the alley entrance, where an explosive confederate awaits him at the wheel of an explosive Ferrari, all wired like Lisenbury. But most probably, I think, he just saw one of those Las Vegas Chamber of Commerce ads like the one I read in the *Wall Street Journal* the other day, about Las Vegas, the great "Convention-Vacation Location . . . *Wonder-full* Las Vegas . . . Year-round boating, fishing, golfing, swimming, hunting, sunning, star-studded entertainment, excitement . . . the *wonder* of the resort world." The poor guy needed a holiday.

Reading about ordinary crime again will seem pretty tame when the New York papers come back, if ever. There are parts of the country where people have more fun.

Offers and Demands

JANUARY 26, 1963

The Sunday, January 13, issue of the New York *Standard* prefigured the American newspaper of the future, once we have been reduced to a single newspaper ownership in each city. (There are only 58 towns and cities in all the United States where more than a single ownership persists; all the rest have gone the way of monopoly.) New York, with seven papers of six different ownerships—although this is a decline from fifteen papers within my own reading lifetime—alone maintained at least a surface appearance of that variety which is essential to a healthy journalistic life. Then, when the printers' union struck four of the papers—the *Times,* the *News,* the *Journal-American,* and the *World-Telegram*—and the three others refused to publish, all disappeared from the kiosks. That was on December 9; on January 6, the *Standard* appeared as the sole *remplaçant,* like a windblown weed growing in a crack in a bombed street. It thus inherited, temporarily and without payment, the monopoly position for which Samuel I. Newhouse recently paid $42,000,000 in much smaller New Orleans and offered over $40,000,000 in Omaha, where he was turned down.

The *Standard,* a product of opportunism, disclaims any intention of continuing after the other papers come back—for one thing, its scratch staff consists almost entirely of regular members of theirs—but in the meantime it provides a glimpse of what is likely to happen within a couple of decades: the January 13 issue consisted of 120 tabloid pages, 110 of them advertising, which should have brought in between $100,000 and $150,000 at its current page rates. If the stoppage lasts until February 1, the *Standard*'s publishers should clear the expenses of starting the

86

paper and begin to make money seriously. The ten other pages included news, amusements, a book review, a couple of byline columns, sports, stock tables, fashions, and television listings. They were all gobbled up with gratitude by readers who had been reduced to a diet of out-of-town newspapers, supplemented by specialized organs like the *Wall Street Journal* and the *Journal of Commerce,* which carried a few smatterings of general news crammed in among such headlines as UTILITIES FEAR REGULATION and HOGS ACTIVE IN CHICAGO. (The *Journal of Commerce* at first entranced me with its ship cards, listing the ports of call of freighters with names as exotic as their destinations, but since December 23, when the longshoremen called their own strike, even the ship cards have gone blank. The *W.S.J.*'s column of humorous quips, "Pepper . . . and Salt," began to pall after three and a half weeks, although it had seemed as funny as all getout in the beginning. A typical joke was about how a single man's life is just "one undarned thing after another.") New Yorkers' forced experience with out-of-town newspapers left them with a full appreciation of John Macy's forty-year-old dictum in "Civilization in the United States": "On the whole, the American newspaper is amazingly uniform from Portland, Maine, to Portland, Oregon." The respects in which they are not uniform, however, are those that readers care most about—the identity of the persons mentioned in the obituaries, for example. To me, the most striking proof of the inadequacy of electronic media for the communication of essential facts was that until I read about the rise in postal rates in the *Standard* I was unaware that one had been in the making. I am sure that it must have been mentioned often on the air, but the trouble with television and radio news is that you have to be there at the moment the announcer says it, and unless you have gout, you may be somewhere else. The ads and the modicum of news offered by the *Standard* constitute the public-utility function of a newspaper.

The *Standard* of January 13 also served as an illustration of what a newspaper *doesn't* have to be to win acceptance in the absence of a better newspaper. One nonessential is wit. There was a headline on page 5—AN IRISHMAN STARS AT THE PLANETARIUM—that would have been worthy of "Pepper . . . and Salt." The "Irishman" was "Orion, pronounced O'Ryan"—see? The first-page story on the newspaper stoppage to which the *Standard* owes its existence was as slanted as if the paper had been carrying eleven times as much advertising as news every Sunday for half a century. BLASTED, PRINTERS WILL TALK was the headline, the very clear intimation being that *because* they had been "blasted," or scolded, by a "fact-finding" committee of three judges, the officials of the typographical union, chastened, had agreed to meet with the publishers and Secretary of Labor W. Willard Wirtz on the following day. The story showed, if you read it hard, that the phenomena were unconnected, since the union never accepted the authority of the judges. "The board found that the printers had not budged in fifteen post-strike negotiating sessions from their original demands," the *Standard* said. It did not include another sentence from the report: "All of those meetings can be summed up with the statement that *neither party moved.*" (Italics mine.)

When I find the *Standard* a bit bland during the week, I enrich my diet with a few vitamins from the *National Enquirer,* a publication where they are the *spécialité de la maison.* When there were newspapers on the newsstands, the *Enquirer,* which is a weekly magazine that looks like a tabloid newspaper, used to lurk around the edges of the display. With the disappearance of the papers, dealers moved the *Enquirer* into one or another of the vacant spots, where it attracted the unwary news hunter by its newspaperlike makeup. To add to the confusion about its status, it once *was* a newspaper, appearing every Sunday afternoon under a Monday dateline; it was then called the *New York Enquirer,* and my old journalistic patron Colonel John R. Stingo lent luster to its pages with his column "Yea, Verily." A few years before the Colonel's retirement in 1961, at eighty-eight, it adopted its

new national policy, epitomized in a recent headliner:
MURDER! ASSAULT! THEFT! Or another:

DOCTORS TOLD MOTHER ...

YOUR CHILD WILL DIE TONIGHT
BUT DOOMED CANCER GIRL
LIVES TO DANCE THE TWIST!

Not long ago, it ran a corking series on a lady who
told how she had buried her nine illegitimate children
in her garden. That she did so in Derbyshire several
years ago detracted only slightly from the pleasure of
the narration. The *National Enquirer,* although it appears only once a week, is available on the newsstands
all seven days, and the stories can be taken as desired, before (but not advisedly) or after meals—SET
FIRE TO HIS HOUSE TO GET RID OF FAMILY, or BLINDS
WIFE HE CAUGHT KISSING A STRANGER. It also features
an educational columnist named John J. Miller, who
tells you how the greats of this world, particularly
Hollywood greats, really live—slugging, kicking, spit-
ting in faces, Twisting with no pants on. EDDIE FISHER
DATES DIETRICH THE GRANDMA and HEY, LIZ—BUR-
TON'S DATING LOLLOBRIGIDA! were the headlines on his
two latest columns.

The *Standard's* wholesale capture of advertising
should at any rate reassure *Editor & Publisher,* the
timid handmaiden of the newspaper industry, which in
its issue of January 5 feared that newspaper readers
and advertisers might lose the habit and that the press
might perish, its charms forgotten like those of the
Buffalo Bill Wild West Show: "For the last four
weeks, metropolitan New Yorkers have been without
their usual newspaper reading fare and have been subjected to a barrage of substitutes. Neither the newspapers imported from other cities nor the makeshift
dailies that have sprung up in New York have ade-
quately taken the place of the struck papers. In fact,
they might be doing irreparable damage to the reputation of newspapers, both in the city and nationwide,
instead of performing a service for newspaper-starved

New York. . . . How long will it be before New Yorkers,
without their choice of several excellent morning and afternoon newspapers, compare what they once had with
what they have now and decide it isn't worth the
price? Once these readers are lost to newspapers—out
of the newspaper habit—will they ever buy one again?
Is it possible that after several weeks and months of
living on capsulized news from radio, television, and
other substitute sources they may decide it is adequate? And if the former reader also happens to be an
advertiser, will he be a 'former advertiser' also?"

After a couple more Cassandrine paragraphs,
E. & P. wound up, "Congress couldn't do it. The
President of the United States couldn't do it. Even the
courts can't do it. Only a striking union abetted by
other unions can close down the newspapers in the nation's largest city, not to mention the newspapers in
the nation's eighth largest city." (The Cleveland papers
are also shut down.) The publishers can do it, too, as
those of the *Herald Tribune,* the *Post,* and the *Mirror*
have proved.

What disquiets me more than the possibility that
newspapers *qua* newspapers will disappear is the increasing uniformity of the survivors as they wait to
coalesce. The stoppage has illuminated this, just as the
conjugal reaction to a stranger's interference illuminates the essential solidarity of a loving couple. The
"competition" among the six New York ownerships
has proved a pale and sometime thing compared to
the competition of all of them against all of their employees. It seems naïve now for Bertram Powers, the
leader of the striking printers, to have offered the
financially weaker papers a separate peace—or separate individual peaces—when he struck the *Times* and
the *News* and the *Journal* and the *World-Telegram.*
The Hearsts, for example, own both the unstruck, because deemed "weak," *Mirror* and the struck because
deemed "strong," *Journal-American.* It is hard to
imagine them running one of their papers while a
strike is on against the other. As for the *Herald Tribune* and the *Post,* at a more competitive period in
newspaper history they might have been expected to

run, restoring their failing strength with the Christmas
advertising revenues made available to them by the
printers' generosity. They had ground not merely to
hold but to make up if they were ever to get back
into contention with their rivals. Their loyalty to their
rivals, who are also their prospective purchasers when
the pinch comes, was touching. It is all very sad, because the surest way for the seven papers to anesthetize the public to future monopoly is to make it evident
that they are already alike. Even a sham battle might
have improved public opinion of all seven. (Mrs.
Dorothy Schiff, the publisher of the *Post,* and John
Hay Whitney, the publisher of the *Tribune,* if we are
to adopt *Editor & Publisher*'s point of view, might also
have done their colleagues a favor by continuing to
print, and so making sure that the public would not
lose the habit of newspaper reading.)

As for who is to blame for the weary length that
the stoppage has attained, I can give no judgment beyond juxtaposing headlines in the *Guild Reporter,* the
organ of the American Newspaper Guild, and in
Editor & Publisher:

Guild Reporter:
>#### N.Y. PUBLISHERS SHUNNING
>#### COMPROMISE IN STOPPAGE

E.&P.:
>#### PUBLISHERS ACCUSE
>#### UNION IN STALEMATE

I have a personal hunch, too, that Amory H. Bradford, the spokesman for the Publishers' Association
of New York City, and Bertram A. Powers, the
printers' president, both suffer from the overcompensation that frequently afflicts boys with flossy first
names, requiring them to fight so often to defend their
schoolyard dignity that fighting becomes an adult habit.
(For a negotiator I should always prefer somebody
named Jack or Mac.) As for the issues in the strike
against the four strong papers, I can only say that, as
a habitual employee, I would, if offered a choice on a

6-to-5, pick-'em basis, naturally take Mr. Powers's position. As for the *causes* of the strike, which are, naturally, quite distinct from the issues (an issue may be minuscular; a determination to fight over it is a cause), I found the report of the three-judge Board of Public Accountability astonishingly informative. I say "astonishingly" because I had first read of their findings in news stories published by the *Standard*, the *Wall Street Journal*, the *Brooklyn Eagle*, and the *Journal of Commerce*. All of these papers excerpted from the much fuller excerpts sent out by the Associated Press and United Press International, and all of them deformed the content.

The *Wall Street Journal* wrote, "The report said the printers didn't present their total demands until fifteen minutes before their old contract expired," but did not reprint, "It was not until 6:40 on the evening of December 7th [with the strike set for 2 A.M. December 8] that the publishers made a complete offer to the printers. That offer totalled, in increased benefits and costs, $9.20 per man per week," including 55 cents a week in cash for the first year. (The employer, in strike stories, always "offers" and the union "demands." A publisher, for example, never "demands" that the union men agree to work for a four-bit raise; the union never "offers" to work for more.)

None of the papers that I saw quoted in full even the excerpts that U.P.I. furnished from the supplemental opinion filed by Judge Joseph E. O'Grady, the only member of the panel with much labor experience. (He used to be City Labor Commissioner.) All three of the judges named to the board—Harold R. Medina, David W. Peck, and O'Grady—signed the full report, but O'Grady also issued a supplemental report, excerpts from which follow:

The newspaper publishers sought to maintain the pattern of bargaining carried on for some years and which had proven reasonably acceptable and successful to them. Mr. Powers was determined to break that pattern, because his members had become dissatisfied with the results of that pattern of bargaining.

I do not believe that I can find fault with either position, and I have not even attempted a moral judgment of which one had the equities on its side. It was inevitable that two such diametrically opposite positions, each supported by a strong protagonist, would result in a strike. To have prevented such a result, one side would have had to abandon its fundamental position. Neither did, and the result was a strike. How long the parties will continue to test their strength and positions I do not know. However, I believe that both forces will have to give some ground before a settlement will be reached. I do not think that either is in the position of bringing the other to his knees.

That is about the way I read the situation. Forty years ago, Macy, in that symposium that so perturbed young American intellectuals at the time, wrote, "Almost invariably, the news of a strike is, if not falsified, so shaped as to be unfavorable to the workers," and this has been a particularly bad one journalistically, because it is a newspaper strike reportedly by ancillary or makeshift newspapers, which have the ready excuse of insufficiency or inexperience to cite for their omissions. (The *Wall Street Journal,* though, expresses pretensions to more serious quality.) The *Times,* ironically, would have covered the strike and the stoppage more thoroughly. It would surely have at least published the full text of the unofficial fact-finding report and Judge O'Grady's supplementary opinion. The reporting has been notably deficient, too, in exploiting obvious lines of inquiry. The *Wall Street Journal,* in the four-line sixth paragraph of its stoppage story on December 19, for example, reported, "The newspapers have a strike-insurance fund said to cover a 29-day strike." (The existence of this fund had been previously reported in both the timid handmaiden and the *Guild Reporter.*) "The insurance covers only cost of maintaining skeleton crews and upkeep of idle equipment, however." But this highly significant feature of the situation was then dropped from notice, not to reappear even on the expiration of the 29 days, on January 6.

How did this affect the prospects for settlement?

The expiration coincided—although I read no comment on the coincidence—with the appointment by the
mayor, the governor, and the Secretary of Labor of
the three-judge "blasting" board, and preceded by less
than a week the announcement by the suspended newspapers of a cut in the salaries of non-union non-
locked-out personnel, and the first offer by the publishers of a slight raise over the work-for-55-cents demand. Nor was there any inquiry into whether the
Herald Tribune, the *Post,* and the *Mirror,* which were
acknowledged to be losing money before they quit
publication, actually cut their losses by ducking out or
whether, after the 29-day period, they would lose more
by staying out and paying overhead than by going into
business again. Yet these are surely interesting matters; the mutual-aid arrangements of the unions whose
members refuse to cross picket lines or are locked out
has come in for a great deal of publicity, the consistent implication being that they, as distinguished
from the newspapers, are ganging up. And how about
the publisher of the *Post,* who announced soon after
she stopped the paper—again according to the *Wall
Street Journal*—that "a long shutdown might put the
liberal *Post* out of business"? How long? I would say
it's time for a checkup. And how about the effect on
the strikers' resolve of their approaching eligibility for
New York State unemployment insurance, which begins, for workers made idle by a labor dispute, at eight
weeks? The stoppage is past its sixth week now. On
none of these points do we see any of the bright speculation that papers carry about, for example, the next
baseball season or the future of Yemen. The subject is
too sacred.

The conflict between union work rules, designed to
conserve jobs, and automation, designed to decrease
them, is not, apparently, a major, direct issue in this
row, though it may be the cause of it. The object of
automation on newspapers is not to increase production, which would be quite senseless unless the papers
could abruptly increase circulation, but to increase
efficiency, and thus income. And the fight—because
complete newspaper automation is not yet ready to be

introduced—resembles those obstinate and bloody inter-trench combats of the First World War, whose declared object was to establish "dominance" over the enemy before the big push began. Big pushes, though, seldom did begin, and usually bogged down, like the automated electric train in the Times Square–Grand Central shuttle, over which the *Times* editorial page was willing to go to war with the Transport Workers Union when the thing was introduced a year ago. "The unpartial arbitrator has made an incredible, incomprehensible decision," the *Times* editorialized when the arbitrator, Theodore Kheel, ordered the Transit Authority to postpone putting the robot train into service. Then, when the dispute was settled by installing a motorman on the train for a six-month trial period, the *Times* said, "The Transit Authority paid a stiff price . . . for retaining the clear legal right it had always had to automate." The only trouble with all this is that the train does not run consistently, and is *still* operating under dual control, with the motorman ready to put her on manual when she stops dead between stations, which is often. "Against a labor demagogue who recognizes neither law, contract, nor his union's pledged word," the *Times* said, like Patrick Henry ordering beer, "the Wagner administration should carry this arbitration decision to court on appeal as a matter of principle worth defending to a finish," and, earlier, "Mr. Quill cannot be allowed to bluster this shuttle train to a stop." But the car, like the papers, stopped dead.

Back

MARCH 16, 1963

The reappearance of the *Post,* on Monday, March 4, marked the first break in the long newspaper famine that began last December 8, when the International Typographical Union Local No. 6 struck the *Times,* the *News,* the *World-Telegram,* and the *Journal-American,* and when the *Herald Tribune,* the *Mirror,* and the *Post* declaring their unfading loyalty to the Publishers' Association of New York City, suspended publication. The union had offered from the beginning to allow these "weaker" papers to run on the basis of the expired contract, pending the negotiation of a new one with the "strong" papers. It is hardly likely that the printers thought the weak papers would continue to publish, but the offer allowed the printers to say that not they but the publishers as a group were perpetrating the blackout. It also gave them room for maneuver, and, after twelve weeks, this paid.

The *Post* does not have the strong financial position of the *Times* and the *News,* and it is not a member of a great newspaper chain that continues to operate in other cities, as are the *World-Telegram* (Scripps-Howard) and the *Journal-American* and the *Daily Mirror* (both Hearst). Nor, while Mrs. Dorothy Schiff, its publisher, is a woman of wealth, does she seem to be the same kind of colossus as John Hay Whitney, the proprietor of the *Herald Tribune.* After the expiration of the 29 days of strike insurance purchased by the publishers, therefore, she must have looked with increasing pity on the plight of a great city left without a proper advertising medium—a condition harmful to retail business and lethal to the theater and book publishing, and one that deprived the unemployed of help-wanted columns and the newsdealers of newspapers to sell, and forced brokers to resuscitate their old direct-mail sucker lists. All these horrors of a city without newspapers were set forth on television programs, in news magazines, in out-of-town editorials that ordinarily would not be seen here, and in ancillary publications like the *Wall Street Journal,* with the nearly universal implication that only the strikers were to blame. A few of these voices went so far as to complain of the lack of public information. (Less, however, was heard about this, since networks and newsmagazines both purport to *be* instruments of public information, and could hardly be expected to accent their own limitations.) The foremost of a flotilla of emergency-rig accommodation newspapers, the *Standard,* appeared on January 6, with a promise in its first number that it would scuttle itself when the regular papers returned to their beat, but Mrs. Schiff must have seen that it was inadequate to serve all the advertisers who wanted to get in. (The *Standard,* reasonably enough, has announced that it will not commit hara-kiri yet, since it does not consider the blackout ended by the *Post*'s solitary action.) Public figures, including the President of the United States, called for renewal of newspaper life in New York. But the union and the leagued publishers were alike adamant. The impasse remained at a dead end, the dead end at an impasse, and Mrs. Schiff, taking pity on everybody, resigned from the Publisher's Association and gave orders for her paper to appear again, which it has now done, amid expressions of regret from the negotiators for the publishers, who have said that her action will lengthen the strike. (Conversely, it may shorten the strike if the *Journal-American* and the *World-Telegram* get the idea that the *Post* is acclimatizing their afternoon regulars.)

Considering the universal ululation that has gone on for months now, one might have expected the emergence of the *Post* to be hailed like the relief of Ladysmith, but it has not been so. When the publishers' committee and the union arrive at a contract, it will probably be much the same for the *Post* as for the papers that continue to battle for the lowest terms possible. The committee must thus protect the *Post*'s in-

terests while the *Post* protects the interests of the
advertising community—a division of labor that the
Times and the *News* are scarcely likely to relish. The
Post is in the position of a "free rider," which is a
labor term for an employee who stays outside a
union while profiting by what the union gains. (This
may help the publishers understand union feelings
about free riders.)

As for the paper itself, its first issue was something
of a disappointment, though it was not much different
in quality from what it was on December 8. Readers,
I think, had gone along for so long wishing they had
a New York newspaper back that they had formed an
exaggerated idea of what one was like, as compared,
say, to the Philadelphia *Inquirer*. Anyway, March 4
was a bad news day; the editors, who must have been
hoping for a good gang murder, or at least an international incident, could find nothing more exciting to put
on the first page than AUTO LICENSE BOOST IS DEAD,
an Albany story about the state legislature. The sec-
ond-best story was about Frank Sinatra. And the old
familiar photographed faces—Governor Rockefeller
and Sinatra—gave us all the feeling that there hadn't
been any lapse in publication at all; the *Post* was in
its old familiar groove. On the third page there was a
Statement by Dorothy Schiff, which said, "I finally became convinced that the course we were following was
not achieving the purpose of facilitating a just agreement, and that my responsibility to the New York
Post and to the public required decisive action on my
part. We at the *Post* have always taken pride in both
our political and economic independence. We are re-
solved to maintain it. Great problems remain. With
your help we will overcome them, now as in the past."

On the front page, with the auto-license item, was
a vertical listing of *Post* columnists ("All Back"), and
I turned to them one after another. The old familiar
Leonard Lyons ("The Lyons Den") reported that
Norman Mailer was writing a play, and that a cop on
Forty-Fourth Street, not recognizing the Duke of
Windsor, had pushed him. Earl Wilson ("It Hap-
pened Last Night") had a story about a cosmetic-shop

lady in Youngstown, Ohio, who thought up a song
title six years ago and sent it to an honest composer
who has now written a song around it and will give
her half of the money, which is the kind of thing I always like to read about—homespun talent plus sterling
character. Dr. Rose Franzblau, the psychologist, who
is my pinup, had a correspondent who wrote, "I am a
happily married woman with two lovely sons. For quite
some time now I have been jumping and screaming
violently in my sleep." Dr. Franzblau's answer began,
"Dreaming is what makes sleep possible." James A.
Wechsler began, "In the darkness of the newspaper
blackout, many dubious deeds were done in many public places." William V. Shannon started his Washington column with "John Kennedy could say with Richard III, 'Now is the winter of our discontent.' Troubles
great and small have crowded thick upon him in the
last eighty-six days." The *Post* never *was* an exces-
sively cheerful paper. Harry Golden was writing on injustices to left-handed people—a tack that could have
gotten him in bad in the McCarthy days—and Sylvia
Porter, the financial editor, was writing about how to
save money on your income taxes. Of the *Post*'s news
stories, the one that made me truly glad to have a
newspaper again said a man named Joseph McD. Mitchell, the city manager of a small place called Newburgh, New York, was going on trial in State Supreme
Court on a charge of accepting a twenty-thousand-
dollar bribe from a real-estate operator. This is the
same Mr. Mitchell who became a hero of the ultra-
conservatives a couple of years ago by ordering forced
labor for relief recipients (the State Welfare Board
squelched him), and I had not known what had happened to him since a couple of days before the newspaper stoppage, when he was picked up on the bribery
charge. (I hope the *Post* covers the trial thoroughly.)

That first *Post* was packed with ads for low-price department stores and furniture stores, holiday and holy-
day resorts, and supermarkets and airlines, besides a
mass of classified. R. H. Macy & Co., on hearing of
Mrs. Schiff's decision, had made a public statement
that it would not advertise in the *Post* until the other

papers resumed publication, and I noticed that none of the other major-league stores were in. I wondered whether this was coincidence, or reflected their reprobation of Mrs. Schiff's desertion.

The second day's *Post* seemed to catch its stride better; perhaps word to resume publishing had come too suddenly for the staff. The front-page story, GOP AIDE GRILLED BY DA'S LIQUOR JURY, was more like it. It was what I call making the most of things, in default of violent action. "Grill" and "D.A." and "liquor" and "jury" are all good stimulating terms, and so, for *Post* readers, is "G.O.P. aide," since the G.O.P. in Manhattan is usually the party of the pharisees trying to grill its betters. A well-grilled Republican politician has 50 percent more news value than a Democrat done to a turn. With this story was a picture of Judy Garland getting a rousing sendoff to London at Idlewild. Soon, I hope, the *Post* will be running "The Judy Garland Story," or "The New Judy Garland"— one of the affectionately psychological studies it so adores. That day, too, it had one of the second-day disaster stories its readers relish—one that began, "Death and disaster are intimates at every hospital, but this time so were the victims." There are papers that cover a spot story better, but nobody sentimentalizes better. There was also a backslapper, CITY GIVES THE POST A HEARTY WELCOME, with plugs from newsdealers, who said (accurately, I'd think) that they couldn't get enough copies, and from readers, one of whom said, "I have been starved for a paper with good local stories." POLICE RAID NETS 3 IN B'KLYN, about "a $6,250,000 a year business" (police on-the-spot estimate), was a fair sample, and there was a story, as there always is in the *Post,* about the tribulations of a colored theatrical star—this time Sarah Vaughan. There was also a full-page ad for *Cleopatra,* which was almost suitable for framing, though where you would hang it I do not know. The other theatrical ads—the issue was full of them—included a reproduced cutting of Howard Taubman's review of *Hey You, Light Man!* from the Western edition of the *Times*—a roundabout way for a New York critic to

review a New York play. The *Post*'s own drama critic,
the cheerfully urbane Richard Watts, and its movie
man, Archer Winsten, who is better than most, were
around too, though, as they had been the day before.

Mr. Shannon's gloom hadn't lifted: "The new Congress is off to a dispirited and unpromising start. How
serious this laggard beginning will prove depends
upon a rather subtle judgment." But he was, as he
usually is, intelligent. Moreover, Doris Fleeson, my
favorite Washington columnist, had rejoined the colors. (She had missed the first day of recrudescence.)
"The Senate these days is seemingly in love with its
chains and its jailers," she started off. And Marquis
Childs began his comeback column with "Only a
white paper giving a complete account of the Cuban
misadventure, with the Administration putting it
squarely on the line, not glossing over the failures or
exaggerating the successes, could at this late date be
expected to damp down the political quarrel over
American policy." After twelve weeks of the *Wall
Street Journal,* during which all I had read about Mr.
Kennedy was that he was wasting money and plotting
against business, it was a novelty to read that anybody
was plotting against him, or that he might deserve any
sympathy. The Shannon piece appeared under a stun-
ning Herblock cartoon—I had missed Herblock, too
—of a council of war of Republican senators, with a
war map of Cuba on the wall, next to the mottoes
"Hot Pursuit" and "No Let-Up!" The caption is
"Who said anything about driving out Castro? We're
talking about Kennedy."

Max Lerner was writing from France, a little to my
regret, for I like the thought that he is ever at hand,
ready to deal with world problems as they arise, like
Dr. Franzblau in the psycho department. The two of
them are, for *Post* readers, father and mother figures,
the way Cholly Knickerbocker and Dorothy Kilgallen
are for readers of the *Journal-American*. In France,
though, Max had found somebody to write about—a
man "of powerful intellect, of passionate conviction,
and of an almost unparalleled power of persuasion,"
named Colonel Argoud, who had somehow gone

astray, straight into the anti-Gaullist underground. I was happy to note that Max's style had lost nothing. The sports page also looked happier than it had the day before.

It was the *third* day's *Post*, though, that looked like the ante-blackout product on good days. Intrepid *Post* investigators had discovered that a city official fired by Mayor Wagner a couple of years ago for financial deals "completely incompatible with holding office"— he then had more than $56,000 unexplained in a tin box, which he refused to explain—was going back on the city payroll, without any public fuss. This is another kind of story the *Post* is good at:

THE TIN BOX CASE: A SEQUEL
OUSTED AIDE SET
FOR NEW CITY JOB

Coupled with a picture of the father of quadruplets in Lima, Ohio, kissing their mother, this made a vintage *Post* first page. Inside the paper, on page three, there was a pip: A GIRL CHOSEN TO SUCCEED FLUNKS A VICE COP'S TEST. This was about a pretty blonde from Fort Wayne, Indiana, who had won a contest there as the "How-to-Succeed Girl of 1960," which carried a two-thousand-dollar fellowship to carry her to the big city, where she had succeeded only in getting herself arrested on a prostitution charge in an East Side *boîte de nuit*. To make the story even better, from a *Post* point of view, she had been arrested by a vice-squad plainclothesman known as "The Actor" because he is so good at impersonating a non-cop who wants a girl. They had a picture of the veiled Miss How-to-Succeed that at least did justice to her nice legs. The story had about everything: pathos, a paradox easy to point out, sex, graft (the *boîte*-keeper admitted paying protection), a hint of a world of sin right around the corner, and cheesecake. I wound up looking forward to a bit of profound moralizing, not unmingled with sympathy, when the inevitable lady reporter would visit the prisoner in the pen, and also some Freudian exegesis; all the *Post* ladies are deputized Franzblauen.

I wouldn't miss it for worlds, and my only instant
regret was that Mr. Lerner was so far away. He would
surely have had a crack at Miss How-to-Succeed's
relevance to twisted social ideals.

Then, there were THALIDOMIDE FIRM FACES COURT
ACTION and THREE WHO CHARGED BRUTALITY GOING
ON TRIAL IN COP ASSAULT and TEACHER ACCUSED OF
KISSING GIRL, 14—all examples of *Post*-type stories
—and the further chronicle of the Mitchell bribe case
that I had hoped for. The stern poormaster's lawyer
was appealing to the federal courts, on the ground
that evidence against his client had been obtained by
interstate wiretapping. The prosecution denied it. As
for the teacher accused of kissing the girl, 14, he had
put the story on another of the *Post*'s home grounds
when he charged persecution: "Or have Levittown,
L.I., officials trumped up charges against the teacher
because he heads a teacher's union?" To have sex and
civic rights mixed into one yarn is almost as lucky—
from a *Post* city editor's point of view—as to get a
potpourri like the one about the blonde.

With it all there was the announcement, on the
last page: POST EXPANDS RACING COVERAGE. It said
that all results from major race tracks would appear
in the early edition each morning, and scratches, including those at Santa Anita, in the later ones, and
that current results would be published during the day
as they came along.

It may be that the Publishers' Association had a
right to be disappointed in Mrs. Schiff, but within
three days she managed to restore a ray of sunshine
to my life.

Step by Step
with Mr. Raskin

APRIL 13, 1963

The return to print of six of the seven New York dailies of general circulation after an absence of 114 days predictably produced a mass of how-glad-you-must-be-to-see-me-again prose, in which might be occasionally discerned a tinge of apprehension, as in the mien of a newly freed divorcée stepping off a plane from Nevada. Suppose, she thinks, the fellow who is supposed to be waiting for me has formed other habits? She smiles overbrightly, and is not at her best. In this she resembles stories like CITY GOBBLES PAPERS from page one of the newly freed *World-Telegram,* which began: "After seemingly endless months without their newspapers, jubilant New Yorkers saw their world return to normal today as they gobbled up millions of copies of the city's dailies at their newsstands. The 114-day newspaper strike—longest by far in the city's history and costliest ever in the nation —was finally over. The toll in money and anguish was enormous."

The picture of anguished millions stuffing wood pulp into their faces as if they were termites was hardly more depressing than the picture drawn by Richard Starnes, a deep thinker on the *W.-T.*'s split page. "The cost in money can never be calculated, the price in disrupted lives is astronomical, and the loss of the city's identity with itself inevitably will take a long time in being restored," he wrote in boldface, and I found myself taking a long time to wonder what city New York identifies with now, before restoration. Columbus, Ohio? Evansville, Indiana? Covington, Kentucky? They are all Scripps-Howard towns, and if you're reading Mr. Starnes, who appears in the

Scripps papers in all three, you can't be sure that you
are not in one of them. "The terrible need for newspapers (and not just for newspapers with which we
agree, but for all newspapers) was terribly apparent
during the strike," Mr. Starnes went on to remind
us. I felt retrospectively astronomically terrible. He
wound up, "We were missed, we do know it, and we
will continue to try to justify the esteem in which we
are held." At this point, the little lady from Nevada
seemed to have given up on her *promesso sposo* and
turned in to one of the bars in the air terminal for a
couple of jolts.

This whole aspect of the first day's papers could
have been anticipated; some of the happy-to-be-back
headlines looked as if they had been kept permanently in type against such occasions, which have become increasingly frequent with the years. Another
facet that could have been foreseen was that all six
of the recrudescents acted as if there had been no
papers since December 8, when the stoppage began;
they scarcely acknowledged the existence of the *Post,*
which had withdrawn from the Publishers' Association
of New York City and returned to life voluntarily on
March 4, printing eight hundred thousand copies a
day. The *Post,* while it took cognizance of the return
of the other papers, kept the story in perspective, on
page three, reserving page one for MOREHOUSE GOT
18G FROM 'PLAYBOY'. This was a story about the former New York State Republican Chairman, who, it
has been said, helped a law-*cum*-public-relations
client, the *Playboy* complex of enterprises, get a state
liquor license for one of its offshoots—the Playboy
Club. (Naturally, the story had the charm of a sub-
liminal cheesecake association.) The rest of the front
page was given over to a picture of the Kennedys at
Gettysburg and a house ad for the paper's feuilleton
of the week, giving the impression, unless you looked
inside, that the *Post* was still the only paper in town.

The harrying question of the moment for the newspapers' business managers was not, so far as I know,
expressed on any page of any paper. That is whether
the commerce and industry of Babylon, proclaimed to

have languished without stimulus of newspaper advertising, will in fact vault with its return. There has been going about what *Editor & Publisher,* the frightened handmaiden of the newspaper industry, calls a Big Lie, to the effect that retail sales held up during the blackout better than anybody could have expected; the Big Lie is a product, *E.&P.* thinks, of a cabal of salesmen of television and radio time. A month, or a couple of months, will have to pass before space salesmen and time salesmen have comparative statistics from which to drag opposite conclusions for prospective clients. No time at all passed, though, before the *Times* and the *Herald Tribune* raised their prices, from a nickel to ten cents.

"The *Times,* ironically, would have covered the strike and the stoppage more thoroughly," I wrote in January, complaining of the way in which the ancillary papers, like the *Wall Street Journal,* were reporting the struggle. What I did not foresee was that the *Times* would publish, in its first resumption, a story as remarkably good as the one by A. H. Raskin, headlined THE STRIKE: A STEP-BY-STEP ACCOUNT. Beginning with a couple of paragraphs on the front page, Mr. Raskin's piece ran on for just short of eighteen columns—a total, I estimate, of close to twenty thousand words. This would make only a mighty slim book, but Raskin has more to say about the tangle between management and labor than you will find in any four thick books. His piece gives new evidence of what newspapers at their best are for: turning a first-class reporter loose on a story, giving him ample time to develop it, and then printing what he brings in.

Raskin, a veteran labor reporter who has now, except for such special occasions, retreated to the editorial rooms, starts by quoting a bilateral avowal of failure, from an official of the Publishers' Association and from a union officer. The stoppage, both admit, was an uncompensated-for disaster. Raskin then sets out to recount it, but not as the agent of either party —and here the *Times* earns the highest marks for letting him go his way. "New Yorkers, baffled by sixteen weeks of hearing little more than that negotiations were on or off, may find some clue to the answers in the untold story of what went on," he begins. Then, as a historian should, he goes back to the last previous important episode in the relations between his principals: a defeat for the publishers. This was the 73-day strike of the New York Newspaper Guild against the *World-Telegram* in 1950, which was won by the guild "primarily through the strength it gained from a newly forged 'blood brotherhood' with nine other newspaper unions." He might have gone much farther back, to the foundation of the guild, in the thirties, but what he does is enough to establish a perspective. "These unions, representing printers, pressmen and other mechanical employes," he says, "forced the paper to suspend by refusing to cross picket lines set up by the reporters, copy editors, and clerical employes in the Guild." (This is a point that a number of Guildsmen recently seemed to have forgotten, or never even heard of.) The publishers, aghast at this rising of the villein rabble, then welded a united front of their own, Raskin continues, and "the result was a bargaining system, under which a contract negotiated with one union fixed a pattern for all the unions and a strike called against one paper generated an employer-enforced blackout of all the papers."

Raskin does not cry woe over the possible immorality of either arrangement, nor does he decry any advantage enjoyed by one side over the other. (If either side *had* enjoyed such an advantage, the strike could not have lasted so long.) "A chief goal of the strike of the Big Six printers was to establish a single expiration date for all the contracts so that the printers' union would no longer have to accept a follow-the-leader status [the leader in this case being, of course, the guild, which had settled with the publishers in November]. . . . Long before the strike showdown there had been a joint recognition by the publishers and all the unions that they were at the end of the road on the old negotiating pattern. . . ." Last November, five weeks before the strike began, Raskin says, Secretary of Labor W. Willard Wirtz, having summoned a meeting of publishers in the apartment of

Richard E. Berlin, president of the Hearst Corporation, "stressed the danger of a Big Six strike in what
one publisher later described as 'terms far more solemn and far more urgent than any we had ever heard
from our own professionals.'" This, then, was no
sudden flare-up; actually, negotiators for both the
Publishers' Association and the union dawdled from
last July until the strike began, four months later,
never coming to grips with their differences. "Both
negotiating teams recognized that the standards set
here on economic and noneconomic matters would
have a compelling effect on contract terms and on the
survival of newspapers in most major cities," Raskin
writes, and that made them nervous, like two small
champions out to represent rival juvenile gangs.

Raskin next passes to the leaders, the Raoul and
Bernier of this *chanson de geste*. Bertram Powers, the
tall president of the New York local of the International Typographical Union, he says, was described
by "one of the army of Government peacemakers who
got to know him well" as "'honest, clean, democratic
—and impossible,'" and by another as "'cold, ambi-
tious, and utterly incapable of setting any realistic
priorities for himself'" but "'so superior to anyone
he had to negotiate against that it was like matching
Sonny Liston with a Golden Glove champion.'"
Moreover, Raskin says, "Pro-Powers unionists term
him 'incomparably the ablest and most forward-look-
ing of the men in the graphic arts unions.'" Amory
H. Bradford, head of the publishers' negotiating committee and vice-president and general manager of the
Times, is two inches taller than Powers and, on Raskin's showing, just as hard to bear: "One top-level
mediator said Mr. Bradford brought an attitude of
such icy disdain into the conference rooms that the
mediator often felt he ought to ask the hotel to send
up more heat. Another mediator, who called Mr.
Bradford the possessor of the keenest mind on the
management side, said he operates on a 'short fuse.'
. . . With the deadline only eight hours off, Mr. Bradford expressed to other members of the publishers'
group his opinion that there would be no walkout. His

judgment reflected the sentiment of most of the labor relations experts attached to the employers' negotiating committee."

The deadline was two o'clock on the morning of December 8. A few hours before that, after four months of so-called negotiations, the publishers declared their terms—that the printers sign for a small money package and that they drop their demands on what Raskin calls "issues more complex than the money gap . . . underlying the shut-down." Powers presented his counter-offer at 1:45 A.M. Like an Arab with a turnip to sell, he asked for far more than he hoped to get, as he later admitted. This was a completely unrealistic confrontation, at best. Of the underlying "issues more complex"—a common expiration date for contracts between the publishers and the unions, a 35-hour week, and limits on the introduction of automation—the printers were destined to win all three, after a costly and anguished period, during which, according to Mr. Starnes, the city forgot who it was. But in money they were destined to receive very little more than the publishers had demanded that they accept. They got a "package" valued at $12.63 a week instead of the publishers' proposal of $9.20. The magnitude of one of the underlying issues may be judged from Raskin's summary of the shorter work week: "The printers wanted their basic work time cut from 36¼ hours a week to 35, the standard already in force for the Guild." With a five-day week, this means a difference of fifteen minutes a day, but the printers said they would sacrifice, in return, fifteen of the thirty minutes of wash-up time for which they had been receiving pay. "The publishers resisted on the ground that there was no real assurance the printers would actually stop taking the wash-up time," Raskin says. Time clocks in the lavatories might have averted terribly apparent astronomical disruption.

Having oriented the *Times*'s readers and set forth the Lilliputian issues and Brobdingnagian forces involved, Raskin goes into the narration of the feckless squabbles that filled the next 114 days. The first "substantial" bargaining began under the auspices of

Mayor Wagner and Harry Van Arsdale, Jr., who is
the city's A.F.L.-C.I.O. chief, at Gracie Mansion on
December 30, he reports, and it proceeded so hope-
fully that "at one stage . . . discussion centered on
how soon Mr. Powers could assemble the Big Six
members for a ratification vote and how long after
that it would require to get the presses rolling again."
The union president, it seemed, had reduced his package demand to $16.42 a week—$3.79 more than he
would ultimately accept 83 days of seemingly endless
anguish later. But, to pick up Raskin, "Mr. Bradford
asked: 'How do we fit that into a $10 bill?' "—$10
being $2.63 less than *he* would agree to when the time
came. Van Arsdale, having sat through one session
with the pair, announced that he wouldn't walk a
block in any direction to help settle the strike. A couple of weeks later, Powers, acting like the stores that
run penny sales on odd Wednesdays, put $10 back
into his package demand. The publishers thereupon
"turned actively to efforts to crack the union front,"
but "no union ever got a tempting enough offer to
make it want to take the lead." On January 16,
Charles Collingwood, of C.B.S., got Powers and Walter N. Thayer, president of the *Herald Tribune,* together, and Powers came down to $16.42 again,
which at least marked progress back to December 30.
On January 21, Mrs. Dorothy Schiff, publisher of the
Post, offered to sit in on negotiations, but her fellow-
publishers, all of them men, did not invite her, and
the labor people suggested that she send a male representative. History proves that she brooded. "At midnight the next day, Jan. 22," Raskin writes, "another
new face popped into the negotiations"—Pierre Salinger, President Kennedy's press secretary. The Secretary of Labor joined him. "By [the following] evening,
when they were scheduled to meet with Mr. Powers
and Mr. Van Arsdale, Secretary Wirtz was predicting
to Mr. Salinger that a settlement could be arranged
for a $12.50 package. This was within 13 cents of the
figure that emerged when the final peace formula was
hammered out by Mayor Wagner six weeks later."
But "Mr. Powers showed up without Mr. Van Ars-

dale." This was a bad omen. Powers "began ticking
off a list of demands much stiffer than the ones he had
sketched out the night before . . . [and] asserted that
he had been misunderstood." New face Salinger then
popped out.

This is the real fabric of history. Negotiators do not
reach a deadlock, which would be static, but a wiggly
relationship, in which they continually set up propositions that they go on to modify or withdraw or that
are not meant to be accepted. (It would be priceless
to have this sort of account of the test-ban conversations at Geneva.) Governor Rockefeller now came
briefly on the scene, with a proposal to set up by law
a State Commission of Public Concern to recommend
terms for settling strikes in unspecified vital industries.
Nobody knew quite where this might lead, and it got
no encouragement. But it spurred Mayor Wagner into
another try. On January 25, Theodore W. Kheel, the
mayor's labor expert, called Wirtz in Washington and
asked what Wagner could do next. Wirtz, according
to Raskin, came up with the suggestion that eventually
paid off: to summon publishers and union representatives to continuous negotiations in City Hall, that
1811 survivor of the Era of Good Feeling. "The publishers got their telegrams on their return from a private meeting with the Governor, at which they had
informed him they had no use for his bill," Raskin
says. "Their initial reaction to the Mayor's intervention was no more cordial. In fact, Mr. Bradford telephoned the Mayor at once and told him his action
was the most foolish he had ever taken." Wagner
persisted. Bradford then told his fellow-members of
the Publishers' Association that he was opposed to
accepting the mayor's summons, because the mayor
would lean to the printers. The big bosses overruled
him, because, they said, it would be bad public relations to turn the mayor down when the strike had
gone on so long. "Confronted with their unanimous
decision . . . Mr. Bradford put on his hat and coat
and said he was not going," Raskin says. For the publishers, it must have been like delegating a man to
patch up a quarrel and then finding out that he

thought you wanted him to act as your second in a
duel.

The next day, Bradford was persuaded to change
his mind, and now the long grind began. "Both sides
came to City Hall with meager enthusiasm," according to Raskin, but "the first few days at City Hall were
unusually fruitful." Powers came down to $13.75, the
publishers went up to $11.04—respectively $1.12
above and $1.59 below where they were going to meet
in a couple of months. "Just when a new optimism
was taking hold, the talks started moving backward
again on the 35-hour week." (Wash-up time.) Kheel
came up with a new formula, perhaps based on the
substitution of a cheaper brand of soap. "At this Mr.
Bradford told the Mayor that he was sick and tired
of the whole proceedings and could see no reason why
the publishers had to keep wasting time by coming to
City Hall. 'If that's the way you feel,' Mr. Kheel exclaimed, 'why don't you leave? Because if you don't I
will.' . . . The next day Orvil E. Dryfoos, president
and publisher of the *Times,* visited the mediator at
his home and assured him that the employers wanted
him to stay. Mr. Kheel, in turn, told Mr. Dryfoos that
it was very important that Mr. Bradford also remain
in the negotiations." But the meetings went into the
doldrums, without even a good fight. Powers got on
his bicycle again and began to escape. Kheel described
him as a " 'jitterbug bargainer—he giveth and he
taketh away.' " Everybody, on both sides and in the
middle, complained about Powers' changes of mind.
Unionists began snapping at unionists, and publishers
at publishers. The head of one morning newspaper
said to the head of another after a meeting of the Association, " 'That was like trying to move around in
a barrel of molasses.' "

On February 6, the International Typographical
Union voted to assess its members everywhere to support the strike, and this put the printers in a virtually
impregnable economic position. The war had now
reached a fortress period, with both belligerents safely
entrenched and flying flags that read, "I'm all right,
Jack!" It wiggled through what Colonel John R.

Stingo would call endless episodia ending in nothing,
such as the near-intervention of Justice Arthur J.
Goldberg, of the United States Supreme Court, who
remembered just in time that his status had changed
from player to referee, and a near-agreement on the
35-hour wash-up, which failed when the Hearst and
Scripps-Howard papers, "concerned about the impact
of a 35-hour schedule on their papers in other cities,
exercised their veto." Unanimity is necessary before
the association can agree to anything, which makes it
effectual, apparently, only when a majority stands for
the negative, like the Polish Diet of the eighteenth
century, with its *liberum veto*. (In this case, the anguished New York public seems to have been sacrificed
to the higher necessity of the budgets of the chain
papers in Cincinnati and San Antonio.) Rockefeller
Republicans tried to infiltrate the mayor's show but
couldn't make it. The unions that had no rich big
brothers like the I.T.U. grew restive. Salinger, still
mad at Powers, induced the President himself to rap
the union leader, which immediately revived sympathy
for Powers among his colleagues, on the principle of
"We must all stand together or . . ." Philip L. Gra-
ham, the publisher of the Washington *Post* and of
Newsweek, attempted to irrupt into the New York picture but was extruded by unanimous petition. From
the way things looked in February, the situation had,
if anything, disimproved from the day before the
walkout.

"The first important power shift," Raskin says,
"came on Feb. 28, when Mrs. Schiff announced that
the *Post* would resume publication on Monday,
March 4. She explained that she believed the tie-up
had gone on long enough, that she saw no evidence of
a quick settlement and that she felt the city should
have at least one regular newspaper." In retrospect,
this sounds sensible. "The Schiff defection and the
arrival of the heavy Easter advertising season injected
a new intensity into the Mayor's revived negotiations," says Raskin. (Seeing the *Post* heavy with that
good Easter–Passover stuff, I imagine, had the same
effect on the other publishers that the smell of jack

mackerel has on a cat.) "The Mayor and Mr. Kheel spent endless hours putting together the intricate mosaic of a contract that would satisfy both sides." It didn't satisfy either side, of course, nor could any contract have done so short of an unconditional surrender, including a deed to the other fellow's shirt, but it is hard to see why a compromise much like it couldn't have been reached without any strike at all. It was a peace of exhaustion.

Powers, however, had some ground for claiming victory. "On all three of Mr. Powers's key issues of principle, the union achieved breakthroughs," Raskin says. It was at this moment that Powers began to give a chilling impersonation of a stunned football player running the ball toward his own goal line. He proposed to reject the settlement that the publishers had already accepted. Here, again, Raskin is good. He quotes Harry Van Arsdale, who said, " 'This is crazy. He'll destroy himself and the whole labor movement. He has all his issues of principle. How much more can he want?' " And experienced labor men like Van Arsdale himself and Elmer Brown, the I.T.U. president, had to persuade Powers to persuade the members of his own negotiating committee to accept what prize-fight people would call a split decision—and a pretty lucky one at that. Like Waterloo, it had been a near thing. After that, the membership of the Big Six further messed things up by rejecting the settlement that their officers had accepted, thus justifying—for one week, at least—the old charge that it's no good dealing with unions because they repudiate their agreements. And then, after the printers had rejected their rejection, a couple of less potent unions that had waited for the printers to settle went into their own acts, all eager to wring a couple of cents more than $12.63 from a presumably exhausted foe. Raskin quotes Kheel on the latecomers: " 'These union fellows are like Janus. They have eyes in the front of their head and in the back of their head. They see what the other fellow got and what he is going to get, and they want it all.' "

In Mr. Raskin's calm piece of reporting there is little credit for anybody but the mayor and his faithful mediators. Raskin's revelation of the world behind the strike is not pretty. ("Both sides deserve each other" was the mayor's own opinion of the principals in the dispute.) "There is virtual unanimity that the indispensable element in nursing the agreement through all its dismal moments of near collapse was provided by the Mayor with the aid of Mr. Kheel and Mr. Van Arsdale," Raskin says, and he quotes "a high Federal official" who said, " 'Nobody sufficiently appreciates Wagner's ability to take a beating when he feels it is necessary to keep the city going. His patience is inexhaustible. He didn't browbeat the parties as Fiorello La Guardia would have done, and he didn't go on TV to read the comics, but he did stick with this through all the frustrations and affronts that came from both sides and finally he made it come out right.' "

Wagner is, for the moment, the fair-haired boy of all the papers he rescued from limbo, and I am waiting anxiously to see which of them will break the truce of gratitude and hurl the first brickbat; almost all of them were sharply critical of him before the blackout. He is anything but spectacular, and observers have often wondered why he attracts the voters. The reason is possibly that they sense his willingness to "take a beating" and get up off the floor.

Great credit, too, redounds to Raskin's superiors on the *Times* for wanting a story that would tell what happened, and for letting him write it. The idea, as far as I can learn, originated with Theodore Bernstein, the assistant managing editor, and Frank Adams, the city editor, who called the writer into conference early in March and gave him the assignment—a story originally intended to fill four columns. Raskin, with a vast accumulation of sources both in labor and in the Labor Department, is a methodical man. He had kept newspaper and press-association clippings on the stoppage almost from the beginning, and these served as a chronological thread along which he made his way backward, interviewing participants. He was working in two worlds he knew especially well—labor and newspapers—and the persistence of the stoppage through March gave him more time than he had expected. When he began to write, he found that he had an awful lot of material, and his bosses had the good judgment to tell him to let it run. Raskin, Bernstein, and Adams, my sources say, had the full support of the *Times*'s managing editor, Turner Catledge, but what I find almost unbelievable is that Raskin's story had the *nihil obstat* of his publishers. I doff my bowler.

3
The
Deserving
Rich

My own approach to newspapers is trichotomous, a word that the boys on the serious quarterlies, who overwork dichotomy, neglect. This is either because they are still working on the first part of the dictionary or because they can't count past two. Trichotomous is, however, 50 percent better than dichotomous. It is at the same time more numerous and less usual. For a man to be pulled two ways is bad enough; when he is pulled three, it is hard for him to maintain a consistent position.

As an observer from outside I take a grave view of the plight of the press. It is the weak slat under the bed of democracy. It is an anomaly that information, the one thing most necessary to our survival as choosers of our own way, should be a commodity subject to the same merchandising rules as chewing gum, while armament, a secondary instrument of liberty, is a Government concern. A man is not free if he cannot see where he is going, even if he has a gun to help him get there.

One alternative to an informed people making right decisions from choice is a correctly informed Government making decisions on the basis of information it cannot communicate to the people. That would be competing with private industry, even in the squalid form that a number of publishers represent, and the preservation of private industry is the principal reason for having a country at all. To make this alternative system work, requires a people imbued with, or cowed into, the habit of blind obedience. We are not ready for it.

The other alternative, a badly informed Government leading a badly informed people, is not an ideal, although it has happened here at times, notably during the Cuban repatriation episode last April.

As an observer from inside, since most of my work has been journalism, I have a rather different view. I am a chronic, incurable, recidivist reporter. When I am working at it I have no time to think about the shortcomings of the American or world press; I must look sharp not to come too short myself. Sinbad, clinging to a spar, had no time to think of systematic geography. To understand perfectly a new country, new situation, the new characters you confront on an assignment, is impossible. To understand more than half, so that your report will have significant correlation with what is happening, is hard. To transmit more than half of what you understand is a hard trick, too, far beyond the task of the so-called creative artist, who if he finds a character in his story awkward can simply change its characteristics. (Even to sex, *vide* Proust and Albertine. Let him try it with General de Gaulle.) It is possible, occasionally, to get something completely right: a scene, or a pattern of larceny, or a man's mind. These are the reporter's victories, as rare as a pitcher's home runs.

A good reporter, if he chooses the right approach, can understand a cat or an Arab. The choice is the problem, and if he chooses wrong he will come away scratched or baffled. (There is a different approach to every cat and every Arab.) The best reporters occasionally fail badly, and the fair ones half-fail often.

I suspect, from my own few shallow dips below the surface of news, that it is reported superficially. I felt, after Suez and Gaza in 1956–57, and Earl Long's Louisiana in 1959, for example, that I might just as well not have read about them before going, because what I found was different. My point here is not that what I see is always exact, and that the harried press association men are always wrong, but that different reporters see different things, or the same things differently, and that the reader at home has a right to a diversity of reports. A one-man account of a crisis in a foreign country is like a Gallup poll with one straw. The same goes for national news.

The critic of other reporters, therefore, takes a mighty risk when he goes out to work with them. I take a humbler tone about reporters than about publishers. There is a healthy American newspaper tradition of not taking yourself seriously. It is the story you must take that way. This applies, of course, equally to the relation between doctor and patient, or soldier and enemy. And if you do take yourself seriously, according to this sound convention, you are supposed to do your best not to let anybody else know about it. (Like bed-wetting.)

When I was a very young newspaperman—about 20 years and 10 months—I worked in a sports department with a fellow who would come in from a football game and before sitting down at his typewriter ask the drunks to shut up so he could hear himself think. The boxing writer christened him "The Genius," and the warning was not lost on me. That fellow wound up on a faculty.

The outside-observing and inside-observing Lieblings consequently speak in different tones. One is Liebling-Elijah and the other Liebling-Sinbad. (Sinbad was the very prince of reporters, and he always went back to take a second look. Up he would get, from those comfortable banquets at which he could have squatted indefinitely in an executive capacity, and back to sea to see what the world looked like. He was interested in money, but more in people. He would never have made a publisher. The publisher in what the *Post* would call "The Sinbad Story" is symbolized by the Old Man of the Sea.)

What reporters can do when an Old Man turns benevolent and gets off their necks was illustrated in Little Rock in 1957, when Governor Orval Faubus staged his successful bid for a third term, at the small expense—to him—of making "Little Rock" a symbol of hypocrisy and intolerance everywhere outside the national boundaries.

John Netherland Heiskell, the proprietor, and his son-in-law, Hugh Patterson, the publisher, allowed Harry Ashmore, the editor, and his staff to fight the good fight. Their performance, before an audience of journalists drawn to the scene from all over the literate world, saved whatever shreds of prestige the United States salvaged. It confirmed the golden legend of a free and fearless press, and so did more for our prestige abroad than all the Eisenhower-Nixon globe-trotting of that unfortunate Administration.

Mr. Heiskell, Mr. Patterson, and their merry men received a number of trifling unofficial honors, such as Pulitzer Prizes, from conscience-stricken colleagues, but they got no recognition from the Federal Government in the shape of citations in orders of the day, special medals, letters from the President or even ¼ of 1 percent rebates on their income taxes. Yet they did more to brake the deterioration of our foreign relations than any dozen political ambassadors who retired with tear-bedewed letters of gratitude from the Chief of State.

(Little Rock, incidentally, is not a one-ownership town. The *Gazette* held with Law and Order—recognition of the validity of the Fourteenth Amendment as interpreted by the Supreme Court—while the *Democrat*, the other paper, took up for Peace and Harmony, which is not the same thing when the going gets rough. The *Gazette* lost, and the *Democrat* gained, in circulation and advertising. The publishers of the *Gazette* therefore made a sacrifice which, in their case, is comparable to that of a Brahmin who permits himself to be run through a sewing machine in order to achieve virtue.

In the third trifurcation of my trifoliate orientation to the press I resemble the late Robert Benchley, who began The Wayward Press department in *The New Yorker*, and carried it on from 1927 to 1937. Benchley, in a passage I cannot forget, told of his joy every morning, when he got up that early, at padding to the front door in his pajamas, opening it, and finding all the morning papers lying on the doormat with the milk. The milk had been delivered by mistake. There were seven New York morning papers up until 1931, instead of our measly four. Benchley was, and I am, addicted to papers, as I was then—I cannot speak for him—to needled beer. This was a delectable drink that disappeared like a newspaper with the repeal of Prohibition. The 20 percent of alcohol that the bootleggers added to this beer will never be replaced in my affections by the picture of Miss Rheingold. Taking the newspapers inside with him, Benchley was quit of the need of thinking for several hours.

Newspapers always offer something to be delighted or concerned or enraged over. Some reporter has done a good job, some editorialist shown a flash of unsuspected spirit. And there is always at least one astonishing story—for example, an octogenarian recluse has starved to death, and nobody has found $212,000 in dirty one-dollar bills hidden in the foul straw of his dingy mattress. In such cases I always figure the cops have stolen the money. Newspapers can be more fun than a quiet girl.

In this tierce of my trichotomy I write my own occasional Wayward Press pieces. I write a case history of how the New York papers—or once in a while out-of-New York newspapers—have handled a story that interested me. If I choose one that they have kicked around the infield it is not done out of malice, but from a hope to instruct. It is true that I get few letters of thanks from editors, but readers sometimes send them. In this I take example from my friend Whitey Bimstein, the educator, who never intervenes when a pair of his professional pupils are going along all right in a sparring bout at the Eighth Avenue Gymnasium, but is ready with advice when one commits a solecism.

"Don't go oncet when you can go twicet," Whitey will then say. "Going oncet is a dirty habit. It leaves you open for a left hook." To me he oncet explained: "Why should I tell him when he done good? It will give him a swelled head."

Like Whitey, I don't want to give the newspapers a swelled head.

In this tridentation of my trifolium I am philosophical, like a lobster-eater who knows that the total number of lobsters in the world is on the decline, but is sure they will last him out. Even in this role I infrequently grow melancholy, remembering that I myself as Sinbad am an inhabitant of this diminishing lobster world; it makes me feel like an Athenian after Syracuse, or my father after Johnson licked Jeffries. I feel as naked as a critic without a fellowship, or a professor of communications without a grant.

Yet who, noting the press's reaction to a given situation, can fail to be cheered by seeing how nearly it matches up with how the press reacted when a similar situation last occurred? Thus, with the word "labor," the newspaper's association (i.e., the publisher's, in this case the same thing) is "stubborn." To Government, "wasteful." To the poor, "pampered"—or malingering or undeserving.

The "taxpayer" is always "overburdened," but it occurs to me as I write that he is always represented in editorial cartoons as a small, shabby man in underclothes and a barrel (the kind of fellow who if he had a wife, two children, and no imagination, would be caught for an income tax of about $8) and never as an unmistakably rich man, like, say, the proprietor of a large newspaper. The man in the barrel is always warned that a frivolous project like medical care for his aged parents is likely to double his already crushing tax burden. The implication is that the newspaper owner is above worrying about *his* parents, and of course he is, because his old man left him the paper.

I once wrote, in a part of *The Wayward Pressman,* about a story I worked on when I was 23, at the state mental hospital in Rhode Island, that resulted in the discharge of an unfortunate impostor who was the only pathologist they could hire for less than the wage of a district reporter. It was a two-thousand-bed hospital. The fellow's chief misfortune was not being a doctor, or he would be there still. We (the Providence *Journal* and *Evening Bulletin*) broke the story and won a factional fight in the state Republican Party. It then became incumbent on the reformers to find a *real* pathologist for a dollar-and-a-half less. (Spur-of-the-moment note on American usage: reporters, talking about their papers, or ex-papers in the past tense, say "we" like boxing managers talking about their fighters. These usages are not an exact parallel, because the managers own the fighters, but the papers own the reporters.) I append "The Wayward Pressman" note on the aftermath at the asylum.

Things there improved considerably for a time. But the appeal to the taxpayer of "rigorous economy" is inexorable. I was talking to a Providence psychiatrist 20 years after my triumph and happened to ask him about the state hospital. "The treatment is substandard again," he said. "They don't want to spend any money."

If the wife of a wealthy Rhode Islander fell ill he would send her to some place like Butler or the Hartford Retreat or Chestnut Lodge. This is cheaper, for a large taxpayer, than paying a proportionate share of the upkeep of an adequate hospital system.

The public-school system in any city, whether Providence or New York, has to combat the same form of negative larceny. The man of property sends his kid to a private day school when young, to a preparatory school and an endowed but expensive college later. His only interest in the public schools is to see that as little money as possible is spent on them. Schools never fare worse than during a "reform" administration.

My then wife, not a particularly rugged woman herself, took a Red Cross Grey Lady course a score of years ago and was sent to Bellevue to do volunteer nursing. She came home one evening and said she had been on a ward where there were 54 chronically ill, bedridden women— and one professional nurse. With my customary arithmetical magic, I calculated in time that this meant that if the nurse worked eight hours without a break for lunch or once sitting down to rest her legs, she could devote less than nine minutes to each patient. She would of course have to arrange that no two patients should need her at the same time. A mere matter of organization.

It wouldn't matter very much on a ward like that if the nurse were 100 percent efficient or just 95, or 60. She couldn't really do a damn thing for that many patients anyway, and the same is true of a public-school teacher with a class of 50 or 60 children. When people barely in the economic middle class become ill their families send them to voluntary hospitals, just like the wealthy. This is not cheaper for them than it would be to pay a pro-rata share of a higher tax rate, which would provide decently maintained public hospitals. They have no alternative. The rigorous economy grafters, and the newspapers that are their mouthpieces, have shoved the level of public education and public hospitals so low that the poor little white-collar gulls have to shun them, too. Then, since the public schools and hospitals are no good to them, these invertebrates dissociate themselves from the fate of public institutions. And the economy hogs let things run down some more.

I often wonder what would have happened if all men of military age hadn't been compelled to go into the same public armed services during the most recent war, and if there had been a nice private auxiliary army available for the sons of large taxpayers. I believe that rations, clothing, medical attention, and pay would have been lousy in the ranks of the public army. To compensate for these drawbacks, discipline would have been much more severe, and the newspapers would have been full of editorials against coddling public soldiers.

There was no attempt to run war on that system, and I sometimes doubt that we should run peace that way.

The crusade against the destitute is the favorite crusade of the newspaper publisher, because it is the safest.

In 1946, Thomas E. Dewey, the publishers' all-time favorite candidate, had been re-elected Governor of New York and was building up a head of steam for his great run for the Presidency in 1948, when he was to be unanimously elected by Walter Lippmann, *Time,* Inc., the Chicago *Tribune* headlines the day after election, and a columnist in the Detroit *Free Press,* ditto. The electorate's defection from all these authorities ranks, as a black mark against the United States, with the repudiation of the Confederate debt and the decision they gave Willie Pep the second time he fought Sandy Sadler and the referee stood on Sadler's feet.

Dewey therefore investigated the City of New York, which is Democratic, incessantly. This is an old Republican tactic, based on two considerations: one, to keep a jab in the enemy's face, and two, to distract attention from what is always going on upstate, where the rural politicians steal one another's eyes for breastpins after they have stolen everybody else blind.

The alliance against the city administration between the big taxables in New York City and the "lazzaroni" upstate is traditional, like the Old Alliance between France and Scotland against England. The Apple-knockers, like the Scots, get in addition to a subsidy (in their case a disproportionate share of state revenues) a license to snitch whatever they can lay their hands on. For this they trade a solid vote including all residents of their shires not dead more than 300 years, and what is even more important, the control of a gerrymandered legislature. So that when there is an investigation of graft in a county like Suffolk, state funds for it run out before a fast talker could say, "Stop, thief."

The newspapers, naturally, cheered on the emissary from Dewey's New Jerusalem. The editorial writers took the Cross. City editors promised plenary absolution to any reporter who caught a repeater on a bread line, and with a great clash of shields the Holy War began.

Horsefeathers
Swathed in Mink

NOVEMBER 22, 1947

There is no concept more generally cherished by publishers than that of the Undeserving Poor. Newspapers may permit themselves a bit of seasonal sentimentality, like the *Times*'s 100 Neediest Cases at Christmastide or the *Herald Tribune*'s Fresh Air Camps in summer, in which their readers are invited to send in money while the newspaper generously agrees to accept the thanks of the beneficiaries. But the governing factor in most newspapers' attitude toward the mass of people out of luck is the tax rate. One way to rationalize the inadequacy of public aid is to blackguard the poor by saying that they have concealed assets, or bad character, or both. The words "reform" and "economy" have for so long been synonyms in newspaper usage that a newspaper plumping for economy often feels that it has a license to fake a bit in a good cause.

Reporters and headline writers have a way of cooking up descriptive titles for women involved in celebrated newspaper cases. To name a few that I can think of as I write, there was the Pig Woman, witness in the Hall-Mills murder inquest; the Woman in Red, who betrayed Dillinger to the law; the Bobbed-Hair Bandit, a lady stickup man of the twenties; the Broadway Butterfly, who was strangled to death in 1924; and the Black Dahlia, a woman unpleasantly done in about a year ago in Los Angeles. Sometimes these inventions become generic labels for types of crime, as when, last summer, New York headline writers began calling the taking off of Mrs. Sheila Mannering a Butterfly Murder—an allusion to the similar taking off of Dorothy King, the Broadway Butterfly—and one of the tabloids recently referred to a local cadaver as a Black Dahlia Murder Victim because the killer had written on it with lipstick, in the manner of the dispatcher of the Black Dahlia out West.

New York newspapers added another title to their list a short while back when they invented the name the Lady in Mink for a woman who was reported to have received relief payments from the New York City Welfare Department though she was possessed of a mink coat. (It may be expected that "the Lady in Mink" will soon be contracted to just "Mink" and, as such, will become a part of headline language, like "Butterfly" or "Dahlia" or "Ripper" or "Raffles." The Welfare Department is prevented by law from divulging the names of relief clients, and as a result the reporters felt justified in using the Lady in Mink sobriquet in practically every paragraph of every story they wrote about the case. On October 30, the *Times* called her, on first acquaintance, merely the woman in mink, but on November 1 it yielded to the vogue and recognized her as a lady. The apparent triviality of the story did not prevent the *Times* from giving it, on the day it broke, the best spot in the paper—the right-hand column of the front page—under this three-column head: WOMAN IN MINK WITH $60,000 LIVED ON RELIEF IN A HOTEL, INQUIRY BY STATE DISCLOSES. (The report of the President's Committee on Civil Rights, which was issued on the same day, got the second-best place—a three-column head on the left side of the page.) The drop under the *Times*'s "Mink" headline read:

42 CASES ANALYZED

INVESTIGATOR SAYS CITY AGENCY HELD
"CLIENT IS ALWAYS RIGHT"

ONE "FRONT FOR BOOKIES"

DEAL APPARENTLY INVOLVED HER LIVING ON AID
WHILE HUSBAND PAID $14,000 IN BAD CHECKS

The story that followed was written by a man named William R. Conklin. I discovered, on reading it, that the all-important "with $60,000" in the head-line had been based only on the opening paragraph—a single sentence—of Conklin's report. This sentence read, "The story of a mink-coated, mink-hatted 'relief client' [the necessity for the quotation marks is ob-scure, since relief client is an accepted term in social-welfare work] who lived at city expense in a hotel at $7.50 a day despite assets of $60,000 was spread on the record of the State Board of Social Welfare yester-day as it opened an attack on administration of a $142,000,000 relief program by the New York City Welfare Department." Nothing in the rest of the piece supported the statement that the relief client had "as-sets of $60,000." The body of the story stated, begin-ning near the bottom of the first column, that in 1940 the woman had been awarded a divorce settlement of $40,000 in California, of which $3,400 had never been paid, and "in addition" had sold $20,000 worth of stocks in 1942. It was not made clear whether she

had bought the stocks with part of the divorce settlement, nor did the story show that she had all, or any,
of the $56,600, or $36,600, whichever it was, in June,
1946, when she applied for relief in New York. As a
matter of fact Benjamin Fielding, the newly appointed
welfare commissioner, announced a couple of days
later that he considered the woman, as she had reported herself to be, too poor to support her child. A
fairer headline for the *Times*'s story might have read:
WOMAN WHO ONCE HAD $x NOW ON RELIEF.

Conklin, of course, must have known that his story
didn't bear out his lead, but some reporters do this
sort of thing impulsively, like poker players who occasionally try to steal a pot. It is up to the editors to
spot such discrepancies, especially in the case of
stories to which they decide to give a big play.[1]

The mink coat in the case—as most newspaper
readers know by now, for Fielding showed a nice flair
for publicity in his handling of this detail—was appraised by a fur expert of I. J. Fox & Co. The expert,
a Mr. Herman Peroff, said that the coat was from six
to eight years old, had a torn lining, and was worth
about three hundred dollars at the present market.
Fielding allowed news photographers to make shots
of him and Mr. Peroff handling the coat—shots in
which, after all the fuss, the coat looked so mangy
that they proved irresistible to the picture editors of
the two-cent tabloids, hostile though they were to the
"pampering" of the poor. The *Times* very sportingly
took cognizance of the appraisal in the last line but
one of the last bank of the headline over its October
31 story—"One Coat Valued at $300," it said—and,
on the next morning, gave the following handsome,
though slightly equivocal, one-column display to
Commissioner Fielding's announcement that the
owner of the coat had no funds: GRAND JURY TO SCAN
RELIEF; CITY BACKS THE "LADY IN MINK." I am aware
that to half retract, in half of a one-column head,
what you have fully stated in all of a three-column

[1] This is one story on which *The New Yorker* did not receive
a complaining, or explaining, note from the late Edwin L.
James, managing editor of the *Times* and a prolific note-writer.

head is decidedly better than standard newspaper practice.

To return briefly to the Conklin story and the headings over it, the line "42 Cases Analyzed" did little to help the reader understand that this number represented only about one-thirteenth of one percent of the department's burden. (The 42 cases involved a total of 207 persons, for whom social workers contended that only hotel lodgings could be found, out of the average of 263,300 persons on the department's rolls in 1947.) As to the "Front for Bookies" line, the incident it referred to was completely refuted within a couple of days. And the lead sentence, beginning, "The story of a . . . 'relief client' who lived at city expense in a hotel at $7.50 a day," seems to me inexcusably ambiguous. It implies (*a*) that the woman was living alone in the hotel and (*b*) that she was paying $7.50 a day just for her room, whereas the fact is that she had her five-year-old daughter with her and the daily $7.50 was to provide for all expenses, including food and clothing, for the two of them. To be sure, you could learn about the existence of the daughter if you read far enough down in Conklin's story, even though he did make her four months old instead of five years—an error that I am willing to ascribe to inadvertence. If you read all the way off the first page and deep into the runover of the story, you found out that the woman and her daughter had long before been moved out of the hotel room they had been occupying and had since then been receiving only $162.20 a month from the department.

The editors of the *Times,* if called upon to explain the play they gave this story, would doubtless say that they had been actuated not by the details of an isolated case but by the principle of the thing. It would be interesting in this instance to know the nature of the principle upon which the *Times* proceeded. I am afraid that a hint as to the answer may be contained in a further passage from Conklin's story, in which he wrote, "Explaining that state law forbids identifying relief clients by name and address, Mr. Shapiro [the state investigator] summarized twelve cases accepted

as eligible for relief by the city's Welfare Department.
They included a married woman indicted for grand
larceny; a mother who entertained men in her hotel
room while her children played in the lobby at all
hours; alcoholics; a divorcee with an out-of-wedlock
child; an unmarried mother with two children; a male
bigamist [if he was a practicing one, why wasn't he in
jail, or if he once served time for bigamy, was he returned by the law to both his spouses?]; and a man
separated from his wife and three children who was
living with another woman on city relief."

None of these descriptions has any legal relevance
to an applicant's eligibility for relief. No law specifies
that a woman must be blameless to qualify for a food
grant at the prevailing rates of $16.45 a month if un-
employed and living in a family group and $21.65 if
pregnant—to cite a couple of examples of the "liberal" allowances referred to in a report put out by
Commissioner Fielding himself last week as attracting
relief cases to the city. All the woman in question has
to be is without means. The principle involved in the
treatment given the Mink story—if, indeed, it was a
case of principle and not of sheer ineptness—seems to
be that the poor are poor because of their sins and
whatever they get is too good for them.

This is a lot of space to devote to one newspaper
story, but I think that Conklin's piece and the headline over it justify detailed consideration. I was saddened by the whole thing because the *Times* is in
many respects a sound newspaper, within the translucent mass of which one may occasionally discern the
outlines of commendable purposes, fixed like straw-
berries in a great mold of Jell-O, and of good men
struggling feebly, like minnows within a giant jelly-
fish. The *Herald Tribune,* although officially Republican, covered this investigation by the State Board
of Social Welfare (Republican) of the City Welfare
Department (Democratic) with considerably more
reserve. The *Sun* (Republican) was also more re-
strained than I had, perhaps unjustly, expected, even
if it did at one point take a strong anti-gypsy position.
"Gypsies, alcoholics, unmarried mothers, persons in

difficulty with the law, neglectful parents and employables who would not work were maihtained in hotels," the *Sun*'s October 29 story began, as if Romany blood were per se a reason for reproach.[2]

The *World-Telegram,* claiming credit on October 27, the first day of the investigation, for having inspired all the commotion over the Welfare Department by its "revelations" last spring (WORLD-TELEGRAM'S CHARGES CONFIRMED BY CITY'S REPORT), referred editorially to the since-resigned Commissioner Edward E. Rhatigan's "nervy request for an $82,000,000 boost in the $142,000,000 Welfare Department budget," which was, I imagine, getting rather near the *Telegram*'s chief preoccupation with the matter. In view of a recent 25 percent boost in the number of persons on relief, and an additional 25 percent boost since March 1945, in the cost of living for all of them, such a request would seem to me to be less than "nervy." It is true, however, that an increase in the Welfare Department's budget would bring nearer the day when the State Constitution will have to be amended to permit an increase in the city's real-estate taxes, and that obviously one of the most effective ways of keeping relief costs from rising is to shout that the people on relief don't deserve to be there and to imply that officials of the Welfare Department are Communists who are packing the relief rolls to run down free enterprise. "But," the *World-Telegram* editorial said, "we hope Mr. Fielding, who calls himself 'a plain blunt guy,' also sees the necessity of releasing key positions and policies in the Welfare Department from the grip of the Communist-dominated C.I.O. Public Workers of America." Next day, the *Telegram* was announcing on its front page that a Republican city councilman had "assailed the appointment of Commissioner Fielding, who, he said, was a member

---

[2] Hitler thought so. He ordered gypsies and Jews exterminated. Can anyone imagine a New York newspaper writing "Gypsies, Jews, alcoholics," etc.? Just because mitt joints (palmreading establishments) don't advertise, must Papers Pick on Petulengro's People? The gypsies may have put a curse on the *Sun.*

of the Communist-dominated American Labor Party."
On October 29, the paper returned to the picayune
cruelties of its original "revelations" by running these
headlines:

PROBE OF STATE
CONFIRMS W-T
WASTE EXPOSE

SHOWS WELFARE DEPT. PAMPERED
CHISELERS IN LUXURY HOTELS

and under them, a story beginning, "Former convicts,
alcoholics, neglectful parents, and women who entertained men in their rooms . . ." (All of these, of
course, are types to be found in higher economic strata
as well.) The reporter, Walter MacDonald, had evidently not heard about the gypsies. On November 1,
by which time even the *Journal-American* reached the
conclusion, inconspicuously, that "the case of the celebrated 'Lady in Mink' apparently had fizzled today
into just welfare routine," *Telegram* headlines read:

STATE AID ACCUSES FIELDING
OF SNIPING AT RELIEF PROBE

CITY'S DEFENSE OF RITZY DOLE
IS UNDER FIRE

This, by the way, was on the day that Mr. Fielding
collapsed and was taken to a hospital as a result of
overwork, causing veiled merriment among old-time
Welfare Department employees, who told one another,
"Now he knows what it's like to work here." The department is chronically understaffed.

A day or so ago, I saw a *World-Telegram* advertisement in another newspaper. It was headed, SURE, NEW
YORK HAS A HEART, and read, in part, "There are three
W-T staff writers in particular who are on most intimate terms with New York's tough-but-soft heart.
Their roving job is to peer between the skyscrapers and
under the chromium to find the hidden stories—the

ones that have a special color all their own. Watch for their sketches of New York's real heartbeats." Maybe this trio, rather than Mr. MacDonald, ought to have been turned loose on the Welfare Department.

Out of sheer perverseness, I suppose, I have leaned backward in an effort not to give *PM* unduly frequent good marks in these random pieces about the press. Perhaps it is because the paper reminds me too often of the repulsive lines forced upon a young American actor, Penrod Schofield, in one of the books I like best to remember:

> "*I hight Sir Lancelot du Lake, the child,*
> *Gentul-hearted, meek, and mild.*"

If *PM* were a girl, her face would be shiny, and she would be conscientiously and resolutely promiscuous and tell all her boyfriends about their complexes. But on a story like this curious investigation *PM* does a beautiful job. "Buried obscurely in the testimony, which dealt exclusively with the now-famous 42 'hotel cases,' " John K. Weiss, of the *PM* staff wrote after a day of "revelations," "were such details as these: many of the hotel cases involved mentally disturbed or depressed persons; press hysteria about the hotel cases forced many persons into substandard housing; one case concerned an immature mother who was moved from a hotel directly into a mental hospital. Not once during the day was the fact mentioned that the State had approved the hotel procedure." And Mr. Weiss's colleague on *PM*, Albert Deutsch, wrote, "Well, what does one do with such people, subject them to euthanasia? . . . Incompetence in public agency workers and inefficiency in public administration cannot be condoned. Periodic inquiries and exposures of maladministration can only be welcomed by the citizenry. But such inquiries must be conducted on the basis of fair play and sound judgment; it is a nasty business to make a political football out of public relief, and to run a headline-hunting campaign under the guise of a fact-finding inquiry." I can't fault him on that.

Almost two years after the press crusade referred to above, the late Don Hollenbeck, in his Columbia Broadcasting program "CBS Views the Press," brought up the subject of the Lady again. I quote part of Mr. Hollenbeck's talk:

The Lady in Mink has taken a solid place in the history of New York City, and historians cannot well ignore her in any notes they make on certain aspects of our social life. What actually became of the Lady in Mink we have no idea, but her wraith is back again, and for the story we tell now, she provides the counterpoint. For some time earlier this winter City Editor Paul Sann of the New York *Post* had been receiving complaints from destitute persons seeking relief; they said they were being made to wait in some cases more than a month before any help was given to them by the Department of Welfare. Reporter Joseph Kahn was assigned to get the story. Kahn had earlier got his hands on a copy of a report by the New York City Youth Board's Bronx Pilot project, checked with officials and gone on from there; the Youth Board is a city project, and its panel includes members of civic, church, welfare and educational groups. On it and his own findings Kahn wrote his first story for the *Post;* it appeared February first under a headline reading "City's needy wait weeks for relief as new system bogs Welfare Department," and the story began with these words: "Thousands of destitute men, women and children in need of home relief are being forced to wait weeks for help. Indigent families who apply for relief must now wait a week for an interview and another two weeks for a visit from a case investigator. Under the law, anyone asking for relief is supposed to be visited within 48 hours; this ruling is being ignored because the depart-

ment is bogged down in a complete re-investiga-
tion of its caseload." Kahn's story went on to say
that the department advised these persons to borrow, stretch their food, go to their friends. And
finally, it revealed that the department was behind
in its investigations of more than three thousand
new requests for relief.

The original story about people living on luxury
relief in hotels involved 37 families—about 120
people—a not appreciable proportion of the
233,000 persons at that time on the relief rolls of
New York City. This time, with 275,000 persons on
the rolls, three thousand more were affected—a
really serious welfare problem—and new applica-
tions being received at the rate of three thousand
a week. But where two years ago the papers hardly
let an edition go by after the first mention in the
Telegram before they were howling in concert
about the relief scandal, it was different this time.
Not a single newspaper bothered to follow the
lead of the *Post.*

The theme of the undeserving poor recurs as often
as Groundhog Sees His Shadow or Tommy Manville
Takes Another Bride. One of the things that puts me
off doing the Wayward Press for years at a time, in
fact, is its inevitable repetitiousness—given the same
opportunity, newspapers will always do the same
wrong thing. But in the spring of 1959, when I was
asked, with Louis Lyons, the Curator of the Nieman
Foundation, and Dean Ed Barrett of the Pulitzer School
of Journalism at Columbia, to judge the New York
Newspaper Guild's Page One awards for work done
during the year, I am damned if the *Daily News* did
not present, *for a prize,* a series on the same thread-
bare nonsense. This time, I think, it had something to
do with Puerto Ricans eating up the profits of the
Daily News by getting two bottles of milk for one baby.

STOP PRESS. Latest bulletin—The city manager of
Newburgh, N.Y., has just announced that he will refuse
food to unmarried mothers and their children. He is,
accordingly, being hailed as a Messiah by the *Herald*

Tribune, World-Telegram and *Daily News,* who propose him as a candidate for Vice-President in 1964, to run on a ticket with Barry Goldwater.

Once we had a Mayor of New York named Gaynor, who lived in Brooklyn and used to walk the Brooklyn Bridge every morning to City Hall, attended by the reporters for the afternoon papers. I was a child then, but when I went to work in 1924 I met a lot of the fellows who had walked with His Honor. There were crusaders then, too, on another pet subject, though for another reason: prurient interest.

"And what about Vice, your Honor," some poor devil would have to ask every morning, because his editor had instructed him.

"What vice?" the Mayor would ask. "Avarice?"

He had hit the publishers' favorite.

The next exhibit combines several advantages. It illustrates the press reflexes to labor—"stubborn"—*and* Government—"meddlesome," "wasteful." It also recalls a historic episode, now dimming, that may have something to do with the beginning of that great press bugaboo, the INFLATION, which many a lad and lass now on campus may have been told by parents suffering from self-induced amnesia was started by Harry Truman, *against* the advice of the current anti-inflationists. Above all, though, it is an exposition of an art form, the unconducted symphony in jive, or jam session, in which each of the principals picks up the main idea and embellishes it, with a rapid development from representational to nonrepresentational reporting. In painting this took a half-century to achieve, but a newspaper can often manage it overnight.

(It is probably necessary to inform the lads and lasses that during World War II and for a couple of years thereafter, there were price controls, which were removed, one by one, as an old-fashioned aeronaut used to drop sandbags out of the basket of his balloon when he wanted it to go up. Rent controls, in most cities, are about the only ones left, but it is hard to convince *les cochons de locataires* that their removal would be instantly followed by a voluntary general reduction of rents by their landlords. The *locataires* in rent-controlled apartments are preponderantly old and stubborn, and may remember when they too could afford an occasional steak that wasn't hamburger. Our curtain rises on a period when the American economy, pinioned like Gulliver, lay prostrate, feebly struggling for a two-dollar pork chop, while tiny men like Arthur Krock scurried among the threads piping "Cut him loose!")

The Great Gouamba

DECEMBER 7, 1946

It is too early, as I write, to present a detailed critique of the way our press handled the news about the coal miner's latest abstention from work. I sometimes fancy, however, that I detect a shift in the papers' economic line since October, when the meat producers were abstaining from the sale of any meat at ceiling prices. Jack Werkley, a *Herald Tribune* reporter who flits about the country in what his paper reminds its readers, every time it runs one of his stories, is a twin-engine Lockheed Lodestar flying newsroom, did, it is true, call the October episode a farmers' strike, and Will Lissner, in the *Times,* wrote accurately, if inconspicuously (page seventeen), that "the main reason why feeders are buying and growers are holding cattle is that it appears to be profitable." But there was a note of understanding approval—even, I might say, of affection—in most of the stories about the cattlemen, who were represented as rugged, wholesome, humorous individual enterprisers standing with their gum boots solidly planted in hog slop while they told the rest of the country to meet their terms. Maybe it is just my imagination, but the papers seem to me to be taking a bleaker view of the coal miners, who are using exactly the same tactics. The cattlemen held on to their beasts until they got their price (whereupon meat

appeared in quantity), the miners are withholding their
labor; but the press seems to have missed the parallel.
The *Herald Tribune,* which on October 14 published
a long piece about how decontrolled grain prices would
affect the cost of raising hogs (if consisted entirely of
quotes from a handout from the Republican Congressional Food Study Committee), has so far printed no
companion piece on how decontrolled meat and other
prices affect the cost of raising miners.

The *Herald Tribune* has me in its debt. It was a
Herald Tribune editorial of November 26, warning
labor against starting an inflation, that sent me scurry-
ing back among my souvenirs to disinter some notes I
had made on the journalistic episode I call the "Great
Gouamba" ("gouamba" is an African word meaning
"meat hunger") to verify my impression that the newspaper line had changed. I first encountered "gouamba"
in *Stories of the Gorilla Country,* by Paul du Chaillu,
an African explorer, lecturer, and author of boys'
books who lived toward the end of the last century
and whom in my youth I read with the rapt attention
I now reserve for the daily press. Dormant for 30 years
in some stratum of my unconscious, the word popped
to the surface on October 9 while I was reading a piece
by John O'Donnell, the political columnist of the
Daily News.

"Come what may," O'Donnell predicted, "this battle for the control of Congress will go down in our
political history as the meat campaign." "Gouamba,"
I suddenly heard myself saying. Later in the day I
checked, in the public library on my recollection of the
word's meaning. "On our return to Obinji," du
Chaillu wrote, in a prose I admire even more than
O'Donnell's, "we were overtaken by my good friend
Querlaouen, who had shot a wild pig of which the
good fellow gave me half. The Negroes feasted on the
koo loo meat [Du Chaillu described a *koo loo* as a
"new type chimpanzee"], which I could not touch. So
the pig was welcome to me, as indeed it was to Quen-
gueza, whom we found almost crying with an affection
which is common in this part of Africa, and is called
gouamba, but for which we happily have no name.

Gouamba is the inordinate longing and craving of exhausted nature for meat. For days, and sometimes for weeks, a man does not get any meat at all; and whenever any other food is brought before him you will hear him say, looking at the food with disgust, 'Gouamba,' which means literally, 'I am sick of food; I have a craving for meat; I care for nothing else.' "
Ever since that day I have thought of the period from October 7 to October 14, 1946 (President Truman decontrolled meat on the night of the fourteenth), as Gouamba Week, or the Newspaper Mardi Gras.

Gouamba Week began, for me, with a picture layout and story on the first page of the *Sun* of Monday afternoon. The *News* [1] was caught more or less flatfooted at the beginning of the week, and it looked as if the other publishers had not told Colonel McCormick, way out in Chicago, what was going to happen. The *News* devoted its front page on Monday to a wedding picture of a bride who had dropped dead a minute after being photographed, and it didn't really seem to grasp the horror of the meat situation until Wednesday. The feature of the *Sun*'s Monday layout was an Associated Press wirephoto of William Saier, of Detroit, a man who clearly lacked two lower molars, sitting in a restaurant in Windsor, Canada, and shoving a large piece of steak into his widely opened face. Mr. Saier appeared to be in little need of nourishment, since he rather resembled the late William Howard Taft (minus the mustache), but the *Sun*'s headline on the Associated Press story it ran alongside brought out the pathos of the situation. AMERICANS DINE WELL—

---

[1] The New York *Daily News*. Capt. Joseph Medill Patterson, its founder and Colonel McCormick's unloving cousin, had just died, and the Colonel had inherited control. He sternly eradicated what he considered a tinge of Pink in the *News*—for instance, the staff's refusal to believe that Lord Howe's fleet was not lurking off Sandy Hook. The Colonel wanted to stretch a chain across the Narrows. Franklin D. Roosevelt, the Colonel believed, had planned to sell the country to George the Third, but had been poisoned by Stalin, from whom he had already accepted a down payment. The Colonel, although not a Stalinist, approved. "There should be honor, even among thieves!" he frequently said.

IN CANADA, it said. The caption under the picture read, " 'Yum-mm—Detroit is NOT like this,' William Saier seemed to be saying as he feasted on a large, juicy T-bone steak in a nearby roadhouse inn yesterday." How Mr. Saier could seem to be saying all that with a large piece of steak stuffed in his mouth, the caption writer did not explain. "A thick, juicy steak, luscious pork chops, tender roast beef, remember?" the A.P. story began. There was a second photograph in the layout, showing American automobiles from Detroit lined up at the customs station in Windsor and filled with people who wanted to get into Canada to satisfy their gouamba.

On the following day the papers published the report (which recommended decontrol) of the Beef Advisory Committee of the O.P.A.,[2] which was composed of representatives of the industry, and on Wednesday the *Sun*'s headline on its leading gouamba story read, POLITICAL STORM SWEEPS NATION IN MEAT SCARCITY. On Thursday a piece on the front page of the *Sun*, headed ILLEGAL DEER BAG LAID TO MEAT LACK, told how gouamba-maddened poachers pursuing deer in the Adirondacks had accidentally shot to death a seventy-three-year-old farmer, a clear case of homicide traceable to the mistakes of the Administration. It should be noted that the headline writer did not get the farmer into the headline, presumably because he was not edible.

The *Times,* which had got off to an early start with a rush of stories that seemed a bit heavy, hit its stride, I thought, on the same day with a piece headed QUEENS RESTAURATEUR, WORRIED OVER MEAT, DIVES OFF BROOKLYN BRIDGE AND SURVIVES. The restaurateur's wife, interviewed by a *Times* reporter, did not say what paper her husband had been reading. Some of the other *Times* entries for Miss Gouamba of 1946 (which prove that the *Times,* as I have often contended, is not nearly so unimaginative as people think) were MEAT HUNTERS BEAT PATH TO JERSEY HAMLET,

---

[2] Office of Price Administration. Occupies the same place in the history of American business as the Inquisition or the Sherman Act.

BURGLAR IN BUTCHER SHOP FINDS CUPBOARD ALL
BARE, and CHINESE VISITORS EAT BEEF AT CITY LODG-
ING. This last was the headline writer's way of saying
that some Chinese police chiefs had tasted the stew at
the Municipal Lodging House on East Twenty-Fifth
Street.

The *Herald Tribune*'s most ambitioous contribution
to gouamba was the aerial voyage Mr. Werkley made
through the West in quest of meat, but I thought that
a brief and simple improvisation by the paper's ship-
news man, headed STELLA POLARIS IN, 106 BID MEAT
GLUM FAREWELL, had a much more gouambaceous
effect than its airborne reporter's expensive set pieces.
The ship-news man described the terror in the faces
of the passengers disembarking after a 19-day Carib-
bean cruise and confronted by life in a meatless New
York. The cruise rates ranged from $425 to $1,475 a
passenger, and I felt sorry for people with only that
kind of money to spend faced with the sort of hell
they were coming back to. The best Mr. Werkley could
do was tell about a ranch owner who fed him meat off
a roast of beef as big as a medicine ball, but since I
had never wanted to swallow a medicine ball, my
gouamba was not stimulated very much.

The *Journal-American* made a double enveloping
advance on the subject of the week. It ran one series
of articles from Canada by a reporter named John C.
Manning, designed to prove that there was meat in
that country (where rationing has been in force almost
continuously since 1943—a cogent argument for the
abandonment of control here), and another series, by
a reporter named Kent Hunter, that was meant to indicate that *our* meat had gone, via U.N.R.R.A., "into
the larders of the Russians and their satellites." Mr.
Hunter, who not very long ago was Gen. George Patton's uniformed press agent with the Third Army in
France, announced on October 9 that 375,490,719
pounds of "the meat, sugar, butter, and concentrated
foods that American housewives cried for" had been
shipped to Austria, Czechoslovakia, Hungary, Finland,
Poland, the U.S.S.R., Yugoslavia, and Albania. That

works out, if you are good at figures, to one and one-third pounds of food, mostly cereals, per inhabitant of those countries, and could have provided every American citizen with a good buffet lunch. But it is much more impressive if you put it in pounds instead of tons. In tons, it is, to be specific, 187,500, or about three substantial shiploads per country. Incidentally, Hunter might have said that it was more than six billion ounces (6,007,851,504), or 170,322,590,138.40 grams, figures that obviously would have been more important to the stimulation of metropolitan gouamba than any stories about the number of beef cattle in the hands of the ranchers.[3] The head on the story was SENATOR CHARGES FOOD DIVERSION FROM U.N.R.R.A. TO RED ARMY USE.

This piece of Hunter's was surpassed, however, by one he wrote a couple of days later. It was headed SENATOR BRIDGES CHARGES U.N.R.R.A. STEAKS SOLD IN EUROPE BY BLACK MART. The *Journal* editors must have had as high an opinion of it as I did, for they moved Hunter up from page two to the front page. "Civilians on the ship [the aircraft carrier *Franklin D. Roosevelt*] brought back a detailed report," Hunter wrote, "of two-inch-thick steaks served in black-market-supplied restaurants in Naples, in Athens, and along the Morocco–Algiers coast, at a time when American housewives cannot buy hamburger." Naturally the implication was that the steaks must have come from the U.N.R.R.A. Mr. Manning's Canadian jaunt had produced mostly photographs of hunks of meat, the idea being that there were no hunks of meat

---

[3] Precisely the same chestnut has reappeared this year. Wholesale butchers in New York, chided because meat has risen far above the 1946 black-market prices, blamed the "shortage" on the export of meats to Europe. The *Sun* followed up with a "revelation" from its Washington bureau that 300,000,000 pounds of meat had been shipped out of the country during the last six months. This would be about two pounds per inhabitant of the United States, or less than an ounce of meat a week diverted from each individual American. It would be less than a tenth of an ounce subtracted from each meat meal. You could hide that much meat behind a green pea.

on this side of the border to photograph and that we
knew whom we could blame for *that*.

The *Mirror,* ever a younger sister in Hearst journalism, produced little notable gouamba stimulus during
the festival. Its best offering was a story by a reporter
named Henry Hillman, headed MEAT FAMINE HAS
STATE ON GUARD FOR RUSTLERS and explaining, "The
arrest Wednesday of a Manhattanite for a butcher-and-
run assault on a docile, three-year-old Holstein cow
near New Paltz seemed to justify the jitters, and many
farmers have reached a state of sirloin tremens where
they're about to move their cattle into the front parlor
for safety. A high State Police official at Albany, however, informed the *Mirror* that the scare is without
foundation." This sort of marched-up-the-hill-and-
then-marched-down-again journalism would never have
started the Spanish-American War.

The *World-Telegram* proved disappointingly unin-
ventive. Its Frederick Woltman, the fellow-traveler-
collector, was apparently miffed because Hunter had
beaten him to the Red angle, and he sulked behind
his file of the *Daily Worker* all through Gouamba
Week, not even bothering to go out and see if he
could discover a soup bone concealed beneath the
plinth of the Independent Citizens' Committee of the
Arts, Sciences, and Professions. The *Post* whimpered
a few quiet suggestions about measures Mr. Truman
could take against the meat men if he felt like it, and
then subsided when it became evident that he didn't.

The white-horse team in the chariot race, which
overtook the whole field, after being left standing at
the start, and passed them all in a cloud of flying
gouamba, was, as any connoisseur of the kiosks might
have anticipated, the *Daily News.* The issue of
Wednesday, October 9, which I keep pressed between
rose leaves, served notice on all lesser newspapers that
since Colonel McCormick and Mrs. Patterson [4] had
now taken cognizance of the emergency, it damn well

---

[4] The late Cicely, a cousin, then publisher of the Washington
Times-Herald, since gobbled, like a decontrolled chuck roast,
by the Washington *Post.* It was such a bad paper that a book-
maker would have made it odds-on to survive, but it didn't.

was an emergency. The front page carried a picture of a band of steers tottering out of a freight car in Flushing, where, according to the publicity man of a company out there that manufactures steel lockers, they were to be knocked on the head and distributed in bits to the firm's employees. Mr. O'Donnell, in his column about this being the meat campaign, had apparently blown the whistle for all hands to turn to, and they did, with the alacrity of so many *koo loo*s. That day the lead Washington story opened with "A ray of hope for the meat-famished East appeared today." The lead editorial, headed LET 'EM EAT HORSE MEAT, began, "The above should be the slogan of the Truman Administration, according to Representative Charles A. Halleck (R.-Ind.), chairman of the Republican Congressional Campaign Committee." The editorial cartoon showed a flabby, dissipated-looking pugilist, labeled "New Deal Crackpot Economy," supine on the floor of a ring and shouting "Conspiracy! Conspiracy! Conspiracy!" while a handsome young boxer, ticketed "Facts of Life," stood victoriously over him.

On the following day, DEMS, FEARFUL OF VOTERS, ACT IN MEAT CRISIS shared page three, the *News*'s equivalent of the right-hand side of the first page in a standard paper, with SLAIN PAIR FOUND IN DEBRIS, a story about a double murder in Florida. Mr. O'Donnell played a reprise on the viola da gouamba, and there were two divertissements, called COOKIE PLANT MAY CLOSE [FOR LACK OF LARD] and MEAT STOPS MINE WALKOUT. The second was about how fifteen hundred miners quitting their jobs in Logan County, West Virginia, had been lured back by a promise of free pork chops—a trick that has not yet been tried in the new emergency. On Saturday a photograph of the Duke and Duchess of Windsor had to share the front page with a picture of a meat queue in the Bronx, captioned "Grand Illusion." Saturday's biggest gouamba feature was, however, a mighty funny photograph of a straw-hatted butcher in Johnson City, New York, who happened to be named Harry Truman and who was quoted as saying, while he held a cleaver over a carcass of lamb, "Get rid of those price ceilings and we'll have meat." He evidently considered lamb a vegetable.

With all the newspapers except the gently sniffling *Post* and an imminently apoplectic *PM* joining in the crashing chorus of "Gouamba! There is no meat!" like a refrain by Vachel Lindsay, the week rolled on to its predestined end. The *Sun* cried, in one frantic sub-head, SCARCITY SWELLS HOURLY! In another hour, it would have been a matter of minutes. Mr. Werkley's climactic *Herald Tribune* story was headed CORN BELT FATTENS FLOOD OF BEEF, WAITS FOR O.P.A. DAM TO BREAK. On the second Monday evening of the Great Gouamba, the dam went out.

PM, very ungenerously, I thought, used the front-page headline TRUMAN SURRENDERS to record the event. What the President had done was simply yield to a spontaneous demonstration of public opinion. Personally, I much preferred the *Journal-American*'s triumphant paean: HOG PRICES SOAR TO ALL-TIME HIGH.

Not all publishers are hopeless, however, as the following piece, an almost-anniversary sequel to "The Great Gouamba," proves.

The Impossible Headline

OCTOBER 18, 1947

The recent headlines and stories about food prices in the newspapers here have reminded me of the French newspapers I read in 1940, when I was in Paris and the Germans were advancing on that city. Every day the Parisian press would report that the enemy had been hurled back, or at least contained, at some point, and a couple of days later it would develop that he

had advanced an average of 25 miles along the whole
front. The military experts would predict a great coun-
teroffensive, and the commanding generals would issue
bulletins adjuring everybody to stand fast, as if one
could solve a concrete dilemma by making fancy
statements. Old-timers who remembered the First World
War kept insisting that things would not be really
serious until the Boche reached the Marne. At last,
the reading public, including me, began to realize that
the struggle was lost.

It was with a nostalgic sense of familiarity, there-
fore, that I read these front-page headlines in the
Times of Saturday, September 20, over a story by Will
Lissner:

MEAT PRICE DROP
NEXT WEEK SEEN;
GRAINS FALL AGAIN

BREAK, SHARPEST IN MONTHS,
SENDS CORN DOWN THE LIMIT
SECOND CONSECUTIVE DAY

BUTTER FAILS TO RECOVER

BUYER RESISTANCE FORCES EGGS DOWN AT
WHOLESALE HERE AND ON
CHICAGO EXCHANGE

Next week came and went, and the headline over
the *Time*'s lead food story on the thirtieth read: MOST
FOOD PRICES CONTINUE TO RISE.

As I square away to my typewriter, the headline on
Mr. Lissner's latest food story in the *Times* reads:
BUTTER PRICES DROP SHARPLY AS OTHER ITEMS CON-
TINUE UP. The story begins: "Price-conscious consum-
ers from New York to San Francisco scored a re-
sounding victory yesterday against one of the leaders
of the food price spiral, butter, although the price
level of basic commodities continued to advance; hog
and cattle prices climbed again and grain prices gyrated. [By "gyrated," Mr. Lissner apparently meant

that grain prices rose, or perhaps that they fluctuated; at any rate, wheat was about 25 cents a bushel higher at that writing than it had been on September 20.] The housewives of the nation were in the position of winning one battle and losing the campaign, for meat prices were heading higher, a 1-cent rise in the price of bread was imminent and other retail prices continued at high levels."

Mr. Lissner's "gyrated" is not the only product of the mental exhaustion caused in newspaper offices by continued daily efforts to find synonyms for "rise." At about the same time, a headline writer in the *Wall Street Journal* described cocoa prices as "careening," meaning, it turned out, not that they were tilting over on one side but that they had increased 850 percent in a few years. The *Herald Tribune* ran a front-page head on September 26 saying: HALT IN SPIRAL OF PRICES LED BY MEAT, EGGS. Leading a halt, I imagine, would be rather like winning a race at a standstill.

The Marne, which a few optimists, like Arthur Krock of the *Times,* kept on telling their readers had not been reached again, is the 1946 level of black-market prices. "In this space, in the issue of September 23," Mr. Krock wrote in his editorial-page column on September 25, "one phase of [the argument over responsibility for present high prices] was examined—comparisons of the last prices for certain foodstuffs under OPA with prices being asked last week for the same viands. And it was pointed out that these comparisons (prime beefsteak 64 cents a pound then, $1 now, etc.) were deceptive for several reasons. One reason is that most of the OPA prices in that period and for some time before were meaningless because the shelves in retail shops were empty of the articles. Another is that in numerous instances the black market prices at that time were as high as or higher than at present."

I am in a position to inform Mr. Krock that a restaurant which in 1946 provided an excellent sirloin steak at the unlisted price of $3.50 now has a legally listed counterpart at $4; a more modest place, which used to charge a sub-rosa $2.50 for a similar article, now gets a super-rosa $2.85.[1]

Affronted by the "soaring" (*World-Telegram,* September 29), "skyrocketing" (*Post,* September 30), "whirling" (*Times,* same date) prices, reported in the *Times* (October 3) as having "spiraled" to higher levels, a newspaper that had opposed the O.P.A. engaged in a variety of diversionary antics, which made me think of a man I knew in the Poplar district of London during the war, who played hymns on a portable harmonium to cheer people buried alive by bomb debris. The *World-Telegram* ran a United Press story by Harman W. Nichols informing that "in the Klondike, after gold was discovered in 1897, a man paid $10 for a plate of eggs and a slab of ham." The *News* offered a consolatory story by a woman reporter named Edna Ferguson, which began, "With housekeeping purses drained by the high prices of meat and other fresh foods, a survey by the *News* yesterday disclosed a housewife's paradise in the canned food market, in which prices generally are much lower than last year. Eye-opening items included boned chicken, which sells for 55 cents for a 5½ ounce can this year compared to 85 cents last year." Boned chicken at 10 cents an ounce seemed to me a perfect solution of the budget problems of a low-income family.

Editors, turning back to the assignment books of September and October, 1946, hauled out a number of the feature-story ideas that they had worked up during the mass appeal to the American "gouamba," or meat hunger. The *Herald Tribune,* which in 1946 had sent a reporter named Jack Werkley on a tour of the West to find out why no meat was coming to market, in 1947 dispatched a reporter named Kenneth Koyen to approximately the same territory to find out why prices were so high. Werkley had reported that cattlemen were holding their stock for higher prices. Koyen reported that the cattlemen were now getting higher prices. The device Koyen employed for tangiblizing— if I may borrow a verb from Father Divine—this diffi-

---

[1] As of this writing (1961), $5.

cult concept was the biography of an Aberdeen Angus steer that he chose to call Hector. Koyen reported that Hector, born in northwestern Nebraska late in the summer of 1945, and then valued at $5, had been sold to a cattle feeder in eastern Nebraska on October 22, 1946, for $114, having grown a lot in the interim. The feeder sold him about a year later for $468, having spent in the intervening time, according to his own calculations, $164 on the animal. This represented a profit of 68 percent. Shipped East, the beast passed through the hands of a packer, a jobber, and a retail butcher, none of whom, as far as Koyen could determine, made much on him. Hector reached the consumer in the form of about seven hundred pounds of beef, worth anywhere up to a dollar a pound when the *Tribune* went to press with Mr. Koyen's story, and perhaps a couple of cents more now.

Koyen reached two conclusions: "First, that there appears to be no individual culprit who can be accused of deliberately raising Hector's price. Second, the biggest margin between costs and prices is being enjoyed by the producers, specifically, the ranchers and farmers." Koyen did not bother to point out that a year ago the ranchers and farmers were making a collective effort to raise Hector's price by getting rid of O.P.A. controls, nor did he say that his paper was then doing its best to help them.

A while back, the *Sun* sent a man named D. G. Lawrence up to Canada to check on the food situation there. (Plenty to eat at low prices.) Lawrence, in the course of reporting an interview with a French-Canadian taxi driver in Quebec, wrote, " 'Oui, sir,' he continued in a curious mixture of French and English. 'We get along.' " (A *Sun* copyreader, ever solicitous lest a reader miss a point, placed over this quotation a subhead that read, "Polyglot Answer.") Lawrence went on to Ottawa, from where he reported, "One inflationary factor—high wheat prices—is not affecting the Canadian economy to any great extent. Wheat is one of the few commodities still under direct price control." The paragraph containing this statement appeared while newspapers here were chronicling the rejection by the Chicago Board of Trade of the Administration's initial suggestion that the board lend its support to increasing marginal requirements for speculation in grain futures to 33⅓ percent.

The most depressing aspect of the New York press to me, at least, during this inevitable sequel to last year's "gouamba," is the daily-menu feature prepared by the municipal Department of Markets' dietitians for a "low-to-moderate-income" family of five. The menus, which are printed in a number of newspapers, offer a diet that suggests the regimen of a well-conducted poorhouse. The breakfasts almost invariably consist of cereal and milk, fruit juice (usually canned), bread and margarine, and coffee (milk for children). A typical lunch is pea soup (canned or dehydrated), a cottage-cheese-and-raisin sandwich on whole wheat bread, grapes, and milk. A dinner may be built around a main dish of "wheat germ fish fry," "tuna fish puffs" (whatever they are), or a fish chowder made with dried skimmed milk. The big, five-star meat meals (about four of which are suggested a week) offer something like lamb stew, made with three pounds of stewing lamb for five persons, which, considering the percentage of bone in stew meat, would barely flavor the potatoes.[2]

If a man earning a low-to-moderate wage can provide only what the Department of Markets' menus allot, the plight of the family with a rock-bottom income is obvious. I cite a Washington Associated Press dispatch of September 27, published in the *Herald Tribune:* "Senator Ralph E. Flanders, Republican, of Vermont, said today food prices have climbed so high in New York City and some other large metropolitan areas that some white-collar workers and low-salaried job-holders are 'seriously undernourished.' Senator Flanders has been directing two weeks of public hearings by a Senate–House subcommittee investigating

---

[2] Here I seem to have spoken out of turn. Several women wrote to me that this was quite enough lamb to put in a stew for five, and while I am glad I am not married to any of them, I probably would be slimmer if I were.

high costs of food and clothing. 'It is my personal opinion that there is a submerged population in New York City and some other large cities,' he told a reporter. . . . He defined 'submerged population' as those persons whose 'family incomes have not kept pace with the rise in the cost of living.' " Senator Flanders can hardly be accused of looking for votes in New York City, or of playing politics with Left Wingers, the Left Wing vote in Vermont being what it is.[3]

It is not apparent what "waste"—to use the President's word—a Department of Markets' family could wring out of a diet so stringent (I'm referring again to those daily menus) that the precise number of vegetables for each dish is specified (four onions in the lamb stew, one stalk of celery in the Waldorf salad). As for less fortunate families, Senator Taft's suggestion that they could, or should, eat less puts me in mind of something William Cobbett, the English political writer and grand old man of journalism, wrote in 1823 of a depression that had swept his country: "The fashion became to cry up spare diet, and to preach content with hunger. One of the Tracts put forth by canting hypocrites who pretended to exclusive grace was entitled 'The Life of Peter Kennedy, who lived on, and saved money out of eighteen pence a week.' And this to his praise, mind! . . . The gist of the whole of the 'Tracts' was to inculcate content in a state of misery! to teach people to starve without making a noise! What did all this show? Why, a consciousness on the part of the rich, that the poor had not fair play; and that the former wished to obtain security against the latter by coaxing."

The *Wall Street Journal,* a publication that has lately

---

[3] Mrs. Roosevelt in 1948 called attention in her newspaper column to a Gallup poll report that one out of seven Americans interviewed admitted having had to go hungry during some part of that year. While, as Mrs. Roosevelt noted, there is no particular reason to take polls literally, they may be more accurate about nonpolitical matters than about elections. (Also her observation.) Senator (then) John F. Kennedy in his debates with Vice-President (that was) Richard Nixon, used a similar figure for 1960.

begun to fascinate me, indicated in a recent front-page
"Commodity Letter" the aspect of the food situation
that worries it most. "Food prices ride high on full
employment and foreign hunger," the letter began.
"There's little to suggest a big break in the cost of
eating before one of these key props begins to sag.
There are now 15 million more people in paying jobs
than in 1939. This means there are 33% more bread-
winners putting money into family pockets now than
then. It means millions are eating better now than ever
before. Specific example: The average American now
eats 115 pounds of meat for every 100 pounds he ate
in 1937–41."

The *Journal* offered no evidence that anyone who
ate a reasonable amount of meat in 1937 is eating any
more now, and it overlooked the fact that more employment gave millions of Americans who had been
living mainly on boiled potatoes a chance to get their
teeth into an occasional chop or roast. Nor did it consider the possibility that the rise in the price of meat is
demoting these people back to the boiled-potato class.

"Runaway food prices," the *Journal* continued, "if
sustained, can help cut the full employment that sup-
ports them. Department store executives already blame
declining sales on heavier grocery spending. Lower retail sales eventually mean restricted manufacturing—
less employment." [4]

The *Journal,* I gather from its editorial page, would
like to see us pay a minimum of attention to "foreign
hunger," believing that a high level of employment,
and department-store sales, can be maintained here no
matter what happens in the rest of the world.

All the newspapers I read seem to be handling the
facts of the food story well enough. Most of them give
decent positions to statements by public officials, such
as Commissioner of Hospitals Edward M. Bernecker
and Commissioner of Welfare Edward E. Rhatigan,
that high prices are endangering the health of pregnant
mothers, hospital outpatients who need special diets,
and school children in low-income families. *PM,* the

---

[4] Has this happened? (1961)

Cassandra [5] of metropolitan papers, and, except for
the *Post,* the only one to fight against the anti-O.P.A.
agitation last year, goes on being right and being ignored. Most of the papers give some prominence to
the remarks of such public figures as Mayor O'Dwyer
and Chester Bowles blaming the Republican Party for
ripping off the controls and imposing "involuntary rationing, Republican style" (the Mayor's crack) or for
"taking orders from the National Association of Manufacturers" (Mr. Bowles's). Even more prominence is
usually allotted to the remarks of Senator Taft, who
naturally blames the Democrats. President Truman is
in a poor position to blame anybody, having thrown
in his hand when he abolished meat controls last October. Seeing a political fortune go to waste, he must
sometimes be sorry that he didn't at least call. [6]

When the O.P.A. was dying, some of its editorial
opponents were inclined to side with the *Mirror,* which
proclaimed that "the worst threat of inflation has
passed"; others shared the more cautious view of the
News, which conceded that "some prices most likely
will go up" for a while, and of the *Times,* which spoke
of a possible "higher plateau"; [7] all appeared to face
the future confidently and there was a general feeling
that a little price raising might be on the whole salutary. But something must have slipped up somewhere;
otherwise, how can one account for the signs of hysteria and near-panic in the wording and presentation
of today's front-page price-rise stories? It almost looks
as if the O.P.A.'s enemies never expected matters to
turn out this way. What chokes me up is that not one
of the papers that last year plumped for the abolition
of the O.P.A. has yet come out with an editorial admission that it may have been in error. That, it seems
to me, would be great journalism. And what a head-

---

[5] Like Cassandra, *PM* came to a sad end.

[6] This is an example of an analogy that turned out to be
inexact. President Truman had not thrown in his hand on this
issue, it developed during the late campaign. He had merely
passed. In the late summer of 1948, he cashed in handsomely
by blaming the Republicans for high prices.

[7] The plateau turned into an escalator.

line it would make: PUBLISHER ADMITS HE MAY HAVE
BEEN WRONG.

I did not write this seriously, of course; it seemed a
forlorn hope. But within a week I received a communication from Mr. William N. Barto, managing
editor of the Lewisburg *Journal-News,* of Lewisburg,
Pennsylvania, which boasts that it is "Union County's
Leading Advertising Medium." Mr. Barto's letter is by
way of being a unique document:

> I am enclosing a short editorial regarding OPA . . .
> You will see that although but a small country weekly,
> the Lewisburg *Journal-News* has had the courage to
> about face. We had been numbered among the loudest
> critics of OPA, and long had our paper demanded its
> demise. We got that for which we worked—and we're
> sorry. . . .
>
> > *Very truly yours,*
> > WILLIAM N. BARTO
> > *"Another who was wrong."*

The editorial enclosed by Mr. Barto read, in part,
"When we saw that OPA was on the way out, we
joined in the snake dance that was led by the National
Association of Manufacturers and unwittingly swallowed the platitudes put out by the organization that
the end of price control would increase production and
lower costs. After several months of eye-rubbing, during which time prices continued their steady climb
(after an oh-so-brief drop), we began to awaken to
the fact that the NAM eyewash was irritating rather
than soothing, and not too long ago we had the courage
to ask for a return of the OPA if prices could not be
controlled."

I never thought I'd live to see the day.

The next selection from *The New Yorker* of last
August, 1960, shows that little has changed in the
ranks of Labor as seen from the business office. It is

still stubborn, selfish, unreasonable, overpaid, grasping, domineering, un-American, irreverent, blind to its own interests, and living in an unreal world. It is also inefficient, undemocratic, and gangster-ridden, although the newspapers, in the following set piece, commendably kept the gangsters on the sidelines for once.

Inflamed, but Cool

AUGUST 20, 1960

In the community where I live in summer, I am distracted by a pushing bird who introduces himself with vulgar insistence as " Bob *White*." When I hear him, I am reminded of a cloying anecdote about some meddlesome Middle Western children who attended a session of their state legislature to support a bill designed to protect the quail from bird shot by classifying him mendaciously as a songbird. When the bill was introduced, according to this legend, the children quavered, "Bob *White!* Bob *White!*" and the legislators, seeing no other way to terminate the ghastly racket, voted against the evidence of their senses. Now I want to shoot the children. At any rate, here I live in East Hampton, vainly trying to write, and going into town once a week to talk about what I will try to write after I finish what I am not writing. (Stendhal wrote two masterpieces in hotel rooms above the cheerful, noisy, crowded streets of Paris. On the Rue de Richelieu in 1830, Bob White couldn't have heard his own voice for the rattle of carriage wheels.) The cost of each of my transitions from country to city is normally $9.67. This is divided into $2 for the taxi from my house to the East Hampton station of the Long Island Rail Road, five miles away; $7.52 for railroad fare, including parlor-car seat; and a 15-cent subway token for the ride between Pennsylvania Station and Times Square, which is a block and a half

from my office. The fare by day coach is $4.85, but
since the journey lasts just under three hours, I indulge
myself.

Every now and then in the past, some portion of the
Long Island personnel would threaten to strike, but
until this summer such threats had generally evapo-
rated. So when, at one minute after midnight on Sunday, July 10, a strike of conductors and trainmen
closed the road down, I was as surprised as most other
residents, permanent and seasonal, of Suffolk County,
which covers the eastern two-thirds of Long Island
and has a population of about eight hundred thousand
in summer and six hundred and fifty thousand the rest
of the time. From the Sunday *Herald Tribune,* the first
paper I saw, it was clear that the strikers, like those in
practically every account of a strike I have ever read
in a newspaper, were wrong, and dead to the public
interest. The *Times,* which arrived by mail next day,
confirmed this. The trainmen and conductors, it appeared from both papers, wanted to work five days a
week, instead of six, at no reduction in wages, and the
company said that any five-day week would have to
be accompanied by a pay cut. The union had rejected
the company's proposition, and the company had rejected the trainmen's proposition. In newspaper practice, this situation, which occurs pretty often, is treated
as a tie in favor of the company. It looked to me like
a reciprocal rejection, but the union's was the only one
mentioned in the *Tribune* story, by Joel Seldin:

UNION BARS RAILROAD'S
LAST OFFER

After a six-hour, personal effort to settle or postpone the
Long Island Rail Road strike, Gov. Rockefeller announced
late last night that the union had rejected a last-minute
company offer and decided to strike at 12:01 A.M. . . . The
Governor said he regretted "deeply" the union's decision to
reject a last offer which would have provided the trainmen
with a five-day week at a cost of $200,000 annually. [I.e.,
cost to the railroad, for extra employees; the railroad

wanted the trainmen to accept a reduction in wages, amounting collectively to $150,000 a year, in order to help pay the $350,000 that a changeover to a five-day week would cost. This aspect of the negotiations was not mentioned in the *Tribune* story.] Mr. Pryor [the union chairman] insisted, Mr. Rockefeller said, on a settlement that would cost [the company] $350,000 a year, and also rejected a request by the Governor that the strike be postponed. The union had already postponed the strike three times previously.

The *Times*'s story, by A. H. Raskin, its labor expert, was equally unappreciative. He wrote of "a company offer of a five-day week," as if the idea had originated with the company instead of with the union. "It would have been the first on any major railroad in the country," he noted.

Both papers carried boxes listing "Facts in Dispute," but both omitted a lot of what I, or any ordinary curious reader, would have liked to know. An odd aspect of the omission was that, in all papers I saw, it continued right through the 26 days of the strike. The *Times,* which is representative, noted in its box, "Basic wages range from $19 to $20.64 a day." Under "Issues," it said, "The union's central demand is for a five-day week with no cut in the seven days' pay that passenger and freight trainmen get on a six-day schedule." The implication was that the men wanted the same pay for five-sixths the amount of work they had been performing, or, fundamentally, $140 for $100's worth of work. Reading the news stories, however, I gathered that the men were paid by the hour, not by the day, since the wage awards cited were all on an hourly basis. Yet I never came across a story that specified how many hours constituted a day's work—seven, eight, nine, twelve—or whether the six-day week for which the men received seven days' pay was a six-day, forty-eight-hour week, or a six-day, thirty-six-hour week, or something in between. If the men wanted to swap a six-day, forty-eight-hour week for a five-day, forty-hour week with no cut, they were asking for a raise of 20 percent in their hourly wage

—a whopper that would have cost the railroad in the neighborhood of $1,500,000 a year, and a statistic that Mr. Thomas M. Goodfellow, the president of the Long Island, would hardly have been shy about revealing. If, though, they wanted to work the same number of hours in five days that they had previously worked in six, they were demanding only a rearrangement. The seven-day week went out with Thomas Gradgrind and King Cotton. Now you get, say, $100 a week, which contains seven days, for working some part of that time. If the phrase "seven days' pay for five days' work" has some occult meaning in railroading that it hasn't in ordinary life, it was doubly the reader's right to have it explained to him. In any case, I never did find out from the papers how many hours there are in a basic railroad work week or day.

I am willing to believe that this omission was inadvertent (as might be the omission of a score of a ball game), but it made it harder, especially in the first few days of the strike, to judge between the two contending causes. The newspapers may have reasoned that anybody sufficiently curious was at liberty to call up the union or the Department of Labor, but if a reader has to do his own investigating, why should he buy a newspaper?

Editorially, the two newspapers got to the strike on Monday, with phrases that the editorialists had been bringing to a slow boil over the weekend. "If there ever was a strike that victimized the public, this is it," said the *Tribune*. "We urge the strikers [not, I could not help noting, the management] to remember that this is a stoppage that hurts the entire community— the community of which unions [but not, apparently, railroad managements] are a part." Compared to the *Tribune,* the *Times* reminded me of a story the late Alben Barkley used to tell about the husband and the lover at the woman's grave: "The husband wept freely, but the *lover!* He howled and tore his hair and wanted to jump into the hole." The *Times* man, tearing his hair, wrote: "The 1,350 trainmen whose strike yesterday stopped all traffic on the Long Island Rail Road have angered more than 100,000 people who

wanted and needed to use the railroad. These feelings
will be widened and inflamed [like broad noodles
flambés] today as some 85,000 commuters are hampered in getting to and from work. . . . Even if Mr.
Pryor and his trainmen don't care what the public
thinks now, they may well ponder the long-run effects
their walkout will have. For what they are doing is to
use their power to cause intolerable disruption of the
daily lives of myriads of innocent bystanders in labor-
management rows."

Here, I suspected, the editorialist had forgotten that
Mr. Goodfellow might also have used *his* power to
prevent intolerable disruption. At any rate, he didn't
mention it. (I cannot resist quoting at this point from
the *Times* editorial of August 5, after the strike
ended: "There probably never was a strike on an essential railroad that stirred so little public indignation,
and hence so little pressure for a settlement." Had the
angry hundred thousand cooled off, the widening,
flaming feelings narrowed and sputtered out? Or is it
possible that the public has ceased to accept the doctrine of unilateral original sin in labor disputes?)

Beyond a sense of wonder that the railroad men,
with their supposedly strong union, had not already
won a five-day week, of however many hours, long
ago—all the commuters have done so, including editorial writers—I had no inflamed reaction to the dispatches until I remembered I had an engagement in
town on Thursday, July 14, that I had made months
before and could not possibly change. With the strike
just beginning, I would ordinarily have stayed out in
the country and waited for a break, meanwhile trying
to train a cat to catch Bob White. Now there was no
way out. I therefore engaged the East Hampton taxi-
man to take me into New York on July 13 and leave
me there. The regular taxi tariff is $45 (the distance
by road is well over a hundred miles), and you can
take several members of your family in with you and
send several right back with him for the same charge,
if you happen to have a large family living half in
New York and half in East Hampton. Otherwise, it is
more expensive than the railroad. There was, how-

ever, a strike-stranded woman at the Huntting Inn, in
East Hampton, who wanted a ride into town that
morning, and she bore part of the expense, so I had to
pay only $35. The difference between $35 and $9.67
is $25.33. Madella, our maid, who has children in
New York, had been going into town every weekend
by day coach. She had left East Hampton, as usual,
on the previous Friday afternoon; the strike had always been postponed before. She was consequently
marooned in New York. So I recuperated her and sent
her back with the taxi on Wednesday evening. Since
she had been due on Sunday night, we had by that
time lost three days of her work, evaluated at $21.42.
Not being a corporation, I did not feel entitled to lay
her off when the strike made it impossible for her to
work, as the Long Island had done with its non-strik-
ing employees. This put me $46.75 down by the time
I reached my desk in New York, and found on it a
copy of the *Times* for the previous day, with a story
by Raskin:

COMMUTING EASY
IN L.I.R.R. STRIKE

Seventy-seven thousand commuters stranded by the Long
Island Rail Road strike swept in and out of the city yesterday with little strain on their nerves, feet, or pocketbooks.
Only minor inconveniences were reported [here I wondered
whether Raskin ran an inconvenience-report bureau, and
whether I should phone him about my $46 and change] as
suburbanites turned to buses, subways and car, boat and
airplane pools to escape the impact of the two-day-old
walkout by 1,350 Long Island trainmen. . . . The home-
bound tide moved out as smoothly. . . .

Airplane pools sounded dashing, but no mass solution. They also sounded like "Let them eat cake."
    An unsigned story on an inner page said: "Long
Island commuters adapted quickly to bus and subway
transportation yesterday, and many even expressed a
preference for substitutes for traveling on the Long
Island Rail Road. . . . For much of the day, the ease

of travel puzzled the 77,000 persons who normally commute on the Long Island in the summer." Like the editorial's hundred thousand angry men, the seventy-seven thousand was a slightly uncertain figure, because it was based on the number of people the Long Island might have been carrying on an average Monday if it had been running. The Long Island, according to its own figures, carries two hundred and sixty thousand riders on an average weekday (five days a week, naturally). Of these, eighty-five thousand commuters count twice—going to work and coming back—but a certain number of commuters (four-day workers for seven days' pay) apparently take Monday off. Commuters have special weekly or monthly tickets and they live near town. The ninety thousand other passengers travel on single or round-trip tickets. I fall into the latter class when I ride the train, as do most residents of Suffolk. So although I was glad to hear that the commuters were having such a lark, I felt a bit left out of the *Times*'s strike reporting. For me and my neighbors there were no alluring buses or subway cars to learn to prefer standing in, and even motorboats didn't help, though the *Queen Mary* might have. We are too far out. There are indeed airplanes, but they are more costly than transportation by train. The newspapers simply dropped us out of the story.

I went back to East Hampton on Saturday, paying the full $45. I might have flown, but I had a couple of cartons of books that I wanted in the country and would ordinarily have sent by American Railway Express for around $5. By putting the books in the taxi, I cut my strike loss on the run to $30.33—the $45 minus the $9.67 I would have paid out in subway, railroads, and taxi fares and the $5 I would have paid the express company. This brought my total strike loss so far to $85.66, and I was happy to learn from the driver, on the way out, that a woman he knew had discovered a cheaper route to New York. She had come in by a succession of buses, changing at Riverhead, then at Center Moriches, then at Patchogue, then at Freeport, where she had found a bus that brought her all the rest of the way.

"It took her five and a half hours, instead of three," he said.

I asked whether she had expressed a preference for this substitute for the railroad and he said no.

While in New York, I had had a chance to read all the newspapers, and had learned not to complain about what the strike was costing me, because I was suffering for a principle. It was a principle of Mr. Goodfellow's, not mine, but it would be a poor world if men insisted on suffering only for principles they subscribed to personally. Mr. Goodfellow said that the trainmen were welcome to the five-day week but that they must absorb the expense of it—the $350,000. Otherwise, the railroad would have to pass the bill on to the passengers in the shape of a rise in fares, and this Mr. Goodfellow would on no account do because the passengers were already overburdened. I must confess to an unworthy astonishment at the Long Island's squeamishness about applying for another rise. It occurred to me that it had already swallowed a lot of them without gagging—a recollection that I verified by checking through the *Times Index* for recent years. To be sure, the railroad had not changed its fares from 1918 to 1947, but between 1947 and 1954 it had raised them 89 percent, and then, struggling successfully against its scruples, had accepted further boosts of 8.4 percent (of the 189 percent) in 1955; 5.4 percent (of the accumulation) in 1957; 5.9 percent (of the snowball) in 1958; and 4.6 percent (of the total tumescence) in 1959. And there have been applications for further raises since, including one that averages out at $24 a year. I estimated that Long Island fares had gone up roughly 150 percent since 1947. (In the same period, the railroad workers' annual earnings had gone up just short of 100 percent.) I might even have expected the railroad, with its passenger income of seventy million a year, to pick up the tab for a mere three hundred and fifty thousand without further troubling its riders, but Mr. Goodfellow said that *that* was impossible, and I was not prepared to challenge his statement. Neither were the newspapers.

The finances of the Long Island are a proper subject of public interest, as they have been of private curiosity on Long Island ever since the first potato, but I saw not one newspaper story on a topic so essential to a proper understanding of the strike. I was mean-spirited enough to reflect that a fare rise of $350,000, divided up among the seventy million or so passengers that the Long Island carries each year, would add half a cent to the price of each ride, and that even if Mr. Goodfellow succeeded in breaking the strike immediately and saving this money for us customers, I would now have to ride between East Hampton and New York 17,142 times to make up for the $85.66 that his devotion to principle had already cost me. This would require a total of 46,000 hours—1,916 days, or nearly six years, even if I did all my sleeping on trains.

I stayed in the country, saving up money against the next time I might have to go to New York and looking at whatever newspapers came my way. On July 18, Francis A. O'Neill, Jr., the United States mediator in the case, suggested that the trainmen give up 2½ cents of a pay increase of 5.4 cents an hour that they had already acquired. That would pay roughly half the cost of the changeover to a five-day week, and the company, he suggested, should pay the other half. The union accepted. At that point, I took from my wallet, where they reposed useless, a sheaf of tickets for parlor-car transportation that I had bought before the strike; in my eyes, they reassumed beauty. I began to shine my city shoes. But Mr. Goodfellow rejected the proposal on the twentieth. I waited for the next day's papers, which were sure to be full of criticism of him for keeping the public from the cars, that, according to the same papers, it now preferred to do without. There wasn't any.

What the case wanted now, the *Herald Tribune* said editorially on July 22, was arbitration (WHAT'S SO WRONG ABOUT L.I.R.R. ARBITRATION?). The selection of an arbitrator agreeable to both sides would consume more time, and it would take a new man quite a while to examine the evidence, but the "stoppage that hurts the entire community" was no longer the *Tribune*'s primary concern. It was now more interested in who would get the decision on points than in what happened to the victimized public. As for the *Times,* when the Long Island presently offered to cut down to $25,000 its own outlay in the settlement, the paper called the proposal "an extension and amplification of the plan announced . . . by Mr. O'Neill." This, it seemed to me, was as if two men shared a lunch costing $3.50, and after one of them said, "Let's go Dutch," the other answered, "Fine. I will extend and amplify your suggestion. I'll pay a quarter and you put down three dollars and twenty-five cents."

By now it was apparent that the picayune sums involved were important to neither the railroad nor the union except as symbols. The two contestants had been chosen by their factions—the national railroad associations and the national railroad unions— to settle in single combat the battle of the five-day week, and the results would set a precedent for bigger adversaries. The railroads had conceded in advance that the five-day week itself was inevitable, because it has become standard in other industries and public opinion cannot be turned against it. But the Battle of Long Island would determine to what degree the railroads could make the unions share its initial cost. The shadows of the bigger conflict got into some news stories, particularly those about how strike insurance for the railroad and strike benefits for the trainmen took the sting out of the struggle for both; it was like a gymnasium boxing bout, with headguard and heavily padded gloves. But in their main news stories—and particularly in their editorials—the papers continued to handle the dispute as if it were a real fight, and as if Pryor and Goodfellow were championship contenders instead of preliminary boys.

What frustrated me, and most of my neighbors whom I talked to, was that in this manufactured

main-bout atmosphere not one paper carried a story
mentioning the fact that the Long Island Rail Road
is what they call in New England a public charge. A
fellow down the road who keeps tabs on the Long
Island from pure ancestral animosity told me that in
1953 the City of New York had forgiven the railroad
$7,000,000 in taxes. The railroad then owed Nassau
County, where most of its commuters live, $3,000,-
000 in taxes; Suffolk County, where I pay $472 and
some odd cents in taxes on my house, $1,000,000;
New York State, which won't let me forget my income taxes, another $1,000,000; and various towns
and villages in Nassau and Suffolk Counties, including East Hampton, yet another $1,000,000. They all
settled for about half. This put the bite on all of us
on Long Island; I got bit in three places—Albany,
New York and East Hampton. Like an old drunk,
my neighbor said, the railroad was always promising
to reform if we would just lend it something to get
back on its feet. It had also been granted a 50 percent reduction in tax assessments—in Nassau County
alone this amounted to $8,000,000—and in 1954 the
state legislature had given the road a nine-year tax
reduction of $2,500,000 a year. Daily, while training
my anti–Bob White cat, I waited for a newspaper to
give us word of what had happened to this thirty-odd
million dollars, but never did word come. I had
thought that the *Post* would find in the strike an opportunity to air the financial affairs of the Long Island,
but the *Post* was sticking close to its pre-empted field
of civil rights in Alabama, where the foe is far away.

On August 1, I had to go into town again, and this
time I flew, incurring an expense of $3.50, instead of
$2, for the initial taxi (the airport is five miles far-
ther from my house than the railroad station); of
$18, instead of $7.52, for the main leg of the trip;
and of $4.35, including tip, for the taxi from La
Guardia Marine Terminal to my office, instead of the
15 cents that gets me there by subway when the
Long Island is running. Loss on this trip: $16.18.

On Wednesday, August 3, the strike ended. The
railroad accepted the O'Neill proposal that the union

had accepted and the railroad had rejected on July 20, but I could not learn from the newspapers just how it differed from the proposal that the railroad had accepted and the union had rejected the night before the strike began. The *Herald Tribune,* under the eight-column headline L.I. STRIKE ENDS, FARES TO GO UP AGAIN, smote its public with the news that "Thomas M. Goodfellow, president of the line, said the immediate result would be an increase in passenger fares of $1 or $2 a year over the $24 yearly increase already scheduled." This confirmed my estimate of the immense additional expense Mr. Goodfellow had been battling to save us from. Mr. Goodfellow said that only the personal intervention of Governor Nelson A. Rockefeller had brought him out of the trenches. "Harold J. Pryor, general chairman of the Long Island lodges of the B.R.T. [Brotherhood of Railroad Trainmen], called the settlement a 'victory,' " said the *Tribune.* It quoted Mr. Goodfellow to the effect that he had made a better offer at the beginning of the strike than the one the trainmen had settled for, and added, "Mr. Pryor . . . pointed out that the offer had also contained various work-rule changes that were unacceptable to the union. He said the settlement agreement did not include those changes." This reminded me of the arguments between fighters' managers in the sports pages back in the days of no-decision bouts. Both would claim they had won easy.

The *Journal-American* mourned editorially: "The trainmen won their demands for a five- instead of a six-day work week, adding $162,041 to the Long Island RR's annual labor cost. . . . This, of course, will be passed along to the already hard-pressed commuter, who faces an immediate fare increase ranging from $25 to $26 a year, with the prospect of still higher fares in the years to come. [But, as the *Tribune* said, the rise attributable to the strike settlement would be $1 or $2; the remaining $24 had nothing to do with it.] It is ironic that the settlement now accepted by the union bosses represents a considerably smaller package than the one they were offered just after the strike began."

The *Times*'s news story on the settlement said that "in contrast to the smiling Governor, Mr. Goodfellow was grim as he faced the cameras and the reporters' questions," and that "Mr. Pryor was the last to come out, and he, like the Governor, was smiling and affable."

The *News* editorial on August 5 said of the settlement, "No doubt the Governor acted conscientiously, but the episode reminded us strongly of old Truman Administration times, when the U.S. Government used to put the squeeze on employers to give strikers everything they wanted, and too bad about justice, inflation, and the general public." The front page was covered by a picture of a smiling Mr. Goodfellow holding against the poop of a day coach a placard reading "L.I.R.R. Rolls Again." He looked a winner all over.

The *Mirror* said on its editorial page, "The union leadership has been shown up not only as pigheaded but stupid [as distinguished, no doubt, from pigheaded but scintillating] by the acceptance after 25 days of a lesser package than it could have had at the start. The railroad management, headed by able and progressive Tom Goodfellow, is faced with the challenge of winning back customers who found, perforce, that there are other ways of doing business."

The truth appeared to be that neither side had got all it wanted, and that what newspapers call pigheadedness in a railroad conductor is what they call devotion to principle in a railroad president.

In case you think that anything has changed suddenly, I include the following "Notes and Comment" Department that I wrote for *The New Yorker* in February 1961, after a strike of tugboat crews employed by the railroads to haul barges around the harbor.

Notes and Comment

FEBRUARY 11, 1961

There was a time, during the prime of the late Senator Joseph McCarthy, when a large section of the press held that to say a man had a right to a fair hearing was equivalent to approving of whatever he was accused of—Communism or subversion or consorting with Harvard professors. We hold no brief for "featherbedding," a catchword with an aura of having been invented by a company public-relations man, or for "labor-sweating," a practice ascribed to management by the public-relations men for unions. But we cannot agree with the newspapers here (all of them) that in the strike of railway-towboat workers that spread to dry land last month "featherbedding was the issue," any more than we would agree that murder—i.e., its desirability—was "the issue" in a murder trial.

The issue, as the newspapers almost surreptitiously stated in the news columns, was the towboat unions' refusal to let management decide, on its own hook, what *constituted* featherbedding—whether or not it would be a good idea to cut the present standard crew to five. To yield would have been like agreeing to let management decide which it would prefer—a twelve-hour day or an eight-hour day, for the same money. We are not experts on towboat management, but when we looked out through our window and the falling snow toward the swatch of North River we can sometimes see between the Paramount Building and the Hotel Dixie—we couldn't see that far then, of course—we remembered the last time we had been out there in like conditions, some years ago, and it didn't make us think of a bed, even a foam-rubber one. We are beginning to worry, for the newspapers' sake, about their custom of ruling, in every strike, that labor is wrongheaded, as if they were a panel of arbitrators appointed by a Higher Power. A fortune cookie is not worth buying when the strip of paper inside always carries the same legend. This time, the newspapers were all outraged because "664 maritime workers" could tie up the town by their stubbornness in a dispute with eleven railroads and terminal companies. The corollary, that eleven railroad presidents were being equally stubborn, with as good (or bad) reason, was left for the reader to figure out for himself, and in most cases, we imagine, he did.

In the task, both delicate and rugged, of handling oil and freight barges in a river as wide as a lake and as thronged as Fifth Avenue, plagued by submerged floating matter, and often nearly blanked out by fog or snow, the number of men aboard a tug is of more than cheese-paring interest. It may mean the difference between a routine day on the river and catastrophe. Automation is seldom what it is cracked up to be, afloat or ashore. In the building where we work, machinery has replaced the fallible human beings who once operated the controls of the elevators, and is 88 times as fallible. Bus service has been miserable since they took the conductors off. We are all for copilots on airplanes, waiter captains as well as waiters (and lots of busboys), grocers' delivery boys (down with go-carts and supermarkets), barbershop shaves, and bookmakers instead of pari-mutuel machines. In brief, plenty of manpower. Let the railroads beware of eliminating anybody at all; they run badly enough already.

This tempered objurgation, asking only a modicum of fair play for labor in New York, provoked a reaction of gratitude so exaggerated that it broke my heart. No newspaper anywhere in the nation, apparently, has had a kind word for the working man since about 1936—on this point the press is not lopsided, but unilateral, monolithic, solidary, and unanimous.

The Carpenter, national organ of the carpenters' union, ran the Note under the not completely flattering head:

TRUTH CROPS UP IN THE STRANGEST PLACES

The *New Yorker* is not a magazine you normally look to for penetrating conments on economic or political affairs. Its field is sophistication and entertainment. However, in its February 11 issue the magazine neatly applied the needle to New York newspapers for their persistent failure to report strike news fairly and objectively. Because newspapers everywhere throughout the United States and Canada are as biased and as opinionated in the handling of labor news as the New York newspapers are, the *New Yorker* editorial is herewith reprinted in full. . . .

The *AFL-CIO News,* of Washington, editorialized, before quoting:

THE ONE-SIDED PRESS

The recent strike of the railroad-tugboat workers in New York provided another demonstration of how the press and other communications media come down on the side of management with an almost automatic regularity.

In its issue of Feb. 11, the *New Yorker* magazine, in its "The Talk of the Town" column, comments . . .

The *Guild Reporter,* national publication of the American Newspaper Guild, said:

WRONGHEADED

The monotonous regularity with which this country's press editorializes against labor and for management brought a refreshing protest this month from *The New Yorker*—[and then quoted . . .]

Labor, The Machinist, the *Oregon State Labor Journal,* felicitated and quoted in full. Letters came from labor union officials and simple members. One that would have startled Harold Ross was from a machinist in Chicago who had read me first in *The Machinist,* published by the International Order of Machinists, and who wrote:

> *The New Yorker* is the only Magazin that I know of, that fights for "All the People, All then Time." You can make use of his quotation if you do desire—I wish you would.
> I just finished reading the enclosed Editorial [the *Machinist* clipping] of your estimed Magazin and had to come to that conclusien. Therefore allow me to congrate you and please: Send me your Magazine for one year, and a bill, wich I will promptly pay per check

> Respectfully Yours Truly,
> Max R. Paulick

Ross, founding and operating *The New Yorker,* never thought of it as the People's Champion, and neither, I am sure, has Raoul Fleischmann, the proprietor. I occupied the position in its behalf, timidly, unwittingly, and by default.

It is depressing evidence of what labor thinks of the deal it gets—here, you will note, I am my urbane, supercautious self, not even hinting labor may be right about it—that a casual, measured comment in a medium that cannot be familiar to many unionists causes such a welling-up of hosannas.

4
The
Press
Mess

On subjects less closely touching the publishers' mass preoccupation—their pocketbooks—in theory, newspapers are less predictable. But the same mass preoccupation, in practice, often keeps them from covering news at all. When I worked on the *World-Telegram,* 1931–35, the paper, although posing as a Metropolitan daily, never sent reporters out of town any farther than Flemington, N.J., 50 miles away, and that was for a unique occasion, the trial of Bruno Hauptmann for kidnapping the Lindbergh baby. A wave of economy followed this unwonted expenditure—reporters using the subways were required to bring in signed notes from the platform guards before submitting a voucher requesting reimbursement of their nickels.

For anything that happened more remotely, we depended on United Press, United Feature Service, Newspaper Enterprise Association, and a syndicated science service—all Scripps-Howard sources geared to the modest demands of the chain's papers in Youngstown, Ohio, and Oklahoma City. Since "percentage of use" by subscribers is the measure of syndicate success, a story used only by the Scripps-Howard chain stores in its more sophisticated locations, New York, San Francisco, and Washington, rated as wasteful. Instead of the kraals profiting by a big-time service, which might in time have stimulated curiosity about the world outside, the Scripps-Howard entries in the big cities were therefore held down to a coverage no wider than Youngstown wanted. If a race riot occurred in Birmingham, Alabama, let us say, a special request for information would be routed by third-class mail to the pitiful trading post in that city, where there was a boy publisher scratching hard to ingratiate himself with the savages and make excuses for being a Yankee. He hoped if he could show a profit, to get promoted to Toledo. This footling proconsul would be asked to see if he could sell an ad to Western Union, get a due bill for it, and send, subject to rejection by the *World-Telegram* if not acceptable in toto, not more than eight words, including punctuation, by night letter.

The awful sensation of working for a grain-and-feed store in an automotive age afflicted the New Yorkers on the staff—I never left the city room without taking off my jacket and slapping the lapels to dislodge hayseed. The boss himself, in his purple shirt, looked like a cotton-candy man at the Delaware County, Ohio, Fair, and the shop was continually cluttered with bright boys shipped in out of the woods for eight and a half days of big-town polish so they could go back to the Sierra Nevadas as managing editors with New York experience. Out of the $5 a week they would get out there they would repay Scripps-Howard, 50 cents at a clip, for the round trip on the Greyhound bus.

This should have taught me not to expect too much, but by the period of the following exhibits, I had been out of newspapers for 13 years, had covered five years of a war in which nobody questioned my expense accounts, and in retrospect took an almost sentimental view of life in the transplanted corncrib on Barclay Street. (My father, who spent his boyhood on the East side, used to talk nostalgically of the tenement where he had grown up. One Sunday in 1933 he walked me down there to have a look at the old place. He had the look—one—and then he couldn't get away fast enough.)

The M.B.I.

JANUARY 3, 1948

A couple of months ago, I had occasion to subscribe to 20 out-of-town newspapers, and the copies have been piling up in my office ever since. Though depressed at encountering the same syndicated features in one paper after another, I sometimes read four or five of these papers at a stretch when I have nothing better to do, and even when I have. It is like eating pistachio nuts from the shell—unrewarding, but hard to stop once you have begun. I'm not really interested, for example, in why the editor of the Portland *Oregonian* gave a first-page play, with photographs, on November 7 to a story, datelined Hollywood, naming the ten most eligible bachelors in America, as selected in a poll of women dancing teachers throughout the country. Nor do I especially care why the editor of the Cincinnati *Enquirer* chose for his first page on October 9 a story about a man in Pittsburgh who had been tube-fed for 26 years and was now about to eat normally. Nevertheless, I moon about such matters. I took a livelier interest in a brief item in the Atlanta *Constitution* headed VISITS HUSBAND, THROAT IS CUT, about a woman named Mrs. Seay, in Thomaston, Georgia, who went to see her husband in the Upson County jail. "They were left to talk with jail bars separating them," the story says. "Sometime later Mrs. Seay screamed. . . . Fifteen stitches were taken in her throat and twenty in her arm at a local hospital. An attending physician said that although Mrs. Seay's condition was serious he believed she had a chance to recover." It interested me that the *Constitution* didn't say how the husband got the knife, or whether knives are standard equipment for prisoners in Georgia jails, or how he got the blade through the bars and into position for such a long slash. The city editor of the *Constitution* seems to be blessed with plenty of good homicides; this gives his paper a certain special flavor. When I read papers from less favored regions, I sometimes have to look up at the masthead to remind myself which one I am reading.

Looking at the New Orleans *Times-Picayune* for November 14, I found my attention caught by a story on the first page about something odd that was happening in the neighboring state of Mississippi, which the *Times-Picayune* considers to be in its circulation territory. The headlines said:

POLICE POWERS
GRANTED WRIGHT

WHITTINGTON CHARGES FORCE
WOULD BE "GESTAPO"

I suppose "Gestapo" was the word that nailed me;
we have all grown sensitive recently to stories about
secret-police forces.[1] The story, signed by W. F.
Minor, a *Times-Picayune* correspondent, began.
"Over some protests of 'Gestapo' in both houses, the
Mississippi Legislature today gave final passage to a
far-reaching measure granting the Governor police
power through investigators to suppress violence."
Not having the least suspicion that Mississippi was
having more than the usual amount of violence, I
read on with some curiosity. "The legislature, key
measure of seven bills presented to the extraordinary
session which was convened Wednesday," the story
continued, "was the outgrowth of recurring incidents
of violence which have accompanied a six-month-old
strike of drivers of the Southern (Trailways) Bus
lines." Now, in any of the states in which I have re-
sided long enough to learn local customs, a strike
sufficiently bad to cause the governor to call a special
session of the legislature to cope with it would be an
impressive event, and I wondered why I had not read
anything about this Mississippi rebellion before. I
decided that I must have seen earlier stories in the
New York papers but that I avoided reading them
because of my resistance to any Southern dateline,
and that I had forgotten that I had seen the headlines.

The police power that the legislation at Jackson
had granted the governor empowered him to create
an organization that did not appear to be exactly like
any state force with which I was familiar. It was to
consist of investigators, appointed by and known
only to him, who would have the power "to investigate and make arrests in crimes of violence or in-

---

[1] A year or so later the tide shifted. The identiy of the informant, in civil rights cases, became, for F.B.I. and Congressional investigators, a secret unthinkable to violate. Anybody
who asked to see his accuser was ipso facto considered an
enemy of constitutional government.

timidation." "Regular" investigators were to post
bonds of $2,500 with the governor, Fielding L.
Wright, and the governor might also name any temporary, unbonded investigator he pleased. Among
the six other proposed bills was one making it a jail
offense for two or more persons to conspire to interfere with the operation of a transit line. Another
made it a crime punishable by death to place a bomb
in a bus, truck, or filling station, whether anybody
was killed or not. Still another proposed a penalty of
as much as five years in the penitentiary for anybody
who had in his possession "dynamite caps, fuses, det-
onators, dynamite, nitroglycerine, explosive gas, or
stink bombs," unless he was conducting a lawful
business. After a moment's speculation about what
lawful business stink bombs could be employed in, I
decided that a law making the mere possession of
dynamite prima-facie evidence of felonious intent
was a stiff bit of legislation. My concern was evidently shared by some of the Mississippi legislators.
Senator Luther A. Whittington, of Natchez, had
asked, "Isn't this the same kind of law which dictators of Europe started and then began terrorizing the
people with a secret police or Gestapo?"

I read on, eager for a hint of the horrendous doings that had led Governor Wright to ask such powers and the legislature to grant them. I recalled that
Huey Long had once called the legislature of the
Times-Picayune's home state into special session to
clothe himself with unusual powers, but the troubles
preceding this event had had a considerable notoriety
in the nation's press. It was difficult to believe that
even such a superficial reader of newspapers as I
could have missed all reference in the metropolitan
dailies to what struck me—and, apparently, the editor of the *Times-Picayune*—as an important story.
So I set a young man who occasionally helps me to
checking through the New York newspapers for
November to see if there were any stories on the
Mississippi special session or a notably violent strike
preceding it. Meanwhile, I dived into the great
mounds of nearly identical provincial newspapers that

are gradually walling in my desk in search of the
Times-Picayune for the few days before and after
November 14. The *Times-Picayune* of November 8
had a first-page story by Mr. Minor about an announcement Governor Wright had made to the effect
that he would call a special session to ask "broader
power and additional laws" to deal with the strike.
The story also said that a brick had been thrown into
the waiting room of a bus station and that a bus had
been shot into but no one had been hit. I further
learned that Mississippi already had a State Highway
Patrol. An Associated Press dispatch run as a shirt-
tail to the special story informed me that the striking
union was the Amalgamated Association of Street
Car, Railway, and Motor Coach Employees of
America, A.F.L., and that the strike had been on
since May 20, when the company's contract with the
union had expired. The *Times-Picayune* of November 12 said that Governor Wright had called the
session on the ground that "the laws of the State had
been trampled upon." A couple of legislators named
Henley and Shanks had asked the Governor, "Is the
legislature going to be convened every time there is a
strike?" The *Times-Picayune* of November 13 carried
a story on the governor's specific legislative requests.
It indicated that the members of the secret special
force, to be called the Mississippi Bureau of Investigation, were to have the right to arrest without warrant any person whom they suspected of intent to
interfere with a bus line, and to search him. The
M.B.I. was to be provided with arms by the governor.

The *Times-Picayune* of November 15 had a two-
column story, again on the front page and again by
Minor, summing up the legislation passed. Out of
seven emergency bills introduced during the session,
only one had not been enacted—a bill that would
have made it a penal offense for two or more persons
to conspire to intimidate anybody engaged in a lawful occupation of *any* kind. A bill making it a penal
offense to conspire to intimidate an employee of a
bus company had become law, as had bills to estab-

lish and pay the M.B.I., to set a penalty of up to five
years in prison for flinging a stone at a bus, to make
possession of dynamite prima-facie evidence of a
crime, and to empower a judge to impose the death
penalty on anybody convicted of placing a bomb in
a "building, ship, vessel, boat, railroad station, train,
bus station or depot, bus, truck or other vehicle, gas
and oil stations and pipe lines, radio stations or radio
equipment or other public utilities." It seemed to me
that this kind of legislation deserved prominent space
in newspapers throughout the country, if only because of the sanguinary anarchy that must have
reigned in Mississippi for months to justify anything
like it. My state of mind, therefore, verged on astonishment when my file reader reported that in all the
New York newspapers from the thirteenth through
the sixteenth of November—including the *Daily
Worker,* which surely would have welcomed the opportunity to play up this kind of news—he had found
only one story about the Mississippi special session.
That was a short piece on page twenty-one of the
Times of Sunday, November 16, under the headline
BILL TO CURB LABOR FAILS IN MISSISSIPPI. The lead
said that the legislature had passed "all but one of six
measures aimed at ending violence," and I noticed
with amusement that the copyreader had based his
head on the one bill that failed instead of the five
that passed. The *Times* story had a Jackson deadline
and was slugged "Special to the New York *Times.*"
There was no mention in it of the death penalty,
which I would have thought newsworthy. Theretofore,
I had been aware of only four offenses that were
punishable by death in the United States: murder (in
most states), treason, kidnapping, and (in some
Southern states, like Mississippi) rape. These penalties are intended to protect, respectively, human life,
the nation's existence, children, and the purity of
American women. Now Mississippi had added
trucks, buses, and filling stations to this sacred roster.
Nor did the *Times* story mention the peculiar character of the governor's investigating force. Had this
same story appeared, even inconspicuously, in other

papers, I would have concluded merely that nothing
that happened in Bilbo's and Rankin's home state
any longer had power to astonish news editors, and
that they had just underplayed it. The near-totality
of the blackout stumped me.

I considered two possibilities: one, that I had
misinterpreted the stories, although I could not understand why, if they really lacked weight, the
Times-Picayune should have devoted so much space
to them; two, that the New York editors had simply
never known about the yarn. The *Times* dispatch, a
full day late, looked like something ordered from a
Jackson correspondent, who had queried them and
been told to send a couple of hundred words. Since
the United States is presumed to be completely covered by the fine-mesh network of the great press
associations, which supposedly keep their members
informed of everything important that happens anywhere within its boundaries—such as the selection of
the ten bachelors by the woman teachers of dancing,
or the man in Pittsburgh with a tube in his stomach
—I could scarcely accept the second hypothesis.

Just for the hell of it, I called the news and telegraph editors of one New York daily to ask if they
remembered seeing the story. They said they had
seen nothing. That was not, of course, conclusive.
Such a volume of stuff comes in on the press-association machines that nobody can remember it all. Still,
a news editor is seldom unaware of a story that is
covered on three successive days, as the Mississippi
story would have been if the press associations had
carried it. My helper phoned the Associated Press to
ask what the people there knew about it. The answer
was simple and direct: nothing. An official said that
they hadn't seen anything of the story in the New
York office. Two papers in Jackson, Mississippi, are
members of the Associated Press, and so is the
Times-Picayune, and presumably one or another of
them sent out *something* on it, but not all stories put
on the wire by Southern members come as far north
as this. A news-association editor in Atlanta may
decide that a story has only regional importance. An

official at the United Press said he thought he remembered seeing the story, but he couldn't swear to it, and it would involve digging through bales of copy to check up on it. He said he didn't think it was worthwhile. He did ask the U.P. string man in Jackson, who said he had sent out five or six hundred words a day during the session but couldn't say how far up the line his stories had gone. I wired the U.P. bureau chief in Atlanta, but I got no answer. I knew that if the story did get to Atlanta, the *Constitution* didn't use it, because I dug up the *Constitution* for the proper dates from my newspaper pile.

To clear up my other doubt—that I had misinterpreted the stories—I sent a wire to Mr. Minor, who, to judge by his stories in the *Times-Picayune,* is a straightforward reporter, asking him to summarize his series for me, give me some of the background of the governor's emergency call, and tell me what, if anything, had happened in Mississippi since November 14. I further asked him to send copies of the the bills passed at the special session. Minor came through with a confirmation of my interpretation of the *Times-Picayune* stories. "Buses occupied by passengers were being fired on and stoned in various parts of the state," he wired. "No injuries, though. The most important piece of legislation to come out of the session was the creation of a Mississippi Bureau of Investigation. The membership of the M.B.I. is to be kept secret." The death-penalty law against placing bombs in filling stations, Mr. Minor said, amended and continued "a wartime statute that applied to public utilities, radio stations, etc." He continued: "The M.B.I. began organization the day following the adjournment of the legislature under an ex-Army colonel who had been executive officer of the Mississippi National Guard. However, where instances of violence against the Trailways were occurring every few days prior to the enactment of the new laws, not a single such act has been reported since. Down in Hattiesburg, a city of about twenty-eight thousand with a large labor and pro-labor population, three C.I.O. locals ran a full-page advertisement stating that they would pay the legal expenses of the first 'innocent' person arrested by the Bureau of Investigation, all the way up to the Supreme Court. The unions also threw a few accusations at the Governor for setting up such a force when present authorities were adequate to cope with the situation."

The bills arrived in my office a day later. They were as reported.

[Note: I may claim credit for having in this story introduced to a non-Mississippian public Governor Fielding L. Wright, who was later to issue a call for the first Dixiecrat convention, which nominated Governor L. Strom Thurmond of South Carolina for President and Governor Wright for Vice-President.]

The story of the M.B.I.'s creation and of the establishing of a new crime subject to capital punishment seems to me to have merited space in any American publication pretending to be a newspaper. (The prospect of 48 state Bureaus of Investigation, with armed personnel not of public record—a C.B.I. in Connecticut, an N.Y.B.I. here, an R.I.B.I. in Rhode Island—should have given the papers something to think about, too.) If editors the country over had this story in their offices and rejected it in favor of the fluffy wire stuff most of my specimen newspapers are filled with, then the national press is in a low state of health. It has been tube-fed a long time, and, like the man in Pittsburgh, ought to relearn how to chew. If the story never came over the press-association wires to where the editors could see it, or if it came in such feeble form that it could not be properly evaluated, somebody ought to begin mending that fine-mesh news net that the heads of press associations are always bragging about. From where I sit, that net looks more like a toothless rake.

The next piece is a sequel.

Goodbye, M.B.I.

FEBRUARY 7, 1948

A letter I received from a man named Talbot Patrick a couple of days after the publication of my piece nicely supported my point. Mr. Patrick, who is editor and publisher of the *Evening Herald* of Rock Hill, South Carolina (population 15,009), wrote:

Your report on this case should jolt wire-service staff members out of a sort of hypnosis in which, while handling masses of words in a routine way, they lose alertness for everything except surface accuracy and a chance for speed. A jolt like this forces an appreciation of the meaning to human lives of ideas behind the words they handle —and what makes up human life is the important part of the medium- and smaller-size American daily newspapers.

The press associations are miracles of modern mechanics. No wonder that sometimes the servants of the machine fail to think through, beyond, past the machine and radio stations and newspapers, to the men and women who work and eat and worry and try to go forward.

From Mr. Patrick's letter, I assumed that the *Evening Herald,* although a member of the Associated Press, had not received much, if any, coverage on the Mississippi Bureau of Investigation, or, as it has since come to be known, the M.B.I.

A day later, a letter reached me from Miss Rita Livingston, who publishes the *Courier-Democrat* in Russellville, Arkansas (population 5,927), together with a copy of the front page of that paper for November 15. The news on this page included an

Associated Press story of about 150 words giving a synopsis of the legislation that had just been passed in Mississippi. "I hang my head in shame for printing but not emphasizing the ridiculous portent of such a news dispatch," Miss Livingston wrote. She added, a bit irrelevantly, I thought, that "as long as an alert Northerner points out its idiosyncrasies, the South merely puts another hypothetical chip on its shoulder." I hope that in this instance no Southerner will put a hypothetical chip on his shoulder, because my object was not to criticize the South. I was simply trying to find out how the press had all but kept the story a secret, and I have since dug up most of the answer.

Both the Associated Press, which is a cooperative organization of 2,398 member newspapers and radio stations, with, in addition, 1,490 subscribers, and the United Press, its chief rival, which is a privately owned enterprise selling news to 2,947 customers, have permanent bureaus at Jackson, the capital of Mississippi. Before the appearance of my piece on the Mississippi Bureau of Investigation, an Associated Press editor here in New York told me that he could not remember having seen anything come over the wires about those laws. Apparently, though, something did. Paul Mickelson, the A.P.'s general news editor, has since informed me that the A.P. man in Jackson sent out a pretty fair 340-word story on the night of November 13, immediately following the passage of the legislation in question. This, the crucial story of the session, went out to Southern morning papers. (If Patrick, in South Carolina, did not receive it, that would be because his paper is an evening one.) The press-association empires are divided into regional satrapies, and to reach New York, for wider distribution, copy out of Jackson must be passed upon successively by bureaus in New Orleans and Atlanta. The New Orleans and Atlanta men waved the November 13 story on, and it came into the Associated Press main office, in New York, that night. Here, however, nobody thought much of it, and it was cut down to two hundred words, losing its moderate punch in the process. It was then, for some mysterious reason, sent out on a subsidiary circuit serving only newspapers west of New York City. It was not sent to newspapers here or in several other large Eastern cities at all.

After the appearance in this department of my somewhat bewildered speculations, the Baltimore *Sun,* an important member of the A.P., wired the association's New York office asking why it hadn't received a full account of the Mississippi situation and requesting that it be supplied with one. The New York office, endeavoring to comply, got after the Atlanta, New Orleans, and Jackson A.P. men, who must have been astonished at the sudden flare-up of interest in the story after a month and a half of apparent unconcern. Jackson sent out a quite good six-hundred-word story on January 3, telling about the M.B.I. and adding that the legislature would meet in regular session on January 6 and that Governor Wright was now saying that he didn't want his secret-police force anymore and was willing to swap it for some other kind of police department. I was unable to find this story in any New York City paper, but a scout sent me a clipping of it from the Milwaukee *Journal,* and it seems reasonable to assume that the Baltimore *Sun* used it, too. On January 9, both the A.P. and the U.P. bureaus in Jackson sent out accounts of an interview with Governor Wright in which he said that the idea of a secret-police force had been the legislature's, not his. Moreover, the governor said, the M.B.I. had accomplished its purpose. (So far as is known, it had neither received a single complaint nor made a single arrest since its inception.) What he really wanted, Wright said, was a permanent uniformed police force to help county authorities enforce the state's prohibition law. (I haven't come across anything anywhere yet, though, about the governor's asking for repeal of the death penalty for those who leave bombs on bus-company property or of the other special strike laws the M.B.I. was created to enforce.) In New York, the A.P.'s version of the Wright interview made the *Herald*

Tribune, under a two-column head, the following day, and a much-condensed, warmed-over version of it, also by the A.P., appeared in the *Times* a day later.

National interest in the Mississippi legislation was growing. Soon after Wright's talk with the press, I received from an agent on the Pacific Coast a clipping of an A.P. story that had appeared in the San Francisco *Chronicle* under a Jackson dateline of January 11. It was by far the longest and most comprehensive story about the M.B.I. that I had seen in any newspaper except the *Times-Picayune.*

The whole incident was recently reviewed, from the A.P. point of view, in a report to the publisher-members of the organization. A copy of this document, passed along to me by one of my more adept operatives, is here quoted, entirely without permission.

The fact is we booted general service delivery of a significant news story, last Nov. 13, reporting actions by the Mississippi state legislature, featuring establishment of a secret police force.

The legislature's action was a climax of developments in Mississippi connected with a protracted and violent strike of bus drivers. From Jackson, Miss., in the night report of Nov. 13, we did transmit a comprehensive news story, but it was (a) transmitted in full only on the south regional (GGG) wire, and (b) cut so sharply on the west wire (BBB) relay that the really significant news details were lost. On top of these misjudgments, we slipped up entirely on relay to New York City members, and failed to discover the actual facts of this foulup in time to tell The New Yorker, which quizzed us.

All of this is the subject of intensive staff review, for object lesson purposes. . . . It is particularly a lesson to control bureaus (in this case, New Orleans, Atlanta, and New York) not to permit even the crush of an extraordinarily big news day (which Nov. 13 was) to sidetrack or overlook the national significance of news having its roots in regional situation.

The United Press was less contrite about its handling of the M.B.I. story. I was told by U.P. editors in New York that their man in Jackson had sent out five-hundred-word stories to Southern clients every day of the legislature's special session, but they were, regrettably, unable to show me copies of any of them. They did, however, produce the parts of them that had been sent along by the Atlanta Bureau for their Round Robin, or main trunk wires. These amounted to a couple of hundred words a day, sent in scrappy, fragmentary form—"first leads," "second leads," and "adds" of a few words each, none of which could have given an editor who was not familiar with the situation much idea of what was happening. There was no mention, for instance, of the peculiarly anonymous character of the M.B.I. A woman who acts as a news editor of a New England radio station that receives U.P. service has written me that she "used several stories but finally gave up as they became more complicated and bizarre. You can't do as much explaining on radio news as in a newspaper . . . so the Mississippi-type stories are just a headache." After I looked over the U.P. stuff out of Atlanta, I saw the lady's point. The lead on one bit read, "Efforts to modify or expand a bill which would give the Governor special investigators with police powers were defeated in the Senate. . . ." The impact of this sort of thing, with a Jackson, Mississippi, dateline, on an editor in another part of the country would obviously be fairly feeble. The news and telegraph editors of the *Herald Tribune,* to whom I spoke before writing my first story on the case, could not remember having seen any of the U.P. material It even made no impression at *PM,* always on the alert for the liberty-in-peril type of story.

Unfortunately, most of the belated interest in the M.B.I. story, while gratifying, has nothing to do with the point I originally wanted to make. The newspapers have by now given considerable publicity to the threat implicit in an organization like the Mississippi Bureau of Investigation; they probably have bolstered, if they did not inspire, Governor Wright's decision that he can get along without it. Furthermore, they have added some interesting information about criminal law in Mississippi. It appears that there were already three capital offenses in that state —murder, rape, and armed robbery—before the legislature added bomb-leaving. (Incidentally, I have received some correspondence about capital offenses elsewhere. A fairly new one—federal—is the handing over of atomic secrets to "any individual or person . . . with intent to injure the United States or with intent to secure an advantage to any foreign nation," even in time of peace. Another is first-degree burglary—in North Carolina. Entering a home by night with intent to rape constitutes first-degree burglary in that state, which means that judges and juries must be skilled at reading a man's mind.) What impresses, and depresses, me, though, is that by looking through a few old newspapers I was able to find a pretty big story that the main organs of news distribution had completely muffed. I can't help wondering how often stories of general importance appear in full solely in local papers and get out to the rest of the country only after they have been compressed into insignificance. This reflection leads me to another, still more depressing: I wonder how many important stories never got into the newspapers at all. The American press makes me think of a gigantic, supermodern fish cannery, a hundred floors high, capitalized at $11,000,000,000, and with tens of thousands of workers standing ready at the canning machines, but relying for its raw material on an inadequate number of handline fishermen in leaky rowboats. At the point of contact with the news, the vast newsgathering organizations are usually represented either by a couple of their own harried reporters, averaging, perhaps, twenty-two years and eleven months old, or by a not too perceptive reporter on a small-town paper whose version of an event, written up for his employer, may or may not be passed on to the wire services by someone in the office. Not all the newspaper owners' towers of ma-

sonry, with their ingenious insides, like the Daily
News Building, or all the tons of newsprint covered
with red and black ink and pictures of women jumping out of windows, can add anything to the quality
of what these reporters regard as significant.

Press-association reporters are warned when they
start in of the necessity of keeping down the volume
of news and sending only what a fairly large number
of newspapers are likely to use. This sometimes
seems to mean a story about a dog that refuses to
leave its dead master's newsstand or a child who has
swallowed a whistling teakettle. I do not doubt that
November 13 was an extraordinarily big news day,
as the A.P. report to its members says it was, but I
could not help noting that the Chicago *Sun* and the
St. Louis *Post-Dispatch* of November 14 both carried a two-hundred-word A.P. story datelined College Park, Georgia, about a woman who, upon being
fined $7 for driving past a stop sign, insisted on
serving seven days in jail instead of paying, and
made such a nuisance of herself that they finally let
her go. This must have been part of the news that so
crowded the A.P.'s wires that the M.B.I. story had
to be cut down to two hundred words and incoher-
ence.

After the first M.B.I. story I began to receive mail
with clippings enclosed from people all over the place
who evidently thought I was running the N.B.I., or
Newspaper Bureau of Intelligence, asking me to right
the wrongs inflicted upon the body politic by publishers from Compton, Cal., to Yonkers, N.Y. Most of them
wanted to know how I had missed some awful thing
that their local paper had done. I have never made any
attempt to cover the whole press of the nation, of
course—it would take a staff of 30 or 40 people just to
read papers every day, and the results might or might
not make a fascinating publication. I am inclined to

think not. I rather think that the most common newspaper faults are the same in their broad outlines, in
Texas as in Maine, and that the details of the Maine
instances wouldn't interest people in Texas or vice
versa.

Ever since my adventure with the M.B.I. I have wondered how many of the stories worth knowing slip by
us fortnightly, weekly, or perhaps daily, so that when
their sequelae flare up irresistibly in headlines, we are
stupidly astonished. The segregation mess in Louisiana, for example, was predestined from the moment
that Jimmie Davis, the present governor, won the Democratic gubernatorial primary last January after selling
his soul to the racists. Newspapers throughout the
country, however, missed the point almost as completely as they missed the M.B.I. They recorded the
result of the primary, of course, but they treated it as
a repudiation of the ghost of Huey Long, who has been
dead since 1935.

These failures are not the result of a press conspiracy, however, as Left Wing critics in the past have
frequently charged. The newspaper proprietor who will
spend only a dead minimum on reporting is like a slum
landlord who maintains a firetrap. The landlord does
not want a fire. He hopes there won't be any, and he
will save the cost of fire escapes. He is not an arsonist,
but a tightwad. And the owner of the fishery described
in an above essay undermans his boats not because
he doesn't want them to catch fish, but because he
hopes that the fish will jump into the boats unassisted,
the cost of nets being what it is. Most newspaper
owners will print exciting news if they get it on the
blue-plate special: the press services that they have to
buy by the year.

"Conspiracy" would be less disquieting than the
present state of affairs, because the newspapers could
not possibly conspire as fast and as often as they now
manage to keep the news out of circulation through
their miserly ineptitude.

When they appear to take positive action with common accord, it is by instinct, like a school of mackerel

chasing sardines, rather than by predetermined plan, like warships attacking an enemy fleet. The common objects of their ire—unions, taxes, public welfare, and the Democratic Party—require no pointing out by scout planes. They take secondary action—akin to the union secondary strikes, which they continually denounce—against any phenomenon that they associate with these primary targets. They are anti-egghead because most intellectuals are Democrats and few publishers are either. They oppose public expenditures on colleges because colleges breed eggheads.

Guided by these simple, pre-vertebrate reflexes, most newspapers accepted and spread a doctrine of universal treason during the first postwar decade, because they thought it would discredit the then Administration. They believed with the simple faith of the silly, that anything discreditable to such an Administration must be true. It followed then that anybody who said it might not be true was a traitor. This reproduced exactly the atmosphere of the Papist Plot time in seventeenth-century England. To doubt that the Jesuits plotted to kill the King was to establish a presumption that the doubter was himself a Jesuit. In that case, he must be a plotter against the King, because all Jesuits were, according to the charge, which would establish a presumption that the doubter was a Jesuit, too. Naturally there were few expressions of doubt, because the sentence pronounced *against* plotters against the King, who were presumed to be plotting because they had been presumed to be Jesuits or presumed to be Jesuits because they had denied a plot, was: "That you be drawn to the place of Execution upon Hurdles, that you there be severally hanged by the Neck, that you be cut down alive, that your Privy Members be cut off, and your Bowels taken out, and burnt in your view, that your Heads be severed from your Bodies, that your Bodies be divided into Quarters, and those Quarters be disposed at the King's Pleasure; and the God of infinite mercy be merciful to your souls."

Skepticism was hardly worth the price.

Meanwhile, the testimony of witnesses like Titus Oates, who admited they had perjured themselves in the past, was accepted against defendants with honorable pasts. Twenty-two defendants perished, dismembered like chickens in a pick-your-own-parts poultry store. Some were Jesuits, who said they had not plotted. This proved they had, because, the judge reminded the jury, all Catholics were liars; if they were not they would plead guilty. Some denied being Jesuits, which proved they were, because Jesuits were taught to lie. The rest were just people that the informers said they had heard say they wondered if there was anything in the charge.

The chief witnesses in the trials of the Jesuits, true and presumptive, were rogues who said *they* had been Jesuits and so knew what was up. Titus Oates, the worst of the lot, claimed to have been a courier for the Black Pope, or head of the Order.

Lord Chief Justice Scroggs, charging the jury at the trials of five accused Catholics in 1678, handled this point neatly when he said: "It may seem hard perhaps to convict men upon the testimony of their fellow offenders, and, if it had been possible to have brought other witnesses, it had been well; but, in things of this nature, you cannot expect that the witnesses should be absolutely spotless."

In the congressional witch-hunt that began here in 1947—by coincidence, the Republicans had captured both Houses in the elections of 1946—the witnesses, like Oates and his colleagues long ago, panted with eagerness to denounce their own pasts. All claimed to have been Communists who cursed God every morning before they brushed their teeth, and then went out and looked for secrets to betray. This drew from their straight men the same reaction as in 1678. Congressman Herbert of Louisiana, in a meeting of the Committee on Un-American Activities, said of Whittaker Chambers, the Time, Inc., editor who beat his breast to a pulp in every session of self-accusation: "Some of the greatest saints in history were pretty bad before they were saints. Are you going to take away their sainthood because of their previous lives?"

By constant repetition, with reiterated editorial endorsement by most of the press, this line grew so strong that by the summer of 1949, when Chambers appeared as a witness against Alger Hiss in Hiss's first trial for perjury, the easiest way to get a job with Luce, or Hearst, was to say one had been a Communist. Lloyd P. Stryker, Hiss's attorney, found that he strengthened Chambers's position with the jury every time he got the *Time*-fellow to admit an instance of past perjury. Stryker had a long history of victorious cross-examination in criminal cases, where he had destroyed witnesses' credibility by proving they were experienced liars. Now he was at a loss.

After two years of newspaper Oates-thought, all the courtroom values of the three centuries that intervened between Oates and Chambers were reversed. The witness improved his credibility every time he said he had lied.

At the end of the first Hiss trial, which finished with a hung jury, 8 to 4, in favor of conviction, the section of the press that had failed to obtain the political result it wanted took its case outside the courtroom. This is a practice known in Arab countries as "going to the street." It precluded a second disappointment.

The following Wayward Press piece, which was written directly after the first, indecisive trial, proved unhappily accurate.

Spotlight on the Jury

JULY 23, 1949

The trial of Alger Hiss, which produced some of the best and some of the worst newspaper copy of our time, inspired none more effective than an account by John Chabot Smith, in the *Herald Tribune* on Saturday, July 9, of how the jurors reached their final disagreement. Mr. Smith, basing his story of the scene on talks with two of the eight jurors who voted for conviction, wrote:

A documents expert called as a witness by the government
had testified that the spy papers had been typed on the
Woodstock machine [once owned by the Hisses], and the
defense had contested this evidence solely by testimony
that the machine was not in Mr. Hiss's possession and was
not being used at the time. The defense had not called a
documents expert of its own to dispute the government
expert's testimony, nor had either side considered the question whether the same person had typed both the spy
papers and the "standards of comparison"—letters admittedly typed by Mrs. Hiss on the same machine. This
question the jury settled for themselves. [Here Mr. Smith
discovered a peculiar aspect of the cast that, so far as I
am aware, eluded the other reporters.] During the last hour
of their deliberation, according to two of the jurors who
voted for conviction, the jurors studied the typewriter, the
spy papers, and the standards. They observed many instances of similarity between the standards and the spy
papers indicating that they had actually been typed by the
same person—such as the same slips of the finger occurring again and again, and the same habit of crossing out
errors by overprinting a certain letter. When this was demonstrated, these two jurors said, all the eight who were
against Mr. Hiss solidified in their determination not to
acquit him. Even the four who wanted to acquit Mr. Hiss
had to admit that he or his wife might have typed the
papers, they said. But these four still clung to the conviction that there might still be some other explanation of the
way the papers fell into Mr. Chambers' hands; that even
if Mrs. Hiss typed them Mr. Hiss might not have given
them to Mr. Chambers for espionage purposes. When the
eight saw that the four would not recede from their doubts,
they gave up arguing any further, the two jurors said.

This passage was in the second-page runover of Mr.
Smith's lead story on the ending of the trial. Also on
page two of the *Tribune* was a story headed HISS JU-
RORS TELL OF LONG HOURS OF WRANGLING. This
quoted Mrs. Helen Sweatt, a real-estate broker and
one of the jurors who voted for conviction, as saying,
"We tried the typewriter out and went over the docu-

ments. We took a long time tonight because we went over the documents again, word by word."

A box on the same page carried the information that during the trial the government had called 43 witnesses and the defense 30, the government had introduced 224 exhibits and the defense 33; and a total of 2,851 pages of testimony, running to 570,000 words, had been transcribed. After doing its best to evaluate the significance of all this, the jury had tried, it seemed, to decide the case on the basis of a point on which no expert testimony was introduced: the identity of the person who operated the typewriter. I have since read through a transcript of the testimony of Ramos C. Feehan, the Government's typewriter man, and confirmed my impression that Mr. Smith's statement of the facts was correct. Mr. Feehan's testimony was no more revealing than Mr. Smith said it was, but it was nevertheless the closest any witness came to helping the jury answer the all-important question. What Mr. Feehan had to say made rather a small ripple on the river of newspaper copy about the case when he was examined on June 16. It received modest headlines in early editions of the afternoon papers, but these disappeared in later editions. In the morning papers of June 17 it rated only a couple of paragraphs tucked away near the bottom of the lead story, for it was overshadowed by the more dramatic appearance in court of Henry Julian Wadleigh, the fellow who, following Feehan on the witness stand, said he had stolen papers from the State Department but didn't know whether or not Mr. Hiss had.

On page two of the same day's *Tribune* that carried Mr. Smith's story about the jury there was an intimation, in the form of a statement to the United Press by Congressman Richard M. Nixon, Republican, of California, a member of the House Committee on Un-American Activities, that it is un-American not to convict anybody Congressman Nixon doesn't like. Mr. Nixon was quoted as saying that there should be an immediate investigation of Judge Samuel H Kaufman's conduct of the trial. Judge Kaufman's "prejudice . . .

against the prosecution" had been "obvious and apparent," according to the congressman.

By Saturday afternoon, less than twenty-four hours after the jurors gave up, the *World-Telegram* and the *Journal-American* were devoting eight-column headlines to the attack on Judge Kaufman: HISS JUDGE PROBE DEMANDED and DEMAND CONGRESS PROBE HISS JUDGE "PREJUDICE," respectively. Congressman Nixon, reinforced by a couple of other Republican congressmen, was still doing the demanding.

The jurors, both pro-conviction and pro-acquittal, had by now become public personages. Already, on Friday afternoon, while the jury was still out, the *Journal-American* and the *World-Telegram* had broken a story of how early in the trial the prosecution had complained about one of the jurors, who, however, had remained on the jury. Saturday's papers elaborated: someone had telephoned to the F.B.I. on June 2, the second day of the trial, to report a rumor that the wife of the foreman of the jury, Hubert E. James, had told a visitor to a Catholic convalescent home in New Jersey that her husband believed Mr. Hiss innocent. The F.B.I., it was said, relayed the information to Thomas F. Murphy, the prosecutor. Mr. Murphy went to Judge Kaufman in chamber and threw the problem in the jurist's lap. He declined to ask the judge to remove the juror but hinted that it would be a nice thing if the judge did. The judge didn't, and Mr. Murphy later, during his summation, took pains to warn the members of the jury that they shouldn't let the foreman influence them any more than any other juror. After the dismissal of the jury, it became public knowledge that Mr. James *had* voted for acquittal, along with two other men and a woman, about whom the prosecution hadn't been tipped off in advance. Mr. James, a tall, prematurely white-haired man, had been welcomed to the jury box by the government on the first day of the trial. I remember that, after having been accepted, he himself raised the question of whether his eligibility as a juror would be affected by the fact that he holds a reserve commission in the Army. He was assured by the court, with the tacit

approval of counsel for both sides, that it would not.
Mr. James is an executive in the General Motors Acceptance Corporation and looks the part. His deprav-
ity, from a prosecution point of view, went unexplained
until the arrival in New York of the Chicago *Tribune*
for Saturday, June 9, which, in a story about the jurors, carried the subhead "Son of Professor." The foreman's father, the paper reported, was James Alton
James, retired head of the history department at
Northwestern.

The most articulate of the pro-conviction jurors—
at any rate, after the dismissal—was James F. Hanra-
han, an accountant employed by a shipping corporation, who told the *Journal-American* on Saturday that
the four acquittal jurors were "so stubborn you could
have knocked their heads against the wall and it
would have made no difference. The foreman was emotional, two were blockheads, and one was a dope.
Eight of us pounded the hell out of the four since
Thursday night, but we couldn't get anywhere." Han-
rahan, a pale young man with a long chin, had given
no indication in the jury box that he was a man of
such dynamism. Of the two women on the jury (they
voted against each other), Mrs. Sweatt, the real-estate
broker, was the more specific as well as the more talkative. She said she had been unable to believe that
Mrs. Whittaker Chambers was lying, because Mrs.
Chambers had testified in such detail about the interior
of the Hisses' home. The other woman juror, Mrs.
Louise Torian, a dressmaker, confined herself to gen-
eralities. "We just didn't see things the same way," she
said. Two of the pro-conviction jurors said that they
had been antagonized by the long procession of character witnesses for the defendant, including United
States Superior Court Justices Frankfurter and Reed,
which could serve as a hint for the defense when it
prepares for the retrial. One of the pro-acquittal jurors, Arthur L. Pawliger, said that he couldn't believe
Whittaker Chambers could remember the pattern of
the wallpaper in anybody's house after twelve years;
just as the detail in Mrs. Chambers's descriptions made
Mrs. Sweatt sure that the witness was not lying, in

Chambers's case the detail made Pawliger sure that the witness *was* lying.

Sunday's papers recorded more Nixonian dicta. The congressman said he thought that Judge Kaufman should have allowed the prosecution to call a couple of eleventh-hour witnesses whom the judge had ruled out—Mrs. Hede Massing, the divorced wife of Gerhart Eisler, and William Rosen, an officer of a second-hand-automobile firm in Washington. "Perhaps the Judge had good technical grounds for barring those witnesses," the *Times* reported Nixon as saying in a radio interview with Bert Andrews, of the *Herald Tribune,* "but I think those two witnesses should have been permitted to testify about their knowledge, if any, of Mr. Hiss. For all anyone knows, their testimony might have made a great difference in the minds of the jurors." The *Times* took care of the radio interview in six inches of type.

The Sunday *Journal-American* played up a pair of front-page stories under these headlines: REPUBLICANS ALSO DEMAND FULL PROBE OF JUDGE KAUFMAN and HISS TRIAL CONDUCT WIDELY PROTESTED. The latter appeared over a story by Leslie Gould, the *Journal's* financial editor, and the wide protests turned out to be mostly his. "To this report," Mr. Gould reported, "it appears there is ample evidence that Kaufman's ruling and attitudes during the trial were detrimental to the Government's case." In its day-to-day reports of the trial, the *Journal-American* occasionally commented upon Judge Kaufman's handling of the case, finding it, in one instance, at least, "unusual." On June 28, when the trial was little more than half over, the *Journal's* Westbrook Pegler, in a column the editors decided was worth breaking on the front page, dismissed the judge as a "a New Dealer and an organization Democrat."

The *Herald Tribune,* whose coverage of the trial was admirably impartial, did not at the time indulge in any such side excursions, but in the days immediately following the trial it became intensely preoccupied with statements criticizing the judge. On the Sunday after the dismissal of the jury, a story in the right-hand

column of the *Tribune*'s first page, headlined HOUSE
GROUP SPLIT ON HISS INQUIRY, began: "Reopening of
the Congressional investigation into the Hiss-Chambers
case and inquiry into the conduct of Judge Samuel H.
Kaufman was urged today as a result of the hung jury
in the perjury trial of Alger Hiss, and promptly encountered sharp criticism. . . . Reopening of the investigation by the House committee was urged by
Representatives Richard M. Nixon, of California;
Francis Case, of South Dakota; Harold H. Velde, of
Illinois, Republicans; and Morgan M. Moulder, Democrat, of Missouri." The first 16 inches of the story
were fairly evenly divided between the point of view
of the urgers and that of their "sharp" critics: Representative Emanuel Celler, of New York, chairman of
the House Judiciary Committee, and former Secretary
of War Robert P. Patterson, president of the New York
City Bar Association. Twenty of the succeeding
twenty-seven inches of type, however, were given over
entirely to the radio interview between Representative
Nixon and Mr. Andrews, the *Tribune*'s correspondent.
Mr. Nixon again said that Judge Kaufman's "prejudice
against the prosecution" had been "obvious and apparent," as he had done in his United Press interview
printed in the *Tribune* of the day before. (He is obviously unaware that the two words apparently mean
the same thing.) Mr. Nixon said he thought "the average American wanted all technicalities waived in this
case," and that "the entire Truman administration was
extremely anxious that nothing bad happen to Mr.
Hiss." He also told the already familiar jury-foreman
story. (Mr. James, the foreman, on the same day denied ever having discussed the case outside the courtroom or having carried any bias into court with him.)

Monday's *Herald Tribune* gave a first-page play and
almost two columns of space to a story headed REP.
VELDE JOINS ATTACK ON JUDGE IN HISS TRIAL. Recalling that Velde was one of the four named by the *Tribune* on the previous day as critics of the judge, I found
it hard to understand how he could join something he
was already in. "A new blast at the conduct of Judge
Samuel H. Kaufman . . ." the *Tribune*'s Monday story,

signed by David McConnell, started out, and then it went over much the same ground covered by the Nixon pieces. Mr. Velde, however, had added some new complaints, listing six "flagrant examples" of misconduct by the judge. Flagrant Example No. 3, for instance, began: "Judge Kaufman permitted a psychiatrist retained by Alger Hiss, one Dr. Binger, to sit in a prominent spot as a prospective defense witness, and take notes on the behavior of Whittaker Chambers." It went on to say that the judge had allowed Lloyd Paul Stryker, the defense counsel, to ask a long hypothetical question of Dr. Binger but had refused to allow Dr. Binger to reply. "As Prosecutor Murphy cried, in a raging protest against this most undecorous judicial conduct, the 'damage had already been done,'" Representative Velde said, implying that the psychiatrist's presentation on the witness stand had been a mere feint by Stryker to enable him to ask his question. Flagrant Example No. 4 was that Judge Kaufman allowed Mr. Stryker to ask Mr. Chambers about the suicide of his brother but did not allow Murphy to ask Mr. Hiss about the suicide of his father. No. 5 was: "When Chambers was asked how he had first met Alger Hiss he testified that he had been introduced to him by Harold Ware and J. Peters. When the prosecution asked for further identification of these two men, Judge Kaufman refused to allow an answer. Both were known operators of Washington spy rings." In reporting Mr. Velde's criticisms of Judge Kaufman, the *Times* contented itself with a United Press story, which it printed on page eleven.

On Tuesday the *Herald Tribune* ran a first-page story headed: FIVE HISS JURORS EXPRESS BELIEF KAUFMAN WAS BIASED FOR DEFENSE. This time, the newspaper presented Mrs. Sweatt, the real-estate broker, as an authority on jurisprudence, including the admissibility of evidence. "He should have permitted the witness and testimony that the prosecution wanted," she was quoted as saying. "I was interested in hearing Mrs. Massing and the Cherner Motor Company executive. And it wasn't right for the Judge to allow that psychiatrist to sit there all the while that Mr. Chambers was on the witness stand. At the same time he was watching the jurors and it made some of us nervous. Then I recall that the Judge let them ask questions about a suicide in Mr. Chambers' family but would not permit the same kind of questions about the suicide in Mr. Hiss's family. Then the Judge didn't let the prosecution identify the Communists Harold Ware and Jay Peters." Any coincidence between the Velde bill of particulars and Mrs. Sweatt's complaints is an obviously apparent coincidence. The *Tribune* seemed in danger of catching the *World-Telegram*'s habit of running the same story over and over again indefinitely as news. Mrs. Sweatt's views did not make the *Times* at all. That paper's aftermath story for the day (on page four) bore the heads:

KAUFMAN'S ACTION
IN TRIAL DEFENDED

REPRESENTATIVE HAYS ACCUSES
COMMITTEEMEN OF MAKING
"VICIOUS ACCUSATIONS"

The *Tribune,* by my count, had now run essentially the same story on four successive days, plugging the piece on page one on the second, third, and fourth occasions. In its second Nixon story, the paper had re-quoted what the congressman had said the first time; in its third-day story, it had quoted Velde's elaboration of Nixon 1 and 2, in which Velde had been cited as concurring; and in its fourth-day first-pager, had quoted Mrs. Sweatt's detailed restatement of Velde.

On Wednesday, after the *Tribune*'s third reprise of the Nixon charge that Judge Kaufman was, to say the least, irresponsible, the paper ran a story on page eight signed by Peter Kihss and headed:

COURT RECORD
SHOWS BASIS
OF HISS RULINGS

KAUFMAN CITED FIVE CASES AND
TWO TEXTBOOKS IN BANNING
MRS. MASSING

"On argument in chambers," Mr. Kihss reported, "the judge had cited five cases and two textbooks on evidence to contend the government was bound by the evidence it itself drew from Mr. Hiss 'on a collateral matter,' namely, an alleged 1935 conversation with Mrs. Massing. . . . He added that the testimony would have been admissible if offered in the government's own case, rather than on rebuttal." This was less arresting than talk about judicial prejudice, and the news editor of the *Herald Tribune* had, accordingly, placed it in a less prominent position. In another headline on page eight, the *Tribune* proclaimed: INQUIRY ON HISS NOT TO BE CALLED "AT THIS TIME." (The quotes are the *Herald Tribune*'s.) The story that followed attributed to John S. Wood, Democrat, of Georgia, chairman of the House Un-American Activities Committee, the statement: "There will be no investigation of the judiciary by the Committee on Un-American Activities, and none has been proposed or requested by any members thereof." What Velde and Nixon had wanted, this story explained, was an inquiry by all Congress, not just by their own committee. Representative Francis E. Walter, Democrat, of Pennsylvania, another committeeman, had also made a few remarks, and these found their way into the bottom half of the story on page eight, as follows:

Representative Walter pointed out that the Hiss case has not been concluded. He said that for a Congressional committee to investigate the Hiss trial would be "an interference with and an obstruction of the administration of justice." It is not within the province of Congress, he said, to inquire into "errors of law" and other technicalities of the trial.

"Presumably," he said, "there will be another judge when the case is retried, and the new judge should be free to make his own decision at the time and not be influenced by the findings of any Congressional committee."

In the last two paragraphs of this story, the *Herald Tribune* was right back on the old theme, quoting George A. Dondero, of Michigan, still another Republican, as saying: "When five members of the jury in the New York *Herald Tribune* this morning say that the judge was prejudiced in favor of the defendant, there is surely some basis for the charge that the trial was unfair"—a small but gemlike example of how a ball can be tossed from one hand to another. The effect of this sort of reiteration, which is to be expected of the *Journal-American* but not of the *Herald Tribune,* may well be, as Congressman Walter suggested, to intimidate any judge who in the future presides over a similar trial, or a retrial of the Hiss case. That far-short-of-radical paper the *Christian Science Monitor* got the idea across well in this front-page headline on Tuesday, July 12, at a time when the *Tribune* was running its Mrs. Sweatt story: BLASTS ON KAUFMAN SEEN CHALLENGE TO FREE U.S. JUDICIARY.

The story that followed, by Mary Hornaday, who covered the trial for the *Monitor,* included the statement, "If Mr. Hiss had been acquitted, the attacks on the Judge probably would have been even more violent." It is much the same sort of thing one might write after a trial in Yugoslavia. The great publicity given to the jurors and the violent attacks in the press by jurors voting for conviction upon those voting for acquittal appear likely to make jury service even less popular than it is now. The *Journal-American,* which never puts too fine a point on things, recorded, three days after the jury was dismissed: "All jurors in the trial reported receiving telephone calls and mail commenting on their stand. Those who voted for conviction received expressions of approval while those who stood for acquittal reported 'threats.' " After which the *Journal* gave the names and addresses (of considerable convenience, I imagine, to anonymous letter writers) of two of the pro-acquittal jurors. It quoted one of them as saying that he had received a call from a man who said he (the juror) was going to "get his," and that he had also received a postcard in red ink, calling him a "sucker for the Communists" and "advising him to go back to Russia."

This sort of thing obviously and apparently lessens the chance of a fair trial next time. Perhaps the secrecy of the jury room, like that of the voting booth, should be protected by law.

It did not require my penetrating intelligence to discern the impossibility of ever getting a fair trial for Hiss in New York again. His lawyers asked for a transfer to a United States Court in Vermont, where there are no Hearst or Scripps-Howard papers, and where inhabitants likely to serve on a jury own shotguns and are less susceptible to intimidation by telephone calls from anonymous muzzlers. The United States Circuit Court of Appeals refused the request, and he was brought to trial in the same courthouse as before, in January, 1950.

This time there was no fear of rebellion in the jury box. Any panel-man who felt that he might be reasoned into voting for acquittal and so exposed to Hearst-abetted hoodlum action, would, naturally, have saved himself by saying he had an opinion on the case. Thomas F. Murphy, the assistant United States District Attorney who had prosecuted in the first case, was on deck again, vast, confident, bullying, while Judge Kaufman, who had ventured to rule against him now and then, was gone. It was a blatant advertisement to jurors as well as public that Murphy was cock of the roost. This time he had the equivalent on the bench of a hometown referee.

Courts and Administration, impressed by the hullabaloo, seemed to have decided that the very worst thing that could happen, politically, was for Hiss to be acquitted, since, as Miss Hornaday had deduced, attacks would then become even more violent. The party in power may have thought that, if it chucked him to his accusers, it would show that it disapproved of treason just as strongly as the Republicans.

In 1678, Charles II encouraged his courts to give the Jesuits the works although he did not in the least believe them guilty, because his political enemies, the Dissenters and Low Church nobles, whispered that *he* was soft on Catholics. This was an equivalent of the charge that the Truman Administration was soft on fellow-travelers. Charles thought that if he let the fanatics disembowel a few priests—who *should* be glad of martyrdom anyway, the old cynic probably told himself—the row would die down and be forgotten in the excitement of the new bull-baiting season. The Truman Administration may have had the same thought in 1949–50.

Both were wrong. The two similar "hysterias" that they tried to calm by yielding were politically stimulated, and a politician does not let up when he is being yielded to. He pushes harder. The way to stop him is to knock him flat, a truth the President should have remembered from his campaign in 1948. Knocking flat is the Truman style, and a style is impossible to change. In this instance he looked like Rocky Marciano trying to be Kid Chocolate.

In Charles's case the Protestant nobles, accepting the *émincé* of 22 Catholics as an appetizer, next accused the Queen herself, through her physician, Sir George Wakeman, of plotting to kill the King. This would have made her liable to all but one of the penalties in the sentence cited earlier on, and as Charles liked her, in a dispassionate way, and needed Dr. Wakeman to take care of his gout, he found it a bit thick.

He therefore ordered Scroggs to revert to the normal laws of evidence. The jury, by what amounted to a directed verdict, acquitted Wakeman against precisely the same sort of testimony that had caused the previous juries to hang his predecessors. Another court found the informers guilty of perjury, and they were all thrown into jail and thrashed. I do not know whether Charles regretted not having done this before, but I hope so.

Hiss's new lawyers, coming up to the second trial, faced an insuperable problem, stated in the Titus Oates days by Thomas Whitebread, the doomed Provincial of the English Jesuits: "We are to prove a negative, and I know 'tis much harder to prove a negative than to assert an affirmative; 'tis not a very hard thing for a man to swear anything if he will venture his soul for it; but truly, I may boldly say, in the sight of Almighty God before whom I am to appear, there have not been three true words spoken by this witness."

Mr. Stryker, who had so damaged his client's case by establishing Chambers's mendacity, had withdrawn. The defense had learned from the first trial. Before trial, a lawyer still of counsel had talked with a handwriting and typewriting expert in Pittsburgh who, while he thought the papers produced by Chambers and the controls may well have been written on the same machine, was sure that the characteristics of the *typewriting itself,* were different. The defense had not engaged him then, because it judged that what he said about the machine might hurt as much as what he said about the typewriting might help. Now it knew that the first jury had attached more weight to the nature of the writing than anything else, off its own bat, and had argued it without having received any evidence bearing on the point.

The defense hurried back after the first trial to see the Pittsburgh man, but the public climate had frozen him. He said he would not appear under any circumstances, because his testimony might ruin him in his regular business, spotting fake signatures on checks and verifying sound ones on disputed wills. The F.B.I., working with ubiquitous industry on details of the Hisses' life in Washington and Baltimore from 12 to 15 years earlier, came up with a mixed bag of apparent trivia, to which, working closely with Chambers, it established sinister correspondences.

Agents going through old Hiss bank accounts found, for example, that on a given date Mrs. Hiss had withdrawn $400. Chambers immediately recalled that she had given him the money to buy a car. Previously, he had testified that she had given him only one car, an old one, worth $25. To support his refreshed recollection, however, he pointed out that he *had* bought another car shortly after the withdrawal of the $400 by Mrs. Hiss—he had the receipt.

The price, he acknowledged, did not exactly correspond with the withdrawal, but the Hiss money had formed part of it. It would have been out of keeping with the Oatesian penumbra of the courtroom to suggest that if Mrs. Hiss had withdrawn $8.95 the witness might have testified that she gave it to him to buy a box of cigars. As irresistible corroboration Oates would have produced a cigar box.

The prosecution's new evidence was amusing and the new obstacles placed in the way of defense investigators by the artificially created climate that followed the first trial were instructive, but both were irrelevant to the foreordained result of the second. So was Hiss's extra burden of having been hailed as an honest man by two justices of the United States Supreme Court, while his chief accuser enjoyed the advantage of a self-advertised career as a spy, liar, traveler on false passports, and hider behind so many false names that he acknowledged during the second trial that he couldn't remember which one he had been using at the time of the only contact with the Hisses that they admitted—in 1934. When a handicapper puts enough weight on a horse to make its defeat certain, it does not affect the result if he throws on 20 pounds more. The great attack on judge and jury that had followed the first trial had obviated any chance of getting a fair jury in New York, and Alger Hiss was convicted of perjury on two counts—denying he had delivered State Department papers to Chambers and that he had known Chambers subsequent to 1936.

Since this one circumstance made the actual trial as redundant as the election that follows the Democratic primary in a Deep South state, I will try, if I can restrain myself, to stay off ancillary legal themes.

The defense appealed on a swarm of grounds, some of more and others of less merit, to the Circuit Court of Appeals and the United States Supreme Court, and was turned down, Frankfurter and Reed, still abashed, not voting. One of the grounds was, naturally, the essential one: that although the newspapers had made a fair second round impossible in New York, the Circuit Court had denied a change of venue. The justices found this had no merit, although, to give them their intellectual due, it must have made them think.

In April, 1951, the court heard the appeal, carried up through lower tribunals, of two Negroes whose lawyers alleged their clients had been illegally convicted of rape, a capital offense, in a town called Groveland, Florida, in 1949. The Negroes had then been sentenced to death. The lawyers' novel argument, which would have thrown counsel for the A.N.P.A. into fits, was that the county newspaper in Groveland, a one-ownership town principally notable for a tough sheriff, had published "confessions" the sheriff may have beaten out of the two prisoners, and so inflamed everybody within the county against them as to make a fair trial impossible.

The court unanimously reversed their convictions, and Justice Robert H. Jackson, who wrote the opinion, said, among other things prejudicial to the divine right of holders of an A.P. franchise:

> If freedoms of the press are so abused as to make fair trial in the locality impossible, *the judicial process must be protected by removing the trial to a forum beyond its probable influence.* [Italics mine.]
> The case presents one of the best examples of one of the worst menaces to American justice.
> If the court [in Groveland] had allowed an involuntary confession to be placed before the jury, we would not hesitate to consider it a denial of due process of law and reverse. . . .
> But neither counsel nor court can control the admission of evidence if unproven, and probably unprovable, "confessions," are put before the jury by newspapers and radio. Rights of the defendant to be confronted by witnesses against him and to cross-examine them are hereby circumvented.

Shortly afterward, the Negroes, who had been sweating out their appeal and a new trial in Groveland, were shot to death trying to escape. They had established a legal principle, though, like laboratory rabbits whose deaths serve in the identification of a "worst menace."

The court's decision in the nonpolitical case of the two Negroes, following its refusal to see the point so clear in the Hiss case, confirmed the great Dooley dictum: "The Supreme Court follows the elections." In truth, it went him one better. It proved that the court anticipates them.

In the years since, newspapers themselves have become much more sensible of the threat to justice implicit in the American custom of a pretrial in the press that, like a primary election in the Solid South, predetermines the official verdict. They were heartily stimulated in this direction when jurors in Montgomery, Alabama, found the New York *Times* guilty of "libelling" a pair of regional Dogberries and awarded the plaintiffs a cool million in a suit that anywhere else would have been laughed out of court. The *Times,* its lawyers, and even, save the mark, the Chicago *Tribune,* volunteering as amicus curiae, were quick to point out, among a dozen other reasons, all sufficient for upsetting the verdict, that the inflamed state of Alabama public opinion—inflamed mostly by the press—had precluded fair trial.

And the *Times,* like an oligarch who endows gout prevention after his big toe swells, published on June 11, 1960, an editorial which, though late, I couldn't agree with more:

FREE PRESS AND FAIR TRIAL

Two fundamental principles protected by the Constitution—freedom of the press and the fair administration of justice—come too frequently into conflict. A criminal defendant is often made the subject, before trial, of sensational accounts in newspapers and on radio and television. His guilt is assumed, his past raked over. By the time the trial takes place it may be virtually impossible to find a juror not prejudiced against him.

In the past the Supreme Court has been reluctant to step into this picture to restore the balance of fairness to the defendant. But a decision last week indicated that that reluctance may be disappearing.

The court set aside an Indiana murder conviction because a "barrage" of publicity before trial had fatally prejudiced the jury against the accused killer. Eight of the twelve jurors admitted that they had started out by thinking the defendant guilty, although they promised to be impartial.

Even the most vigorous advocate of freedom of the press can take no reasonable exception to this decision. One of the tests of a society is the fairness of its criminal justice; this need must not take second place to the public's taste for the morbid and sensational.

Because the facts in the Indiana case were so extreme—with the jury admittedly biased—it is impossible to know how rigorously the Supreme Court will apply the rule that criminal defendants are entitled to trials untainted by damaging publicity. But at the least the newspapers of the country, and other means of communication, are on notice that they have an obligation to use restraint in the reporting of criminal cases lest they interfere in the administration of justice, and lead to reversals of convictions. A similar obligation rests on prosecutors, who so often (in the Indiana case, for example) drum up publicity by issuing detailed statements about the crime and the defendant before trial.

Hiss's forced conviction shaped American political life for the next five years, 1950–55, and powerfully influenced it for five more, 1955–60. Through the quotations in "Spotlight on the Jury," the chagrin of a young congressman named Richard M. Nixon shines out like four fireflies in a bottle. The only public im-

pression that Nixon had made in three modest years
in the House was through his association with the
House Un-Ameri an Activities Committee's investigation of Chambers's charges against Alger Hiss. These
began in the summer of 1948, and Nixon had stuck
with Chambers when other members of the committee
showed signs of boredom with the *Time* editor's tale.
It was Nixon who, in Chambers's darkest hour, when
he was being sued for libel by Hiss in the fall of 1948,
had gone out to the ex-Communist's farm at his behest.
There Chambers had revealed to him the scraps of
hand- and typewritten paper that he charged Hiss had
abstracted from the State Department, stashed in
pumpkins like eggs in the ovaries of portentous hens.

After the revelation, there had been anxious weeks,
because Chambers, in previously denying under oath
that he knew Hiss to be a spy, had perjured himself,
unless, indeed, he was perjuring himself again in saying that he *had* known it. The race, then, was to see
which man the Federal Grand Jury would indict for
perjury: Chambers, who admitted it, or Hiss, who
denied it. The Oatesian precedent prevailed: to avert
suspicion, confession is the safest course. But it had,
from some accounts, been a near thing in the Grand
Jury room.

From then until the end of the second trial, Nixon
was in the plight of a young bank teller who has bet
his life savings on a horse that looks like faltering. If
Chambers lost, Nixon would be wiped out, and the
old foxes of his party, like the under-officers of the
teller's bank, would put a black mark against him as
a young man who went too far out on a limb without
testing it.

With Hiss's indictment and Chambers's elevation to
eminence of the sort once enjoyed by Oates, Nixon's
prospects brightened, until he began to take the result
of the first trial and his own party halo for granted.
After the jury hung that time, he thought of Judge
Kaufman and of Mr. James, the jury foreman, less as
personal enemies, whom as a Quaker he should forgive, than as obstacles to the common good, whom it
was a public duty to denounce. Ten years later, during

his presidential campaign, he was to react in the same way to the reporters upon whom he made an unfavorable impression, and to throw himself upon the bosom of Westbrook Pegler after the campaign to bewail their injustice. He is a brave gambler, but not a good one: he sweats, gets angry, and suffers cramps.

The favorable result of the second trial set him up as the perspicacious plunger who had backed an unlikely nag into a small political fortune. He parlayed his win into a seat in the United States Senate. His opponent in California was, fortunately for him, Helen Gahagan Douglas, who expected not be slugged because she was a lady. She might as well have expected her opponent to get up and give her a seat in a Fifth Avenue bus. Nixon is a firm supporter of equal rights for women.

The war in Korea had begun, exacerbating the climate. Nixon arrived in the Senate, made his maiden speech, and then, turning like a bettor with a hot tip on the next race, ran for the cashier's window to collect on his winning ticket and bet it all down again. He bet his new political fortune on General Eisenhower against Taft, and so ran his advocacy of Chambers into the Vice-Presidency of the United States. That first two-dollar bet, in fact, landed him within a heartbeat, a yard of intestine, and 112,000 votes of the White House, on three separate occasions and in that order. Nixon, however, was never of more than almost-importance, since he was running too fast to leave footprints on the sands of time. He just skimmed them, like a coot taking off.

The true beneficiary of the newspaper jury tampering was Senator Joseph McCarthy of Wisconsin, who for four years had been hovering above the battle, waiting for somebody to drop safely dead before he swooped. The conviction of a fairly high former official, a Democrat, like Hiss, gave McCarthy his cue, and a couple of weeks after the end of the second trial, he made his famous first West Virginia speech, in which he announced there were hundreds of card-carrying Communists in the State Department. When anybody muttered that he could not prove his charges,

he would shake his necrophagous beak and croak:
"Who would have believed it of Alger Hiss?"

Pretty soon nobody muttered. Human courage has
not notably increased since the reign of Charles II.

McCarthy ranted and reigned for the next four years.
It was the McCarthy episode, rather than the Sputnik,
that marked the nadir of American prestige abroad.
He frightened our teachers and through them our children, shook the teeth out of our European alliances,
making it morally impossible for any self-respecting
European to go along with us. His touring anti-cultural
exchange, Cohn and Schine, lifting books from the
shelves of American libraries abroad, served to dis-
qualify an American in Europe or Africa from speaking
of freedom. He would be greeted by a howl of laughter.[1]

From a G.O.P. point of view, McCarthy was, like
Carnot, the Organizer of Victory, in 1952. General Eisenhower, like Masséna, was only its favorite son. But
the stultification of justice in the Hiss trial by the press
had given the fearless statesman from Wisconsin courage to be born.

---

[1] The leitmotif of those days was: the Cohn-Schines east,
the Cohn-Schines west, McCarthy knows where the Cohn-
Schines best.

5
Innocence
at
Home

In the field of foreign affairs, newspapers are less trammeled by their owners' mass phobias than at home. Norwegian labor unions cannot affront American employers with impudent demands for money. British income taxes are not levied against American incomes. The Portuguese may be poor, but they have no way of scrounging second bottles of milk that may eventually be reflected in a rise of half a mil in the real estate rate paid by the New York *Daily News*. Nor can any Austrian politico run for President against Nixon next time out, or even for Sheriff of Yolg County, California. The principles of publishers are thus less directly involved, and a reporter abroad might, therefore, have a freer hand than a reporter at home. The trouble is that approximately 1,700 of approximately 1,750 American dailies haven't got a reporter abroad.

The New York *Times,* which boosters of the American press always push forward as a representative of its virtues, is as unrepresentative as possible. It is unique in having a foreign service that is adequate in quantity and of a quality that frequently justifies reading. The New York *Herald Tribune* has a service that makes an interesting supplement to the *Times*—I read them both most mornings—and the Chicago *Daily News* syndicate used to have some crack correspondents, although I note with regret that *Editor & Publisher* yearbook lists mostly, as evidence of their present quality, the names of past stars. There are in addition the Baltimore *Sun,* the *Wall Street Journal,* and a few more who have from one to half a dozen men about, and the Chicago *Tribune* syndicate maintains what I should call a counter-information service of waning efficacity, in decline since the death of its encyclopedic leader, Colonel Robert Rutherford McCormick, the decathlon champion of the human mind. My estimate of 25 papers that have even one man abroad is probably generous.

The three papers that have noticeable foreign coverage—the *Times, Trib,* and Chicago *Daily News* (the same one that is now a Siamese twin of the Chicago *Sun-Times*)—have syndicate services available to any paper that will pay for them, and an aggregate of less than a hundred clients take one, or two, or in a very few cases all three. They do not get full service, but nearly always a great deal more than they use. That leaves about 1,600 newspapers entirely dependent upon the Associated Press and United Press International, one, both, or the other.

There are also available a few syndicated columnists who specialize in international affairs, notably Joseph Alsop, who orbits the earth like a moon, descending for a day or two now and then to lecture an Arabian King or a Bessarabian prelate on his duties. Alsop contributes some useful insights, and communicates—that key word of insight-journalism—a sense that the world is one, and likely to be one less any minute. His column, "Matter of Fact," might better be called "For Whom the Bell Tolls," and he keeps it tolling so continuously that sometimes it sounds like an electric buzzer. He is, for more Americans than any other one man, the sharpest reminder that a rest of a world exists, but he makes it sound rather awful.

News magazine coverage is of course supplementary. *Time* and the David Lawrence thing perform the service of the waiter-captain who meets you in front of the smorgasbord table and says: "Let me help you make a selection." He then fills your plate with all the items the management particularly wants to get rid of. They specialize in *réchauffés* of newspaper despatches, livened with sauces prepared on the premises. At Time, Inc., you are likely to get a bit of Chiang Kai-shek straight out of the deep freeze with every meal.

In *Time*'s beginnings this was all its foreign service consisted of, and since its proprietor made a great deal of money that way, he cannot see any use for reporters of his own. He has a considerable number now, including, for limited spans now and then, some good ones. But he has never been able to bring himself to believe them unless they tell him what he already thinks. That great Louisianian, the late Earl Long, defined Luce journalism incomparably when he said: "Mr. Luce is like a man who owns a shoestore and buys all the shoes to fit hisself."

The next exhibit is an example of what American foreign correspondence still was, only eleven years ago, in the age of the last of the giants, R.I.P.

The Colonel Looks on Marathon

MARCH 25, 1950

Periodically, Colonel Robert Rutherford McCormick, publisher of the "World's Greatest Newspaper," quits his atomic-bomb-proof eyrie in his Symphony in Stone, the Tribune Tower, in Chicago, to soar off into the Wild Blue Yonder on a mission of aerial reportage. These missions are flown in a converted Flying Fortress named, in honor of the World's Greatest Newspaper, the Chicago Tribune. The Colonel bought the flying Chicago Tribune—as distinguished from the printed one, which he inherited—out of Government surplus, in 1948. There had been overproduction of Fortresses during the war, he told *Tribune* readers at the time, and he had got it for less than the price of a small new plane. From the points where he alights, the Colonel tells *Tribune* readers what the world outside looks like to him (pretty dismal, except for few bright spots, such as General MacArthur's Japan and General Franco's Spain). The proprietor of Dick Tracy, Moon Mullins, and John O'Donnell does not permit the syndication of his own contributions. By reserving them for the *Tribune,* he may feel that he is protecting the publication's position *as* the World's Greatest Newspaper. Whatever his reasons, as I have discovered while making Chicago my temporary headquarters, he is unjust to readers in less favored regions. For the Colonel is a travel writer in the great tradition, like De Tocqueville, Lemuel Gulliver, and George Borrow, and he brings back memories of Tom Sawyer and his balloon. The countries he visits merely provide background.

The Colonel is currently abroad on the fifth reconnaissance of importance he has made since the recent war. His entourage includes his wife, her daughter by a former marriage, a woman secretary, and a lady's maid, in addition to five crewmen. On the Christmas card that the Colonel and his lady sent to *Tribune* employees last December was a photograph showing the couple standing beside the flying Chicago Tribune with their luggage. In the upper right-hand corner of the card was the line, "To the ends of the earth we go, go, go—Kipling." Although he was British, and an Empire man at that, Kipling is one of the Colonel's favorite poets.

A map and timetable of the Colonel's itinerary are published in the *Tribune* before each departure. On the present journey, which has been called by WGN, the McCormick radio station, "a three-continent fact-finding flight," the Colonel was scheduled to inspect Bermuda, the Azores, Spain, Greece, Egypt, Saudi Arabia, Pakistan, India, Burma, Thailand, Iran, Turkey, Italy, France, Denmark, and Iceland, in that order. On March 4, however, at which time the Colonel had reached Karachi, it was announced that he would skip Burma, because of "discouraging reports," and the *Tribune* of March 11 let it be known that he would also omit Iran. The latter news was carried in a modest Reuters dispatch, datelined Teheran, that read: "Col. Robert R. McCormick, editor and publisher of the Chicago *Tribune,* has notified the American embassy here that he has canceled his visit to Iran scheduled for March 14. He had already had 'satisfactory talks' with Shah Mohammed Riza Pahlavi in Pakistan, where he attended a dinner in the Shah's honor, he said."

The same day's *Tribune* carried the following Associated Press item from Bangkok: "Col. Robert R. McCormick, editor and publisher of the Chicago *Tribune,* left today in his private plane for New Delhi, India. Col. McCormick, who during his two-day visit here had talked with Premier Pibul Songgram, said he be-

lieved the premier is conscious of the Communist
threat to his country. He added that Thailand appears
relatively prosperous."

These are not oustanding examples of the Colonel's
knack of reaching and communicating conclusions rapidly. In an interview granted to Percy Wood, a *Tribune*
correspondent, and some Egyptian newspapermen, in
Cairo on March 2, the Colonel engineered a scoop of
sorts by reporting on the condition of France, which
he was not scheduled to visit until March 24. "France
is atheist and anarchic," he said. "Her greatest hero,
Pétain, is held in prison by his political opposition."

There is, though, evidently some limit to the Colonel's power of reporting by anticipation—a journalistic innovation, incidentally, almost as important as the
method of judging newspapers by their gross weight,
which the *Tribune* revealed in 1946.[1] He can report
on a country three weeks before he goes to it, but not
a full year before. "Asked to comment on the British
election results," Mr. Wood wrote, "the publisher said,
'Ask me a year from now. I'm going there next year.'
He said that a Truman–Stalin conference would be
useless, because 'no statesman ever keeps his word.'
The publisher added, however," Wood continued,
"that 'we can lick everyone, including Russia.' Declaring that individuals bring on war, Col. McCormick said, 'The last one was caused by Hitler and Roosevelt; maybe the next one will be brought about by
Truman and Stalin.' " (Colonel McCormick then went
in for one of those historical digressions that are his
specialty. "Empires, except the Roman, don't last," he
told Mr. Wood and the Egyptians, whose land was
once the seat of a fairly durable empire itself. "The
Turkish empire didn't last, nor did that of Louis XIV,
nor Hitler's. The British Empire didn't last, and the
Russian empire won't." This marked a slight switch in
the Colonel's historical line. On February 20, he had
told the Associated Press in Newark, "There has never

---

[1] This story, besides recording an epoch-making discovery in
journalometry, is an outstanding example of the *Tribune*'s
depth-reporting. Their foreign correspondent, like his patron
and pattern, is historically minded.

been a successful empire since Charlemagne's." By March 2, he had apparently decided that Charlemagne was a bust.)

In Madrid, on February 23 (I'm making no effort here to keep Colonel McCormick's observations in chronological order), the publisher told Spanish reporters and the Associated Press that he believed the dangers of atomic warfare to be overrated (despite his preparations for protecting Tribune Tower workers against atomic radiation). "It would be hard on little, concentrated countries like England," he said. "In the United States we have lots of space."

On March 6, in Karachi, Reuters reported, and the *Tribune* duly noted, Colonel McCormick invited Liaquat Ali Khan, the Pakistani Prime Minister, to have lunch with him at Cantigny Farm, the publisher's estate near Wheaton, Illinois, sometime this spring. After lunch on the forthcoming occasion, according to the dispatch, "a number of Pakistani women in the Prime Minister's party will go shopping in Chicago with Mrs. McCormick." The Colonel was reported to have "commended the self-reliance, energy, and high purpose of Pakistan's statesmen." (It was Liaquat Ali Khan who arranged the dinner with the Shah, a providential visitor in Karachi, and thus made the Colonel's trip to Iran unnecessary.) The Egyptian statesmen didn't come off so well. Once he had left Cairo, the Colonel, a Reuters man wrote, "denounced the new Egyptian constitution as a complete phony." In Bombay, the Colonel, as filtered through Reuters, "denounced President Truman's civil-rights program as a new form of slavery." He said, "I believe every employee must have freedom to choose his employer and every employer freedom to choose his employee." (He did not say, as far as I could make out, what happens when the choice is not reciprocal.) The *Tribune* headline on this story read: COL. MCCORMICK HITS AT TRUMAN ON CIVIL RIGHTS. It must have made many of that newspaper's readers think the Colonel was already back home.

All these third-person dispatches, even though most

of them include quotes, are dilute stuff for straight-McCormick addicts, however. We prefer the species of first-person journalism that he sends along under his own bylines: "By Col. R. R. McCormick," to fit in a single column, and "By Col. Robert R. McCormick" when he has a double. This, for us, is the Real McCormick.

The Colonel, as a travel writer, points for one big Sunday piece each week, which is also read over WGN at nine o'clock, Central Standard Time, on Saturday evening, as part of a radio program called "Chicago Theatre of the Air," which he has sponsored since 1940. The reading is sandwiched in between halves of a cut-down version of some operetta or musical comedy, the director accelerating the tempo of the performance if there is an unusually large amount of McCormick to be squeezed into the middle. When in residence, the Colonel appears at the studio, and generally reads an address on some historical incident in British–American relations—the Battle of New Orleans, for example. When he is on the wing, he carries on by recorded voice or by deputy. Collections of the Colonel's addresses, well printed on heavy paper, are to be had free of charge at the Tribune Tower, but a request for them there, I have found by personal experiment, elicits a certain amount of astonishment.

Colonel McCormick's weekend piece does not always absorb all his creative energy while traveling, and he sometimes can't wait to jack up the standards of the World's Greatest Newspaper. The first McCormick byliner of the present *tournée,* under the head COL. MCCORMICK TELLS ABOUT HIS BERMUDA FLIGHT, appeared on Wednesday, February 22. It was briefer than many, but it set the mood for a trip through space with the man who has admitted introducing the machine gun to the Army, light opera to the American public, and aspirin to atomic warfare. It read, in part: "After a tiresome delay which one experiences only from New York customs officers and posing for a few pictures in the cold wind [a *Tribune* photographer, Al Madsen, is also a member of his party], we took off yesterday for Bermuda at 4:30 P.M. . . . followed by a 55-mile-an-hour wind, we lost sight of land in 15 minutes more. . . . Over the ocean, of course, there are no landmarks, but we passed four checkpoints where the navigator pinpoints his position by triangulation. From above the clouds we could see no ships. After dark, the northern lights came out. I have not asked whether they are used as navigational aids. . . . The lights of Bermuda appeared at 8 P.M., New York time, and I said what I had not mentioned before—that, with a 55-mile-per-hour wind, our survival equipment would not be any better than a 5 cent cigar."

The Colonel is intrepid, but he knows *Tribune* readers worry about him. In 1948, when he bought the winged Chicago Tribune, he sought to reassure his public by devoting most of a "Chicago Theatre of the Air" address to a review of the safety factors involved. "Hot and cold food and coffee will be taken on at the different stops, as we do not propose to risk the additional hazard of a stove," he said then. "Neither will there be any smoking on board, and matches taken along for emergency will be in hermetically sealed metal boxes. . . . Calculations indicate that in a four-engine plane two engines will fail together once in 250,000 flights. The same odds are that one could make a million flights before three or four engines would fail simultaneously. . . . If one or two of my engines go out I can make port on the others. Stationed in the North Atlantic Ocean are seven weather-rescue ships on a full-time basis and another on a half-time basis. . . . All these ships have experienced crews aboard . . . constantly standing by for rescue, should their assistance be required. . . . If it were conceivable that both of the pilots should become incapacitated, any one of the other crew members [radio operator, engineer, and navigator] can make a safe landing on an airfield. . . . If all of the crew should become incapacitated, I can hold the plane on an even keel and hit Europe somewhere, in which event the passengers and crew will have to bail out." Happily, the assistance of the rescue ships was not needed. Since then, *Tribune* readers have grown accustomed to the Colonel's flights, and now, when he takes to the air, they are able to bear the strain.

The Colonel followed his dispatch from Bermuda with a byliner, twenty-four hours later, headed: COL. MCCORMICK REACHES MADRID. The piece ran about two columns. The Colonel did not miss the chance for another shot at Gomorrah. "After New York City . . . it was pleasant to get here where there is plenty of water and you don't feel you are depriving someone else when you take a bath," he wrote. "The first stop on our aerial tour was Bermuda," he continued, by way of recapitulation. "Everybody knows that Bermuda is a first-class winter resort." After a short disquisition on the geology of the islands, the Colonel noted, with perhaps a wistful thought for Chicago: "There is segregation of races in the schools and a rather small minority of white people keep control of the legislature by a heavy property qualification. All of the police are white. On the other hand, the colored people are contented and extremely well off."

"We had a little turbulence as we left the island," the report from Madrid also noted. "Then it became extremely cold. . . . From this, and from habit, I was up several times in the night. Of course, legally, I was only a passenger and all five [members of the crew] were vastly superior to me in air knowledge, but the years of responsibility could not be shaken off." The Colonel got the plane safely to the mainland, after a stopover in the Azores, with which he was not greatly taken, finding the peasants poor. "Our soldiers make the best ambassadors we have, with their polite manners, their high education, and high standard of living," he wrote. "The Portuguese, however, are suspicious of their intentions, due partly to the fact that when the English came to Portugal to fight Napoleon they shipped all of the Portuguese industries to England and kept them there, and also because they learned of Roosevelt's plan to occupy the Azores in times of peace."

The Colonel said nothing about Madrid in that dispatch (aside from announcing that he had arrived there), probably because he wanted to save his best stuff for the Sunday paper. But an Associated Press interviewer at the airport there quoted him as saying his present tour would be the end of his travels. "I have been everywhere else," the Colonel declared. "This will be my last big trip." I was sorry to hear it, and glad to read a week later that he had apparently reconsidered and would be going to Britain in a year. The A.P. story from Madrid also recorded for *Tribune* readers the embarrassing mistake about the Spanish Republican flag that had been painted on the Colonel's plane instead of the Franco flag. The Colonel had evidently forgotten to read copy on his fuselage.

In Colonel McCormick's first Sunday piece from Madrid, he wrote that he had had an interview with General Franco, whom he called "the originator of war as we have known it for the last fifteen years." Franco, according to the Colonel, "originated the maneuver of moving troops by air." (This innovation, by the way, has also been credited by the Colonel to Ulysses S. Grant. At the time he gave Grant the laurels, he explained that the Civil War general had moved troops by train but pointed out that the principle was the same.) The Colonel also wrote that Franco had invented dive-bombing. (Colonel McCormick never cites authority, being it.)

Elsewhere in his report after interviewing Franco, the Colonel executed two journalistic maneuvers that were as innovational, in their way, as the martial ones he attributed to his subject. For one thing, he began his story, "I have just come from an interview with Gen. Franco," and then didn't tell anything the general had said. And he displayed even more originality in facing a problem that has long baffled many other reporters: how to present a colorful introduction without pushing the main part of the story down to the bottom of the page. The Colonel accomplished this by simply leaving out the introductory material and running it a week after what it was supposed to lead up to. His first piece, the main part of the story, consisted of an account of the Spanish Civil War as the flying publisher sees it in retrospect. The American Government, he said, sent "a Communist brigade, outrageously named Lincoln, to fight with the Spanish Communists. These men fought well, but did as much harm to their cause by their cruelty to civilians." Despite the presence of this expeditionary force, the Colonel continued, Franco, with some German and Italian assistance, "originated the original blitzkrieg, broke through the defense, and rushed on without stopping to the capture of Barcelona. This practically ended the resistance. Franco granted amnesty to all nationalist soldiers who were not convicted of atrocities. Perhaps his trial of those guilty of atrocities furnished the example for allied trials of war criminals after the World War, but not for Justice Jackson's legalized murder of German political leaders. Franco's strategy was in the best tradition. His tactics were original. Whether Guderian or Patton improved upon them is open to question, but no one denies that they imitated him. [No one except the Colonel, so far as I know, has even suggested it.] So Franco remains the greatest general to appear on the European scene. MacArthur's great strategy of the Pacific was of a different nature. . . . Whatever we think of [Franco's] political principles, no one can question his idealism or his patriotism. In addition to being a great general, he may turn out to be a great statesman."

The second weekend piece from Madrid, in which Colonel McCormick presented the introductory material about his visit there, was entitled SPAIN AND GRECCE and shared the WGN bill with *No, No, Nanette,* after which it went a double-and-a-single on the editorial page. With it, I thought, the Colonel really hit his stride. "The time of the last broadcast did not permit me to give my full impression of Madrid," he started off. "The approach to Generalissimo Franco's home presented the most dramatic peacetime picture I have ever seen. He lives in a former royal hunting lodge, I should say about the size of the late Potter Palmer mansion. [The reference is to a large and hideous Chicago residence that has just been torn down.] Following a straight avenue, we [I assume he means himself and Mrs. McCormick] first perceived two horsemen who, on closer approach, were seen to be

two Moorish cavalrymen on Arab horses. On their
heads were octagonal steel spiked helmets. Their robes
covered the lower part of their faces. Reins and ac-
coutrements looked like the middle ages. Two flags
were at the end of the lances which they dipped in
salute as we passed by." After describing three more
sets of guards and some tapestries, the Colonel reported
that he had been "introduced into the presence of the
Generalissimo, who, in his capacity of chief of state,
was in civilian clothes." He then continued: "Last
week, I told of the interview. [He had apparently forgotten that he hadn't.] As we departed, the guard of
honor was dismissed. . . . How different it was some
years ago when I called on King Alfonso at his massive palace in Madrid." Alfonso had been guarded by
"pikesmen in shabby clothes who clashed their hal-
berds on the floor as they had done in the time of
Henry V," the Colonel reminisced, and this had given
him the tipoff on Alfonso—"an energetic, clever man
who, however, could not resist the changing times."

"Taking off for a night flight, we passed first over
Barcelona and then over Rome—the grandeur that
was Rome," the second Sunday report continued. "The
ghosts of the Caesars are grinding their ghostly teeth
that their capital has become a checkpoint for airplane flights." En route to Athens, the Colonel learned
that his pilots had received some faulty weather information from the Azores. "When we come back
across the North Atlantic, I hope the same joker will
not be on duty," he said; and then, "Returning to
Athens after 30 years, I recognized only the old palace, much like a New England summer hotel, the
Stadium, and, of course, the Acropolis. The Acropolis, obviously, has not changed. Except for when it
was blown up by the Venetians in the 17th century, I
do not suppose it has changed since Pericles built it
with money from the subject states that should have
been used for self-defense and caused the fall of
Athens. . . . The E.C.A. (Economic Cooperation Administration), anxious to brief me on its efforts, pointed
out the roads it had built, so superior to those of Illinois, and the railroad it had rebuilt with money taxed

from American railroads. . . . My informants appeared
intelligent and were clearly sincere. Like others, they
have taken the best jobs they could find and were performing them to the best of their ability. It is at home
that the 5 percenters are doing the collecting. Our
[nation's] presence in Greece was the work of the
English wing of the State Department. . . . The Hitler
plan to get control of the Suez Canal route to India
was being adopted by the Russians. . . . The State Department plan to use the American Army to protect
this British pipeline was, of course, backed by the
beneficiaries of E.C.A. expense. . . . How futile it has
all been is perceived when we see Egypt, India, Cey-
lon, and Thailand all free and the Suez Canal of no
further use to a vanishing empire." Some good may
yet result, though, the Colonel decided. The Greeks,
he observed, are learning from the Americans "a way
of life they could not have learned otherwise."

"The [American] Army has shown them the power
of the Republic," the Colonel said. "The navy, also in
the Mediterranean to protect the lifeline to India,
points out to the nations along its shores that Columbia rules the waves. . . . The elaborate plans under a
clever deception, to return our Republic to European
control, are defeating themselves. The Republic is
pushing forward in Europe. And so, as I take off across
the ancient battlefields, I recall the words of Byron:

> The mountains look on Marathon
> And Marathon looks on the sea;
> And musing there an hour alone,
> I dreamed that Greece might still be free."

Maybe Colonel McCormick is going to become a
convert to the Truman Plan, after all.

Aspirins for Atoms,
Down with Babushkas!

JANUARY 7, 1950

The most invigorating feature of life in Chicago, otherwise a fairly placid city, is one's daily encounter with the World's self-admittedly Greatest Newspaper, the *Tribune*. The visitor to Chicago, awakening unalarmed in his hotel room and receiving the *Tribune* with his breakfast tray, takes a look at the headlines and finds himself at once transported into a land of somber horror, rather like that depicted by the science-mystery magazines, with additional points of resemblance to *True Detective* and *The Musket Boys of Old Boston,* a book about the Revolutionary War that I read when I was young. As he turns the pages of the *Tribune,* the stranger is likely to get the feeling that some of the people and events he is reading about superficially resemble people and events he remembers having read about in the world outside, but he never can be sure. Comparison with other Chicago papers only adds to the confusion. Not long ago, for example, when the Chicago *Daily News* carried the headline HOPKINS, WALLACE DEFENDED—SOUGHT NO ATOM SECRETS, SAYS GROVES, and the Chicago *Sun-Times* head read, GROVES ABSOLVES HOPKINS AND WALLACE (both page one), the *Tribune* headline (on page four) ran DEMOCRATS HIT FOR "WHITEWASH" IN ATOMIC PROBE —REPUBLICANS LEFT OUT; GROVES TESTIFIES. The texts of stories printed by the *Tribune,*. on the one hand, and by the *News* and the *Sun-Times,* on the other, are even more disparate than the headlines; the only points on which the *Tribune* agrees with its two rivals are those reported scored in basketball and hockey games.

The effect on the adrenal glands of the morning dip into the *Tribune*'s cosmos is amazing. The *Tribune* reader issues from his door walking on the balls of his

feet, muscles tense, expecting attacks by sex-mad foot-
pads at the next street corner, forewarned against the
smooth talk of strangers with a British accent, and
prepared to dive behind the first convenient barrier at
the sound of a guided missile approaching—any minute now—from the direction of northern Siberia.

Thus, when the World's Greatest Newspaper recently carried the headlines on its front page:

NEW TRIBUNE TYPE
EASIER ON THE EYES

SPEEDS READING; CUTS FATIGUE

to announce that it had adopted a larger body type—
8-point instead of 7—Chicagoans swiftly realized that
the change was a war measure, for another headline,
a couple of columns over, read, A-BOMB EXPLOSION
HELD SERIOUS TO 2 MILE RADIUS, and the back page
of the paper was entirely devoted to plans for the in-
stallation of atomic-bomb shelters in the Tribune
Tower, where the World's Greatest originates. The
atomic-bomb-shelter story, it seemed clear, had been
timed to coincide with the story about the new type
and the one about the two-mile radius, so that readers
racing for the protection of distance or of the Tribune
Tower would not lose time trying to decipher small
print.

In the center of the page outlining the bomb-shelter
plans was a drawing, two feet high, by Curt Gfroerer,
a staff artist, showing the Tribune Tower sliced down
the middle, with what looked like rows of dimes in the
corridors (we'll get to those later) and, next to each
floor, two sets of digits, which, a legend explained, indicated the number of refugees the floor could accom-
modate and the number expected to use it. (S.R.O. on
most floors.)

"The plans are the result of conferences of *Tribune*
department heads, based on the best scientific advice
available," the caption under Gfoerer's drawing read.
The *Tribune,* it developed, didn't care for the treatment it had received from certain potential sources of

scientific advice. "In devising the world's first atomic-bomb protection program, the *Tribune* has been compelled to rely upon its own resources," Roy Gibbons, the author of the story accompanying the drawing, wrote reproachfully. "When a *Tribune* reporter, more than two years ago, called on Maj. Gen. Leslie R. Groves and the special-weapons section of the joint chiefs of staff, he was virtually laughed out of the Pentagon Building. . . . Because of . . . the fact that the Truman administration still is withholding engineering specifications on how to build scientifically-constructed A-bomb shelters, Col. Robert R. McCormick, editor and publisher of the *Tribune,* instructed designers of the *Tribune*'s refuge areas to do the best they could with natural resources available to them." (The *Tribune* would be a likely first target for an aggressor, the Colonel doubtless had assumed, reasoning that without it the country would be simply a brained giant.) It was realized, Gibbons continued, that in the event of a hit within a crucial radius everybody in the building would probably be killed. Nevertheless, possibly acting on the artillerist Colonel's conviction that Russian gunnery is seldom what it should be, the *Tribune* proposed to go ahead anyway and line its corridors with rolls of newsprint, in order to get as much mass as possible between its employees, tenants, and reader-refugees and the radiation of the bomb. This accounted for the rows of what looked like dimes in the cross-section picture.

"Ordinarily these rolls are 5½ feet high, 40 inches wide, and weigh around 1,800 pounds," Gibbons explained. "Because objects of this size could be moved only with difficulty through doors leading to the shelter sites, Park [the *Tribune*'s production manager] received permission from Col. McCormick to have the *Tribune*'s mills at Thorold, Ont., turn out special size rolls 36 inches in diameter. The smaller rolls contain almost five miles of paper and weigh 1,550 pounds. Orders for their manufacture already have been placed, and when the rolls are received they will be stored in readily accessible places for distribution throughout Tribune Tower. . . . Under present plans, the rolls of paper would remain in storage until, for example, the present 'cold war' generates alarming heat or a warlike move indicates open hostilities may develop." Here Colonel McCormick seems to be discounting the chance of a sneak, or Pearl Harbor, type of attack with supersonic missiles." Then thousands of the rolls of paper would be moved to various shelter locations."

Should the cold war begin to get hot, the *Tribune*'s publisher is going to let his people know about it at once. "To inform the *Tribune* population and others in the neighborhood of Tribune Square that an atomic-bomb attack is imminent, a steamboat whistle soon is to be installed on the seventh floor," I learned from Gibbons's story. "The whistle to be used is 4 feet high, 10 inches in diameter, and weighs 200 pounds. It was taken from the steamship Yale [Colonel McCormick is a Yale man], a vessel constructed in 1906 by the Delaware Shipbuilding and Engine Works, Chester, Pa. . . . In tests of the whistle in the *Tribune*'s machine shops, using only 90 pounds of compressed air, it emitted an earsplitting sound."

Colonel McCormick, Gibbons continued, had suggested to officials of the Illinois Bell Telephone Company that, instead of relying upon his earsplitting whistle to warn the whole community, they ring all the telephone bells in town simultaneously—a special short ring—to signal an attack. The officials had rejected the idea (with regret, they had informed Colonel McCormick) because "under present conditions it would not be possible to accomplish multiple ringing without passing so much added current through the wires that the telephone cables would be melted."

Not the least remarkable feature of the Colonel's plan, it seemed to me, was its attention to details. "In equipping the shelters," I again quote Gibbons, "it will be necessary to provide thousands of items such as medical supplies, excavating and demolition equipment, and apparatus for extinguishing fires. Capron [manager of the Tribune Tower] has made an inventory of all these needs, *even to the number of aspirin tablets that must be stockpiled.*" It was this last demonstration of prescience, which I have italicized, that really staggered me. I would have been unable to predict even the number of headaches likely to result from an atomic-bomb attack combined with an ear-splitting whistle, or from either separately, and here was a *Tribune* man who knew, down, presumably, to the last five grains, how many aspirins would be needed to cure the unborn *Katzenjammer*.

The aspirins, the warning whistle (dating, significantly, from the administration of Theodore Roosevelt), and the rolls of paper weighing 1,550 pounds apiece (as much as 775 Sunday *Tribunes*) offer an example of the *Tribune* gift for tangibilizing a situation, to borrow a verb from Father Divine. In drawing up and announcing his unique plans for insulating the Tribune Tower's interior, he has helped to spread still further the fame of a building that he considers Chicago's chief architectural glory. All visitors to the Tribune Tower, a thirty-six-story specimen of Business Gothic, may obtain, on request, a free 64-page heavy-paper brochure telling exactly where the edifice belongs in the hierarchy of mankind's creative efforts. "Words cannot describe the beauty of the Taj Mahal," the brochure begins. "Man fails to voice the true impression of the magnitude of the Great Pyramid. To say that Tribune Tower is a stone skyscraper which is square in plan and isolated on all sides is to describe a Brahms symphony as a musical composition written for a number of instruments. To appreciate the music of this great master you must hear it. To appreciate the symphony in stone which is Tribune Tower you must see it, experience it, live in the same community with it. . . . It is an impulsive flame of beauty caught in a mold of stone!"

Chunks of older buildings that the Tribune Tower rivals—Westminster Abbey, Notre-Dame, and the Taj itself—are embedded in its façade. There are also a number of chunks from edifices of merely romantic or historic note, such as the Castle of Chillon, the Alamo, and the old General Post Office in Dublin, where the Easter Rebels defied British tyranny in

1916, as the *Tribune* has been doing since long before that.

Esthetics, however, has not been the Colonel's chief consideration in his contemplation of the Chicago Taj. "While Tribune Tower is the most beautiful commercial building in the world," the booklet states, "it is primarily the workshop of the world's greatest newspaper." So the Master of the Tower, although a renowned patron of the arts (he sponsors an hour broadcast of operetta every Saturday evening), is primarily a man of wide vision. How wide, anyone with no more than a novice's experience in *Tribune* reading could begin to guess from a piece the paper printed a couple of weeks after the publication of its defense strategy in 8-point. This was a front-page story by Walter Trohan that appeared under a Washington dateline and the heads:

PLAN DICTATOR
IF WAR WIPES
OUT CAPITAL

ARMY WOULD TAKE OVER RULE

"The defense department has plans for a military dictatorship if war should come with a devastating atomic attack upon the national capital," Mr. Trohan started off. "One of the nation's outstanding military leaders told the *Tribune* that the military will take over under disaster plans if civil government is blasted. . . . The military leader acknowledged that the military . . . can run war efficiently and economically if it is not hampered by too nice a regard for civil laws." Experts had told him, Trohan said, that "one atomic bomb, no more powerful than that which destroyed Nagasaki, would finish Washington as a useful seat of government." The *Tribune*'s plot line was becoming distinguishable: the Colonel was once again getting ready to snatch the ball as it fell from the numbed fingers of the unprepared and fumbling East and run to a touchdown, as he so often has in the past in the pages of the World's Greatest Newspaper.

Three days after Trohan's story, the *Tribune* ran an editorial headed A SLIGHT ITCH OF DICTATORSHIP. This began: "A highly-placed military leader has described to Mr. Trohan, of the *Tribune*'s Washington Bureau, the Army's 'disaster plans' under which it would take over control of civilian affairs in areas subjected to surprise attack by atomic bombs. If an atom bomb in Washington destroyed the civilian personnel of the Federal government, military control probably would be imposed on the whole nation, this officer said. This is a suicidal policy."

Decentralization is the answer, the *Tribune* concluded: let authority return to the civilian governments of the individual states and let them reconstitute a federal government. Although Colonel McCormick hasn't publicly made the offer yet, I suspect he'd be willing to let the new government take shelter behind the rolls of newsprint in the Tribune Tower, from the seventh floor of which the S.S. *Yale*'s ear-splitting whistle could function as the nation's new Liberty Bell. He is a man with a sense of destiny.

Working to tangibilize the national emergency for a younger segment of McCormick readers, Jimmy Savage, who runs a column in the *Tribune* called "Tower Ticker," has been waging an attack on what he considers an insidious, Sovietizing headdress, the babushka. This, I have learned through personal inquiry, is a colored kerchief that girls, especially schoolgirls, put over their heads and tie under their chins, producing an effect that does not strike me as specifically Russian; instead, it has a vague association with the way all immigrant women used to be dressed, in book illustrations.

"We propose a citywide burning of the babushkas!" Savage wrote one morning not long ago. "These regimenting rags, which convert pretty, young Chicago faces into moon-round parodies of peasants, have made the teen scene resemble potato digging time on a Soviet collective. Watching those farm-fresh, 4-H club visitors to the livestock show [one of Chicago's great annual winter events], we noted that not one

of them wore that sloppy substitute for headgear. . . .
Those youngsters were American farmers, too proud
of their heritage to wear the slave-scarf symbol of
European field hands. Are our Chicago kids less smart,
less proud? To the torch then, and the burning of
the babushkas!"

Five days later, the *Tribune* proudly reported the
first positive result of Savage's crusade, leading off
with "To cries of 'Down with babushkas,' 60 girls
of the senior class at Jones Commercial High School
huddled around a blazing fire in the schoolyard yesterday and heaved their bright-colored headgear into
the flames." Savage attended the burning and made
a speech. "Down with babushkas!" the *Tribune*
quoted him as crying. "Down with the slave-scarf
symbol of the steppes! To the torch, to the flames!
Down with babushkas!"

Norma Lee Browning, a *Tribune* reporter assigned
a few weeks ago to pose as a wayward girl and find
out whether Chicago has a heart, wore babushkas
most of the time as she threw herself, day after day,
on the mercy of the city. The serialized narrative of
Miss Browning's adventures began under these two-
column headlines:

WAYWARD WOMAN FINDS
CHICAGO HAS A HEART

SHE DISCOVERS FAITH AND IS GIVEN
HOPE BY UNFORTUNATES DWELLING IN
THE CITY'S SLUMS

Miss Browning's first lead was bolstered by a column of boldface citations from Luke and Matthew,
subheaded "Golden Rule," "Good Samaritan,"
"Mercy," and "Charity." Throughout her pieces, she
professed to be "seeking the truth in the poet's immortal lines: 'Alas for the rarity of Christian charity.'"
Miss Browning introduced herself by writing that she
had been instructed by her editor to learn what it
was to be alone and penniless in the cold, cruel city.
She found that it was pretty nice, and that no need

of a welfare state was indicated. The only place, in fact, that did not receive her with instantaneous warmth was, as all readers familiar with the *Tribune* undoubtedly had anticipated, the State Department of Public Welfare, "supported by taxation, not contribution," where "the reporter, dressed like an urchin," had to wait patiently for five minutes "while the Government employee finished her social telephone chat" and then "looked up, slightly bored." Miss Browning didn't even hit this relatively chill spot until the third day of her wanderings, and when she did, the Government employee she encountered there sent her to an agency that helped her—by referring her back to private charity, as any seasoned *Tribune* reader could have anticipated.

As it happened, Miss Browning brought the immortal poet up only to knock him down; she found charity everywhere—a 100 percent endorsement of the *Tribune*'s belief that, for all the ominousness surrounding Chicago, the city has a heart of gold. On her first time out, she wore "red shoes with runover heels, a short yellow dress, white sweater sleeves extending beyond the too-short sleeves of a shabby red coat, and a black straw hat adorned with huge gardenias." She also painted her face. Even so attired, she reported, "as a down-and-outer in the cold, heartless big city," she found it anything but heartless. Within three hours, she had been offered "free shelter and food, carfare, a potential job, and the friendliness of complete strangers in Chicago's Skid Row missions."

In an attempt to augment her repulsiveness, Miss Browning abandoned the black straw hat with huge gardenias and took to the babushka, which she favored in most of her subsequent forays. The results of the change were negligible. The headlines on successive stories supply a measure of her failure to repulse: "INDIGENT" GIRL FINDS FRIENDS AT EVERY TURN —"COLD CITY" WARMS TO HER WOES; WAIF IN NEED FINDS CHARITY REALLY EXISTS; PASTORS OPEN THEIR HEARTS TO SEEDY MISS; BIG CITY OPENS ITS HEART; WAIF GIVEN FOOD, JOB, HOME; and CLERGY GIVE SHABBY WAIF TRUE CHARITY.

Wearing, in the adventures chronicled in one installment, "a wrinkled babushka, faded blue coat, shabby
and too short in the sleeves, and toeless shoes with
runover heels," she had, within an hour after appealing to a minister, "found friends, food, and shelter
as an anonymous vagabond in one of the largest
cities of the world." In another installment, she told
how, "dressed as a poor, shabby woman of the
streets . . . in a wrinkled babushka and frayed coat,"
she had gone about putting the bite on a clergyman.
" 'Haven't you ever—worked?' he asked hesitantly.
. . . It was obvious he thought [the reporter] a strum-
pet." But he wished her good luck anyway and suggested that she might get a job in one of Thompson's
Restaurants. I kind of wish she had.

Two Pounds for a Dime

NOVEMBER 2, 1946

It is always salutary to find out how we look to an
acute observer from outside our own cultural area—
a De Tocqueville, an H. G. Wells, or even a Lin
Yutang. I was therefore delighted at the opportunity
to read a series of three articles by Charles Gotthart,
a Chicago *Tribune* foreign correspondent assigned
to New York, which recently ran on the front page
of the Sunday edition of the "World's Greatest Newspaper." I had been going along in my effete, Eastern
way, feeling fairly well pleased with my environment,
and then, bang!—the Gotthart trilogy arrived in a
lump, each installment embedded in a heavy Chicago
Sunday *Tribune,* all three issues bound together with
baling wire by a scout I had sent out into the Sears,
Roebuck country to trap specimens for this department. Mr. Gotthart, an accompanying note from my
scout explained, had been dispatched to New York
by his employer, Colonel Robert McCormick, to do

a series on the newspapers and magazines of the East. The headlines on the first piece read:

THE ALIEN EAST:
A THING APART
FROM AMERICA

ITS MILLIONS LOYAL TO
LANDS THEY FLED

Gazing at this simple message, I could see Mr. Gotthart (whom I pictured wearing a coonskin cap) feeling as out of place in Times Square as Ilya Ehrenburg or Konstantin Simonov, and trying to attune his ear to the harsh-sounding speech of the natives as he sized up the merchandise on the newsstands.

This article was mostly background stuff, designed to acquaint the reader back in America with the ecology of Eastern journalism. Mr. Gotthart delimited what he meant by the East at the very beginning. "Geografically speaking," he ruled, employing the Chicago *Tribune*'s simplified orthography, "the east is east of the Hudson." Having thus annexed Sneden's Landing, Woodstock, Newburgh, and Kingston to the Chicago *Tribune*'s American intellectual empire, though leaving Riverdale, Beacon, and historically blighted Hyde Park to the East, he got busy punching.

"The midwesterner who accepts the east as something apart knows from his history book that all of the seaboard states had their foundations from England," he wrote, making no shrift at all of any Dutch pretensions to a hand in settling the area. "The Tory influence was always strong in them, and in New York in particular. When the Declaration of Independence was approved by the Continental Congress in Philadelphia, the last to sign was New York—after considerable hesitation. Historians have attributed this reluctance to the fact that New York was the most strongly pro-British of the thirteen colonies. Many of the Tories exiled from the seaboard states for treasonable attempts to hamper the Revolution returned afterward. In New York City they have remained dominant. Those who pushed across the mountains became purely American, but those who remained on the seacoast never did. . . . In the entire country, three out of every ten persons are foreign born or the children of foreign born. In New York the proportion is six out of ten." Consulting United States census figures, I discover that in Chicago it is also six out of ten.

In his second article Mr. Gotthart introduced the story that British influence still fouls the alien Eastern press. The headlines on this one were:

ONCE GREAT N.Y.
PAPERS HIT NEW
LOW IN ESTEEM

REPLACE PATRIOTISM
WITH ANGLOMANIA

At the outset Mr. Gotthart made one rather grudging concession to our papers. "With all its shortcomings, the eastern press is still superior to that of England, where journalism is not acknowledged of equal rank with other professions," he admitted; and somewhat later he added, "In New York there is a barrier between newspaper owners and workers not found in the west, but even so, the city's reporters are vastly better off than their British brothers, who call themselves 'journalists,' and who have to use the back entrances and servants' stairs because they are not accorded equal rank with other professions." By coming out into the open with all this, Mr. Gotthart called attention to a lamentable state of affairs which I became aware of while living in London in 1941 but which I was not allowed to mention because of wartime censorship. In those days, whenever American correspondents went into London pubs with English "journalists" they had befriended, they were compelled, by social law, to leave these ragged, low-caste acquaintances in the three-ales bar, where there were shavings on the floor, while they themselves went into the saloon lounge, where there was a carpet. One of my own English-press protégés, a man on the *News Chronicle,* had to rise before dawn every morning to soap his publisher's hunting boots. Another had to serve his publisher tiffin when the old man clapped his hands three times. To clinch his argument that the press is discriminated against in Britain, Mr. Gotthart pointed out that English publishers, when they are made peers, seldom get anything higher than a viscountcy. "Viscount," he added acridly, "is the title given unsuccessful soldiers like Generals French, Montgomery, and Alexander."

All this had the tone of a man who intended to make no other concessions, but Colonel McCormick's nuncio, surprisingly, reported that he found the Eastern daily press in pretty good shape: "The *Sun* and the *World-Telegram* now reflect all of the best in the eastern rich, a characteristic also of the *Times,* which presents the best of the eastern point of view and extends its influence well beyond New York City. . . . The New York masses are reached by the Hearst papers—*Journal-American* and *Mirror*—and by the Sunday and Daily *News,* the phenomenally successful tabloid, all of which reflect the midwestern and western origin of their publishers." This, I took it, meant that the Chicago *Tribune* had given its imprimatur to six of the nine major New York dailies, with a total of 4,994,238 circulation out of the city's 5,763,444 circulation. I had always feared that most New York newspapers were editorially out of bounds, from a Chicago *Tribune* point of view, and I was pleased to discover that so many of them were acceptable.

Mr. Sulzberger, the publisher of the *Times,* may have been less pleased, because shortly after the Gotthart series appeared, the *Times* sent Felix Belair, Jr., out to Chicago to write a comical interview with Colonel McCormick. It looked like an attempt to get him to withdraw his endorsement. But perhaps Mr. Sulzberger never even saw the Gotthart series and I am just reading meanings into the Belair interview.

It was then revealed that the New York papers of which Gotthart disapproved were the *Herald Tribune, PM,* and the *Post* (plus the *Daily Worker,* which he included just for laughs). The *Tribune* (the alien-Eastern one), he said was an "anglomaniac supporter of all 'causes' intended to promote the British empire," and he had an unanswerable explanation of how it got that way. It is the product of a merger of the old *Herald* and the old *Tribune*. James Gordon Bennett, Jr., who inherited the *Herald* from his father, was "horsewhipped by his fiancée's brother after his engagement was broken off in 1877. Thereafter he lived abroad. . . . The *Herald* became completely a British newspaper (it was violently pro-war in 1914) and has remained pro-British ever since." As for the pre-merger *Tribune,* it belonged to the Reid family, as it still does, and "in promoting internationalism under the influence of worship for everything pertaining to the British nobility, whom they fawn upon, the Reids have aligned themselves with domestic crackpots who have become expert in the art of smearing American citizens." You put two papers like that together and what have you got?

Mr. Gotthart has little to say of the *Post*'s motivation, but he does call it "a vicious paper, reflecting mental turpitude."

The headlines over his third story read:

REAL AMERICA
A MYSTERY TO
PAPERS IN EAST

BRITISH-RED BIFOCAL
VIEW NO HELP

This, one might assume, referred only to the three excommunicated papers, but most of the space beneath it was devoted to magazines. Mr. Gotthart bore down harder on the Eastern weeklies than on the newspapers, possibly because the weeklies have a larger circulation in the Chicago *Tribune*'s territory.

"The pattern of Anti-Americanism is found again in such magazines," he writes, "as the Luce trio: *Time, Life,* and *Fortune;* in *Look, New Republic,* the *Nation,* and *New Masses;* and considerable pink has colored the political complexion of *Collier's,* the *Saturday Evening Post,* and *Harper's.* . . . *Life,* most successful of the Henry Robinson Luce periodicals, heads the procession of 'cheesecake' magazines. . . . *Life* frequently publishes lengthy textual matter to justify its sex appeal photografs and drawings." I noticed that the *Tribune* uses the spelling "photograf," though the *News* has an inquiring "Fotographer," and wondered whether it was a difference over how to spell this word that for ten years had come between the *Tribune* publisher and his cousin, the late Captain Patterson. But I was glad, in any event, that someone had offered an explanation for the text in *Life.*

When Mr. Gotthart got on to the *Saturday Evening Post* and *Collier's,* he made what I was quick to recognize as a major contribution to the apparatus of criticism. "Pink has colored the formerly great weeklies of large circulation—the *Saturday Evening Post* and *Collier's,*" the Man from America wrote, restating his thesis. "Lacking in qualities inspired by the midwest brand of Americanism, these weeklies fail to offer their readers anything remotely approaching the physical content of a good Sunday newspaper. The CHICAGO SUNDAY TRIBUNE, for example, weighs 32 *ounces; these magazines, five.*" The italics are mine; I use them because I immediately realized that Gotthart had discovered a tangible basis for the appraisal of journalistic values, and, what was equally important, a procedure for its application. Under Gotthart's Law, it was no longer necessary to read a publication in order to evaluate its contents. It was enough to weigh it. There had been no comparable boon to humanity since the discovery of anesthesia. I raced to the laboratory and, picking up the first magazine to come to hand, the then current issue of *The New Yorker,* I threw it on the scales. I was slightly chagrined to find that it weighed but ten ounces, which put it in the same relation to the Sunday *Tribune* as a panfish is to a two-pound sucker. It was scant consolation that, as I directly ascertained, the *Morning Telegraph* weighed only five and a half ounces, *Marvel Comics* three, and *Laff* three and a half. *A Daily*

Worker I borrowed from the polo editor weighed but two ounces, a figure that should assure Colonel Mc-Cormick. But when I placed the latest Sunday *Times* on the scales, I began to wonder whether the *Tribune* proprietor would stand by *la méthode Gotthart*. The *Times* weighed two pounds and fifteen ounces, exceeding the *Tribune* cited by Gotthart by just one ounce less than a pound.

I then weighed a Chicago Telephone Directory for June, 1943, the latest available in the laboratory. It came to four pounds, fourteen ounces. A Manhattan Telephone Directory weighed three pounds, eight ounces; a Brooklyn one, two pounds, five ounces; a Queens one, a pound, twelve and a half ounces; a Bronx one, a pound, five and a half ounces. Aggregate for the city, exclusive of Richmond, whose directory I couldn't find in the laboratory: eight pounds, fifteen ounces, or as much as the Chicago Telephone Directory and *two complete Sunday Tribunes* combined; I didn't know what to make of these findings until I decided that Mr. Gotthart might have had in mind the division of publications into weight classes, like boxers or game chickens. *The New Yorker* may be O.K., after all, for a welterweight periodical. I hope so.

Post Scriptum: Pursuing the subject of weights, I have just learned from the Museum of Natural History that Mr. Gotthart's brain, if of normal size, weighs approximately forty-nine ounces, or as much as one complete Sunday *Tribune* and the news, sports, theater, and first advertising sections of a second.

The publication of Mr. Gotthart's *grande inchiesta* provoked no demonstrations in front of the Chicagoese Consulate here, possibly because nobody in New York was strong enough to lift a copy of the Chicago Sunday *Tribune,* much less read it—I used a block and tackle in my own manipulation of the formidable co-agulation of agglutinated sapience.

When I, innocently retracing the path of Mr. Gotthart's plane, attempted a simple reportage upon Chicago four years later, however, its appearance in *The New Yorker* produced an effect like dropping a whole bottle of Eno's sparkling salts into a goldfish bowl. Of the letters I received I append only one mild example, which I subsequently reproduced in the preface of "Chicago: The Second City," a book made from *The New Yorker* pieces, published in 1952. The book is out of print, but still survives as an ectoplasmic itch, causing Chicagoans even now to scratch themselves. It was intended as a soothing ointment, but they are hard to soothe.

It is, and most apparently so, that Chicago is not what is should or could be. It is not, however, in need of more bitter criticizing, rather in need of intelligent aid at the front.

I should like to know Mr. Lieblings true humanitarian capacity—if any! It is hardly likely that he throws automobile tires at his wife, beats same, plus children,—nor would he, upon encountering a person of lowest circumstances,—"a beggar on the street" (New York version),—"a bum" (Chicago version) and quite the more vivid and descriptive term—probably be captured with the near obsession of just how he could lead this be-beggared one into still further depths of any worse condition which might be possible to bring about.—It is entirely enough that there are now, so many others, world wide, who are only too willing to trample any of the falling, hesitant, or be-clouded—without dwelling so long, hard and sarcastically upon such an abundance of dowdy and brutal remarks, which in the end, are certainly not much of a shock to anyone. . . .

Is Mr. Liebling forming a "Be Nasty to Chicago Club"??? Is he perhaps trying to gain followers—those who are also inclined towards sarcasium, slicing throats.—Or is he by some maddening theme—perhaps without knowing, himself endeavoring to inspire helpful people to action at the

Chicago front!! If this is so and I almost entirely doubt such a pleasant ulterior motive, then I should adore to board the next plane possible and be first in line to tenderly and encouragingly grasp the hand of Mr. Liebling as he staggers (I hope) backward from reading such reactionaries as this one of many of which he must be in recipience daily!

Leave us not without exception, stamp on the discarded cigarette—if it is out, it's quite ridiculous.—

Sincerely,

A first emotional letter to the editors writer.

That the discarded cigarette of resentment is *not* yet out was borne in on me five years later, when I visited Vassar for a couple of weeks as a living inspiration to student writers. While the majority of the girls thought I was fine, I found in nearly every section one or two sullen beauties who scowled throughout the period and waited for me at the door when the class broke up.

"Oh, Mr. Liebling," they would say, "how could you write such awful things about Chicago!"

What flattered me about this was that these girls could have been no more than 13 or 14 years old when the stories appeared, and had probably never read them. The resentment had been transmitted to them by their parents, a tribute to the durability of the itch I had implanted.

I would say to each of these pouting charmers: "You're not from Chicago, you're from Winnetka, or Lake Forest," and it always turned out so. The people who most resent reporting on Chicago are those who wouldn't be found dead there after dark. They inhabit the better-cushioned suburbs, where, if Chicago should ever revolt against its squalor, it couldn't tax them.

My living monument in the Colonel's once-domain is a nightclub named, after my book, The Second City, set up, in 1959, nine years after my departure, to refute what some natives have interpreted as my aspersions on their wit. If I went there they would serve me a Mickey Finn.

The following report is from the Chicago *Daily News,* August 4, 1960:

SECOND CITY

Less than a year ago, a new entertainment venture opened in the Old Town area, with the ironic title, "Second City." The name was taken from A. J. Liebling's sneering "profile" of Chicago in the New Yorker magazine a few years ago.

Proving once again that Chicago has an almost inexhaustible fund of talent, "Second City" became an immediate success, attracting national attention with its sardonic skits and its off-beat commentary on the contemporary scene.

The readers of the 1,600-odd newspapers who depend entirely on the two surviving press associations for their foreign coverage are in the position of motorists on a state throughway that is served only by Howard Johnson restaurants. What they get will not make them eager for more.

It is not hard, therefore, for the newspapers to satisfy their appetite for foreign news, and for editors and publishers both, at annual conventions of their peer-groups, to say that they already use more press association stuff on foreign countries than their readers want. Of the stories papers do run, a considerable proportion are simple human-interest yarns that have happened in Norway or Yugoslavia but might just as well have occurred in New Jersey—quadruplets, say, or mass murders. Others are on a favorite theme— what foreigners think of us and our gifts to civilization. We are passionately interested in ourselves, and all press-association correspondents regularly file a story called "Mirror, mirror on the wall/Who are the fairest ones of all?" It cannot miss, because if the anonymous aliens interpellated say, "You Americans, who else?" it is gratifying and increasingly unusual. Most papers will use it, and the hard-boiled Chicago

Trib type of editorialist can comment that they are sucking up to us for a loan. If, however, they say "Us Arabs"—or Europeans, or Koreans—it proves what a dirty lot they have turned out to be. Most papers will use it, and the editorialist can then renumerate all the scraps of food we have thrown their way, as evidence of how hopeless it is to be kind to jerks.

The following specimen, from *The New Yorker* of September 6, 1947, will serve as an illustration of a genre that seldom varies much. It is about the press associations' favorite foreign character, "the little man."

A British crisis began, according to our two largest press associations, when the Labour Government imposed a 75 percent tax on the net earnings of American films imported into Britain. An Associated Press man, writing under a London dateline of August 8, announced, "The icy wind of the economic crisis blew smack down the neck of the British little man—and his little wife—today with the news that no more Hollywood movies would be crossing the Atlantic. You can water his beer, up the price of his cigarettes, cut his candy ration, and still the little man who dodged the buzz bombs will grumble, grin, shrug, and carry on. But deprive him of his weekly bath of celluloid and glamour![1]

" 'This is the last straw!' declared the wife of an electrician. 'Going to the films is the only recreation I have. If they take away American films— well, I'm patriotic and all that, but there's nobody like Clark Gable in British pictures.' "

---

[1] Time, Inc., as one might expect, maintains the largest stable of little people, all anonymous and often quartered in pubs. Let a Time man ask, "And what do you think of free medical service?" and a little man in a pub will pop up and shout: "It's all a bloody fraud Guvnor 'Ip, 'ip, 'urray for 'arley Street, wot tikes such good care of us perishers for three guineas a consultyshun! And put in a good word for Chiang Kai-shek, Guv, whoile you're at it. 'E's our favorite Hamerican stoitsman."

The *News,* in which I read this alarming dispatch, ran it under the headline: WHAT! NO CLARK GABLE? CRISIS IN ENGLAND'S A REAL CRISIS NOW.

Thinking back on the time I spent in England during the war, I could not recall any dominating attachment of the British to American films. In those days, Britons seemed to take beer and cigarettes more seriously than slush, and also seemed not to be in need of looking at any more bloodshed than the Luftwaffe thoughtfully provided them with. But I decided that they must have changed. The A.P. man, being on the scene, was in a position to know better than I.

The *Post* that afternoon confirmed the story of British despair carried by the *News.* The *Post*'s item was also an A.P. product and, although datelined a day later, bore certain similarities to the earlier dispatch. The headline was: "LAST STRAW," CRY BRITONS ON LOSS OF U.S. MOVIES.

"Britain's economic crisis," the text began, "was brought home sharply to the ordinary man and woman today with news that they could no longer seek escape from their troubles in Hollywood movies." I was glad to note that the A.P. correspondent had removed the icy wind from down the little people's necks, and I pressed on in the hope of finding that their plight had been in other ways bettered since the filing of the dispatch in the *News.* The *Post*'s A.P. report continued: "Some Britons, already short on food, beer, and other consumer goods, were irate to hear that they were to be deprived altogether of Hollywood films. 'This is the last straw!' said an engineer's wife. 'Going to the films is the only recreation I have—and if they take away American films . . . well, I'm patriotic and all that, but there's nobody like Clark Gable in British pictures.'"

I found it a little odd that the engineer's wife in the *Post* story shared so completely the taste, and even the language, of the electrician's wife in the *News,* but decided that it was due to the drab sameness of all little people, as quoted by big newspapermen.

During the next couple of days, I suffered damnably, though vicariously, with the British people, little, big, and middle-sized, especially when I happened on a United Press dispatch in the *Journal-American* that stated, in part: "British moviegoers face the bleak prospect of never seeing Amber in her marathon amours." The head over this read: U.S. BAN DISMAYS BRITISH FILM FANS.

"The news that no new American movies would be sent to Britain to be subject to the 75 per cent tax on their earnings brought the economic crisis home to the fans with dismaying impact," the story continued. "A streamer headline in the *Evening Standard* said: 'Forever Amber and Joan of Arc may never be seen in London.'"

For a while, the only relief was afforded by Louella O. Parsons, motion-picture editor of the International News Service. "A bright spot in the dark movie news over the levy of the British tax is that Darryl Zanuck has bought the film rights to the life of William S. Hart," Miss Parsons wrote. For me, this was not quite enough. I was heartened, therefore, and also just a trifle astonished, to read in the *Herald Tribune* of August 12, over a London story by Don Cook,[2] the headline: BRITISH PUBLIC INDIFFERENT TO HOLLYWOOD BAN.

"Most comment on the government's action has been laudatory," Mr. Cook wrote. "There has been no editorial demanding for any relaxation. . . . The *Evening News* today conducted a man-in-the-street

[2] Cook is one of the best U.S. correspondents.

poll, and while the question admittedly was a leading one, 'Do you prefer British or American films?' the results were interesting. Only two people out of twenty said they preferred American pictures. The reporter added that 'nearly all were agreed that the loss of American second-feature rubbish would be a good thing.' "

Faced with a choice between the *Herald Tribune*'s and the press associations' version of British public reaction, I allowed myself to be governed by my memory of what Britons are like and by what I know of their present situation. And somehow, I found myself thinking of a comic police inspector in a British film I had happened to see a few days before. "Scotland Yard, I'm afraid," the inspector says deprecatingly when he introduces himself. "Poppycock, I'm afraid," I decided that I should have to say to the news associations.

The coverage of this British dilemma made me wonder about the quality of news coverage we should get if all newsgathering in foreign parts were left to the press associations. At present, if you live in New York, you have your choice of several newspapers and can decide for yourself which of their writers to believe. It is an extremely limited choice, but still an appreciable one. If you live in one of our smaller cities, where publishers don't feel that they can afford to send correspondents overseas, you have no choice at all, because the press associations have you free and clear.[3]

Variants of this story are "German Girls Say Yanks Make (Best, Worst, Lazy) Husbands"; "G.I.'s Say European Girls (Dumb, Best, Make Best Wives)"; "Hot

---

[3] Since this was written the New York *Evening Post* has closed its London bureau, reducing New Yorkers' choices slightly. (The *Post* had one man there.) *PM* and its successor, the *Star*, which used to print the very good London correspondence of Frederick Kuh, have disappeared, narrowing the choice still further. The staffs of all the bureaus are being steadily reduced.

Dogs Big Hit in Persia"; "Arabs Like American Cars"
—in fact, you can do it yourself. Between filing the
human-interest bits he finds in local papers and this
narcissistic junk and a few things that actually happen
—change of government, for example—the press-
association man has neither time nor encouragement
to learn or write about the essential nature of the
country to which he is assigned. Big news, whether
of a revolt in Algeria or of a Guatemalan purchase of
Communist arms, always comes as a colossal surprise
to the reader (who has never been told even that the
Algerians are angry, or that the Guatemalan Government, a Socialist affair, first has been refused permission to buy arms here.)

This helps keep all matters of foreign policy, as far
as the captive newspaper audience is concerned, a
distasteful mystery. The Associated Press, in angry
refutation of a charge by a Fund for the Republic man
a week or so ago, said it had *80* full-time correspondents abroad, instead of 60, the figure he gave, and
that it had, besides, 140 full-time foreign native correspondents in capitals abroad. This is, with a ven-
geance, the story of the handful of fishermen and leaky
boats. There are 99 member nations of the U.N.O.,
besides a couple of sandlot states, like China, that
cannot get in. This works out to one correspondent
for every nation-and-a-quarter, although there are
some countries, like Great Britain, Russia, and Japan,
that it would strain the capacities of a man-and-a-
quarter to cover. Naturally, with four-fifths of a man
doing, say, India, a lot of nuances get lost.

As to the foreign stringers, since their necks are in
imminent danger if they deviate from the Government
line in many countries, and their livelihoods are in
peril if they do so in others, it is the Government line
that they stick to. This is one strong reason why the
American press seems to foreigners always to be on
the side of the party that is in.

From Batista to Salazar to Syngman Rhee, whoever
is in power is reflected in the fragmentary mirrors of
the American press as a "grand old man," "the father
of his people," who, the informants confide, are not

educated up to democracy. This is not because American newspapermen are easy to fool, or even because the member publishers of the Associated Press in America favor Batistas and Salazars. (They might if they knew who they were, but the last is unlikely.) It is because American newspapermen are not present, except occasionally, between planes, to send a spot dispatch. The men in the field often, indeed generally, know a great deal more than they ever have occasion to write, but they have no time, and no instructions, to dig in and confirm the evidence of their eyes and ears.

The stringers themselves are often the source of excellent tips and leads, for they are seldom in sympathy with the regimes they must live under. This is a characteristic of the newspaperman in an authoritarian environment. But they take risks even in hinting. I knew at least one in North Africa who got hit on the head because the regime suspected him of such private confidences.

The small bits of news we get out of most foreign countries are, thus, by a margin of 140 to 80 just what their governments want to send. To make matters a bit worse, the "minor" countries, in which the press association is sure to be represented only by natives are, in general, precisely the countries most likely to be under the thumbs of benevolent army officers or Uncle-Tom kings. A Britisher, for example, would not labor under the same disadvantages if he represented an American paper in England, as an Egyptian who represented it in Egypt.

There was a time, that lasted most of the way through the nineteenth century, when American newspapers, more numerous and competitive, but distinctly less rich than today, retained literate citizens who were resident in a foreign land or were going abroad, on their own affairs, to write about the countries they had opportunity to study. This was a simple and relatively inexpensive process. The man used his legs, his eyes, his judgment, and a pen.

In time, his letter arrived at the office of his employer in New York, or Boston, Cincinnati, or Hartford, and when the editor had an appropriate amount of space available he shoved it in. I do not pretend to have spent my life among old newspaper files, but in the course of looking up old stories I have hit on, and lost myself in, examples of this kind of correspondence that make even "interpretive" reporting today look sketchy.

This is a cheap expedient, perhaps more available today than ever, because more Americans seem to go abroad, and it provides an individuality of approach that a paper never gets if it must depend solely on a syndicate. Often, in the old days, I am sure, the paper in Hartford or Charleston got a better picture of the events in Schleswig-Holstein or the Caucasus than the big paper in New York, simply because it had a more intelligent letter-writer. (This was, of course, the original meaning of correspondent; the full-time kind came later.)

It is more essential, and usually more interesting, to understand what is going on somewhere else than to apprehend the outside world exclusively through news flashes that mean nothing to you when you read them, and to which you are indifferent *because* they mean nothing.

The transatlantic cable and the successive speed-ups of communications that followed knocked news values askew—the emphasis was displaced from information to speed, until for one newspaper or news service to beat its competitor by 13 minutes became more of a triumph than to have a better story. This substitution of a duel in mechanics for one in intelligence is the essence of an age: the fidelity of reproduction takes precedence over the merit of the music, the speed of transmission over the accuracy of news. Luckily the Russians are of the same mind as we are about this. The cold war, in its most publicized aspect, has become a competition in gadgetry, like a weight-lifting contest: who can put how many pounds of metal how high?

Neither party, while both are so preoccupied, will venture the introduction of a new thought, which would be stigmatized as a sneak punch.

In the newspaper game 1918 was the year that sealed the pre-eminence of speed over thought. Roy Howard of the United Press reported the end of World War I three days early, and instead of getting the sack, rose to heights seldom scaled in his industry. It was an omen.

The competition in speed in which both are engaged keeps the correspondents of the Associated Press and United Press International locked closely, like the escaped convicts, one white, one black, shackled together in a recent motion picture. In a great many instances it cancels both out, since neither can stray from the source of handouts for fear that the other will get one while he is away trying to see what goes on.

The two press associations, however, represent the maximum collective effort and expense that the American publishers are likely to put forward in the field of foreign news. There is constant pressure from most of them, as A.P. members and as U.P.I. customers, to cut *down* on the free lunch, because it is better than the bums deserve.

* * *

The lazy mind, faced by recurrent but changing problems, takes refuge in a formula. This may be a religion, a pill, or a system for playing the horses. When dullness is compounded with avarice, it is even surer to happen. The farmer who won't see a doctor takes Carter's Little Liver Pills for every ailment. The bettor who has neither the imagination to see nor the intelligence to treat every race as a new problem, buys for $5 a "system," based on progression in wagering, or track condition, or astrology.

Nothing so infuriates the dullard as the failure of his formula, which always occurs. Nothing so delights me as the spectacle, if I am safely clear of the wreckage. I find no ballad more exhilarating than the one about the railroad train that blew, she blew, with its delightfully detailed description of the individual consequences: the flagman, for example, who rolled on the grass, and where his flagpole lodged. When one is a passenger on the train, though, it is less amusing, and we are all dependent on this rambling wreck of an industry for our sense of direction.

The formulas most newspapers have fallen back on for foreign news are few. One is, "Man go to church, good man, no lie. Man not go to church, bad, lie." Ergo "Franco, Salazar, Adenauer, Christian Democrats, good truthful. Communists, bad, whatever they say lie." In handling any story outside the United States, then, it is necessarily true, and you have solved your problem in reporting without trouble or expense.

Thus, as an example of formula thinking, if Sicilians riot because living conditions are ghastly, and a Communist leader says, later, "Look at Sicily, living conditions are ghastly," then *living conditions cease to be ghastly.* By agreeing with *any* charge the Communist takes the truth out of it, first, because he is trying to turn it to his own advantage—which, to revert for a moment to nonformula sanity, has not one thing to do with whether it is true or not—second, because even if it were not true it would be to his advantage, so he would invent it. It is therefore a lie, because (a) Communists are liars, they do not go to church, and (b) they invented it. And the Sicilians themselves are liars, because they allowed the Communists to agree with them, thus putting themselves in the position of people who agree with liars. How can you agree truthfully on what is necessarily a lie?

The thing to do for anybody whom a Communist agrees with is to retract his original statement. Else he becomes a fellow-traveler. You are on a train and a Communist gets on. That makes you a fellow-traveler just as much as if the Communist were on the train first and *you* got on.

A second formula is that *all* trouble is the fault of Communists. Trouble means anything like Cubans getting mad because American sailors make water on a statue; they wouldn't have been so particular if Communists hadn't put them up to it. Communists were undoubtedly mixed up in that movie story, too. It was

Communistic not to like Clark Gable. No surer test, except maybe hot dogs and hamburgers and miyulk. Anybody that would rather drink wine than miyulk is a Red, sure as the Chicago *Tribune* is the World's Greatest Newspaper.

These and a couple of allied formulas eliminate the trouble of finding out what the hell is going on, which a number of troublemakers used to say was part of the function of a newspaper. They save money, too. Or perhaps, to preserve the order of importance of these points to newspaper owners, I should switch the two preceding sentences around.

The following exhibit, now fifteen years old, serves as a good example of the formula approach, and its sequelae lend themselves to brief study.

Antipenultimatum

SEPTEMBER 7, 1946

Journalists, and particularly the fellows who write for the press associations, have a habit of using the strongest word they can think of in the lead of a story, even when the word really means something else. Headline writers often base their eye-smackers on the strongest word in the lead. That's the only excuse I can find for the use of the word "ultimatum" by every New York newspaper on Thursday, August 22, to describe the note sent by the United States to the government of Yugoslavia the day before. It was a conspicuously civilized note, telling the Yugoslavs that if they didn't turn loose the surviving occupants of two American planes shot down by them, the United States would complain to the Security Council of the United Nations. This message, to me, marked a great advance in relations between governments—an advance in a class with that of an individual who, instead of threatening to break an irritating neighbor's neck, tells him he will swear out a summons and hale him into court. An ultimatum, I had always understood, is a threat to break the neck, and no country, or man, can submit to one without loss of self-respect. Serbia received an ultimatum from Austria in 1914.

So when I saw the lead on Jay Reid's *Herald Tribune* story, "The United States Government today served an ultimatum on Yugoslavia," and the *News* headline ULTIMATUM GIVES TITO 48 HOURS TO FREE FLYERS (based on an Associated Press story beginning, "In an angry ultimatum . . ."), and the *Mirror*'s YUGOS GET U.S. ULTIMATUM (built on an International News Service story beginning, "The United States served a forty-eight-hour ultimatum . . ."), I felt that we had left the diving board and would hit the surface of the third World War any second. As soon as I read the text of the note itself, I felt a whole lot better. There must have been millions of people, however, who didn't read the note, newspaper reading being as perfunctory as it is, and these millions must have spent the next day or so in a Pearl Harborish gloom.

Even the *Times* story by Anthony Leviero, who is ordinarily a conscientious chap, had "ultimatum" in the second paragraph. The three-line, eight-column banner across the front page of the *Times* said, U.S. GIVES BELGRADE 48 HOURS TO FREE FLYERS OR FACE ACTION BEFORE U.N. SECURITY COUNCIL; REJECTS RUSSIAN SHARE IN STRAITS DEFENSE. That seemed to me tying the note to Yugoslavia rather closely with one to Russia about the Dardanelles, as if the two were facets, and comparable facets, of the same dispute. Whatever I thought of Russia's ancient pretension to Constantinople, I didn't think it was an outrage—whereas I thought the killing of our fliers was—or that, considered separately, it would have rated more than a one-column head on a dull day.

The *Sun,* that afternoon, carried an eight-column head, U.S. SET FOR SHOWDOWN ON YUGOSLAV ULTIMATUM, which made it look, at first glance, as if Marshal Tito had sent an ultimatum to *us.* The *World-Telegram,* often one step ahead of the rest of the world in looking for trouble, had a first-page streamer announc-

ing, TITO REPORTED SET TO DEFY U.S. ULTIMATUM ON
AIRMEN. It wasn't ahead of the *Post* this time, however, for that paper proclaimed, SPOKESMAN SAYS TITO
TO SNUB ULTIMATUM. The heads were based on United
Press stories, datelined London and Belgrade, that
quoted "an informed Yugoslav spokesman." In both
cases he turned out to be ill-informed. *PM* also used
the word "ultimatum" in the lead of its story, supplied by the Chicago *Sun* syndicate.

The *Daily Worker* used a United Press story about
an ultimatum. (It is strange to think of Roy Howard
accepting Moscow gold, but the United Press is a
profit-making service.) It also carried a covey of
headlines, among them UNITED STATES SWINGS "BIG
STICK" *and* U.S. THREATENS YUGOSLAVIA IN NEW NOTE,
with leads such as "Secretary of State James F. Byrnes
took a hand in the 'crisis' manufactured over the
American violation of Yugoslav sovereignty yesterday." (Next day, Friday, the *Worker* performed the
remarkable squiggle of filling three pages with squawks
about the "ultimatum" with only one obscure reference to the fact that some Americans had been killed
before the note was dispatched.)

A fairly late edition of the Thursday *Journal-American* managed to change its headline to TITO RELEASES
YANKS, ACTS AFTER U.S. ULTIMATUM and to insert a
bulletin to that effect, but it had not had time to
change its lead on the story, which remained "London,
Aug. 22 (I.N.S.)—Yugoslav sources in London predicted today Marshal Tito will reject the U.S. forty-
eight-hour ultimatum on Yugoslavian armed action
against American aircraft." (The I.N.S. seems to have
discovered the same Yugoslav source as the United
Press—perhaps a member of the anti-Tito ex-govern-
ment in exile.)

After reading newspapers about the "ultimatum"
all day, I began to wonder whether I *did* know what
the word meant. It was as if I were in one of those
dreams in which familiar words become dissociated
from their usual meanings, or as if I were listening to
Whitey Bimstein talk double-talk. So I got down a
ninety-five-cent dictionary which I bought one time in

a cigar store and which gives only one meaning for each word, and that the commonest one; it is an excellent guide to everyday usage. It says, "Final conditions offered as the basis of an agreement, prior to the declaration of hostilities"—which is how I have always used "ultimatum." Only in part reassured, I carried my research to Webster's unabridged, which says, "A final proposition or condition; esp., the final propositions, or terms, offered by either of the parties in a diplomatic negotiation; the best terms that a negotiator will offer, the rejection of which usually ends negotiations." It was evident in the note to Yugoslavia, though, that the United States contemplated further negotiations, via the United Nations, in the event of a rejection. To make surer than sure, I went to the 13-volume Oxford Dictionary. It defines "ultimatum" as "In diplomacy, the final terms presented by one power or (group of powers) to another, the rejection of which may lead to the severing of diplomatic relations, and eventually to a declaration of war." The rejection of the note to Tito could have led immediately only to a complaint to an international tribunal, and while that might have eventually led to a break, and that to war, the note could at worst have been described as no more than a kind of antepenultimatum.

The appearance of the word "ultimatum" in all the stories makes it look, I freely grant, as if the papers had some common excuse for its use—perhaps permission from a State Department public-relations official who, asked at a press conference "if it is all right to call this thing an ultimatum," may have answered, "Sure, boys, go ahead." But public-relations men do not originate meanings for words; nor, fortunately, do they compose the diplomatic communications that pass between the United States and other governments.

I fear that I detected, in their taking the gloomiest possible view of the situation, a certain eagerness on the part of most of the newspapers. The *Times,* for example, in attempting to chart for its readers the probable course of events, interviewed the Premiers of Italy and Greece—two countries on the outs with

Yugoslavia. It also carried a long dope story by Herbert Matthews, who said that "the violent incident with the Yugoslavs is considered in these [diplomatic] circles as merely the beginning of a long series of incidents calculated to maintain the tension." The "circles," the "well-informed spokesman," and all the other anonymously ominous sources had a clambake. The *Mirror,* on Friday, went as far as to express editorial regret that the American note had mentioned the United Nations and implied an even more profound sorrow that the Yugoslavs had complied with its terms.

Marshal Tito, whose unfortunate photographic resemblance to the pre-Nuremberg Göring was impressed that week on newspaper readers as never before, did nothing throughout the incident to win international esteem. His complaint, reported in the papers of August 26, after he had yielded up his prisoners, that "a hundred and ten American aircraft, ninety-one of them warplanes," had flown over Yugoslavia between August 9, when his men shot down the first unarmed transport, and August 19, when they dropped the second, set one musing about the fiery, unbridled temperament, as the Yugoslav apologists called it, of an air force that passed up ninety-one potential opponents to await one safe target.

The complaint also set me, personally, to remembering a fellow I knew who was killed quite a while back, during the war, while riding in an American transport plane over the territory of a country with which we were not at war. I have always considered him, like the five boys in the second American plane shot down over Yugoslavia, the victim of a cowardly and malicious act. The transport, a lumbering C-47, like the jobs shot down by the South Slavs, could not possibly have been mistaken for a bomber or a light, fast photo-reconnaissance plane. The pilot had lost his way while flying across some mountains and thought he was over an American field, so he started to land. When he was 150 feet from the ground, the fiery, unbridled heroes who were jealously protecting *their* sovereignty cut loose with a machine gun. One of the bullets went through the head of this man I knew, a radio correspondent—he was a French-Canadian and an obliging sort—whom I last had seen in Algiers, acting as spokesman for a group of correspondents in a long squabble with General Giraud. The shooting took place on January 25, 1943, over Spanish territory in North Africa, and the plane was on its way from Algiers to the Casablanca Conference, carrying a full load of war correspondents. The pilot managed to get away from the field, though his plane was full of holes, and to make French Morocco. I didn't see any American newspapers, since I was in Africa myself then, but I had always assumed that the shooting must have caused great indignation in the United States. The other day I looked into the files of the *Times* to see how the newspapers in 1943 had handled this incident, and this is the full, and the only, story I found (with a one-line head of minimal size):

CANADIAN BROADCASTER KILLED

Mrs. Edouard Baudry has been advised of the death of her husband, thirty-three-year-old Canadian Broadcasting Corporation correspondent, in North Africa. It was learned here today that Mr. Baudry was killed by anti-aircraft fire when the plane in which he was a passenger flew off its course and appeared over Spanish Morocco.

News values seem to depend very largely upon who does the shooting.

The last sentence remains one of the basic truths of journalism. There are counties in the South, for example, where if a white man shoots a Negro it doesn't even rate inclusion in local notes. On the international scene, the 20,000 shootings by Batista got considerably less space than the 700 by Castro that followed Batista's un-shot exit, and other examples are not hard to find. In Palestine border incidents between the first war there and the Suez invasion, for instance, Arab casualties were considerably higher than Israeli, yet the news services disseminated a contrary impression.

The reader's reaction to the above story, I hope, will include a brief gasp of horror at the notion of what might have happened if the State Department had allowed itself to be pushed into sending a *real* ultimatum.

The Yugoslavs, in 1946, were outwardly orthodox, Stalinist, Moscow-line Communists. Underneath the surface, though, they were resisting pressure and preparing the split of 1948. Had we broken off relations with them, we would have forced them back into complete dependence on the U.S.S.R., and so prevented the Soviet Union's greatest single defeat. By 1948, when he moved, Tito had been able to assure himself of Western support, and in return for it he closed his Greek border, cutting off the Greek Communist armies from their source of supplies, after which they collapsed.

The Russian advance in Europe was pushed back from the Adriatic to the Yugoslav and Greek frontiers with Bulgaria. The newspapers would have shot Santa Claus. The practical moral here would seem to be that when the State Department says "Yip!" it wants the newspapers to say "Yip!" and nòt "Yip! Yip! Yip!"

Since we are on the subject of shooting, I include another brief example of foreign coverage that I like better.

Miracle in Palermo

My newspaper-reading compulsion is even greater, if possible than it used to be, and in consequence I have added *Il Progresso Italo-Americano,* an Italian-language daily published in New York, to my list of required reading. A story that I came across in it more than a month ago is still lodged in my memory, with, I believe, some reason. The headline over it was: SHOOTS AT THE CARABINIERE WHO HAD SKILLFULLY SEDUCED HER WITH A PROMISE OF MARRIAGE. The story, attributed to "Our Special Service," begins:

PALERMO—Some months ago, Signorina Francesca Paolo Troia di Pietro, of 26 years, made the acquaintance of Armando Ionta, a carabiniere of Castelforte Latina, attached to the station of Pallavicino. Ionta did not delay getting himself in with the alluring girl, to whom he swore and swore ever harder that he would soon marry her. One evening of April last, with the pretext of taking a walk in a garden near San Lorenzo Colli, using violence, he possessed her.

The fact came to the attention of relatives of the seduced young one, who threatened death. In a little time, all was hushed up, because the carabiniere pledged himself to atone at the soonest by matrimony, but in three months the situation returned to becoming more acute, because Ionta not only commenced to keep his distance but made known to the deceived one that he was no longer able to keep his promise, showing himself hostile and indifferent. Signorina Troia had divers conversations with the seducer, advising him to repair the wrong and warning him that otherwise she would have to make a scandal, but the military coxcomb did not wish to acquiesce. In a moment of pain, having also learned that her seducer was preparing to leave for his home district, the seduced approached the seducer one more time, exhorting him to keep his promise. At his refusal, she extracted from her handbag a revolver, shooting at the soldier, who was left miraculously unhurt.

That, in my opinion, is the snapper: she missed him.

This sequence of events is in direct contravention of the theory maintained for years by my friend the late Jack Curley, a wrestling promoter, who had a shoe box filled with clippings on cases of women who had never handled a revolver in their lives until they killed their lover with one shot. "You take a detective that has been practicing pistol-shooting all his life," Jack once said, "maybe with medals for marksmanship, and he shoots at a stickup man escaping with the whole Saturday-night take of a high-class saloon, and he misses him and kills an old lady on top of the Third Avenue 'L,' waiting for a train. But you take some doll that has never soiled her fingers even with brass knuckles and she buys a gun and has to ask the clerk to show her how to load it and she points it at a guy that is maybe trying to squeeze himself up into a very small target and bang! —every time, right through the heart. I never knew one to need two shots."

Jack would have agreed with the Sicilian reporter that the carabiniere's escape was a miracle.

* * *

The advantages of foreign coverage by formula are more numerous than I have been able even to suggest. The essential is, as I have explained, that it eliminates all but the most nominal expense; in the words of a book of Japanese prints that I picked up long ago in a bookstall by the Seine: "It permits, without spending money or tiring travel, to see manifold beauties while staying home." This thought is as soothing to publishers as would have been, to old-time saloon keepers, the discovery of a kind of free lunch that was as free to the fellow who put it out as to the customer who ate it. But it also preserves mental health.

During the Korean War, for example, it became clear that we weren't licking the unmentionable Chinese fast enough. When the Truman Administration was so reminded, it asked for more men and more money. By not examining the army of Chiang Kai-shek on Formosa, however, it was feasible, without knowing you were lying, to assert that there was a large, ferocious, lovable army of mentionable Chinese waiting to spring into action if permitted and whale the tar out of the unmentionable Chinese—having, presumably, by now saved up enough money to buy back the American matériel they had sold to the unmentionable Chinese previously.

This permitted the publishers *and* their readers—the publisher thinks of the reader, too, when it is free—to stay happy. It also permitted the publishers to lay into the Administration for wanting to spend more money to lick a few ragged, dispirited, unmentionable Chinamen that Roosevelt had set up in business in the first place, and it stained old Harry Truman's head with the blood of every American boy he had permitted to get uselessly killed when that lovable, ferocious army on Formosa would have been glad to do the job. (It was a cheap army, too. You could get it, for $2.67, with 26 issues of *Life* if you took advantage of the big trial offer.)

The Chairman of the Joint Chiefs of Staff, over in the Pentagon, knew that there wasn't enough of any army on Formosa to hold the place, if seriously attacked, but you could avoid finding that out if you sent nobody to ask him. Not-reporting, like charity, begins at home. He kept on asking to be asked, but Senator Robert Taft, who led the campaign to utilize the lovable, ferocious army, knew it was a trap. He wouldn't ask, and the newspapers wouldn't, either. They didn't want a name for being snoopy.

If you start permitting reporters to visit the Pentagon for information, the whole point of not-reporting is lost. It is like letting the camel put his nose in the tent and giving him an inch that will soon be an ell. Next thing you know, some radical will suggest that not-reporting is not reporting.

Well sir, the way that army grew was a caution, and I with my innocent interest in the military, began to take a count, of which the following specimen was the first installment.

The Rubber-type Army

APRIL 7, 1951

When General Douglas MacArthur made a statement early in March that the war in Korea would reach a point of theoretical stalemate unless the United Nations' army received major additions, I looked forward to the deployment, in newspaper type, of the army of Chiang Kai-shek. I was sure there would be a breakout because Chiang's army had been out of print for more than a month—unless I missed a minor story or two about it—and I wanted to know how big the new edition would be. It had consisted of 800,000 men when it went into winter quarters in the editorial offices—where it bivouacs between its campaigns—following a discourse by Representative Joseph W. Martin, Jr., of Massachusetts, the Republican leader of the House of Representatives, on February 12. This marked a decrease of about 15 percent from its top (printed) strength of "nearly a million" (George E. Sokolsky, in the *Journal-American* on January 4), but it was an agreeable advance over the 500,000 reported by Senator Robert A. Taft in a speech on January 9. The Taft–Martin discrepancy seemed to call for an intercameral Republican conference, with perhaps an eventual compromise on 650,-000. I felt let down when the *World-Telegram & Sun,* on March 15, placed the number at half a million. This, I supposed, was a genuflection to Senator Taft, but undoubtedly discouraged Chiang, and conceivably, to judge from what shortly followed, General Mac-

Arthur himself. For on March 24, the general, as reported by the Associated Press, said he was ready to talk things over with the Chinese commander in the field. On March 26, Major General Claire Lee Chennault, retired, in the first of a series of articles in the *Herald Tribune,* reported a further slight decline in Chiang's forces. He said there were only "nearly half a million."

The extreme expansive-contractile capability of the Nationalist Army trapped on Formosa by the United States Seventh Fleet began to impress me early last fall. At that time, I still thought the fleet was protecting the Nationalists from the Communists, but I have learned since, from various journalistic military experts, that it was the other way about. Reading a signed piece by John Osborne in the October 2 issue of *Time,* which estimated the army at 700,000, I thought I remembered that in *Life* not long before he had put it at 500,000. He had, I found on checking up, on August 7 and September 25. Two hundred thousand in seven days struck me as a fair rate of recruiting for an army isolated on an island, but I assumed that, like the fellows in *Kon-Tiki,* the new chaps had rafted off the mainland, possibly inspired by a couple of good, rousing *Life* editorials. But a month later, on November 6, Parker La Moore, a Scripps-Howard columnist whom I always think of as "Toujours," noted, in the *World-Telegram & Sun,* a defection of 200,000 men from Osborne's augmented army and put its strength at 500,000 again. The cut seemed, in turn, to indicate a high percentage of desertions from an army stuck out there so far from the mainland, but Mr. La Moore did not appear to be depressed by the gravity of his discovery. "If . . . a [general Pacific] war is in the making anyway, as many people are beginning to suspect, Chiang Kai-shek's army of 500,000 veteran troops might become very important to the Allied cause," Toujours wrote. In the next day's *World-Telegram & Sun,* a correspondent named Jim G. Lucas, cabled from Formosa that Chiang claimed to have 600,000 men (100,000 less than Osborne had conceded him in *Time*) but that "Americans here" (Americans unspecified) put the figure at around 450,000. It was then that I organized a small pool among my friends, with six numbers from 450,000 to 700,000, and high and low field. Two days later, Lucas, to show that the troops on Formosa did not stand alone, quoted Nationalist Prime Minister Chen Cheng as claiming to have 6,000,000 agents and guerrillas on the mainland. I decided to organize a guerrilla pool, too.

On November 18, the *World-Telegram* brought Chiang's army back to full *Time* strength, in a United Press dispatch quoting the Reverend Dr. Daniel A. Poling, who had told an audience in Buffalo that there were 700,000, all right—well trained, well fed, but lacking equipment. A Mrs. Geraldine Fitch, of Leonia, New Jersey, subsequently confirmed this figure in addressing the Overseas Press Club, and it appears to be standard on the lecture circuit. The *World-Telegram* editorially detached the 200,000 from the main body of type on November 30, just when General MacArthur's need was sorest, declaring, "Chiang Kai-shek has half a million trained troops in Formosa which he is ready to throw to our support."

On December 9 the *World-Telegram* editorialist, apparently estimating casualties at the rate of 5,000 a day since November 30—high for troops not committed to combat—gave the Nationalist strength at 450,000. Later in December, Chiang's army, its flank digits pushed in by the volume of Christmas advertising, was stabilized at this figure throughout the Scripps-Howard domain. This was its Valley Forge. A quarter of a million of the troops supplied by the *Time* organization had become a lost army, and any theory that they had been sent on a secret expedition to the mainland was invalidated by a report, relayed by Harry Ferguson, United Press foreign news editor, on December 27, to the effect that guerrilla forces had declined. If the 250,000 had slipped through the Seventh Fleet blockade, the guerrilla total should have been 6,250,000 by that time. But Mr. Ferguson quoted Nationalist sources as saying there were only 1,000,000 guerrillas—a drop, although he said nothing about it, of 5,000,000 since Mr. Lucas's piece of November 9. The guerrilla forces, however, are even more subject to in- and de-flation than the regular establishment. On January 8, the United Press quoted the Nationalist government as saying that forces on the mainland had tripled in size in the last six months and now totaled 3,000,000 men. This was a rare understatement; they had tripled in the twelve days since the appearance of Mr. Ferguson's dispatch. If they have increased at the same rate since then, they now amount to 6,500,000,000 men, which is quite a lot.

On January 9, Senator Taft, speaking at a luncheon of the National Press Club in Washington, set his figure of the regular army at 500,000, his estimate jibing with that of Miss Marguerite Higgins, of the *Herald Tribune,* whose census was cabled from Formosa, where, apparently, she had been counting the soldiers. Senator Taft described this army as "the only force . . . that anyone can see" that could prevent the loss of southeast Asia. His speech must have stimulated recruiting, for Andrew Tully, in the *World-Telegram* of January 27, had the army up to 600,000 again. This, in my opinion, showed a certain lack of respect for a more celebrated journalistic contemporary, unless, by chance, *World-Telegram* writers do not read the *Journal-American.* For on January 4, Sokolsky, the old China hand of the King Features Syndicate, had blown the lid off the Girondist plot to minimize Chiang's forces by disclosing exclusively that Chiang's army consisted of "nearly a million troops." He added, sneering, obviously, at the Luce and Scripps-Howard underestimates: "The time has come for Americans to know the facts." There is an old-China-hand maxim, perhaps never reduced to English until now: "In time of crisis, moderation in mendacity may be only less disloyal than strict adherence to the truth." Representative Martin's 800,000 seemed, in the light of the revealed facts, moderate enough, and as soon as I read General MacArthur's statement last month, I bought a ticket on high field on both pools.

No sooner had I done this than I read in a *World-Telegram* editorial, on March 15, that the guerrilla force had declined by 50 percent in a couple of months, to "a total of 1,500,000 throughout China," according to "Nationalist sources." "But our government is doing nothing about it," the *Telegram* man wrote, apparently undiscouraged by this evidence of mass defection from the as-of-January-8 estimated guerrilla force. "We're passing up a momentous opportunity. . . . We won't even let the Nationalists airlift supplies to their own people or bomb the common enemy. Nor, under the Truman–Acheson neutrality order, will we permit the Nationalists to throw another half million trained troops into the fight." That "half million" floored me. It reflected a loss of 300,000 trained soldiers since Representative Martin had closed his mouth. But it helped me understand why the United States government hadn't moved. Just Pentagon inertia. Suppose you were a staff officer and you had to arrange a lift from Formosa for an army that might be 700,000 (*Time*), 450,000 to 700,000 (Scripps-Howard), 500,000 (Taft-Higgins-*Life*), 800,000 (Martin), or nearly 1,000,000 (Sokolsky). How would you know how many ships to send? And then that Intelligence problem. Are you going to make contact with 6,000,000 or 1,000,000 or 3,000,000 or 1,500,000 guerrillas after you get to the mainland? Clearly, under the circumstances, any Pentagon drone would prefer to sit on his hands.

PENTAGON "WARRIORS" SIT ON HANDS, as it happens, was the headline on a *World-Telegram* Washington story on March 12. Roger Stuart, the author, did not say he had seen anybody literally do this, but he said he had seen an officer rub his shoes with a rag on government time. Others, he said, lolled in their chairs and swapped jokes—possibly like rewrite men between stories. "Turning away from that office," he wrote—the one where he had seen the lollards—"I accidentally bumped into a girl who had come silently along the hall with a tray of sandwiches and Cokes. A few minutes later I was on the fifth floor." It seemed to me that he skipped the high point of his piece. Did the girl remain silent after he bumped into her? And what became of the sandwiches and Cokes? The whole incident looks like a plant to enable him to put them on his expense account.

Of course, it's possible that staff officers have never read any of the estimates, and they'd be silly to, since they know all about the Nationalist Army. The lowest figure quoted above is too high, and the number of useful combat troops is low in relation to the army's total strength. This is information easily to be had by any of the newspapermen regularly stationed at the Pentagon. The exact figure cannot be made public, for the Nationalist force on Formosa may someday have to fight as a garrison, and it is not customary, during a war or threat of war, to proclaim the strength of garrisons. Maybe the beat men have told their editors and have been ignored. On the other hand, maybe a beat man isn't supposed to tell his boss the facts of life anymore. But those responsible for getting this country to assume a posture of defense have been hampered by the stories about the army that could be expanded or contracted to fit any headline, like the rubber type of copyreaders' legend. Congressmen held back on bills to call up the sons of their constituents when the mail became filled with letters from the constituents enclosing clippings about how a superb army of 700,000, 450,000 to 700,000, 500,000, 8000,000, or nearly 1,000,000 was spoiling for action. The ballyhoo for this army wasn't even consistent with friendship for Chiang, since if we are going to invade China and put the fellow in again, we will need an army of our own to do it with. And we can't make that kind of army out of rubber type.

To be sure, it could be that the publishers and politicians who are pushing hardest aren't friends of Chiang's at all. It is always the loser in a barroom fight who yells, "Let me at him!"—after his friends have rescued him and stood him in a corner. If they are true friends, they keep him there and tell him he's lucky to be alive.

Seldom has story coincided better with news. *The New Yorker,* which takes a Saturday date, always appears on the stand on the Thursday preceding. The following piece continues the military epic.

The Rubber-type Army
—A Postscript

APRIL 28, 1951

By a historic coincidence, the forces of Chiang Kai-shek chose April 6, the day after my discussion of them appeared, for their most important amphibious operation. They made simultaneous landings on the front pages of all the New York newspapers, and within five days succeeded in dislodging General of the Army Douglas A. MacArthur from his position in Tokyo. Chiang's soldiers accomplished this without getting their feet wet, surely the most spectacular achievement ever chalked up by a hypothetical force at a range of ten thousand miles. The Rubber-Type Army, though its role was bloodless, thus won its place in history.

When it debarked in the papers on April 6 it was back to the strength of 800,000 that Congressman Martin had warranted in his February address. This was not surprising, since the medium of its reappearance was another speech by Congressman Martin, delivered in the course of a debate on universal military training in the House of Representatives. He said, as quoted by the *Times,* "Because of adherence to policies long since proven disastrous, our State Department today is blocking the use of the fullest resources available to us. I refer to the failure to employ the 800,000 anti-Communist Chinese troops on Formosa under the command of Generalissimo Chiang

Kai-shek." This time, as everyone knows by now, Martin produced a letter from General MacArthur, which he said supported his plan to use the R.T.A. for an invasion of the mainland. The general had not previously made public, nor did he make public in that letter or at any other time until he reached Washington, his personal estimate of the R.T.A.'s size. Whether he was aware that his letter was to be used as an argument against universal military training was not established. Inasmuch as he has since made it clear that he advocates holding both Europe and Asia, it hardly seems likely.

The row over the letter, as everyone also knows by now, led to the President's dismissal of MacArthur, and whither *that* will ultimately lead, it is difficult to divine. One thing it has led to already is some of the hottest prose and poetry of the age. "The furiously boiling political situation created by MacArthur's ouster is, of course, violently exciting and important," John O'Donnell, the political columnist of the *News*, declared on O(Ouster)-Day-plus-1, in what, compared to most of his subsequent copy, was a tone of ponderation. "But even more important is the fundamental issue—life or death for the republic as we know it." I was glad to see O'Donnell less final than Westbrook Pegler, who pronounced the republic dead in the *Journal-American* in 1948, after the Truman election, or than I. F. Stone, who laid it out in the *Compass* early on in Korea. It is nice to know O'Donnell is still holding the mirror to the nation's lips—or at least the *News*. It is, of course, Walter Winchell who holds the *Mirror*.

On April 18, a *Journal-American* poet, Harry H. Schlacht, wrote, "We Thank Thee, Heavenly Father, For Gen. Douglas MacArthur," and on the eleventh, a *Mirror* poet, Nick Kenny, contributed a stirring ballad about how the arrows of the envious glanced off the general's stalwart breast while his back, apparently unarmored, was exposed to the knives of those at home. Going into the homestretch, Mr. Kenny wrote:

*"Great soldier, statesman, diplomat,
Keep high your shining sword!"*

and he got under the wire with the line, evidently intended to rhyme:

'Tis your name that they applaud!"

These are pretty posies, but Hearst readers were also given to understand that the picture had its ugly side. The *Journal-American,* for instance, on April 18 ran an editorial hinting that the President lay in a drugged sleep—"Maybe the State Department gave him some kind of mental or neural anodyne"—while Dean Acheson and Assistant Secretary of State Dean Rusk did the firing themselves. "Thus," *Journal-American* readers learned, "a page in history—a dark, disgraceful page—was written in the midnight hours of April 11.[1] General MacArthur was fired—no doubt about that," the editorial added. "But did *the President* fire him? That is doubtful."

The R.T.A. was not overlooked by this gruesome editorialist. Our State Department policy, he wrote, was "dictated by the British Socialists," and "Socialist Britain opposes the utilization of the large and strong Formosan army against the Reds." So if there hadn't been any R.T.A., Dean Acheson wouldn't have had to drug President Truman in order to fire General MacArthur to prevent him from using the R.T.A.

All of the four principal New York morning papers, in their accounts of Martin's speech and the MacArthur letter that was admittedly responsible for precipitating the struggle, picked the reference to the R.T.A. as the nub of the story. The headlines were: M'ARTHUR WANTS CHIANG ARMY USED ON CHINA MAINLAND (*Times*), MACARTHUR BACKS USE OF CHIANG'S

---

[1] This indicates a lapse, since 1951, in the temperature of Hearst journalism. When Mr. Rusk's name was brought up for confirmation as Secretary of State, Congress was permitted to forget how he had drugged Mr. Truman and fired Mr. Truman's great friend. This omission, it seems to *me,* is a dark and disgraceful page in the history of the patriotic press.

LEGIONS (*News*), and MAC WOULD USE CHINESE (*Mirror*). This was the logical result of the long public-relations campaign to build up the "large and strong" Chiang army, which was conducted mainly by the Scripps-Howard and Hearst newspapers, with their affiliated press associations, and by the Luce magazines. Catching the ball from the creators of this force, the Republican leaders in the Senate and House —Robert A. Taft and Martin, respectively—had for some time been referring to the existence of the "large and strong" army as a fact. These references had, in turn, been considered worthy of headlines even by newspapers that had taken no part in the buildup, as when, last January, the *Times* devoted two full columns to a speech by Senator Taft in which he spoke of the Chiang army as "the only force . . . that anyone can see" able to "prevent the loss of southeastern Asia."

When it came to statistics in the Martin–MacArthur story, the *Times* quoted the minority leader's "800,-000" unquestioningly, as did the *News*. The *Mirror* omitted figures. The *Herald Tribune,* atfer quoting the 800,000, added, "Pentagon officials said Chiang's forces, which they estimated at 500,000 to 600,000, were equipped and trained for the defense of Formosa rather than for a campaign on the mainland."

On April 7, the day after the R.T.A.'s landing, the *Herald Tribune* carried an editorial, entitled "Fog over Korea," that was remarkable because it disclaimed the customary editorial omniscience. "As to the Chinese Nationalist Army in Formosa," it read, in part, "there is no authoritative estimate available of their numbers, capabilities, or even of the morale which they might bring to an invasion of the mainland; how, then, can one intelligently debate the question of their 'use' for such an operation?" The editorialist apparently had not read the articles by the *Tribune*'s own Marguerite Higgins last January, which placed the number at 500,000. In other papers, too, the R.T.A. passed to the defensive. A *News* headline on the same day read, WHITE HOUSE SNUBS MAC BID TO USE CHINA NATS. Jack Doherty, the author of the story that followed, wrote: "Presidential press secretary Joseph Short . . . said there had been no change in the announced policy of isolating the Chiang Kai-shek garrison on Formosa. He refused to comment on a report that President Truman was considering the recall of MacArthur." That afternoon, the *World-Telegram & Sun* and the *Journal-American* brought up an important reinforcement. "Rallying to Gen. Douglas MacArthur's support," a United Press Washington report on the front page of the *Telegram* read,

Sen. Robert A. Taft (R.,O.) said today it is "perfectly idiotic" not to unleash Chinese Nationalist troops for forays on the Communist-held China mainland at once.

The Republican policy chief expressed this view to a reporter. "It is ridiculous," he said, "not to let Chiang Kai-shek's troops loose to conduct raids on Communist China on the mainland and thereby take some of the pressure off our own troops fighting in Korea. I just can't understand it. It is utterly indefensible and perfectly idiotic," Sen. Taft said.

(In the *Journal-American,* the quote was "idiotic, *ridiculous,* and utterly indefensible." [2])

TAFT BACKS MAC'S PLEA TO USE CHIANG'S FORCES was the *Mirror* headline for the same interview. And the *News* editorial on the same day was headed, MAC HAS A PLAN—WHAT HAS HARRY GOT? In the Sunday *Mirror* of April 8, Senator Joseph McCarthy spilled the beans on why the administration wouldn't allow the use of the R.T.A., "estimated," according to the *Mirror,* "at over 500,000 on the Island of Formosa and perhaps 1,500,000 in Southern China." "The Truman Administration hopes Gen. MacArthur will be destroyed in Korea so that he will then be dis-

---

[2] Aides of General Omar Bradley, the Chairman of the Joint Chiefs, had repeatedly waited on Sen. Taft to ask him to listen to the truth about the politically inflated paper tiger. He refused, apparently so that he could tell himself he was not consciously lying. Bradley, Taft told me, was "George Marshall's man, and Marshall would do anything Roosevelt wanted." This clinched the case for the nonexistent army.

credited among the American people and the Administration can move him out," the *Mirror* paraphrased Senator McCarthy as saying, in a "special" dispatch from Milwaukee, where there is another Hearst paper. "He declared the Administration and the 'Yalta crowd in the State Department' hope for this, even though this means 'dooming to death vast numbers of our boys in Korea.'" (One might think that the senator would have rejoiced at the general's release from his death trap three days later, but he didn't.[3]) In the Sunday *News,* also of April 8, Frank Holeman wrote, "MacArthur said he agreed with Martin that the 800,000 Chinese Nationalist troops on Formosa should be thrown into the war in Asia." This is an illustration of how assertion shades into newspaper fact. MacArthur hadn't agreed with Martin that there were 800,000 troops on Formosa; in fact, when he finally addressed Congress last week, he put the figure at "some 600,000."

The same weekend brought the first deployment of another statistically volatile army—the not-armed South Koreans. "Sen. Ferguson (R., Mich.) wrote the Secretaries of State and Defense asking what 'political considerations' are blocking the use of South Korean reserve forces needed in the Korean fighting," the *Mirror* reported on April 8. "MacArthur said Friday that release of 120,000 South Koreans from U.N. service last month 'involves basic political decisions beyond my control.'" The *Herald Tribune* said Senator Ferguson wanted to know about 500,000 South Koreans. These new expeditionaries also had a part in the final amphibious assault on MacArthur, when the White House issued, as part of the ouster release, a report that the general himself had turned down a proposal by the Joint Chiefs of Staff to utilize the South Koreans. But I think that Chiang's hypothetical soldiers have a right to regard these putative South Koreans as Johnny-come-latelies.

The *Times* of Monday, April 9, carried an Associated Press dispatch from Fort Atkinson, Wisconsin,

---

[3] He might at least have sent Cohn and Schine to the rescue in a helicopter, but he didn't.

where Senator McCarthy, worried for the safety of General MacArthur, was reported to have said, "It is high treason to refuse General MacArthur permission to use Chinese Nationalist troops." But the *Herald Tribune* stated editorially on the same day, "Chiang's troops have never been suggested by serious military thinkers—and General MacArthur did not so suggest them—as offering a limitation on America's liabilities in the Far East or materially reducing the burden upon this country's armed forces. . . . The entry of Nationalist China into the present fighting would mean an extension, not a contraction, of present American responsibilities." That same morning, the *Mirror* ran a cartoon entitled "Ally in Chains!" in which a small boy, in pajamas decorated with the hammer and sickle, was kneeling at his bedside in prayer and saying, "Bless Stalin and the U.S. State Department!" On the wall of the boy's room was a poster captioned "Formosa," showing some soldiers and a couple of formidable tanks, all done up in chains. The *World-Telegram* carried a front-page cartoon, by Talburt, with a title borrowed from Ernie Pyle: "Here Is Your War." It was a lumpy drawing of two hands bound together with rope at the wrists. The right hand was labeled "MacArthur," the left hand was unlabeled, in token of Talburt's respect for his reader's intelligence. (He trusted them to know that was MacArthur's, too.) The lead editorial in the same day's *Telegram,* headed THE MACARTHUR ISSUE, asked, "Why should Americans bear the brunt of the fighting when there are Asiatics who could do so, if they were given the equipment and permitted to fight?" The editorial also declared, "Gen. MacArthur would have been relieved of his command long ago were it not for the fact that his return would focus the attention of Congress and the country on questions he has raised which the Administration would rather not discuss. The very thought of the colorful commander relating the untold part of his story to a Congressional committee, and the vast audiences such committees now command, could cause sleepless nights in some high places."

The R.T.A. had become the symbol of the Struggle for MacArthur. It wasn't a tangible army, but it sounded as if it might be tangible. The repeated references to it reminded me of all those stories about steaks that the newspapers ran during the weeks preceding the final dispatch of price controls in 1946. Steaks tangibleated the controversy, as Father Divine would have put it. And now there was a large and strong Chinese army that would do all the fighting if we would just "unleash" it. Precisely how this remnant of a really big but completely defeated army— back in its peak days on the mainland, it was reported by the Nationalist Government to number 6,250,000 —had grown large and strong in its island exile was not explained, any more than it was explained in 1946 precisely how steaks would grow cheaper if butchers were allowed to charge more for them.

But on Tuesday, April 10, the day before the big sensation, two New York papers, the *Times* and the *Herald Tribune,* launched stiff counterattacks against the R.T.A.'s beachheads. Michael James, a *Times* correspondent on Formosa, contributed a story on the army there. Mr. James wrote that it was estimated at 600,000 men, "half of them ground combat troops," the rest apparently being Navy, Air Force, and supply and technical-service troops. The number ready for unleashing was, however, according to Mr. James, pitifully small. "Except for shortages of fuel and ammunition for their rifles and mortars, it is believed, the Nationalists might be able to load twelve to fifteen battalions aboard their twelve operative L.S.T.s and head for the mainland," he reported. (Twelve to fifteen battalions represent 12,000 to 15,000 soldiers.) "But except as an emergency measure to relieve intolerable pressure in Korea, it is regarded as unlikely that this would be seriously considered by either the United States, the United Nations, or the Nationalist command in view of the pathetic state of [Chiang's] Air Force and Navy. . . . The Navy . . . is considered by United States observers other than naval as probably the weakest link. It is pointed out, however, that China has little naval tradition and that besides, con-

ditions are steadily improving in naval matters. The
Navy, it is pointed out by Western experts, no longer
indulges in widespread smuggling operations, for which
it was notorious until last year."

In the *Herald Tribune* of April 10, Walter Lippmann, whose admirer I frequently am not, went after
the whole legend. "Sen. Taft is talking about Korea
and Formosa in a way which sounds as if he had not
understood Gen MacArthur," Mr. Lippmann started
off. "The Senator seems to think that there are 800,-
000 anti-Communist Chinese troops on Formosa who—
if only we permitted it and gave them 'arms'—would
march into the transports. . . . But who told Sen. Taft
about this army on Formosa, and about how big it is,
and about what 'arms' it could use? . . . Not Gen.
MacArthur in his many public pronouncements. [This
was before General MacArthur's speech to Congress,
of course.] . . . He wants to wage an all-out war
against China instead of the localized war he is now
waging in Korea. . . . Those who believe in a general
war with China know perfectly well that if Chiang's
army were able to invade China it would be only because there was an American army in front of it."
Compared to what the R.T.A. had had to face in the
newspapers up to that date, this was a bayonet charge.

On the next day, when the blow fell, Frank H.
Nichols, a clerk, of 15 Erie Street, Jersey City, one
of the Men-in-the-Street interviewed by the *World-
Telegram* (DISMISSAL ANGERS MAN-IN-STREET; SOME
ASK TRUMAN'S IMPEACHMENT), told the interviewer,
"And if Chiang Kai-shek has an army of 800,000 on
Formosa, for God's sake, let's use it." Once you get
a round figure started, it rolls.

Even if Mr. Nichols doesn't read the *Times* or Walter Lippmann, I consider it probable that Senator Taft
does. The basis for my theory is an Associated Press
dispatch datelined Washington, which I read in, of all
papers, the *Journal-American,* on Sunday, April 15.
"All I want—and I am sure the General shares these
views," the senator told a reporter, "—is for the United
States to furnish some equipment and supplies to the
Chinese Nationalists on Formosa to conduct raids on

the mainland. I have no idea that the Nationalists could gain any toehold that they could maintain, but if such raids diverted even a few divisions from Korea, it would help take the pressure off American forces there."

The discrepancy between Senator Taft's R.T.A. force in January, when he called it the only visible power capable of protecting Asia, and the raiding party incapable of maintaining a toehold sounded to me suspiciously like that between a large and strong army of 800,000 men and 15,000 ill-armed Chinese crowded into twelve old L.S.T.'s. At all events, the general has now given the boys a figure they can stick to, consigning the R.T.A., presumably, to permanent bivouac.

I think now that the rout of the rubber-type army was the apogee of my career as the unheeded Whitey Bimstein of the American press. The publishers' irresistible need, inducing an irresistible belief, of a cheap and easy solution to every unpleasant problem, their editors' failure to take any note of the discrepancies between one another's conflicting stories—word having got around, atmospherically, as in the "Great Gouamba," that nobody would check on anybody else, and the sky was the limit—the priceless story of the drugging of Harry Truman, which I had forgotten until I reread the pieces, thus foiling his plot to have Gen. MacArthur captured by the Reds, the solemn quotation and re-quotation of Taft, who refused to be informed—all seem more disgustingly comical now, *pericolo passato,* than when they endangered our own and the allied United Nations forces in Korea.

If Truman truly planned the capture of MacArthur by the unmentionable variety of Chinese, come to think of it, then Mr. Rusk, by drugging old Doctor Tru Man Chu and forging MacArthur's dismissal, saved MacArthur's life and is the hero of the episode. (This would account for the *Journal-American*'s failure to bring the matter up again this winter.) Rusk may even have been a double agent, planted in the Red-riddled State Department by J. Edgar Hoover to be his Scarlet Pimpernel. I think my exposition of the hoax in the first story may have had something to do with the reservations shortly afterward expressed by the more respectable papers, as noted in the second.

I had, at any rate, a unique chance to rub turpentine in the wounds of the American Society of Newspaper Editors in the interval between the appearances of the first and second stories. They had invited me, God knows why, to address their annual meeting at Washington, which fell midway between. Gen. MacArthur, saved from the President's spidery plot against his life, was by that time in town, expressing no gratitude to his rescuers. (It seems, now, a quaint incident of yesteryear, like *l'affaire Boulanger*.) I spoke, though, with some misgivings, like a fat Republican orator twitting Bonaparte on the 17 Brumaire. I talked from the notes for my forthcoming piece, this Postscript. I found myself among friends. They cheered me, as if I were Spartacus addressing the gladiators, but in low tones, lest their publishers be listening. The American Society of Newspaper Editors apparently had as little to say about what went into print as the American Newspaper Guild or the American Cairn Terrier Club.

I proposed the Society sponsor an annual award to an American newspaper for lying, which would, I suggested, inspire far more interest than the Pulitzer Prizes, the latter having by now attained all the prestige of bean bags, tossed to good little newspapers by other papers that had them last year. The proposal was well received, but has never been activated. I can't imagine why.

Historical note: now that a decade has passed, and the number of lovable, ferocious soldiers on Formosa in 1951 can no longer be of strategic interest to that unmentionable Intelligence Service which then read George Sokolsky with such terror, I can reveal it. There were 450,000, of whom, my army informant said, "Maybe 130,000 might be of some use in combat."

A year or two after Gen. Eisenhower's accession he offered to unleash them against the mainland of China, but, having been once insulted, they declined to perform—in that resembling the racoon the ventriloquist sold in a saloon to the man who admired its vocabulary.

Yet, on their island, they have continued to inspire editorialists, like the one who wrote the following.

Notes and Comment

SEPTEMBER 20, 1958

Nothing is more useful in the conduct of human affairs than the time limit—the count of ten in the prize ring, the five years of the statute of limitations on felonies, and the five years of a husband's absence after which his wife is allowed to presume him dead. Arbitrary such periods must be, but fixed with some regard to the reasonable. If a fighter can't get up at ten, for example, the chances are that he can't at eleven, or shouldn't; if a husband hasn't come home in x years, the chances are that he won't in x plus 1, and anyhow he should have the good taste to stay away. Without devices like these, there would be no steadiness in life; no citizen would know where he was. We are in favor of a reasonable rule of closure in the United States Senate—if a speaker can't convince his colleagues in x hours, it is almost certain he won't in x plus 27 or in $27x$—and in favor of a fixed date for compliance with laws and Supreme Court decisions. (There are fixed dates for meeting taxes and mortgages, and although we hate to think of them, we suppose they are necessary.) What we are getting at, by a long enough route, we hope, to avoid the charge of subversion of State Department foreign policy—and the consequent risk of being denied a passport by a Pennsylvania congressman—is that the world lacks a Count of Ten on Fallen Statesmen. How long after a ruler is checked out on his de-facto ear

by an ungrateful country does he remain de-jure chief
of government, and how far does he have to be
chucked to be out of bounds? If the United Nations,
following a big, rousing debate, set a maximum interval between the time a regime loses effective control
of its country and the time it ceases to be the legal
government, international relations would be simplified. No matter what the U.N. decided—six months,
ten years, twenty years—it would be all to the good.
(As a parallel, there is no immutable reason territorial
waters should extend three miles from the shore, as
they do, or twelve, as the United States claimed during
prohibition, but there must be an international definition of territorial waters or we'd all be shooting one
another.) In the name of decency, we are for a fixed
minimum interval, too—of at least until the palace
charwomen finished wringing the blood from their
mops. There could be adjustments later. No government anywhere today has an unflawed original title:
England's government is based on conquest (1066)
and revolution (1688), France's on a whole pinwheel
of revolutions, ours on a revolution, a forced solder
job in 1865, and the Tilden-Hayes election of 1876.
Yet each of the three would find it intolerable if an
outside power indefinitely withheld recognition and
treated with the Anglo-Saxon Nationalist government
or the House of Valois or the Sons of the Confederacy.
In brief, we're advocating some kind of order. There
would be nothing at all, of course, to prevent the de-
legalized crowd from starting a revolution in order
to get back. After the third out, they go into the field.
A revolution is an internal affair, though, and until
it succeeds outsiders should recognize the regime the
revolution is against. One government, like one husband, at a time. Let the U.N. pass an Enoch Arden
law.

JULY 20, 1959

Last September, we suggested here that it might be
helpful all around if the United Nations instituted a

knockdown count on governments in exile—an arbitrary time limit, after which they would no longer be considered governments of where they weren't. Still, it came as a bit of a shock when the International Olympic Committee, instead of the U.N., expelled Nationalist China as if a bellboy had started being rude to an unfortunate guest before the management officially locked him out. If every Tom, Dick, and Harry of an organization is to decide for himself who is the official government of what, we have come to a pretty pass. The International Olympic Committee had already admitted Communist China as a member. We are in favor of having both Chinas in and drawing the two against each other in the first round of every competition. We once saw Yugoslavia and the U.S.S.R. play an Olympic soccer match when Tito and Stalin were refusing to recognize each other, and it worked fine. The game ended in a 5-to-5 tie after two scoreless overtime periods, the players slugged each other silly, and all the spectators enjoyed themselves. Combined with Stalin's death, the game may have led to a rapprochement between the two brands of people's republics. A good Olympic-style relay race, with plenty of elbows flying, might ventilate hostility between the two brands of Chinese. As for the suggestion of the International Olympic Committee that the Nationalist Chinese reapply for admission as the representatives of Formosa, where they now reside, it doesn't seem to fill the bill, because they are not Formosans. Let them in, rather, as The Chinese Wanderers, or let them plan to join with other displaced athletes—the refugee Hungarians and Czechs and Poles and Balts, the sons of Spanish Republicans whom Franco executed, and the Algerians who don't want to compete for France. (North Africans have won the marathon twice in the last six Olympics.) The list is practically endless. The criterion of eligibility would not be *why* an athlete was in exile but simply *that* he was. The team could also use Negroes who are barred by some African governments from competing with whites, and who would not care to represent those governments anyway. Pooled, these groups would make a powerful squad, strong

in almost every sport. They could be known among
other Olympic nations as The Rest, and their tattered
flags in the procession on opening day would remind
the crowd that the world still has a lot of unfinished
business.

Infantry War Again

AUGUST 12, 1950

Newspaper stories never repeat themselves precisely;
it is simply that one story is often much like another.
For example, a few weeks ago the local papers reported that a man beat his wife to death with his fists
because she was spending all the family's money, and
a week later it was duly recorded that another man
beat his wife to death with his fists—but in this case
it was because she would not give him a divorce. It
is characteristic of our time that the main outlines
of an invasion story have become as banal as those
of a mugging murder, and most newspaper readers
in the days since the North Korean crossing of the
Thirty-Eighth Parallel, on June 25, must have had
the sensation of having read it all somewhere before.
The news broke on a Sunday, like the news of the
German invasion of Russia on Sunday, June 22, 1941,
and of Pearl Harbor on Sunday, December 7, 1941.
The way of the transgressor is trite, and surprise is
always slightly increased by an attack during the weekend.

The way of the transgressor is also helpful to the
ordinarily modest circulation of the New York *Enquirer*, the weekly masquerading as a daily that is
dated Monday but appears on Sunday afternoon. The
late city editions of the *Times* and the *Herald Tribune*
had the Korean invasion story on this particular fate-
ful Sunday morning, but neither had given it an eight-
column spread, or even the best position in the paper;
there was, of course, no way of knowing from the early

press-association bulletins that it would develop into a bigger story than the death of 58 people in an airplane accident, which held the place of honor. The *Enquirer,* which received later United Press stuff, was the first to promote the fighting into the eight-column class. And as I read an editorial in the *Enquirer* of five weeks later that started in boldface type on the front page and ran over, I had an even stronger feeling of déjà vu than I'd had the day it all began. It said:

The reverses which the United States has sustained in Korea are not without precedent in our history, which shows that we have a habit of meeting with ill fortune after we begin to wage war.

But our history also proves that notwithstanding the habit in question, we have emerged victoriously from every war in which we have engaged.

The Truman Administration cannot honestly be blamed for the turn of events in Korea, in view of the pronouncedly abnormal condition in which the world has found itself for so long and the impossibility of our Government's providing against all contingencies amid the vast complexities of our era.

This sounded like January, 1942, when our habitually unprepared forces were being hammered about the Philippines, and people here were being habitually philosophical about it. The rest of the first page of this issue of the *Enquirer* was filled with war news, all from the United Press but livened by such headlines as REDS PERIL TAEGU! YANK FORCE TRAPPED! and DEATH ORDER PRAISED BY WALKER'S MA (Lieut. Gen. Walton H. Walker's mother, 81, approved of his order to his men to fight it out to the death), and EISENHOWER'S VIEWPOINT U.S. MUST WIN IN KOREA— "OR ELSE." The back page carried a biographical piece headed SYNGMAN RHEE IS KOREA'S GEORGE WASHINGTON.

But in the body of the paper, the *Enquirer* ran a second long editorial, this one demanding justice for Charles Thomson, Secretary of the Continental Congress, born in Ireland, who, it said, had signed the

Declaration of Independence but had never got enough
credit for it. "For some reason his noble act of self-
sacrifice has not received from history the recognition
it deserves," the editorial declared. Colonel John R.
Stingo, the *Enquirer*'s turf-and-social correspondent,
writing from Saratoga, reported, "Everything points
to a satisfactory season despite the ominous shadow
of War with its depressive uncertainties." Colonel
Stingo, who is 77, has survived a lot of uncertainties
and is not going to become depressed prematurely,
although, as he conceded in another part of his piece,
"In the happy crescendo there is heard a dolorous note
here and there." A horse-race tipster named A. J.
McKeever advertised:

AMAZING—INCREDIBLE—
BUT TRUE!

ACCLAIMED BY RACING FANS
EVERYWHERE!

YOU CAN'T WIN GUESSING

. . . Find out what the professionals are doing and string
along with them.

The illusion of being back where one had come from
only recently was heightened by the name MacArthur,
scattered through the text. It seemed to me I had
caught this act before.

There have been at least 15 sneak-punch invasions
and aggressions since the Italians marched into Ethio-
pia, and they all have a number of points in common.
For one, the aggressor always claims provocation. The
Germans marched into Poland to avenge Polish atroci-
ties against Germans, and into Norway to forestall an
Allied plot; the Russians went into Finland because
the Finns were preparing an attack on Leningrad;
Franco flew to Spain from the Canaries to save the
Church; the Dutch parachutists dropped on Jogjakarta
because the Indonesians were meditating treachery.
Also, the flash invasion is almost invariably successful.

Only the Italians in Greece and the Russians in Finland met any trouble at the outset, and in both instances the trouble was caused by the attacker's ineptitude. Ethiopia, Albania, Loyalist Spain, Austria, Czechoslovakia, Poland, Norway and Denmark, Holland and Belgium, the British and American garrisons in the Far East—all went down before their respective aggressors, and the German attack on Russia rolled forward a thousand miles, or four times the length of South Korea, before it even began to stop. A third commonplace is that the slugger always spreads the report that resistance is halfhearted, in order to lessen sympathy for the sluggee, to whom, according to the slugger, the result is obviously a matter of indifference. I can remember an age of innocence, between 1935 and 1941, when newspaper readers took seriously the chances of the jumped country to repulse an invasion. Encouraging reports would be printed of the native ferocity of the Harar tribesmen, the high motives of the Spanish Republicans, or the gallantry of the Polish cavalry. This wore thin, I think, after the capitulation of the Finns at a time when they had the newspaper decision well in hand. It perished after the Nazi march through the unconquerable Yugoslavs. It was then that the more materialistic among us began to understand that when a boy hits another boy over the head with a schoolbag full of rocks, he diminishes his victim's capacity to resist.

The affair in Korea began with an orchestral potpourri of these conventional themes. The day the news broke recalled to me a hot Sunday in June, 1941, when I walked about Union Square listening to excited groups discussing the German attack on Russia. The North Korean Government, like the Nazi Government, announced that it had been provoked. On June 26, the *Times,* as befitted a paper of record, printed the texts of the antithetical North and South communiqués, in which each claimed to have been attacked. The main headline of the *Daily Compass* was EACH SIDE CHARGES IT WAS INVADED. The *Daily Worker* of the same date said, RIGHTIST ATTACK RE-

PELLED IN KOREA. And the invasion evidently was going as smoothly as invasions always do.

Within a day or two, the South Koreans, like the Poles and the Loyalists, rallied in the headlines. There was, for instance, the headline of the *Times* on June 30, SOUTH KOREANS STABILIZE FRONT; AIRPORT NEAR SEOUL IS RETAKEN, and the *Herald Tribune*'s extra-prompt SOUTH CHECKS INVASION, on June 26, and SOUTH KOREANS HOLD SUWON, REDS STALLED, on July 2. I don't think many readers took much stock in them. No other generation was ever so inured to the language of unfounded hope. Anybody of voting age can remember that "infiltration" is a military term always followed, after a short interval, by "rectification of the line," and "rectification," in turn, by "orderly withdrawal to a previously prepared position."

The only segment of the New York press that appeared to view the military situation with satisfaction was the *Daily Worker,* and a fraction, varying from $1\frac{2}{3}$ to $11\frac{1}{17}$, of the total columns in the *Compass,* the proportion changing with the positional oscillations of the columnists. Max Werner, the *Compass*'s military expert ("Often alone and almost always right, that's Max Werner"—the *Compass*), displayed from the first a popeyed admiration for the North Korean Army. "There is a kind of inexorable mechanics" of war that the North Koreans have mastered, he announced. But his more profound colleagues found that this efficiency was superfluous. The North Korean successes, they held, were purely spiritual, based on the South Korean lack of will to resist. "It would not be necessary for American boys to die in the mud of South Korea if its own soldiers and people had thought their government worth fighting for," Stone wrote, equating the will to resist with the power to do so successfully. This is the *integer-vitae-scelerisque-purus* theory of self-defense, and among aggressor nations it is an article of faith for export. (The Germans and Russians, although vociferous about their dynamism, never thought it could replace matériel in their armies or in those they equipped for their friends.) A more plausible reason for the South Koreans' initial military failure was advanced by an unhappy American brigadier general named William L. Roberts, who was quoted in the *Times* on July 16. The general, who had been in charge of training the South Korean Army, said the Americans hadn't left it any tanks because they were afraid it would invade the North.

The South Korean Army, as a matter of fact, *didn't* disintegrate. Marguerite Higgins, of the *Herald Tribune,* reporting from the front on July 27, had a lot to say in praise of the South Koreans, and the inexorably mechanistic Werner himself, who had eliminated them from the fighting on about the third day, was again recognizing them as a factor in the situation on July 31. Further reports, by Miss Higgins on August 1, and by William H. Lawrence, of the *Times,* on August 2, quoted American officers who held up the South Korean tactics as an example for our own troops, loath to leave their road-bound vehicles.

With the introduction of American troops into the combat in the second week of the action, there began a sort of reporting that would have been impossible under the formal censorship of the last war, even if there had then been anybody capable of doing it. The first American correspondents with the armies in 1942 had had small experience in the practical aspects of war and were inclined to consider all shortcomings inevitable. By 1944 or 1945, when they had acquired some judgment, things were going so well that there were few faults it would have been useful to call to public notice. Correspondents do not obsolesce quite as fast as infantrymen, and the United States consequently got a rather better report on its military deficiencies in Korea in the first couple of weeks than a nation usually gets before a war is over and military historians begin their autopsies. It is my considered opinion that a small group of correspondents, of whom Homer Bigart, of the *Herald Tribune,* appears to me the most effective, have done much to save the lot of us by pointing out our specific, and remediable, deficiencies in combat. I should like to propose an experienced correspondent as our next Secretary of Defense.

One of the first Bigart combat stories told of an action in which an evidently small American force fought against North Koreans equipped with 40 Russian-built medium tanks (about 35 tons each) and "lost all of their artillery—five 105-mm. guns, two anti-tank guns—and considerable small arms." The essential point of this story, I thought, was not that we lost the guns—since we were in small force—but that we were still shooting the old 105s, which were not too effective even against the German tanks of 1940 design. Now we were shooting them against newer and solider Russian vehicles. "Again and again American gunners scored on the incoming tanks, only to see them roll on," Bigart wrote. "Red turrets resisted penetrating armor-piercing shells. Only by hitting tracks were artillerymen able to halt an occasional tank." It seemed curious that members of our small and presumably select professional army, stationed in a dangerous area, where they would need the army's best weapons, should be using general-purpose artillery that had been thought inadequate against tanks years ago. The shells of the 75-mm. anti-tank guns, Bigart noted, "nicked but failed to stop the tanks." It was a clean, undramatic, pictorial story that included everything but the smell of the rice paddies through which the defeated Americans ran. The escaping infantrymen, he said, had been guided out by natives, an indication that not all South Koreans were happy about what the *Worker* calls their "liberation" by the invading army.

The *Times* carried a story on the same day, datelined Tokyo and written from a headquarters briefing, that illustrated something I have always believed about war reporting: it is better done from where the war is. "United States troops, fighting their first major engagement in the Korean war," this effort began, "successfully stood off the initial attacks of massive tank-led North Korean forces plunging south along the road from captured Suwon." This was not even a definition of what had happened, since a fight is hardly a major engagement, and, besides, the Americans had lost. The headline over the story moved the "major engagement" up one more notch, to a "battle" —U.S. TROOPS CHECK NORTH KOREANS IN FIERCE BATTLE SOUTH OF SUWON; BAR BREAK DESPITE TANK ATTACK. The *next* day's Tokyo communiqué revealed that the Americans engaged in the skirmish where the guns were lost numbered "less than one battalion." The command in Korea said that "less than five hundred" American troops had been engaged anywhere on the front during the day. How "less than five hundred men," less "less than one battalion," could have even fought a battle, to say nothing of winning one, was not explained.

The same spread between affirmation and probability appeared in another Tokyo-datelined story, in the *Mirror* of July 7, which spoke of "thirty thousand armored North Korean troops . . . in a two-day, thirty-five-mile plunge through a thin screen of U.S. troops," and then quoted an American lieutenant colonel commanding the screen (a battalion commander, by his rank) as saying, "We are in good shape—we'll do our best to shoot hell out of them." This would indicate that the battalion commander was insane. Bigart, in his July 7 story, chronicled another minor reverse, and wrote, "It is already painfully apparent that the Americans completely underestimated the enemy capabilities." (The *Times* has since infiltrated nearly a platoon of correspondents into Korea, and they are giving Bigart good competition. Walter Sullivan, Richard J. H. Johnston, and the aforementioned Mr. Lawrence are pretty fine.)

Joseph and Stewart Alsop, in their syndicated column, wrote on the same day, July 7, "Everywhere in America, people are beginning to realize that we are fearfully weak and most dangerously situated." The Alsops, who have been insisting for a good year now that Secretary of Defense Johnson's economy program has been leaving us naked, were being brilliantly vindicated, but they seemed as unhappy as anybody else about it. It was on that day that the *Herald Tribune* reported that General of the Army Douglas MacAr-

thur had assured the President that the position of the
American ground forces was "not considered serious
in any way." The *Post,* encouraged, announced, G.I.'S
HALT RED DRIVE.

A Bigart story datelined July 10 that ran on July
12 began, "American troops in forward positions nar-
rowly escaped another enveloping thrust by North
Korean Communists today, and were able to avoid
annihilation by great luck in withdrawal. The unit suffered severe casualties and was forced to leave all its
heavy equipment behind. This correspondent was one
of three reporters who saw the action, and was the
only newsman to get out alive. . . . It was not an encounter anyone will remember except those who were
there, and the outcome will have no bearing on the
ultimate results. It is worth telling only as an example
of what happens when men are thrown into action
without adequate preparation." The unit, a company,
had been pinned down by its own artillery, and had
finally abandoned its position, at the order of the regi-
mental commander, after a platoon of insufficiently
trained soldiers panicked. Bigart followed his magnificent description of the skirmish with an attempt to
set down what was the matter. The men he had observed did not fulfill the ingratiating concept of a
small professional army of such high quality as to
compensate for its lack of numbers. "Only one man
out of ten had ever heard the sound of a shell passing
overhead. Overhead firing has been banned in peacetime maneuvers lest some of the men get hurt." As a
result, a good number of solders, unable to distinguish
between outgoing and incoming fire, had been un-
nerved by the sound of their own guns. Few of them
had taken part in large-scale training. They were not
"combat-minded." As a result, officers of field grade
—majors and up—had practically had to hold the
men's hands in combat. The casualties among such
officers were heavy. (A dispatch from Washington in
the newspapers of July 30 announced that the Army
had restored maneuvers with live ammunition to the
training curriculum.) "The burning question in their
[the officers'] minds," Bigart wrote, "was why the

United States, having been alerted so long to the danger of aggression in the Far East, was able to commit only a small force inadequately trained and equipped."

When the First Cavalry Division made its unopposed landing at Pohang on July 19, Bigart reported that it was the first cheerful news he had heard since the beginning of the long retreat. It is too bad he could not have been reading headlines in the United States, which presented the country with victories at least every other day. But three days after the landing, he was reporting the hardest knock of all, the "costly" and "humiliating" defeat of the Twenty-fourth Division at Taejon, where it traded too much blood for too little time. I think his brief, unemotional account of the unarticulated effort—communications failed, and in consequence the troops assigned to cover the retreat never moved into position—will be remembered by several hundred thousand people who were not there. I shall not soon forget Bigart's report of his last glimpse of Gen. Dean, the defeated commander, "sitting upon the porch of his command post, the picture of dejection." Bigart drew a useful lesson from this tragedy, and delivered it a week later. "A shocking surprise of the Korean campaign has been the miserable failure of some American Army communications equipment at the battlefront," he wrote. "A frequent complaint is that the materials are often obsolete—roll-back material from Okinawa that has become rotted by fungus during years of storage." After which he went into detail. And in another story, he wrote, "For the human deficiencies, there is no one to blame. Americans like to go soft in peacetime. But there is no excuse for deficiencies in basic field materials. For example, Americans always prided themselves on their knowledge of radio and telephone communications at the front." When he writes so, the unthrobbing Bigart is thinking of the dead at the other end of the rotted telephone wire.

Bigart's type of reporting is rather different from the assurances, datelined Tokyo, that everything is going to be tickety-boo eventually, or from interviews with nerve-shattered men who should be under seda-

tion, in which they tell about the impossible numbers
of the enemy they have killed and the impossible dis-
tances they have run "after the lieutenant said to take
off." The lieutenant, in these stragglers' stories, is always either nameless or dead.

There is a retired major general in west Texas
whom I like to visualize reading Bigart's dispatches
and those of half a dozen other reporters who are now
out in Korea and working along the same lines.
"Good infantry," the old man used to say, "is what
you need a lot of." I am sure the present war has
given him no reason to change his mind.

The Oracles of Mars—Continued*

OCTOBER 28, 1950

Hanson W. Baldwin, the military expert of the New
York *Times,* is not what Max Werner, the military expert of the New York *Daily Compass,* might call a
tank-spearheaded power type. Werner hammers away
inexorably (to use one of his favorite words) against
the nerve centers and Fowler's *Modern English Usage,*
throwing in wave after wave of words in revolutionary, unorthodox tactical formations until he achieves
the strategical *anéantissement,* as Colonel de Grand-
maison would have it, or *Vernichtung,* if you prefer
Oberst Foertsch, of one or the other of the two armies
he is writing about. (Both Baldwin and Werner, and,
for that matter, any military expert, can and do cite
even more sonorous authorities for their dicta.) This
doctrine of the offensive *à outrance,* as Hood found in
1865, Nivelle in 1917, and Graziano in 1946, has its
consequences as well as its rules. Hannibal was a big
man after Cannae, but where was he after the elephants backed up on him? Similarly, Werner, who
seemed spectacularly oracular when, in 1941, he

---

* The first article appeared in the October 21, 1950, issue of
The New Yorker.—Ed.

picked the Russian Army to win, seemed the victim of a double envelopment by his own predictions when the North Korean Army collapsed.

This will never happen to Baldwin, who is a Maréchal de Saxe, or *Times*-editorial, sort of expert, moving carefully among fortress groups of balanced maxims and counter-maxims. "There is an old military maxim that he who commits his reserves last wins the battle," Baldwin wrote on August 9, and promptly illustrated it by adding, "And there is another—still true, with reservations and modifications, as it was in Napoleon's time—that God is on the side of the big battalions." Later in the Korean campaign, he wrote, " 'There are only two powers in the world, the sword and the spirit,' Napoleon said. 'In the long run the sword is always defeated by the spirit.' " He now had Napoleon covering both flanks.

"Thus much of the Naktong River line at the moment is in that state of precarious balance that so often comes in battle," Baldwin, in an incisive mood, began a paragraph early in August. "A breach has occurred and other bridgeheads have been established but, with reserves, the breach could be sealed off, the bridgeheads contained. But—has the United States the reserves?" On August 30, he wrote: "The hard core of the North Korean Army is composed of fanatical, well-trained veterans of either the Russian Army, the Chinese Communist armies, and/or the Japanese Army. . . . North Korean morale, on the other hand, might well be volatile; it could conceivably crack under hard military adversity, although, because of the Communist core of veterans, this seems unlikely." On September 3, Baldwin put the same problem so: "Korean morale is best described as volatile—in victory ruthless and aggressive, but in defeat perhaps uncertain. The North Korean Army is, however, bolstered by a hard core of fanatical Communists—some of them veterans of many battles, some of them possibly Chinese, Japanese, or Asiatic Russians—and there may not be much opportunity for lowered morale to express itself in the hard and practical terms of disintegration, even if the

North Korean Army should endure massive defeats.
Still, no man may gauge the moods of battle; the
North Korean will-to-fight may wane." On September 17, after the Inchon landing, Baldwin still had
not committed his psychological-warfare reserves:
"Asiatic, and particularly Korean morale, is known
to be volatile—up when victory is in the air, down
when the going becomes very tough. But the frame-
work of the North Korean Army is built around a
hard core of Communist fanatics and experienced
veterans of Russian, Japanese, and Chinese Communist armies. Have enough of these been killed to permit dissolution; will the volatile Korean morale
'go to pot' and encourage the quick disintegration
of the enemy forces?" Baldwin steals no bases on
the Dodona circuit, but, on the other hand, he will
never hit into a double play.

The *Times* oracle is an unconventional expert in
at least one way: he supplies his readers with a
considerable amount of information. The *Times* was
the only newspaper in New York in which a reader
last summer could learn the characteristics of the
weapons in the news—weapons like the Tiny Tim
rocket, the 105-mm. high-explosive anti-tank projec-
tile, and the 3.5-inch bazooka—or get sane estimates
of the amount and nature of Russian arms in use by
the North Koreans. "Instead of obsolescent Japanese
equipment plus a small amount of Soviet materiel,"
Baldwin wrote on August 16, "the North Koreans
have proved to be armed with sizable quantities of
good Russian World War II arms, some of them
better than our own. The Russian T-34 tank, the
SU-76, or self-propelled 76-mm. gun, the towed 76-
mm. anti-tank gun, the 82-mm. and 120-mm. mortars, and the 122-mm. howitzer, as well as a Russian
submachine gun or machine pistol, have appeared in
quantity in Korea and have proved to be very effective weapons." The 122-mm. gun, he noted a week
later, outranged our 155-mm. howitzer by five or six
thousand yards. He also impressed me on August 16
with a geographical-meteorological dissertation on
such places as Sovetskaya Gavan '('home base of

the Russian Seventh Fleet . . . ice-locked from December to April") and Petropavlovsk ("base of the so-called Kamchatka Flotilla . . . relatively ice-free except in very severe winters . . . icebreakers keep the harbor open with no great difficulty"). "Vladivostok, home base of the Russian Fifth Fleet," he went on to report, "is ordinarily frozen for about eighty-six days each winter, although icebreakers keep it open for essential traffic." While Werner, at approximately the same stage of the Korean war, was anticipating a quick decision or even a knockout— NEXT 3 DAYS CRUCIAL; SPACE, TIME ARE SHRINKING —Baldwin was equipping his subscribers for a winter campaign.

Being a former naval officer (Annapolis '24, resigned '27 to enter newspaper work), Baldwin got Admiral Mahan, the apostle of sea power, into the campaign early. "Concentration to Admiral Mahan, famed military strategist, was the 'ABC of strategy,' " he informed his readers on July 24, in a piece headed STRATEGY OF COMMITMENT. Then, possibly with some thought to unification of the services on the broadest possible basis, to include the Confederate ground forces, he recalled that "to General Forrest, it was 'to git thar fust with the most.' " "Git thar fustest with the mostest," is the way the mostest military writers quote Forrest. Baldwin was holding a couple of syllables in reserve.

From these maxims, Baldwin did not draw the inference, as Werner might have done, if he had bothered to quote them (the *Compass* strategos usually cites more exotic authorities, like General Brusilov), that the United States should throw its full weight against the North Koreans as fast as possible. Instead, he wrote: "Concentration means a clear view of the objective toward which a nation's main effort should be directed; it means economy of force, or reduction of peripheral or side-show commitments to a minimum. . . . Viewed against the yardstick of these principles of strategy, Korea is a side show. . . . If Russian Communism could be sent reeling to the eastern reaches of the Pripet Marshes and behind the

Dniester, the victory would be far more decisive than
any retreat of the Northern Korean Communists to
the Thirty-Eighth Parallel." The circumstance that we
weren't fighting Russia made a Dniester victory difficult to achieve at that moment, but the *Times* military expert was concerned with the big picture. While
Werner was being awed by the combination of "tank-
spearheaded mobile warfare and stubborn infantry
battle" being waged by the North Koreans "with all
scientific-tactical conclusions," the perils that preoccupied Baldwin were farther-flung. "Formosa is by
no means secure," he warned. "Iran is another trouble zone. . . . What about Yugoslavia? . . . And what
about Western Europe, where perhaps our strength
is needed more than anywhere else in the world? . . .
In other words, we must keep our eye on the ball.
. . . More manpower is needed. This manpower can
come only from two principal sources—Japan and
Germany. . . . The Japanese should be given the
responsibility of the defense of their own islands,
with the right, reserved to us, to retain bases. A Western German police force or army, under allied control, should be formed. And foreign legions of
Germans, Japanese, and other foreigners under
United States or allied high command could well be
organized and offered to the United Nations, to oppose conquest by proxy wherever it is tried."

At this point, it occurred to me that Baldwin might
have forgotten two of my favorite stockpiles of military maxims, *Mercenaries of the Hellenistic World,*
by G. T. Griffith, and *Les Recherches et Antiquitez
de la Province de Neustrie, à Présent Duché de Nor-
mandie,* by Charles de Bourgueville, Sieur de Bras.
De Bourgueville recorded that the lansquenets, the
German mercenaries of his time, declined to bleed
seriously in the cause of their employers, and instead
robbed and bullied the civilian population of Caen
until the citizens had to chase them with rocks. Griffith noted that the mercenaries of the fourth and
third centuries B.C., while they fought well, had the
unfortunate habit of taking over the states that had
hired them. The lesson seems to be that ineffectual

mercenaries aren't worth having and that the only
safe way of handling effective ones is to maintain a
homegrown army capable of licking the mercenary
army at any time. So what you need is two armies.
But since mercenaries are always capable of going
over to the other side, your homegrown army must
be able to beat the hostile army *plus* the mercenaries.
This hardly helps the manpower situation.

In his next piece, on July 26, Baldwin probed
Stalin's aims, and concluded: "Our intelligence has
been wrong in the past; it could be again. . . . The
hour of crisis will come when and if our troops face
an Asiatic Dunkerque, or when we have concentrated in Korea the maximum possible strength we
feel we can commit there. . . . That time has not yet
come, but it may soon come." After that, on July 28,
Balwin returned to a detailed analysis of the peripheral imbroglio in Korea, in which, he said, he dis-
which he said would have an increasing influence on
the campaign. It wasn't until well into August that
Baldwin returned to a detailed analysis of the peripheral imbroglio in Korea, in which, he said, he discerned these two problems: "1. Are we going to be
able to concentrate sufficient ground troops to accomplish our objectives in Korea? 2. What limit
should be set upon the number of troops it is strate-
gically desirable to commit there?"

With Baldwin so uncommitted and Werner, apparently hypnotized by the foe's *mystique de l'offensive,*
descrying every day a new death trap set for our
forces, the Korean affair took on a pretty somber
aspect. On August 20, Baldwin announced the result
of a further squint through the battle smoke. RE-
SERVES ARE THE KEY TO OUTCOME IN KOREA, the
heading over his piece that day proclaimed. And on
August 23 he was still poised for advance or retreat.
"In one sense both pessimism and optimism are justified, but a balance ought to be struck between them,"
he wrote. "War knows no realism save the toll of
dead and wounded. We have certain advantages in
Korea and the enemy has other advantages. . . . It is
still possible that he may call on powerful reserves,

and in any case it is premature to do any 'whoopin'
and hollering.' For as Napoleon said, 'the change
from the defensive to the offensive is one of the most
delicate operations of war.' "

Nearly two weeks later, on September 3, Baldwin
revealed the statistical basis of his misgiving. "The
enemy now has some sixteen identified divisions in or
near the fighting front," he wrote, "and four others
have been reported tentatively in process of formation in rear areas. . . . A three-to-one superiority in
combat effectiveness—some think even a six-to-one
superiority—is, if not essential, advisable to insure
success. . . . We should, to be safe, gird ourselves for
a long struggle." These figures, I immediately recognized, since I read all military experts with equal
avidity, and have reason to believe they read each
other, were meant as a corrective for any public
euphoria based on an *expertise* cabled from Tokyo
by Joseph Alsop, whose home base is Washington,
and printed in the *Herald Tribune* on August 23.
"Certainly, unless the Pentagon is getting ready to
unveil its once famous secret weapons," Alsop had
written, "there seems to be nothing in the facts to
justify such a hopeful Tokyo. It is not sustained by
the facts, which are all too simple and all too bleak.
In brief, no less than thirteen North Korean divisions
are surely in the field. Two more are probably in action, and the intelligence indicates that four new divisions will be ready before long. . . . But the classical
ratio of strength, declared by all prudent command-
ers in order to assume the offensive, is at least two to
one. On the basis of this ratio, we should need at
least twenty-six American and South Korean divisions to undertake a big push northwards."
It had been clear to me when I first read this that
Alsop, in urging us to an attack with only 26 divisions (14 of which we didn't have, in Korea or
anywhere else), was taking dangerous liberties with
his own 2-to-1 ratio. Two days later, Werner quoted
Alsop's statement of the classical ratio. But, earlier,

Werner had said that the North Korean Government could probably muster *fifty* divisions. Now I began to measure the trap into which an Alsop-coached army might fall. On the basis of the Alsop and Werner columns, I could see that not 26 but 100 divisions were necessary for what Napoleon called one of the most delicate operations of war. Never during the Second World War did the United States possess more than 90 divisions, and it was plain to me that we were going to have to cut deep into the ranks of our essential workers this time in order to scrape up more than that. But the Baldwin column that followed the Alsop and Werner pieces showed how grim our plight really was. Striking an average between Baldwin's ratio of 3-to-1 superiority for combat effectiveness and the 6-to-1 ratio the expert said some thought, if not vital, certainly advisable, I arrived at the ratio of 4½-to-1, or, in betting terms, 9-to-2. Accepting Baldwin's estimate of 20 available enemy divisions, we would need 90, which was considerably more than Alsop's inadequate—and mostly nonexistent—26. On the basis of the scientific Werner's report of 50 North Korean divisions, it now became apparent that, by my adjusted ratio, we might need 225 divisions or even 300 divisions (if Baldwin's "some" were right). Going into a kind of mental arithmetic I used to do a few years ago— 3 divisions, 45,000 men, plus corps troops, make one army corps, 70,000 men; two army corps, 140,000 men, plus army troops, make 180,000 men—I could see that three hundred divisions, with corps and army units, would amount to at least 9,000,000 men, while supply troops, replacements, and a proportionate increase in the Air Force might amount to 8,-000,000 more, and it would take years to build the shipping to carry them, even if the shipyards found an exclusively female personnel reasonably efficient. It seemed too long a struggle to gird ourselves for, and I perceived only one way out—surrender.

There was no quit in Baldwin, however, even though he remained essentially conservative. "To

avoid the mountains, a landing . . . would be logical,"
he wrote on September 10, "but again, until troops
are available and supplies ready, such a move, unless
limited, would be pretty risky. Clausewitz, the great
advocate of ground power, put the pre-conditions
for a strategic offensive succinctly in his 'Principles
of Warfare,' a hundred and thirty years ago. They
have not changed. . . . In any case, we should not
expect unlimited assault, quick decision, or rapid
victory."

A week later, on September 17, after the landings
at Inchon, Baldwin wrote, "No prediction as to the
ultimate outcome of these landings is possible at this
time, for there are too many intangibles to permit
accurate calculation." On the twenty-seventh, he ac-
quiesced in our apparent good fortune, but only for
half a column or so. "One of the boldest gambles in
modern United States military history—the Inchon
invasion—has fully paid off and a large part of the
North Korean Army has been cut up and battered
and seems to be in the process of dissolution," his
story started off on that day. But the second half of
the column began, "Two great questions now dominate the Korean picture. (1) What has happened to
the North Korean Army; in other words, what are
the exact dimensions of its defeat? (2) What do we
do next; do we move north of the Thirty-Eighth Parallel?" With respect to the latter question, Baldwin
stated, "We are in a 'damned-if-we-do and damned-
if-we-don't' situation."

Mr. Baldwin has since gone to Korea to do a
bit of reporting; in flight his plane may well have
crossed that in which Mr. Alsop was flying home to
Olympus after a ten-week stint of war reporting. I
had occasion last week to distinguish between the
reporter, who writes what he sees; the interpretive
reporter, who writes what he sees and what he construes to be its meaning; and the expert, who writes
what he construes to be the meaning of what he
hasn't seen. The shifting roles of Baldwin and Alsop
will, I suspect, bring these distinctions into sharper

focus. Joseph Alsop and his brother Stewart, who until Korea pretty much confined themselves to being experts and interpretive reporters, call their syndicated column "Matter of Fact," even though it often contains a high percentage of opinion. For more than a year before the North Korean invasion, the Alsops carried on an almost continuous attack on the policies and personality of the then Secretary of Defense, Louis Johnson. Their major charge was that our armed forces had, for reasons of economy, been trimmed much too low for safety, and, in the light of this, the first week of the Korean war proved that on occasion experts can be abundantly right.

Instead of staying home and indulging in a long syndicated gloat, however, Joseph Alsop chose to have a close look at the war, and he did a pretty readable job of battlefield reporting. This interfered with his oracular activities and it is perhaps unfair to allude to him any longer as a military expert. The classical-ratio interlude cited above may be excused as a temporary lapse, and anyway he wrote it in Tokyo, not at the front. But even while he was within range of the gunfire, he added at least one to the list of authorities quoted by the more conventionally located experts in New York and Washington. "That evening, glancing through a pocket edition of Plutarch," Alsop wrote about himself at a battalion headquarters, presenting an appealing vignette of the cultured correspondent, "this reporter found a description of the troubles of the Roman republican general Metellus with the wild Iberian tribes in Spain. Nearly 2,000 years ago, the historian wrote as follows: [The excerpt told how the Iberians had scrambled around among the rocks while the legionnaires stuck to the roads.] In the foregoing passage, you may simply substitute the name of Lt. Gen. Walton H. Walker for that of his Roman predecessor, Metellus. You will then have the most succinct possible statement of one of our main difficulties in Korea today." Here is an example of the essential technique of military writing: one attacks by leapfrogging citation over explanation, then pinching out the citation, and beginning all over again. The pocket Plutarch was apparently Mr. Alsop's mobile reserve of maxims. I am glad he never had to commit any more of it.

While at the front, Alsop even acquired the field reporter's anti-oracle complex, which he expressed in the following lines on August 23: "In the matter of the main problem of how we can take the offensive in Korea, all correspondents notice the same singular phenomenon when they make necessary trips from the front to the command post to forward headquarters to this dreary city, in order to send off copy. The farther from the front you get, the more hopeful grow the forecasts, until you reach Tokyo and they talk of victory by Christmas. This makes you wonder just who has gone mad." (Here was one time when the rear may have known something.) On September 1, back at the front but having perhaps been infected by headquarters fever, Alsop wrote, "In short, we *might* get out of this mess in Korea rather more quickly than seemed likely when catastrophe still imminently threatened." But on the eighth, still at the front and cured of the fever, he was down again. "Some may argue that General Walker ought to have shortened the whole defense perimeter," he wrote. "Certainly he was strongly encouraged not to do so by the Pentagon, so hungry for blame-erasing victory, so fearful of the political repercussions of retreat. If he fails now, it will not be his fault. In plain words, it will be the fault of those who defrauded the American people, claiming they were making America strong when they were making America weak." In a dispatch published on the thirteenth, Alsop, back in Tokyo, was moderately hopeful again. "A relatively small increment of force should give us enough to achieve a breakthrough, or could even conceivably be landed in the North Korean rear," he wrote, as if lightly touched by the wing of some prophetic bird. On the twenty-seventh, his column bore the subhead THE CONQUERORS.

I somehow wonder whether Joseph Alsop will ever

be able to function as a full-time oracle again. Down, moderately up, way down, not quite so up as the first time, and, finally, way up, all within the space of a month or so, is not the way for a priest of Eleusis to be. Perhaps he will retain a suspicion that out of combat, as in it, confusion is fairly normal.

6
No-News

Now and then I enunciate a truth with such clarity that I hate to boggle with the wording afterward—it is suitable for framing. Thus:

There are three kinds of writers of news in our generation. In inverse order of worldly consideration, they are:

1. The reporter, who writes what he sees.
2. The interpretive reporter, who writes what he sees and what he construes to be its meaning.
3. The expert, who writes what he construes to be the meaning of what he hasn't seen.

To combat an old human prejudice in favor of eyewitness testimony, which is losing ground even in our courts of law, the expert must intimate that he has access to some occult source or science not available to either reporter or reader. He is the Priest of Eleusis, the man with the big picture. Once his position is conceded, the expert can put on a better show than the reporter. All is manifest to him, since his conclusions are not limited by his powers of observation. Logistics, to borrow a word from the military species of the genus, favor him, since it is possible to not see many things at the same time. For example, a correspondent cannot cover a front and the Pentagon simultaneously. An expert can, and from an office in New York, at that.

This, when written, applied immediately to military experts, but it is even more true of experts on foreign affairs. There are, indeed, some experts, like David Lawrence, who are general practitioners. *Being* an expert is more important than what you are expert in. It is a frame of mind, a vocation, like turnspit. "*On devient cuisinier, mais on nait rôtisseur,*" may be paraphrased:

317

"One becomes, with modesty and practice, a reporter; but one is *born* an expert."

When information is unavailable, the expert comes into his own, as on a fatal day in March, 1953.

Death on the One Hand

MARCH 28, 1953

Inconsiderate to the last, Josef Stalin, a man who never had to meet a deadline, had the bad taste to die in installments. This posed a problem for newspaper editors, who had to decide whether to use their prepared obituary notices and shoot the works generally on Wednesday, March 4, the day Tass, the Russian news agency, announced that the Premier had suffered a brain hemorrhage, which even to the most casual reader looked like the end, or to wait until he officially expired, by which time the story might have lost the charm of novelty. What made it even stickier for the editors was the paucity of news that could be expected out of Moscow, where there were but six correspondents for the whole American press; the three major news agencies were represented, and the New York *Times* had its own man, Harrison E. Salisbury. The number has declined steadily since late 1946, when the Russians began refusing visas to new correspondents. Because of the visa situation, there was no way of sending reinforcements to cover the big event, and because each of the correspondents had to file a lead story for his own employer, their efforts were bound to parallel each other. The wire-service reporters—Henry Shapiro, for the United Press; Eddie Gilmore, for the Associated Press; and an International News Service man who for some reason got no byline in the Hearst papers —and Salisbury did an excellent job qualitatively, but quantitatively their aggregate efforts were necessarily skimpy.

According to newspaper canon, however, a big story calls for a lot of copy. The New York papers rose to the occasion by resorting to a procedure known, variously, as constructive journalism, interpretive reporting, and the crystal ball, but for which I now prefer a term I owe to James Reston of the New York *Times,* one of its recent, and probably reluctant, practitioners. Mr. Reston, in the *Times* of March 5, a day when Stalin lay moribund and so did real news, recounted a conversation he had had with a Democratic senator who had lunched at the White House on the previous day. He asked the senator what the President seemed to think about the situation. The senator told him that the President had discussed the Stalin illness "about the way everybody else discussed it all day, saying 'on the one hand this and on the other hand that.'" This is a perfect description of what the newspapers filled up with, and they ended by completely submerging the news story, which was simple enough: a formidable old man had died and nobody knew what to expect as a consequence.

The annoying hiatus that the old Bolshevik permitted to intervene between his syncope and his demise put a strain on even the ruggedest professional seers, who had to start explaining the significance of his death before he had actually died and then keep on inventing exegeses until he was in his tomb. Altogether, their ordeal lasted a full week, but they stood it better than their readers.

It was the United Press that furnished the lead story for the *News,* the *Mirror,* and the *Herald-Tribune* on the morning of March 4, when the news broke—a sober, factual bulletin beginning, "Premier Josef Stalin is seriously ill, it was announced today," and including the essential clinical details. It was accompanied by the official text of the medical bulletin signed by Stalin's physicians. Caught that way, the papers had no chance to do anything constructive about the story. The *News* gave the story the headline STROKE FELLS STALIN and barely found opportunity for a couple of parenthetical inserts in the U.P. text:

(There was evidence of the morbid suspicion with which Russians traditionally view each other. A government announcement said the eight physicians' treatment of Stalin is "conducted under the constant supervision of the Central Committee . . . and the Soviet Government.")

and

(Diplomatic circles in London began speculating immediately on possible repercussions in Soviet satellite states of Stalin's illness—or possible death. All Eastern Europe was considered facing eruptive consequences.)

It also appended a paragraph to the story that appeared in none of the other papers: "Among those whose names have been frequently mentioned to succeed the dictator are Vyacheslav M. Molotov, the former foreign minister; Andrei Andreyev, the vice prime minister; and Georgi Malenkov, member of the Communist Central Committee and a longtime protege of Stalin."

This, incidentally was the only call Andreyev got during the newspaper straw vote for Despot of All the Russias.[1]

The *News,* obeying the precept to strike first with the maximum force, also committed to the press the obit it had been long preserving against the day of Stalin's death. It began, "For more than a quarter of a century Stalin, 'The Man of Steel,' has lived up to his pseudonym as the ruthless dictator of 180,000,-000 Russians and the most inscrutable of all statesmen in a world continuously on tenterhooks." After that, the story ran on for three tabloid columns—pretty dry.

---

[1] As the attentive reader will note, nobody mentioned a man named Khrushchev to take all. This is not a reflection on the expertise of experts, but on the futility of flapdoodle.

The four-star final edition of the *Mirror* I saw had just the United Press story from Moscow, with an add, probably tacked on in the U.P. office here, quoting from Winston Churchill's Iron Curtain speech in Fulton, Missouri, in 1946. The *Mirror*'s headline on the story read: STALIN NEAR DEATH!

The *Herald Tribune*'s eight-column front-page streamer read: STALIN HAS STROKE; HEART AND BRAIN AFFECTED.

All the *Tribune* had on the story was the U.P. piece, including the Churchill quote, and some biographical matter. It held on to its own prepared Stalin obituary, taking no chances on a treacherous recovery. I felt sorry for the Alsop brothers, Joseph and Stewart, who can turn in as good a job of constructive interpretation as anybody in the business, because their column, "Matter of Fact," had evidently gone into print before they had a chance to tell the *Tribune* readers what the Premier's indisposition foreboded. They had been caught flat-footed with a piece about the perpetual crisis in Iran; they said that it was entering one of its incandescent phases, in which the need was certainly dire and the picture somber (in an incandescent way, I suppose), and that steps had to be taken or the Middle East was likely to burst into flames.

The *Times,* as was to be expected, carried the wariest headline: STALIN GRAVELY ILL AFTER A STROKE; PARTLY PARALYZED AND UNCONSCIOUS; MOSCOW DISCLOSES CONCERN FOR HIM. This was only four columns wide, and topped a bulletin from Salisbury, to which was appended the same United Press dispatch that had appeared in the other papers. The *Times* was first off the mark in the department of speculation, however, with a story by James Reston, under a Washington dateline, that bore the three-column head: WASHINGTON JOLTED BY NEWS, FEARS RISE OF RED EXTREMISTS. "The speculation in well-informed quarters here was that if the Soviet Premier died he would probably be replaced by one of three high aides: Georgi M. Malenkov, Lavrenti P. Beria, or V. M. Molotov," Mr. Reston wrote, and then, going into on-the-one-hand-this, added, "Though Mr. Stalin was a symbol of all the anguish of the 'cold war' period that followed World War II, the paradox of the situation here this morning was that his death or incapacitation might signify an even more tense period in the relations between the Communist world and the free world. . . . It was for this reason that the news of his illness produced some apprehension when it was first received in Washington." Switching to on-the-other-hand-that, he continued, "There was, however, another reaction, no less prominent. This was that the death of the Soviet Premier or his prolonged incapacitation might lead to an intense struggle within the Politburo for control of the Soviet dictatorship." Here Mr. Reston quoted Winston Churchill on how the Mongol hordes had turned back from the conquest of Europe to choose a successor to their Great Khan, and had never recovered their impetus. The story ran about a column and a half. The *Times* carried a box noting that Stalin's stroke was similar to the one that killed Lenin. The *News* said it was like the one that killed Franklin D. Roosevelt.

It was with the afternoon papers that constructive journalism came into its own. STALIN'S LIFE FADING; HENCHMEN TAKE HELM, the *World-Telegram & Sun's* headline read, but the main news story, by Shapiro, saying that Stalin's condition had not improved, interested me less than the interpretive pieces the newspapermen had evolved. For example:

WILL KOREA REDS' MORALE TAKE DIP?

WASHINGTON, March 4—Gen. James A. Van Fleet replied "I don't know" when asked today whether the death of Russia's ailing Premier Stalin might lead to a weakening of Communist morale in Korea.

And:

ROY HOWARD SEES NO ATTACK ON WEST

MANILA, March 4—Roy W. Howard, the first foreign correspondent to interview Premier Josef Stalin, said tonight there probably would be no violent anti-western reaction from Russia as a result of Stalin's critical illness. Mr. Howard, president and editor of the New York *World-Telegram & Sun,* is on an extended tour of the Orient.

Reassured by Mr. Howard, I turned to the first page of the second section, and there found:

STALIN ILLNESS MAY
HOLD PERIL OF WAR

BY PHIL NEWSOM
UNITED PRESS FOREIGN NEWS EDITOR

Taking sharp issue with the president and editor of the paper, Mr. Newsom began, "Josef Stalin near death is more dangerous than Stalin alive and in good health." Together, the two pieces constituted a clear case of on-the-one-hand-this and on-the-other-hand-that.

W. A. Ryser, billed as a United Press staff writer, contributed a much longer piece, headed

IF STALIN GOES, THEN WHAT?

EXPERT SAYS WAR DANGER
WOULD DECREASE AT FIRST

Mr. Ryser was writing under a London dateline. The *World-Telegram,* recommending him to its readers, said, "He has excellent news sources among persons who have lived in Russia and know political affairs there well." Mr. Ryser promised "answers to some of the questions raised by Josef Stalin's illness," and led off: "Q. Will the death of Stalin increase or decrease the chances of World War III? A. It probably will decrease them, at least temporarily." Mr. Ryser touted Malenkov, Molotov, and Beria, in that order, for the succession, and answered Qs about all of them. The *World-Telegram* also went in for a bit of long-range medical diagnosis, under the byline of Delos Smith, United Press Science Editor. "Josef Stalin is on his deathbed, two American physicians concluded today from studying the medical bulletin of his nine attending physicians," this story began. "Even 90 physicians could not save him, they said." This approach must have made quite a hit with the U.P.'s clients, because the Providence *Evening Bulletin,* which I chanced to see the same day, not only ran it but checked with a Rhode Island neurologist to make sure the U.P. doctors weren't pulling its leg. This provided a local angle.

The *Post* devoted its tabloid-size front page to a picture of the patient in Moscow and the simple legend, in type three and a quarter inches high, HE'S DYING. It ran the same United Press lead story as the *World-Telegram* and the same medical story (without credit to Mr. Smith or the United Press, in the edition I saw). In the on-the-one-hand-this department, the *Post,* as I had anticipated, yielded to no competitor. STALIN STROKE MAY PRODUCE WORLD CRISIS was the head over a story by Joseph P. Lash. The illness had plunged "the world into perilous seas," he announced, going on to say that diplomats feared the question of war or peace would become "inextricably entangled with the struggle for Stalin's mantle." I had not yet seen any story that admitted the possibility there might *not* be a struggle; I repressed the fantastic thought.

"Who Will Grasp Power?" the *Post* asked, over a layout of pictures of Molotov, Malenkov, and Beria, reading from top to bottom. The layout man could have got the answer by turning to Max Lerner's column, on page forty: "It doesn't take much predicting to predict Malenkov will be the next dictator of the Soviet Union," Lerner said ". . . What have we of the free world to gain or lose by Stalin's death? This is not as easy as some commentators who shoot from the hip have in the past assumed. . . . But there can be little doubt that Stalin's death will prove a great unsettling force both in Russian internal politics and in the world situation. Does this mean that we can soon expect a popular revolt inside the Soviet Union? I will go out on a limb and say No."

The *Journal-American* had a story by Kingsbury Smith, out of Paris, commencing: "Some West European diplomats believed today that Soviet Premier Stalin might already be dead. . . . Their other immediate reaction to the electrifying news that he was paralyzed and in grave condition was that this lessened the danger of any East–West war in the immediate future."

That made the stargazer count three (Newsom, Lash, and Lerner) for increased probability of war; three (Howard, Ryser, and Kingsbury Smith) for decreased probability of war; and one (Reston) for a draw. It was a split decision, inextricably entangled with the tenterhooks of eruptive consequence.

When I opened my copy of the *Times* next morning, I could see that the editors, with twenty-four hours to turn around in, had been able to lay on a somberly incandescent display of tangential coverage. The four-column headline and one-column drop said:

STALIN'S CONDITION BECOMES WORSE
HIS ASSOCIATES DIRECT GOVERNMENT;
EISENHOWER AND EDEN MEET HASTILY

PREMIER IS FAILING

DOCTORS REPORT DECLINE
AS ARTERIO-SCLEROSIS
COMPLICATES CASE

SECOND BULLETIN GLOOMY

OLD COMRADES OF SOVIET CHIEF
TAKE CONTROL OF REGIME—
CHURCHES JOIN IN PRAYER

This had the disadvantage, from an artistic point of view, of telling practically the whole available story. It was followed by an Associated Press lead, which expanded it somewhat, and the A.P. story, in turn, was followed by one from the *Times*'s own Mr. Salisbury, which said that the doctors were doing their best, that Russia "and most of the civilized world" awaited news, and that since the previous Sunday night—forty-eight hours before the announcement of the stroke—the Government had been directed by a group including Malenkov, Beria, Marshal Bulganin, Marshal Voroshilov, and Molotov. "An Associated Press dispatch that passed Moscow's censorship said it would be extremely foolish to speculate on any change in Russian policy at this time," the *Times* interpolated here. Never was a warning less heeded. All in all, the copy out of Moscow ran to about two columns; to the total bulk of reading matter served up, however, those two columns bore the same relation that the male angler fish bears to the female: a small, scarcely perceptible bump, serving only to fertilize her. The copy that I would class under the heading of on-the-one-hand-this-and-on-the-other-hand-that ran to eighteen columns, or nine times the linage of straight news.

A first-page Washington story by Mr. Reston, headed SUDDEN WHITE HOUSE PARLEY BELIEVED TO CONCERN SOVIET, reported that President Eisenhower had talked with the Secretary of State, the British Foreign Secretary, and the head of the Central Intelligence Agency but that nobody knew what they had said. The *Times* correspondent added, "Dependable information on the situation within the Soviet high command was so scarce that speculation on the dictator's successor could not be solidly grounded." He then quoted about a column and a half of unsolidly grounded speculation on all phases of the situation, winding up with the quotation from the Democratic senator, for which I remain eternally in his debt.

Another first-page story, by a *Times* man named Harry Schwartz, who specializes in constructive interpretation of Soviet subjects, began, "Most available evidence points to Georgi M. Malenkov as the man most likely ultimately to inherit Josef Stalin's power [on-the-one-hand-this] but that result is not yet a foregone conclusion [on-the-other-hand-that]." Mr. Schwartz went a couple of columns, handily. In addition, the *Times* covered the story from Tel Aviv

(Israeli analysis of the situation), the United Nations
Building (delegates shocked, express apprehension),
Berlin (rumors flew there), Tokyo (the news received
calmly), Bonn (where Drew Middleton discovered a
new terror; i.e., that the Kremlin was expected to relax
pressure on West, and thus de-frighten Europeans, re-
tarding formation of European Army), Kansas City
(where Harry S. Truman said he was "sorry to hear of
his trouble—I'm never happy over anybody's physical
breakdown"), Rome (where an "unofficial source"
had little that was encouraging to say about Stalin's
prospects in the hereafter), the *Daily Worker* office
("deepest grief"), Belgrade (convinced hell is busting
loose in Moscow already), Hong Kong ("swift speculation here on what effect"), and Taipei (where I can't
remember what). It also carried interviews with four
former United States Ambassadors to Russia; of
whom Averell Harriman predicted a reign of terror,
Admiral William H. Standley predicted a revolt, General Walter Bedell Smith predicted a rule by a triumvirate (Malenkov, Molotov, Beria), and William C.
Bullitt predicted that if there were a triumvirate it
would "tread softly" in international affairs. A brain
specialist at the Columbia–Presbyterian Medical Center and a neurologist at the New York University–
Bellevue Medical Center assured the *Times* that Stalin's recovery appeared unlikely. (The *Times* insists
on its own, nonsyndicated doctors.) From London, C.
L. Sulzberger, the *Times*'s chief foreign correspondent,
wrote, without straining the bounds of plausibility,
"The apparently approaching death of Premier Stalin
will almost certainly precipitate a period of great uneasiness in world affairs." I had an ungenerous feeling,
while paddling through all this virtually identical speculation, that I was watching a small boy pull a cud of
chewing gum out to the longest possible string before
it broke.

The *Herald Tribune*, which usually does the same
kind of thing as the *Times* but less of it, ran only
eleven columns of creative interpretation in its news
sections, along with the essential two columns of news.
But it supplemented its reportorial crystal-gazers with

a couple of professional on-the-one-handers: David Lawrence and Walter Lippmann. Mr. Lawrence was monitory: ". . . the tendency will be to exaggerate the significance of the occurrence," he warned, "and to assume that the removal of one evil man suddenly makes the other twelve in the Kremlin virtuous. It will take a little while for the disillusionment to come —but it will come." As for Mr. Lippmann, perhaps the greatest on-the-one-hand-this writer in the world today, he appeared to be suffering from buck fever when confronted with so magnificent an opportunity for indecision. "The kind of power that Stalin has exercised cannot be transferred intact," he wrote, for his on-the-one-hand-this. "It is a kind of power that has to be grasped by the new pretender and made his own by his own actions. . . . It is hard to believe that this can happen easily or quickly." Then, switching to on-the-other-hand-that, he added, "If it does, it will be the greatest surprise, and the most disconcerting, that has yet come out of Soviet Russia."

As for the morning tabloids, the *News*'s forthright editorialist went on the on-the-one-hand-this circuit with the gruff declaration, "As we see coming Russian events, the only certainty is that there are going to be changes, and that those switches are bound to affect the world, for better or worse." From the tone of the *Mirror*'s editorial ("There is reason for cautious optimism in the condition of a dying despot whose end may have been hastened by his own realization that the game was up—and his plan of world conquest a bloody failure"), I gained the impression that the writer had personally induced the Russian Premier's condition by punching him on the chin. Hard as nails.

By afternoon, the *World-Telegram* had its crystal ball shining like the Scripps-Howard lighthouse in the upper corner of its front page. Ludwell Denny, the Scripps-Howard foreign editor, filed a story from Bonn that appeared on page seven, headed: HEIR TO STALIN MAY NEED WAR TO HOLD POWER. The head over another exercise in omniscience, by Isaac Don Levine, who was given a buildup as "an acknowledged authority on Soviet Russia," proclaimed, on page

eight: KREMLIN'S NEW RULERS NEED PEACE TO SOLVE
PROBLEMS.

In the *Post,* Mr. Lash, who had plunged the world
into perilous seas on the previous day and got it inextricably entangled in a struggle for Stalin's mantle,
now thought that "no immediate open struggle for
power nor violent shift in Soviet foreign policy" need
be expected. Another *Post* writer, Murray Kempton,
wrote a real artistic piece. "Oh, sun, oh, summer sunshine, oh, Josef Djugashvili, oh, Josef Stalin, oh, Koba
or all the other dozen names a professional revolutionary had occasion to call himself; what do the survivors know of you?" Mr. Kempton apostrophized the
invalid of the day. It reminded me of a song written by
Chris Smith, an old colored man I knew long ago:

"Down in Louisiana, among the sugar cane—
Oh! Oh! Oh!"

The plot of Kempton's story was that Stalin was dying
and that no one remembered what a dirty dog he had
been because he had killed all the witnesses. "Alone
among the old Bolsheviks he would lie in a marked
and honored tomb. He had destroyed them all, and
now he too would go to join the revolution in the
grave." His secret would have been safe if he had remembered to dèstroy Kempton.

One of the points Kempton made about Stalin was
that Trotsky once described him as "the most eminent
mediocrity in the party." The *Post* editorialist said the
same thing about the dying man: "He was our century's most successful bore. Stalin was the Babbitt of
Bolshevism." The *Telegram* editorialist said, "He
spread hate and evil throughout the world, and that
evil will live on after Stalin is in his grave."

Meanwhile, the *Journal-American,* a trifle slow in
getting under way the first day, had picked a long shot
to succeed the dying marshal. (Joseph Newman, the
Herald Tribune's figurator, had, by the way, touted
Molotov.) STALIN'S SON SEEN AS "DARK HORSE," a
head on the *Journal*'s Thursday first page announced.
There was a picture of young Stalin in uniform, wearing earphones, and a caption reading, "Anything can
happen. . . . Heavy-drinking Vassily Stalin (above) is

a 'dark horse' possibility to seize power when his father dies, according to the observation today of Arkadi Svobodin, whose series, 'I was Stalin's Nurse,' appeared in the *American Weekly*." Mr. Svobodin himself had been a dark horse to me until that moment, but I like a handicapper who will pick something at a price. Next to the picture was an editorial by William Randolph Hearst, Jr., the *Journal-American*'s publisher. "Apart from the hypocritical, that is to say, diplomatic, words of regret from various heads of state concerning Premier Josef Stalin," it said, "it seems to us there has never been a more appropriate time for the expression, 'I hope it's nothing trivial.' "

The official news of the death, and of Malenkov's subsequent elevation, came as an anticlimax, I thought. When you fill your news columns with stuff that is only 10 percent news, I suppose you create in the reader's mind a doubt that any of it is news. Anyway, I have formed a definite impression on the one hand that Malenkov is not a man at all but a large articulate dummy, with Leon Trotsky inside him. (That explains the small intelligent eyes peering out from behind the cruel mask.) And on the other hand, when you stop to think of it, Stalin may still be alive.

The above exhibit proves that no-news is more voluminous than news. But no-news has its own perverse charm for the reader who can visualize the expert, squirming over his typewriter like a hen ordered to lay or be fried. Nineteen-fifty-three was a vintage year for no-news, of which the following is another cobwebbed bottle. An advantage of no-news over news is that, since it never happened, it never ages. It can be read today with the same pleasure as when it was written, or as the no-news about Cuba or the Congo in this morning's paper.

More News Behind the News

AUGUST 1, 1953

The arrest of Lavrenti P. Beria, which broke in the newspapers here on the morning of Friday, July 10, offered a great opportunity for the dissemination of the journalistic commodity known as the news behind the news, or on-the-one-hand-this-and-on-the-other-hand-that. In this respect, it resembled the story of the death of Josef Stalin, which produced some of the finest news-behind-the-news-behind-the-news writing in the history of creative art.

Within a week after Stalin's announced demise, the American public knew that he had died of natural causes or been murdered subtly, either on the date named by *Pravda* or several weeks earlier; that the people of Moscow had demonstrated grief but (a *Journal-American* scoop) the demonstration had been a carefully organized fake; that his death portended either a hardening or a softening of policy toward the West, which, in turn, would lessen or increase the chances of open war; and that his death would either precipitate an immediate struggle for power among the surviving leaders or impel them to stand together until they got things running smoothly. It was freely predicted that, in the event there was a struggle, Malenkov would destroy his associates or his associates would destroy him. The subject permitted a rare blend of invective and speculation—both Hearst papers, as I recall, ran cartoons of Stalin being rebuffed at the gates of Heaven, where Hearst has no correspondents—and I have seldom enjoyed a week of newspaper reading more.

So when I saw the first headline on Beria—it chanced to be in the *News*—I felt a pleasant thrill of anticipation, as at the sight of the first circus poster. "*Ademonai, kodemonai*," I murmured to myself happily. (This, a Japanese colleague has informed me, is

331

the Nipponese equivalent of "on-the-one-hand-this-
and-on-the-other-hand-that.") The front page of the
four-star edition of the *News* on B-Day was brilliantly
concise. A little more than half the page was occupied
by three lines of type, each two inches high: BERIA
JAILED BY MALENKOV. Below was a picture of Molotov, Beria, and Malenkov in a reviewing stand, taking
a salute. It was a picture that had been widely used in
papers here at the time of Stalin's death, when editors
decided that the three men constituted a triumvirate. In
the reproduction of the picture printed in the *News,* two
white lines had been superimposed, crisscross, on the
figure of Beria. The caption read: "BIG 3 NOW TWO.
Lavrenti Beria, head of Soviet secret police and Georgi
Malenkov's toughest rival for Stalin's mantle, has lost
his fight for power. The Soviet radio announced that
Beria, shown above with Malenkov (right) and Molotov, third man of Russia's Big 3, has been kicked out
of the Government and arrested as 'an enemy of the
people.' "

This was a masterly use of the tabloid form and
contained almost all the information the *News*—or
anybody else here—had. If the *News* had stood pat on
it, the paper would have made journalistic history. But
a tag line—"Story on page 3"—indicated that the editors had not been content to leave merely superb
alone. They insisted on proving that their paper could
be just as prolix as any newspaper of standard size.
Page three contained a long Associated Press piece
from London, which ran over onto page six. The first
part of the story did not say when or how Beria had
been arrested; a reader seeking this detail had to push
on into the runover before learning that it wasn't available. About all that was added to the front-page caption was some scraps of the fascinating Russian official
gabble that accompanied the announcement from the
Kremlin. A sentence I liked particularly was "Beria,
having become crude and rampant, began to disclose
his genuine face—the face of a malignant enemy of the
Soviet people." In the absence of more facts, the story
had been wadded out with some mild specimens of
ademonai, such as "Beria's downfall *may* [italics mine]

have been quickened by the failure of his security forces to avert uprisings in East Germany and the satellites" and "There was no indication whether shortcomings in [the atomic-energy program] *may* have contributed to his disgrace"—or, the writer might have added, whether there had indeed been any shortcomings.

But it was not until I hit a story by a *News* man named Robert Parker that I knew happy days were here again. Mr. Parker had the real news-behind-the-news touch. He had gathered his material by talking to "diplomatic observers," whom he could not, of course, name, and whose whereabout he left uncertain. The sentence that put me completely at home was, "Fully aware of the fact that Russia has cried wolf often enough in the past to make caution extremely desirable [that was the *ademonai*], these observers, nevertheless, suggested that the explosions in Russia's satellites may have started a chain reaction that could shake the Communist world to its foundations [*kodemonai*]." Beria, the representative of the secret police in the Kremlin triumvirate, having been expunged, Mr. Parker went on, Malenkov, representing the Communist Party, and Molotov, backed by the Red Army, would now have to fight it out. "Beria . . . is apparently destined to be the scapegoat for the now discredited Kremlin policy of terror," he ademonaied, only to kodemonai: "There may be further explosions before Beria can be tried."

Grateful for having had everything explained to me so clearly, I turned to the next piece, a United Press dispatch headed: CAPITAL HOPES OUSTER MEANS RED UPHEAVAL. "The dramatic news that one of the Kremlin's Big Three had fallen came as a surprise to the Government, although the State Department had received reports of dissension among Soviet leaders," this one said. Senator John J. Sparkman, a member of the Senate Foreign Relations Committee, had told the reporter that the jailing of Beria "would indicate some strife among the leaders of the Soviet Government"—a reasonable enough conclusion, it seemed to me. Senator Homer Ferguson, also a member of the committee, had said,

"It explains two things: first, the uprisings all over in the satellite states, and I think there are some in Russia; and, two, the disintegration of totalitarian rule." In explaining the uprisings by the arrest, Senator Ferguson took issue with Mr. Parker's observers, who explained the arrest by the uprisings.

The *Mirror,* the next paper that came my way, had been stuck with an on-the-one-hand problem of its own. The Soviet government, ever alerted for a chance to embarrass a Hearst paper, had chosen to release the Beria news on the very day set by the *Mirror* for a big splash on its Lucky Bucks contest, a circulation-boosting stunt that had entailed a lot of advance preparation. On the one hand, the *Mirror* editors recognized, Beria was a pretty fair news story. But on the other hand, a man in Brooklyn had turned up with a one-dollar bill bearing a serial number that won him a prize of $500 in the contest. Five hundred dollars is not the sort of money you give away without milking it of full promotion value. The editors reached a split decision.

Under the first-page headline, MALENKOV JAILS "TRAITOR" BERIA, they ran another line, FIRST $500 LUCKY BUCKO! SEE PAGE 5 FOR STORY AND NEW LUCKY BUCK NUMBERS, and under that they inserted pictures of two Lucky Buck winners. Beria's picture ran inside, with a United Press story from London, which cited Tass, the Soviet news agency, and the Moscow radio as sources. No home-office crystal-ball boy had been available in the city room to write the news behind the news, it appeared—they may all have been out interviewing Lucky Buck winners—so the *Mirror*'s first-day interpretation had been supplied by the United Press, too. This was by Donald J. Gonzales, writing out of Washington, and it began:

American officials said tonight . . . that a titanic struggle for power has been raging inside Communist Russia. Tito was considered the most important factor for the West in the startling news that Russia's No. 2 Communist had been deposed. [There was no clarification anywhere in the story of this allusion to the president of Yugoslavia.] Cau-

tious hopes were raised in this capital that Beria's fall
might mean escape from a disastrous third world war if
inner conflict is destroying the Kremlin's mighty power.
But there were also grim warnings that any such struggle
might explode into new Russian aggressions as a way to
crush dissension at home. . . .

The State Department said it had not received official
reports on Beria's ouster from U.S. Ambassador Bohlen
in Moscow [actually, Bohlen was in Paris at the time of
the coup] and therefore withheld official comment. News
that Beria had fallen caught the U.S. Government by surprise, even though the State Department has received persistent reports of rumblings within the Kremlin. . . .

Some informed sources believed Beria's ouster would
be followed by a purge of his followers in the Russian
government and Communist Party. The removal of Beria
left the position of Molotov in doubt, as far as American
officials could figure. They wondered whether the Foreign
Minister might be the next Russian leader to go. . . . A
high-ranking State Department official said: "It confirms
the belief that a struggle for power has been taking place
in the Kremlin since Stalin's death and that Premier Malenkov has now come out on top."

This struck me as pretty good news-behind-the-news
writing. The struggle was identified as "titanic" in the
first sentence, which let the reader know it was important; Tito was introduced as an element of mystery
and then ushered out as abruptly as Beria himself;
cautious hopes were balanced against grim warnings;
and Mr. Molotov—of whose Red Army backing Mr.
Gonzales appeared not to have been informed—was
left for a future installment, like something in the bottle for the morning.

I wasted little time on the *Herald Tribune*, which
had again been caught, as on Stalin Day, with all its
oracles in print on less timely subjects; like the *News,*
it used an Associated Press story from London. One
of the things the *Tribune* could use these days is a spot
oracle.

Pushing on to the *Times,* I found things humming.
The *Times* had its own Moscow story, by Harrison E.

Salisbury, its correspondent there. Salisbury's story read like something written for metropolitan consideration, and not like a scrabbled handout aimed at a paper in central Indiana, as so many press-association dispatches do. With inserts made in the *Times* office here, it ran two columns. The *Times* also printed the texts of the two official communiqués on Beria's dismissal, along with a biographical note recalling his part in rewriting Russian history for the greater glory of Stalin—an important step in his rise to favor. The Salisbury story had the place of honor on the right-hand side of the first page. I put off reading it, however, until I had read two other pieces on the front page. These provided the news behind the news. (It gives me pleasure to sneak up on the news that way, so I can understand it when I get there.) The first of these specimens of constructive journalism was by Harry Schwartz, an oracle who always leaves his telephone number with the city desk. This started right off with the bold assertion of a possibility; only an inexperienced on-the-one-hand writer will commit himself to a probability, or even to a plausibility.

The purge of Lavrenti P. Beria from the Soviet high command raises the possibility that the entire post-Stalin conciliatory policy of the Soviet regime may be reversed, or at least seriously modified [Mr. Schwartz began]. Many of the conciliatory measures, both at home and abroad, particularly the former, carried out since Stalin's death have generally been identified by foreign diplomatic sources as the result of Mr. Beria's influence in the post-Stalinist Soviet ruling group. [Mr. Parker, however, had identified Beria with the "now discredited policy of terror."]

Whether or not Mr. Beria's removal has any effect on over-all Soviet internal and external policy, his complete fall from power seems to be the most important single event in the post-Stalinist struggle for power since the death of Joseph Stalin, announced as having occurred last March 5. [Mr. Schwartz, I noted, has not conceded on the date.]

Mr Schwartz went on to say that Beria's downfall

strengthened the position of Malenkov, but that it made Molotov's position "seem uncertain," since "there have been indications suggesting that he had sided with Mr. Beria." EFFECTS UNCERTAIN was the head over his story. That's how I felt, too, as I turned to CAPITAL SURPRISED AT MOSCOW NEWS over the byline of Harold B. Hinton: "Officials who might have been expected to know of the event in advance, or to have some immediate reaction to the event, were either silent or declined to permit the use of their names to what speculations occurred to them," Mr. Hinton wrote from Washington. "The consensus was a warning against jumping to conclusions about the status of Premier Georgi M. Malenkov. There was little inclination, on the whole, to evaluate the development as meaning that Malenkov had unqualifiedly inherited Stalin's mantle.

When I had finished this story, I began to feel the same delightful confusion I felt in those days after the death announced as having occurred on March 5. According to Parker's sources in the *News*, Molotov and Malenkov had ganged up on Beria. According to Schwartz, Beria and Molotov had worked unsuccessfully against Malenkov. As for Molotov, who was no worse than even money to take it all in the *News*, he was "next to go" in the *Mirror*, seemed "uncertain" in Mr. Schwartz's *coup d'œil*, and, at least by implication, still had a chance in the opinion of Mr. Hinton's informants.

I could hardly wait for the afternoon papers, and, as always, when depth-reporting—the kind of reporting that requires no expenditure for carfare—is the order of the day, the afternoons were worth waiting for. BERIA FACES DEATH AS SOVIET TRAITOR was the eight-column banner on the *Journal-American*'s Wall Street Special edition, and under it, confirming Mr. Gonzales and Mr. Schwartz, was the red-letter line MOLOTOV SEEN NEXT TO GO. The *Journal-American*, more conscious of its dignity than its tabloid sister-in-Hearst, the *Mirror*, had squeezed a plug for its own promotion gag into a thin line above the masthead: "$500 DAILY DOUBLE WINNERS—SEE PAGES 6, 15."

(The Daily Double contest is based on picking the winners of trotting races.)

Milton L. Kaplan, an International News Service man in London, was beating the brains out of Beria on the front page. "Lavrenti P. Beria, who climbed to power in Russia over the bodies of those he purged as head of the dreaded secret police, today faces a traitor's death for losing in a convulsive struggle with the Kremlin to succeed Josef Stalin" was the way he got up steam. (Beria's climbing reminded me of a head I had noticed over a *News* story: BERIA BURROWED HIS WAY TO TOP: PRAVDA. The man had been going in all directions.) "There was speculation that next to be purged will be Molotov, third member of the ruling 'Big Three,' " Kaplan continued.

Kingsbury Smith, European General Manager of the International News Service, cabled from Paris, "Reports also were received that Beria was infuriated by the rebellious spirit of the captive .peoples and wanted Moscow to drop its appeasement policy and apply steel-handed terrorism to restore respect for Soviet domination." The reports were clearly not received from the same diplomatic sources Mr. Schwartz had consulted for the *Times*.

An A.P. story from London lived up to its headline, BERIA DOWNFALL SEEN VICTORY FOR MALENKOV. Malenkov, therefore, seemed to me to be sitting pretty until I hit the *World Telegram*'s 7th Sports—Race Results—Wall Street edition. Then I discovered that so far as Scripps-Howard was concerned he was a dead duck. BERIA DOOMED, MALENKOV PERILED, MOLOTOV, RED ARMY TAKING OVER, was what the *World-Telegram* banner said. There was nothing about this in their lead story, a United Press dispatch from Moscow signed by Henry Shapiro, but I could well understand that Mr. Shapiro was not in a position to put the news behind the news in his copy. The big head was based on a story by W. A. Ryser, of the United Press London staff, who, an introductory paragraph said, was "long a close student of Russian affairs, with a record of correct interpretation of events behind the Iron Curtain and with a wide acquaintance among Western diplomats." Malenkov had not wanted to hurt Beria at all, according to Mr. Ryser. They had been pals. "Many Western observers believed that all real power now had passed to the rival Kremlin faction headed by Foreign Minister Vyacheslav Molotov and Defense Minister Nikolai Bulganin," Mr. Ryser elucidated. "Beria's unexpected dismissal from all his government posts and his expulsion from the Communist party has reversed the situation created after the death of Stalin. Then it was Malenkov No. 1 in the government and party and Beria No. 2." (Reversed, this would make it Beria No. 1, and Malenkov No. 2, but Mr. Ryser did not tarry to explain.) "Western diplomats believe that Molotov and Bulganin, in achieving the almost impossible, did it by securing army backing and confronting Malenkov with the alternative of dumping Beria or facing open revolt. . . . Now Malenkov, having sacrificed Beria to save himself, becomes a mere figurehead, in the opinion of many observers here."

This was not the way William L. Ryan, Associated Press Foreign News Analyst, saw the news behind the news on page four: "The party faction headed by Premier Georgi Malenkov holds the power as of this moment," Mr. Ryan had it. ". . . But despite his apparent swift victory over Beria, he has been seriously weakened. . . . The timing seems out of kilter, as if the explosion had burst prematurely."

The deciding vote in the *World-Telegram*'s trio of peerers into the murk had evidently been cast by Leon Dennen, N.E.A. staff writer, peering from Paris. Mr. Dennen's source was "one of the best-informed Western diplomats, who has just arrived from Moscow." According to this fellow, Mr. Dennen said, "Beria, in alliance with Georgi M. Malenkov, had been preparing a wide-spread purge of the Red Army. He believes that Malenkov betrayed Beria's plans and the military acted first. . . . By betraying Beria, Malenkov seems to have saved his skin for the moment. But for how long?" The headline over his story was: RID OF BERIA, RED ARMY BECOMES RUSSIA'S RULER.

The *Post* used the Shapiro story for news—without his byline, however. I found the paper surprisingly

unenterprising in the *ademonai-kodemonai* department. It said in an anonymous think-piece that "there
were almost as many opinions as there were experts
on the meaning of Beria's fall from power but one
prediction was general: Those who chose sides with
the hard-eyed secret police boss . . . will disappear
with Beria." The *Post* made amends to the lovers of
news behind the news by printing a symposium of all
the theories that had been launched up to that point.
Among them was one from the London *Star:* "Beria
was the main advocate of a tough policy with the West
and his dismissal 'will probably lead to improvement
in East–West relations.' "

Next morning, which I could hardly sleep until,
brought news that the State Department, despite its
modest disclaimers of foreknowledge of B-Day, had
known all along what was going to happen. The *Times*
—a trifle vengefully I thought—announced, "For public consumption, the United States Government claimed
advance knowledge from Mr. Bohlen of the probable
elimination of Mr. Beria. . . . The State Department
spokesman, in announcing Mr. Bohlen's hurried trip
to the United States, asserted today that the Ambassador to Moscow had foreseen and reported the probable elimination of Mr. Beria 'several days ago.' This
claim of advance knowledge of the Beria ouster . . .
came as a surprise to many in Washington." The State
Department further claimed, according to the *Times*
story, that Mr. Bohlen hadn't been in Paris on a holiday at all—he had been taking a long lead off base so
he could get home sooner with the news behind the
news when the story broke. "This did not square with
a statement that Mr. Bohlen was reported to have
made in Paris this morning," the *Times* went on. "He
said then that he did not think the incident would interfere with his vacation plans. The comment was made
before Secretary Dulles had directed him to come to
Washington."

Salisbury, the *Times* man in Russia, had sent a dispatch in which he said that no change was expected in
Soviet foreign or domestic policy, but I realized that
he could not tell half he knew, because of the censor-

ship. That is one of the drawbacks of having reporters on the scene in foreign countries. Other reporters can think up more fascinating stories sitting right here at home.

It was with keen interest, then, that I noted an Associated Press story from Stockholm, on page three of the same paper. "The following dispatch was written by Eddy Gilmore, an Associated Press correspondent in Moscow from 1941 until ten days ago, when he and his family left for the United States," an italic introduction said. Surely, I thought, Gilmore, a good reporter, who has spent twelve years in Russia, will be able to tell a lot now that he is free from restrictions of censorship. "Is there a Russian Bonaparte in the background? Possibly, but not likely. Nothing is being heard from the Army," Mr. Gilmore wrote (Ryser and Dennen had been able to tell more about Red Army plans at a distance of several thousand miles.) And of Beria he reported, "I would like to say that I deduced from this [Beria's absence from the opera on June 27] that he had been purged. But I did not. I knew it was a possibility, but I thought he had rushed off to East Germany to take charge of that situation."

That may not be news behind the news, but it's certainly candor.

Who Won What?

NOVEMBER 22, 1952

The fine flush of General Eisenhower's victory was fixed on history's cheek forever in the prose of Cholly Knickerbocker, the *Journal-American*'s "Smart Set" columnist. "When the announcement was made over the loudspeaker in El Morocco at 1:50 A.M. that Gov. Stevenson had just conceded to Gen. Eisenhower, a cheer went up that almost shook Chauncey Gray off his piano bench," Cholly wrote in the Hearst evening paper on November 6, after he had had a chance to collect his emotions. "Then he and his orchestra swung into 'Happy Days Are Here Again.' " (Gray's swing into the old Roosevelt campaign tune must have been an example of pure mechanical reaction.) "The club was jammed with staunch Republicans, in white tie and tails, who had just attended the opening of the Horse Show. As my eye swept around the club, I noticed Count and Countess Rodolpho Crespi with Nina Lo Savio; Johnny Meyer with Mrs. David Legget, Olga and Peppi D'Albrew . . . actor George Raft with Rosemary Colligan; Mrs. George Washington Kavanaugh . . . Laddie Sanford . . . Mrs. T. Markoe Robertson, and many, many others."

The jubilation of the staunch Republican Count and Countess was shared by Robert C. Ruark, of the *World-Telegram & Sun,* who is ordinarily hard to please. Mr. Ruark wrote, "I was sort of proud of my country. . . . What made me jubilant was the elevator operator was sore as hell this morning." A corresponding exuberance was on display in every segment of the New York daily press except the *Post,* which had supported Governor Stevenson, and the inconsiderable *Daily Worker,* which had backed the Progressive Party candidate, Vincent Hallinan. Six of the seven newspapers of magnitude—the *Times,* the *Herald Tribune,* the *News,* and the *Mirror* in the morning, and the *Journal-American* and the *World-Telegram* at night, with eleven-twelfths of the city's total daily circulation between them—had been on the general's side. It troubled me, therefore, to note that the victorious media were already beating one another about the head less than forty-eight hours after the polls had closed on their collective triumph. What they couldn't seem to agree on was who had made the landslide.

Arthur Krock, who wrote the lead story on the first page of the *Times* for November 6, the first day on which a detailed picture of the results could be presented, took the simplest view—that most of the people who voted for General Eisenhower had wanted to vote for General Eisenhower. The victory was "the triumph of a person as contrasted with that of a political party," he wrote, adding: "The verdict was clearly

for a change, but primarily of national leaders. That
General Eisenhower, and not the Republican party,
was the principal reason for the termination of Democratic tenure in the White House that had lasted for
twenty years was made evident by the result of the
contests for Congress. The General and Senator Nixon
obtained a minimum of 442 electoral votes to a maximum of 89 for the Democratic candidate [there was
no subsequent change in the score], and the popular
vote as thus far tabulated was 31,862,042 for the
Republican national ticket and 25,654,348 for the
Democratic. [More complete figures were, roundly,
33,000,000 to 26,500,000.] But though the history of
American politics is that the victors in such a landslide carry into office with them sound working ma-
jorities in the Senate and the House of Representatives, the voters gave General Eisenhower only a tenu-
ous majority of one in the Senate . . . and—on incom-
plete returns—a margin of three in the House. [At
this writing, the margin is ten.]"

This would have convinced me, even if I hadn't
turned to the editorial page and there found Mr. Krock
again holding forth; he had apparently run inside
ahead of me and sat down to his second typewriter.
He was, I discovered, of precisely the same mind on
page twenty-eight as on page one. "It was a personal
tribute," the editorial-page Mr. Krock said in his column, "In the Nation." "And that the result was greatly
influenced by the personality and promise of General
Eisenhower is implicit in the fact that, even with such
a Republican landslide, the party barely has a majority in the House of Representatives. This demon-
strates how much stronger than his party was its candidate for President in 1952." Mr. Krock, I was glad
to see, could not have agreed with himself more heartily.

Joseph and Stewart Alsop, in their column in the
Herald Tribune of the next day, delivered a concurrent opinion. "The outstanding fact of the election can
be very simply and shortly stated [they stated very
simply and short]. It has been an enormous personal
triumph for Dwight D. Eisenhower. . . . As soon as

he found himself as a political campaigner, the job
was done. . . . The only Republican candidates who
ran conspicuously ahead of Gen. Eisenhower were Sen.
Ives in New York, and Senator-elect Cooper in Kentucky. These two were, so to speak, Eisenhower-ites
before the general thought of entering politics. . . . The
contrast is dramatic indeed with the Republicans who
do not stand for the things Eisenhower stands for.
Among these, Sen. McCarthy, of Wisconsin, ran a
whopping 200,000 votes behind both Gen. Eisenhower and Gov. Walter Kohler, Jr. . . . Sens. Jenner,
of Indiana, Malone, of Nevada, and one or two more
men of this stripe were unquestionably carried to victory by Eisenhower's magical coat-tails. Meanwhile
Sens. Kem, of Missouri, Cain of Washington, and
Ecton, of Montana, lost their states while the general
carried them. From Gen. Eisenhower's personal stand-
point, in truth, the one blemish must be the defeat of
Sen. Lodge, of Massachusetts. But this was due primarily to the brilliant campaign of Rep. John Kennedy.
. . . The malice of the Neanderthal Massachusetts
Republicans, who cut Lodge because he fought for
Eisenhower's nomination, was at best only a second-
ary matter.

I would have accepted the Krock–Alsop thesis right
there if I hadn't remembered seeing in the *News* of the
day before, in John O'Donnell's column, "Capitol
Stuff," that General Eisenhower had had little indeed
to do with his own election. Mr. O'Donnell seemed to
feel that the general had been merely an instrument,
like the Chinaman that H. L. Mencken said the Republicans could have licked Roosevelt with in 1936.
The only difference was that, unlike the Chinaman,
the general had had the luck to be nominated. Mr.
O'Donnell wrote: "This America of ours made a
sharp turn to the right on Election Day and never
gave a warning signal. [Probably because of the absence of such a signal, he had declined to predict the
election results, thus missing a chance to get even for
his bad guess in 1948.] In the voting collision that
followed, it completely wrecked that fantastic political
one-man shay created by the diabolical genius of

Franklin D. Roosevelt and inherited by Harry S. Truman. The wreckage of that evil machine is more important than the fact that a former general by the name of Eisenhower now enters the White House after defeating a witty and urbane sophisticate named Stevenson. [You can't be a former General of the Army, by the way, any more than you can be a former John O'Donnell. The rank is permanent.] Those millions of votes for Eisenhower were not cast because there was a flaming belief that Ike is the best possible Presidential timber in the nation. They were cast in an effort—successful, may the Lord be praised—to end the existence of a fantastic creation that came to power 20 years ago. . . . The election pulverized that uneasy but functioning New Deal alliance of old-line Democrats, crackpot radicals, boastful and power-mad labor politicians, farmers who liked to get something for nothing, conservative southerners, angry minority groups, and big industrialists who liked those fat contracts backed up by Treasury checks."

This left me up in the air. I was loath to think of either Mr. Krock or Mr. O'Donnell as a man susceptible of successful contradiction. O'Donnell's thesis appeared to find support in a news story by Homer Bigart I saw in the *Herald Tribune* of November 7. It was not Mr. Bigart but the protagonist of his dispatch, Arthur E. Summerfield, the National Chairman of the Republican Party, who furnished this corroboration. The headline ran: SUMMERFIELD SAYS PARTY, NOT NOMINEE, WON. And the bank was: ASSERTS OTHERS COULD HAVE BEATEN STEVENSON; FINAL COUNT IS 442 FOR GENERAL.

Summerfield, the story said, had told a news conference that even without General Eisenhower the Republicans could have won. "Replying to a specific question, he said he thought Sen. Robert A. Taft, Ohio, Gen. Eisenhower's chief rival for the Republican Presidential nomination [and, I remembered having read somewhere, an old friend of Summerfield's], would have won." But he had added, with what I thought rather handsome consideration for the President-Elect, that he was "not saying that the Republicans could have put up a crackpot and won."

The Chicago *Tribune's* man at the news conference quoted Summerfield as saying that "a demand 'for a change in Washington' was the major factor in the Republican victory" and that not only Taft but "some other Republican leaders" could have been elected. (Taft was of that opinion himself, according to a later United Press story I read in the *Herald Tribune,* which went, "Sen. Robert A. Taft said today he would have won the Presidency if the Republicans had nominated him, and that he would have carried more Republican Senatorial candidates with him than Gen. Eisenhower did.") The Chicago *Tribune's* piece said nothing about Ike's magical coattails, but it included a couple of quotes Bigart may have forgotten, such as: "Asked about the distribution of patronage, and whether the President-elect would seek advice from the committee on job appointments, Summerfield said Eisenhower had said that he supported the Republican organization from top to bottom. Summerfield added that the organization will hold itself in readiness to counsel and advise Eisenhower."

An editorial in the *Herald Tribune* for November 6, the day of Summerfield's press conference, said, "The size of the Eisenhower victory is not only dramatic; it is a fact of utmost political significance for the time ahead. The General polled a record popular vote; outran his own ticket in nearly every state; split the South; appealed powerfully across party lines. . . . No man is able to say that his influence elected General Eisenhower. The new President will come to office without commitments or entanglements." But a Chicago *Tribune* editorial of the same date ventured to differ. (Between campaigns, incidentally, the Chicago paper alludes to the *Herald Tribune* as a British royalist publication.) Colonel Robert Rutherford McCormick, the Chicago *Tribune's* publisher, who had disowned both candidates early in the campaign, in its last weeks accepted Gen. Eisenhower with all the alacrity of a loser in a paternity case. Since the election, he has mellowed slightly toward the general, but he is still patronizing. "Gen. Eisenhower made himself a popular figure," the *Trib*'s editorialist said. "His discussions of the issues were sometimes confusing but he obviously convinced some 35 million voters that Dwight Eisenhower is an honest, sincere, likeable man. . . . The principal issue was Trumanism, with its mink coats, Yalta, Potsdam, and Korea. . . . The turning point in the campaign was Gen. Eisenhower's visit to Sen. Taft. . . . And in the Wisconsin primary, Sen. McCarthy's magnificent victory gave the first indication that the Eisenhower landslide was in the making." And on November 8, the *Tribune* revealed who had *really* started the landslide: "It was a long 20 years, and it will always be one of our greatest satisfactions that the *Tribune* never faltered in all that time in its efforts to bring the country back on the straight road. . . . For 20 years we read the record and helped the people to understand it and to weigh it against their own and their country's interests."

The extra two million votes the Colonel slipped the victor—the total at the time was thirty-three million, not thirty-five—constitute the kind of inexpensive largess he is often pleased to bestow. But it is pretty clear who *he* thinks were the architects of victory: Taft and McCarthy. As for Lodge, the *Tribune* editorialized: "One of the most satisfactory results of the election was the defeat of Sen. Lodge, the Truman Republican. He got what he asked for. In an election in which Trumanism was the issue, he suffered the common fate of Trumanites in both parties. Gen. Eisenhower carried Massachusetts by 200,000 votes, and Mr. Lodge lost it by 68,000. Mr. Lodge's close association with the general in the pre-convention and post-convention campaigns could not save him."

In its news columns, under a Boston dateline, the *Tribune* had a story by William Fulton that said: "Lodge, a well-known trimmer and opportunist, tried to ride several political horses galloping off in different directions, with the result the voters unseated him, both Republicans and Democrats taking part in the debacle. Basil Brewer, publisher of the New Bedford *Standard-Times* and manager of the pre-convention campaign for Sen. Taft in his unsuccessful quest for the G.O.P. Presidential nomination, loomed large in the Kennedy victory. Brewer supported Kennedy but at the same time counseled voters to back the Eisenhower ticket. . . . Another powerhouse in the split-ticket, Eisenhower–Kennedy prize package was the Boston *Post,* which has embarked on a vigorous anti-Communist crusade under its new publisher, John Fox. The *Post* is New England's leading Democratic newspaper. The *Post,* however, recommended to its readers that they vote for Eisenhower for President and then cross over to Kennedy because he had a better record fighting Communism than Lodge. Meanwhile, for weeks the *Post* has been carrying Sen. McCarthy's book, 'McCarthyism—A Fight for America,' daily in serial form."

The *Herald* (or British) *Tribune* said editorially, "It is a harsh irony that has removed from his Senate seat in these elections the man who, as much as any other individual, contributed to the grand outlines of the victory." A *Times* editorial entitled "The New Congress" said, "Senator McCarthy was, unfortunately, re-elected, but at least it is a hopeful sign that he ran far behind the ticket, trailing the top five Republican state officers on the Wisconsin ballot. . . . Not enough voters split their ticket, while too many did so in Massachusetts, where Henry Cabot Lodge, a valued and experienced member of the Senate, lost, even though Eisenhower carried the state."

It hardly seemed possible that all these papers could have been on the same side in the same campaign, and at this point in my reading I was beginning to feel an almost unbearable curiosity about who, or what, *had* won it. But if I had found the divergences between different pro-Eisenhower newspapers baffling, I was completely flabbergasted by the internal riot on the *Mirror*. The *Mirror,* best known as the purveyor of Walter Winchell, has an editorial column unfrequented by the human eye: In this space on November 6, my research disclosed, the editorial writer had said, "The great Eisenhower victory establishes that the American people have tired of 'Deals'—New, Fair, or

mixed. They want an American government without
deals. . . . That is why they came out in droves to vote
for Ike Eisenhower." But the next morning Winchell
kicked his anonymous colleague in the shins. "Some
editorialists concluded the G.O.P. victory was not only
a defeat for Truman—but also the New Deal," Mr.
Winchell wrote. "Such an opinion defies historical
facts. . . . Truman rejected New Deal concepts. . . .
It is well to remember that F.D.R. played the major
role in making Ike a national figure by choosing him
to lead the Allied forces. If F.D.R. had not made that
choice, the American people would not be in a position to choose Eisenhower as President."

I gathered from this that if President Truman had
not rejected whatever Winchell thinks was the New
Deal, the Democrats would have won. But I also
gathered that if the late President had not promoted
the career of Gen. Eisenhower, the Republicans would
have lost. Either way it went, the victory had to rest
with Franklin D. Roosevelt.

On November 5, as you have no doubt read, the
President-Elect departed for Augusta, in Georgia, one
of the few states he didn't even come near carrying. A
layout of photographs of his departure in the *Herald
Tribune* illustrated what seems to be a current American phenomenon: as soon as a man is elected President, people start looking like him. From the day of
President Truman's induction, photographers began
discovering Truman doubles in every city ward and
incorporated village in the United States. Soon after
that, Truman doubles began being noticed, even by
non-photographers, in half the tellers' cages in the nation. Ira Rosenberg, a *Herald Tribune* photographer,
got a picture of a man almost anybody would have
thought was Gen. Eisenhower putting Gen. Eisenhower's golf clubs on an airport baggage truck. It is a
safe bet that there will be more doubles turning up
daily from now on, until it becomes a cliché that every
American over fifty looks like Eisenhower. The explanation, I think, is that everybody who gets elected
President looks like a lot of other people but that,

until he *is* elected, nobody thinks this at all remarkable.

With Eisenhower's departure, the press took to warning the public to expect no miracles. The day after he left, I noticed three no-miracle stories in the *World-Telegram* alone. One, a United Press dispatch from Washington, was headed EISENHOWER FACES THORNS ON TAXES, and said, "Gen. Eisenhower, and most of the Republican Congressional candidates, campaigned on promises to reduce the nation's tax burden as soon as possible. But the G.O.P. also is strongly committed to a balanced budget—and that may mean that tax relief will have to wait a while." A longer follow-up on the same theme the next day carried the head: DON'T EXPECT BIG TAX CUTS BEFORE 1954.

Another United Press piece appeared under the heads:

U.S. ADVISERS TO ROKS
WILL TELL EISENHOWER
TROOPS AREN'T READY

LIAISON OFFICERS FEEL IT WILL TAKE
YEARS BEFORE THEY HOLD LINE ALONE

This was a change from the pre-election week, when the same paper had run a first-page story beginning, "The great campaign debate over sending South Koreans into the line to replace American soldiers in Korea mushroomed like an atomic explosion today, billowing out to Tokyo and Paris." (The *World-Telly,* which had placed glaring headlines, and often full-page streamers, across the weekly Korean casualty list every Wednesday before the election, brought it down to a front-page box the day after Gen. Eisenhower's victory.)

To complete the no-miracle triple, Frank Farrell, in his column, cautioned, "Anyone hoping that President-elect Eisenhower will move in on Washington corruption with let's-get-even vindictiveness may be due for sharp disappointment. Outside of the normally expected changes in Cabinet, Pentagon, and elsewhere, there will be no looking backward for revenge, Ike told us recently." At the *Journal-American,* which had thundered so long about kicking the Democrats out of office to get rid of Communists and fellow-travelers in government, misgivings evidently were fast setting in. A story by one of its experts on subversives, Howard Rushmore, put us all right back on our guard only four days after the election. It was an interview with Representative Velde, the incoming Republican chairman of the House Committee on Un-American Activities, and the headline over it ran: URGES U.S. PURGE; WARNS OF REDS INFILTRATING GOP.

Apparently, life is going to go on about as usual in the world of the afternoon newspapers.

V-Day in Court

FEBRUARY 28, 1953

Every now and then, I find myself falling into the error of considering the daily press a commercial enterprise. Then comes a crisis in which the press freely confesses its devotion to principle, and I feel like writing a round robin of apology to all newspaper editors. That is exactly what happened when General Sessions Judge Francis L. Valente announced on February 9 that prosecution testimony in the case of Minot Frazier Jelke III would be given in a courtroom closed to the press. "For weeks, I have watched with growing uneasiness the mushrooming public anticipation of lurid and salacious details," His Honor said, in part. "The defendant is entitled to a public trial. However, this right does not include the gratification of the morbid curiosity of the public." BAR PRESS AND PUBLIC WHILE V-GIRLS TESTIFY, the *Journal-American*'s head on the story said. "V," a letter briefly associated with victory in a previous headline era, now stands for "vice" in the N-boys' and girls' peculiar language, and the V-girls, as every literate New Yorker knows by this time, were to testify against Jelke, who is charged with being a professional pander.

Up to the moment when Judge Valente announced his decision, the story had not seemed one of national significance, although it had its points. The defendant was what the N-boys like to call a Scion (of a wealthy family of former oleomargarine manufacturers, in this instance), which, in the same idiom, qualified him as a Socialite. Scions are seldom accused of procuring, which gave the case a bit of the man-bites-dog-aspect that the schools of journalism talk about. And Pat Ward, the first V-girl scheduled to testify, had provided press photographers with some C-cake pictures that had a stimulative effect on the circulatory processes of readers and newspapers alike. Still, I had an annoying suspicion that the story was being overplayed until Walter Winchell, in the *Mirror* of February 10, the day following the Valente ruling, apprised me of the case's new stature. "In the Jelke case before Judge Valente, the evidence now is secondary to the question of whether the trial was conducted according to the Constitutions of the State of New York and the U.S.," Mr. Winchell wrote. Farther down in the same column, all devoted to the trial, he noted, regretfully, "Too bad it is the kind of publicity New York City has to get on its 300th anniversary." I could sense Mr. Winchell's reluctance to add to the volume of a kind of publicity he deplored, but the threat to *two* constitutions had evidently forced his hand.

In his column of February 13, he confirmed my intuition. "Pat Ward is not the issue," he began this one. "Nor is her testimony. Neither is the defendant, Jelke. Their sordid stories have been running, with different names, since the first man learned how to write. . . . The name Jelke, and his guilt or innocence, is utterly unimportant. . . . The issue is whether *ANY* defendant in *ANY* criminal case can be tried unconstitutionally, and the exclusion of the press is only one feature of the unusual court in progress. . . . As far as this reporter is concerned, Pat Ward's story is of no consequence. . . . The Constitutional Issue is entitled

HOGAN [The Manhattan District Attorney] *AND VALENTE* versus the *FREE PRESS.*" (Justice Benjamin L. Scheriber, of the New York Supreme Court, who ruled on Judge Valente's order a week later, didn't think *either* constitution was involved, but Winchell will probably overrule him, too.) Since Winchell thought Jelke "utterly unimportant" and Miss Ward's story "of no consequence," I wondered briefly why he had written thousands of words about the case before it assumed its eminence in the history of jurisprudence, but it was probably just one more instance of his smelling a story before it broke.

Meanwhile, on February 11, the official editorialist of the *Mirror* had supported Winchell with a leader that ended, "The most important consideration in any case must be the proper administration of justice and the preservation of the dignity of our courts. . . . It is greater than the various characters in this trial." By way of sustaining the dignity of the courts, that particular edition of the *Mirror* carried a front-page picture of Miss Ward as she "jogged her memory," another as she "tosses a provocative glance at reporters," and a "one-time Viennese munitions tycoon," now a "62-year-old boulevardier," whose name had "burst from behind the court-hung shrouds of secrecy" as an acquaintance of the V-cutie. To judge from the interview, a shroud was something the old boy was hardly ready for.

The *Journal-American,* on the day after Valente's ruling, editorialized, "It appears to us the way to treat a shameful social condition is not to hide it under imposed secrecy but to bring it into the open. The press can be counted on to exercise its time-tested public responsibility." With this it coupled a cartoon showing a black-sleeved, possibly judicial hand using a broom marked "Secrecy" to sweep a pile of dirt marked "Jelke Trial" under a carpet, while a trim vacuum cleaner labeled "Publicity Crime Deterrent" reposed unused in the background. That particular issue labored to deter crime with an eight-column front-page streamer, D.A. REPORTS PAT ON STAND HAS NAMED "12 TO 20" CLIENTS; a two-column front-page lead story with a three-column runover; a front-page picture, four columns wide, of Miss Ward and her attorney, J. Roland Sala, hemmed in by suppliant reporters as they prepared to enter the secret session; and a two-column picture, on the page with the runover, of the "oleo heir" with *his* attorney, Samuel Segal, leaving the courtroom. It also carried one of a series of daily intimate features on Miss Ward by a resourceful reporter named Marjorie Farnsworth, who customarily followed her into the ladies' room outside the trial court. This was headed PAT WARD IS GIRL OF MANY MOODS, and began: "Auburn-haired Pat Ward, 19, chief prosecution witness in the vice trial of her former boy friend, Minot "Mickey" Jelke, is one of the moodiest and most inconsistent women I have ever met. One day she will be affable and smiling, the next haughty and cold. In between, she may be off in some personal dream world or flashing her sloe-shaped green eyes in anger." A sloe is a bluish-black plum, which grows on the label of one species of gin bottle. "Her answers are equally inconsistent, at least so far as her answers to me are concerned. She has directly contradicted herself to me on half a dozen occasions —sometimes within a period of minutes. . . . Today she was in [an] angry mood, as she clung to the arm of her elegantly dressed attorney, J. Roland Sala. . . . Yesterday, Pat was quite approachable when I spoke to her. She said she finds the atmosphere of the trial, with observers barred, to be 'nice and intimate,' and disclosed she was no longer nervous. Pat was humming a gay song while combing her hair and applying lipstick during a recess late yesterday afternoon in the trial before Judge Valente." (As further evidence of its time-tested public responsibility, the *Journal* carried, under the first-page V-spread, an advertisement for a coming Sunday feature, " 'The Story of My Life,' by Christine Jorgensen, the Woman Who Was Once a Man." "Christine's own story of her remarkable transformation from man to woman," the ad read. "The most extraordinary human document of our times, the complete, revealing story barely touched by the daily news dispatches. Illustrated with exclusive photographs.")

The *World-Telegram,* on February 10, displayed a similar editorial contempt for the subject matter of the case, though it carried three portrait studies of Miss Ward, all very pretty, on the front page, over a two-column head, JELKE DEFENSE HAS MYSTERY WITNESS. Reporters for all the papers, excluded from the court, were now haunting the corridors and pumping attorneys for both sides during recesses. Jelke's lawyers were being more than cooperative. "We have no illusions about the sordid nature of the case . . . ," the editorialist said. "Nor do we deny the duty of any reputable newspaper to refrain from wallowing in 'lurid and salacious details.' . . . Nevertheless, we feel Judge Valente impugns the high scruple and sense of responsibility in most of the press. . . . Least of all in cases like this Jelke case should the locking of courtroom doors and the drawing of curtains create suspicion that a judge might be more zealous to shield private names than to protect public morals. Some judges may have less worthy motives than Judge Valente's. Which makes his bar-public-and-press ruling all the more unwise as a court precedent." I thought the next-to-last sentence particularly generous in its disclaimer of any imputation against the judge personally, which might lead to action for contempt.

"Miss Ward seemed to be enjoying herself hugely, pleased with all the attention," the *World-Telegram's* story on the "sordid" case noted. "She smiled when someone commented on the fuss over her and remarked that 'Jelke seems to be the forgotten man.'" On February 11, the same paper ran a second editorial on the judicial outrage, which it called "something far more serious and important than the Jelke case itself." Pending disposition of the paramount constitutional issue, the *World-Telegram* published an interview with J. Roland Sala, whose motion to close the court during his protégée's testimony (a motion he legally had no right to make) had, according to Judge Valente, started the train of reflection on public morals that induced the jurist to kick all the spectators out. Mr. Sala, speaking "in a voice trembling with emotion," told the *World-Telegram,* " 'If I thought only of Pat Ward and not of others whose morality might be influenced, I would have the trial opened to reporters. . . . She would arouse such compassion that tears would come into the eyes of every human being—even you reporters.' " The *W.-T.,* trying to be fair to both sides, recorded farther on, "Jelke, who, after all, is the central figure in the vice trial but who has been ignored to a large extent, timorously ventured the opinion that he would be acquitted because 'they haven't proved there's any case.' "

The ladies' room, now apparently being worked by Miss Farnsworth's competitors as well as by her, yielded another portion of the *World-Telegram*'s coverage of the less serious and important elements of the story. Miss Ward, the paper said, had informed the N-girls that she had "agreed to write an 'Advice to Teen-Agers' column for two metropolitan newspapers (not named)." Since the *World-Telegram* already has a teen-age columnist, it was presumably not considering Miss Ward's candidacy, but one of its qualified L-room representatives had inquired into the witness's literary past. Miss Ward, the *W.-T.* girl reported, "smiled then, still brushing her hair, and said, with a dreamy, far-off look in her eyes, 'I used to write poetry when I was about 8.' "

By now, I felt it my civic duty to read every line the defenders of my rights published about the V-case, just as the editors apparently felt it theirs to publish any available form of damn nonsense. The issue was one on which the *Daily Worker* took the same editorial position as the capitalist press, a circumstance that may someday lead to some nasty allegations of fellow-traveling. NAME THE CULPRITS, the Worker headed its contribution to the defense of the constitutions, which ended, "The Jelke case is not a commentary on 'public morals,' it is truly an exposure of capitalist morals—price-tag morals—and the people have a right to know the real culprits."

The *News* editorial writer, like his confreres, deprecated the case as a case. "The Jelke mess, as practically every American knows already, differed little from similar cases that reach the courts every day in the week," he wrote. "Sex has been kicking around for centuries. Only the Café Society prominence of some of the members of the Jelke cast made the young oleo heir's trial extraordinarily newsworthy." It was the legal principle involved that got the *News* man sore, in his bluff, regular-guy fashion, because "right now, a morals case involving a passel of he- and she-tramps has been blown up into a major stink. We think the courts owe it to themselves to remove that aroma, fast." On Lincoln's Birthday morning, the Four-Star Final edition of the *News* again gave the case top billing over another that had been engaging public attention. The front page read this way:

VICE JOHNS
WILL FACE
OPEN COURT

ROONEY "JUST MET" PAT WARD

ROSENBERGS MUST
DIE, IKE RULES.

The top headline, in letters twice as high as the one about the Rosenbergs, referred to a rumor, subsequently denied, that Jelke's lawyers might call some of the V-girls' customers as witnesses, and "open court" referred to the fact that Judge Valente, as of that moment, had pronounced only the prosecution's case unfit for publication.

The *Post,* carrying on its remunerative mission of being intellectual and sensational at the same time, averred that one of the purposes of its coverage was instruction. "We are occasionally asked whether the headlines appearing on page one of this newspaper are ever motivated by a desire to sell newspapers," its third editorial on the case in a week began. "The answer is yes. A lot of liberal newspapers have gone to their graves valiantly proclaiming that they would not let sex interfere with their serious thoughts. We are more modest in our world view. We believe sex is here to stay and even liberals must face it. . . . The kiddies, we are confident, will take care of themselves; when they are old enough to read about sin, they are likely to be old enough to be told. Pat Ward might be happier now if she had not had to learn about it the hard way." It was the *Post*'s old internal conflict between libidinous and didactic tendencies, Earl Wilson and Max Lerner—what the quarterly-review boys would call its essential dichotomy. Sex with a sociological slant has become a *spécialité de la maison* on the paper which under Godkin, long ago, was so Victorian that, according to a period wit, it "made virtue repulsive every evening"—a mistake the present management appears eager to avoid.

The *Post* began writing about Pat Ward last summer, when an unfeeling state first lagged Mr. Sala's star client, with whom the paper seemed to sympathize.

This is the story of a golden-haired daughter of the Lower East Side's ugly hurly-burly [a *Post* biographical sketch of Miss Ward, by Nancy Seely, began then]. A girl who grew up knowing little of beauty and less of fun, who knew the face of poverty from babyhood as she knew her own. Her New York was not the New York of sparkling lights and laughter, of soft music and gay companions. It was the New York of stifling summer nights and bitter winter days —of crowded tenements and cluttered narrow sidewalks. But that other New York . . . became her dream.

The story was headed PAT WARD: FROM SLUMS TO SOCIETY, and told how Miss Ward, originally a victim of urban ecology, had had her fling on the side of Manhattan where summer nights are bracing and winter days balmy and found it was not worth the price. She had gone home and become a serious-minded bookkeeper, just trying to forget. That, of course, was before her lawyer made the motion to bar the reporters. I was a trifle astonished, when I picked up another depth study of Miss Ward in the *Post* on February 10, by Murray Kempton, to find that the

color of her hair was not the only thing about Pat
that had changed in the *Post*'s eyes since August. This
one said that men "gave her the slow, downcast, furtive look that men give the chick who is known to
have a price tag on her." It also said, "If Little Orphan Annie could blow smoke out of her eyes, those
eyes would look like Pat Ward's. But she still has her
youth, and no man can resist a good-looking chick if
he knows she's a tramp. . . . She was, was Pat Ward,
the queen of the Criminal Courts Building." Then
came the switch: "One flight above, there was no sun
in the bare cubicle of the Women's Court where the
ordinary chippies go." It was what the trade knows
as stark writing. The grim part of it wound up:
"Women's Court closed, still cut off from the sun"—
like Miss Seely's slums—"and one of the probation
officers walked out. 'The thing we do here,' she said,
'is terribly serious. You know, I've been here for a
long time now, but every day I see something that
makes me want to cry.' "

Feeling pretty blue myself, I left Mr. Kempton and
turned with a slow, downcast, furtive look to the day's
assortment of *Post* C-cake.

The only major papers that didn't play the V-saga
big were the *Times* and the *Herald Tribune*. The *Tribune* carried what I thought the best editorial on the
subject, although it ignored the fact, cited in its own
news stories, that there are seven particularly messy
kinds of trial from which, by New York State law, reporters can be barred. It has never been held that
either the freedom of the press or the defendants'
rights were menaced by such exclusion. The *Tribune*
said, "The peril is one of arbitrary judges rather than
pollution by the printed word. As for obscenity, there
is plenty of law on the books, and the public can always choose its own brand of reading matter."

Meanwhile, five newspapers (all but the *Times* and
World-Telegram) and three press associations had pe-
titioned the New York State Supreme Court to set
aside Judge Valente's order. On February 17, Justice
Schreiber ruled that he had no power to tell Judge
Valente what not to do, since the General Sessions

judge was not infringing upon any law. It would be up to a still higher court, he said, to decide whether the disputed order made sense. "The guarantees of freedom of speech and freedom of the press in the first ten amendments to the Federal Constitution are inapplicable to trials in state courts," the justice declared, as quoted in the *Times*. (He had apparently not read Winchell last week.) "The provision of Article 1, Section 8, of the Constitution of the State of New York that 'no law shall be passed to restrain or abridge the liberty of speech or of the press' obviously guarantees only the free and unrestricted right to disseminate knowledge or information possessed by the public or the press. It does not purport to confer upon the public or the press a constitutional right of access to all places, whether public or private, with the object of securing information for purposes of publication. The rights to freedom of speech and freedom of the press were not intended to destroy all rights of privacy or secrecy."

This is revolutionary doctrine in our period, and probably guarantees the justice about as much press support as foot-and-mouth disease if he ever runs again for office. He got even more outrageous, from a publisher's point of view, as he went along. "The claim that petitioners are being deprived of their property rights," he said, was also predicated on the "false assumption" that they had "a constitutional right to be present at all trials and obtain for publication purposes [he had not said, I was glad to note, "business purposes"] all the information disclosed in such trials." COURT UPHOLDS JELKE PRESS BAN, the *Mirror* headed its story of the betrayal of both constitutions. The *News* was so disgusted that it gave a non-V beauty top billing over Pat and her colleagues. MDS CALL CHRIS ALL WOMAN, the headline at the top of its first page read, and Christine Jorgensen, late George, smiled from the spot on page three where Pat had so often attracted the reader's slow, downcast, furtive attention.

But it takes more than one tyrannical judicial ukase to daunt men who are fighting for the freedom of the press, the dignity of the courts, and the infrangibility of the American constitution. And at least two consolations remain to the embattled altruists. No circulations have declined as a result of the V-trial, and the judge has not yet barred women reporters from the ladies' room.

7
Not
Too
Lopsided

The outstanding common characteristic of all the stories cited in the above exhibits is that they contained no information. In this case it was not the newspapers' fault that they *had* no information, since the Soviet Government had strangled foreign press coverage. But the reluctance to admit ignorance, illustrated in the two Russian pieces, is with most of the press as strong as the refusal to accept reality: demonstrated in the two on the R.T.A. [Rubber-Type Army].

My cherished preceptor, Major General Terry de la Mesa Allen, now retired, was once confronted, at the Fort Leavenworth staff college, with a hypothetical problem about how to win a hypothetical battle. One of the questions was: "What are the enemy's intentions?" General Allen wrote, "How the Hell do I know?" and walked out. He is not a hypothetical kind of man.

The masters of the press have smaller minds. Such an admission would kill them. .

In the field, however, Gen. Allen pushed reconnaissance, which is *reporting,* to its farthest limits. He probed like a conscientious dentist, with virtuous satisfaction when he found a sensitive spot. I once saw him turn up eight thousand unsuspected Italians that way in a ravine near El Guettar in Tunisia, when a more hypothetical general would have missed them because the Big Picture intelligence boys (experts) had not reported their presence in the region. The way to find out is go see, and in sufficient strength to have a good, unhurried look. This entails a number of foot blisters and an occasional casualty, but it save battles, and campaigns, and wars, and civilizations, in the long run.

The general would have repudiated, perhaps profanely, the concept of covering the North African rebellion, and adjoining countries involved, without even one man on permanent post in the region—Casablanca to Cairo. That is what both major press associations were doing in the spring of 1956, when I was in Tunis again.

There was a U.P. United States citizen in Tunis at the time, who said he made a trip through North Africa now and again, looking for good, zippy adventure stories, like he was going to get into a town he heard was blockaded, but on a day-to-day basis the U.P. was represented, like the A.P., by indigenous stringers. The stringer for both press associations and a half-dozen European and American publications in Tunis, a highly intelligent Tunisian, was the fellow who got hit on the head. (The New York *Times,* give it its due, had two men stationed in North Africa at the time.)

North Africa, it is true, was a region that produced nothing much in the way of news that would interest a member of the A.N.P.A. just then. The Suez adventure was brewing, the war was in its third and bloodiest year in Algeria, but these circumstances were preparing the fall of the Fourth Republic—in short, nothing. It would have been all right with most of the press associations' members if they had dropped North Africa off the news map and replaced it with a new column on home care for corns. But it was a fraud and a gyp to claim they were covering what they weren't.

The expert, however estimable as a vaudeville turn or *père de famille*, becomes a national menace when he is substituted for the reporters. This is like trying to substitute whiskey for food—it gives the illusion, but not the nourishment. The constant reiteration without assertion hypnotizes; very small noise "may herald" the disintegration of the Russian Empire; the mentionable Chinese "may be preparing a comeback" on the mainland. By employing a small, syndicated gaggle of experts instead of a large, mobile swarm of foreign correspondents the press puts us in the position of a prizefighter who relies wholly on his prospective opponent's death by spontaneous combustion.

As a first spot in which to employ a half-swarm of these reporters, I might suggest that:

Since the relations of American companies with foreign governments are, in many countries, the determining factor in their governments' relations with ours, a carefully reported survey of American holdings and operations in each country of, say, Latin American to begin with, would seem to me an outstanding public service that a regenerated Associated Press might render.

Then we would know what we had to beat in each arena we are contesting with the demons whom our newspaper medicine men, the experts, blame for all international ills from croup to cross-eyes. The difference between this kind of reporting and the current reliance on not-reporting is like that between the best X-rays available at a modern hospital and the diagnostic methods of a pygmy witch doctor, who dissolves a toad's eyeballs in a gorilla's urine and then determines the patient's affliction by how the mixture tastes. (It has often occurred to me that a number of experts get their answers that way.)

After he gets his lead, the witch doctor blows a smoke scented with juniper juice into all the orifices of the victim's body and dances a complete cancan, finishing with the *grand écart,* to expel the malefic demon. This is about as effective as the Chicago *Tribune* method for saving Our Way of Life, and considerably more artistic.

A French weekly said after Mr. Kennedy's election— and to every European, of whatever political color, it is a commonplace of commonplaces—that the new President's hardest task will be to make the great American corporations conform to his foreign policy, instead of letting them make his policy conform to them, as under the previous Administration.

Even the intrepid Mr. Kennedy has not yet publicly alluded to this fact of life, and the press might render him a great service, too, if it let the public know how things stand between, say, the copper companies and western South America, or the fruit companies and Central America. Or the oil companies and the Middle East.

To prove that there is a country where the press, even in foreign affairs, does not always, monolithically, without effort, like a piano falling down a stairwell, follow the official line that also happens to be the shareholders', I present an exhibit from Suez week, in 1956, in London. This country, naturally, is not Communist.

Its papers are published in a language closely akin to our own. The exhibit bears out my thesis that a large number of competing newspapers, permitting representation of various shades of thought, are a country's best defense against being stampeded into barbarism. Implicitly, it bears out the converse of the proposition, that a country with few *competing* newspapers, all plugging the same line of non-thought, may all too easily heed the call of the rhinoceros.

The Suez coup, about which it may be necessary to refresh the reader's mind, was carefully concerted by the governments of Great Britain and France during the summer of 1956, after the Government of Egypt had canceled the last twelve years of the Anglo-French Suez Company's lease on the Suez Canal, which runs through Egyptian territory. The prime movers were French industrialists and politicians of the right, who, since 1954, had been telling their electors that the revolt in Algeria was synthetic, and completely the creation of Nasser. Nasser crushed, Arab and Berber would come to heel again, said these experts. French mismanagement in North Africa had had nothing to do with the attitude of the natives—but in any event, as we used to hear with tiresome regularity from *colons* in Algeria in 1942–43, "the Arab respects only force." A good little thrashing for Nasser, and the rest will kiss our feet. (In September, 1956, in Algiers, I read in the *Echo d'Alger:* "No accord, however equitable, on the canal, can be considered until the question of prestige in North Africa has been settled." This was while French and British were pretending to negotiate seriously with Egypt. At the time, however, I thought that the *Echo d'Alger* expressed only the sentiments of its proprietor, an Algerian Colonel McCormick named Sérigny, instead of those of the Government. In fact, British and French troops were already practicing joint landing maneuvers in Cyprus.)

The prime movers among the British were a number of Tories of the right dizzied by memories of old pleasures, like sentimental Southerners who want one more slave to beat just for old time's sake. This type of Tory happens, in many cases, to be rich; many were

at the same time patriots and large holders of Canal
Company shares. Life seldom affords chances to
serve one's country and oneself simultaneously, and
at such small risk. Nasser, in canceling the lease, had
promised full compensation. The Tory politicians and
press shrieked that he never would, never could, pay,
although, since there were 105 millions of Egyptian
pounds blocked in England, it would have been hard
for anybody else to say how he could avoid paying. (An
impartial board, long after the cease-fire, priced the
canceled lease at £68,000,000, which the Egyptians,
perforce, paid. A shareholder of my acquaintance said,
after the award, that his only regret was that he had
sold his shares too soon; if he had held on he would
have had a profit.)

In promoting the coup, however, the shareholders
and their friends may have hoped that, with Nasser out,
a puppet Egyptian Government would extend the lease
for another century or two.

By dividing 60 by 12, even I can compute that an
extension was worth at least £5,000,000, which is
$14,000,000 a year to them. I leave the odd eight mil-
lion quid as a tip.

The partners continued to pretend to negotiate with
the Egyptians, until the last week in October, when the
Israelis, who had synchronized their watches with the
French, attacked Egypt. The partners then, on October
30, delivered an ultimatum (not an antepenultimatum)
to the Egyptians, ordering them to accept an armistice
with the Israelis far within their borders and to hand
over the canal to the Allied forces for safekeeping,
failing which, the latter would attack.

The British action surprised me more than the
French, because I knew the extreme right was strong
in France—a strength it was to demonstrate fully in
May, 1958, when it terminated the regime. But I had no
notion it was strong enough to carry an outwardly respectable Prime Minister with it in Britain. The British
public was even more astonished, but diversely. Half,
and perhaps a couple of decimal points more—a sort
of Kennedy plurality—was agreeably surprised, like a
woman of 60 who feels her bottom pinched. After all,

it had been so long since they had heard Kipling! The Old Moulmein Pagoda returned to the Hit Parade. This was a feeling that cut across party lines, and cost the Labour Party dearly in the longer run. The other 40 percent plus, including all the Parliamentary Labour Party, reacted more intensely. They had all the old Roundhead fervor, and many of the best of the others had a sense of guilt, like small boys caught torturing a tomcat. On reflection, it didn't seem sporting.

The newspapers, I think, decided the issue, as I indicated in the following dispatch.

Eden Must Go—or Must He?

NOVEMBER 24, 1956

For those in London who read more than one paper, it was hard to tell, on the Wednesday morning after Sir Anthony Eden's cease-fire announcement, whether the end of the shooting in Egypt represented an acknowledgment of political bankruptcy or the magnanimous conclave of an episode of triumph unparalleled in British history.

The apparent difference of opinion among the journalists surprised me when the papers arrived with my boiled eggs and tea, because I had spent the previous evening at a Law-Not-War meeting sponsored by the Labour Party in the Albert Hall. Originally arranged as a protest against the Government's war policy, the meeting, scheduled for seven-thirty, had turned itself into a Victory-With-Vigilance celebration, because of the cease-fire announcement at six. The victory, however, was not that of the troops in Egypt but that of the seven thousand people in the hall. Their satisfaction was patent, they expressed their conviction that Sir Anthony had led the country into a discreditable disaster but that they, and the portion of the press that took the same point of view, had prevented him from turning the disaster into a catastrophe. Mr. Hugh

Gaitskell, the head of the Labour Party and the chief
speaker of the evening, appeared to share this impression. Mr. Gaitskell, who resembles an elegant Huey
Long with an astonishingly different accent, accepted
without demur the intimation of the other Labour
spokesmen that the Tories had made a mess of things.
The audience sang "For He's a Jolly Good Fellow,"
meaning Gaitskell, and then switched to a chant of
"Eden must GO!" Mrs. Gaitskell, small and pretty,
looked proud and happy; I am morally certain that
she thought things were going well. The only discord
sounded after her husband, magnanimously offering a
small concession to Sir Anthony, said, "Of course, we
all know Nasser is a dictator." An Egyptian who looked
like a stranded Channel swimmer rose in the third row
and shouted, *"No! He is not dictator!* You don't know
anything about it." Except for the Egyptian, everybody was happy, and even he cheered up when Mr.
Gaitskell said that although the Prime Minister had
jeopardized the lives of the British residents of Egypt,
none had been harmed. "We are very generous!" the
Channel swimmer shouted. When the Labour leader
said that the Suez Canal was now blocked because of
Sir Anthony's action, the Egyptian crowed, "And now
he will have to undo it!"

I therefore went to bed believing that the Government had suffered a reverse, and the *Daily Mirror,* the
first paper I looked at, did nothing to correct my impression. The *Mirror,* a tabloid, has the largest daily
circulation in Britain—about five million—and is pro-
Labour. It carried a front-page editorial that started
out:

EDEN'S WAR:
BACK TO SANITY

Thank God the shooting has stopped in Suez.
This is a last-minute victory for the forces of decency.
Whom shall we thank for this?
Thank the United Nations.
Thank the Labour Party which challenged Eden at every
move.
Thank America. President Eisenhower's warnings to

Eden played a big part in bringing him to his senses. [To read a kind word for America this week almost startled me out of *my* senses.]

Thank public opinion in this country—and in the free world.

Eden's War, which was launched to depose Nasser and seize control of the Suez Canal for Britain and France, shocked world opinion.

Only four days ago, Eden was still laying down conditions and proclaiming that his attack on Egypt would continue until he had his way.

Last night, he went back to the path of negotiation. What a calamity that he ever left it!

Lord Beaverbrook's *Daily Express* with a circulation of four million, took a different view of how things had gone. The first page placed the accent on military operations, rather than on what I had feared Beaverbrook might consider their premature termination. On the previous morning, the *Express* had called the landings "breathtaking events which testify to a magnificent military operation." But, it had added, "the events at Port Said, immensely satisfactory as they are, can only be a beginning. . . . The whole Canal Zone must be brought under the control of British and French troops, so that the vital waterway may no longer be imperilled by the war between Arab and Israeli. . . . There is still much to do before Britain and France are masters." Now, however, the *Express* felt that the much was done. A streamer over its main, black-as-Nasser's-heart banner announced, "ALLIES HAVE FULFILLED THEIR MISSION," SAYS FRENCH COMMUNIQUE. The banner itself said, ISMAILIA FALLS. Actually, Ismailia, which is a town fifty miles south of Port Said, hadn't fallen, and even if it had, the invaders would have reached only the halfway point of the canal. Instead, they had got no farther than El Qantara, a quarter of the way down. I didn't know that then, but I suspected that the *Express*'s reason for featuring French claims was that the British War Office was claiming less.

The *Express*, in an editorial, attributed to the nation

"immense delight that the essential police operation has been brought so swiftly to an end," and added, "The Prime Minister has accomplished a great part of his mission. He can go forward with heightened confidence." The editorialist confessed to one limited regret. "The Government unfortunately adds to the difficulties," he wrote. "For instead of retaining arbitration in its own hands, and those of our French allies, the Government calls in UN." Toward the chaps at the Albert Hall, the *Express* was pitiless. "On one section of the British public the crisis has reflected small credit—the Socialist politicians," it said. "The Socialists and their allies emerge from the crisis as men who have sought low aims by mischievous means. The nation should not forget their miserable record. Nor forgive it."

I remembered that the *Mirror* had also enjoined the country not to forget something or other, and turned to it again to refresh my memory. What it said was: "This country will never forget that in this day and age Eden started a war in defiance of the United Nations, in defiance of treaty obligations, and without any moral sanction." The two papers couldn't even agree on what not to forget.

The *News Chronicle,* which is Liberal, had been flogging the Government hard all week, along with the *Manchester Guardian,* which is of the same archaic but honorable persuasion. The position of the Liberal journalist in Britain usually is enviable, because he is free to criticize whichever of the great parties he wishes. He must restrain himself only from rejoicing when things are not going too badly, since any expression of pleasure risks reflecting credit on either Government or Opposition. The *News Chronicle* has a circulation of a million and a half or so—more than the total Liberal vote at the last general election—and the *Guardian* has considerable moral authority. When they joined the Labour press in the attack on the Suez plan, they gave the attack a color of nonpartisan virtue. Once their point was won, however, the *News Chronicle* clutched happily at a report that the Egyp-

tians had not accepted the cease-fire, which exempted
it from exuberance.

It was not until two days later that the *News Chronicle* was to publish the bitterest of all appraisals of the
concluded venture, by James Cameron, its chief foreign correspondent. Cameron had just returned from
Anglo-French invasion headquarters on Cyprus, where
his wrath had been bottled up by the censor.

In Cyprus [Cameron wrote], it was forbidden to make a
statement "likely to cause despondency," or to "bring us
into disrepute"—as though any conceivable statement
could do either of these things more completely than the
British Government's behavior has already so abundantly
done. . . . Since whatever it is that goes on in Egypt is
not, by decree, a "war," we were forbidden even to use
the word—even those of us officially emblazoned with the
word on badges: "War Correspondent" . . .

At this stage of history, at this nadir of our country's
name, we have precisely achieved the worst of every possible world. We are exposed as bullies and hypocrites, but
not even as successful ones, for the attack did not achieve
its proclaimed object, and gave the impression of being
called off by a Soviet threat. We tore up the goodwill of
three-quarters of the world to bring about—what? The
immobilisation of the Suez Canal, a rupture of the Commonwealth that may be irreparable, and a burning hatred
throughout the Middle East that will take generations to
erase.

Cameron's story, spread across four columns at the
top of the *News Chronicle*'s editorial page, had more
force than a leader.

The *Daily Telegraph* of that historic Wednesday
morning was positive, as it always is when the Conservative Government is in hot water. (In political
matters, the *Telegraph,* although outwardly prim, is
like an *Express* in small body type.) BRITAIN "HAS
ACHIEVED MAIN AIM," a headline on its front page
said, and you had to read into the story to find that
the quotation marks were around what its Diplomatic
Correspondent, Michael Hilton, thought "a summary

of British official thinking" would have been if available. "Britain has achieved what was the main object, namely to get effectively established in the area in effective strength," was the way Hilton thought official opinion might run. "This operation, it is hoped, will stimulate the United Nations to do something instead of talking; if the United Nations continues only talking, British forces will remain in Egypt."

On the editorial page, the leader writer declared it to be "a plain fact . . . that British and French action has stopped the spread of a conflict that would have served Soviet ends," and went on: "Those are the realities of a very grave situation. The feelings of relief —they cannot and should not be feelings of exultation —that a cease-fire has been secured must not dominate the nation's reaction. We have achieved the first purpose of the police action, which was to separate the combatants. . . . If the United States were at this moment capable of single-minded, long-sighted, and courageous action, the picture would be reassuring. (That cancelled out the *Mirror* plug.) But there will be tremendous efforts made, by friends as well as enemies of this country, to get our foot out of the door. . . . To resist that demand will need strong nerves. . . . There has been time enough to argue on the morality and wisdom of the Government's action. People who are divided in that debate can continue it —later."

It was an exceedingly long editorial, and I have retained only its vertebrae. I felt that the writer got closest to what he was thinking about near the bottom of the page, where he said, "It is tempting—and will remain tempting—to speculate on the effect of the cease-fire decision on the strength of the Government and the standing of the Prime Minister." The foot in the door I thought a slightly unfortunate analogy, since it suggested the tactics of a tramp, rather than a policeman, but otherwise the editorial sounded quite well-bred—almost genteel. It is the tone that has made the *Telegraph*'s fortune with readers who want a tuppenny *Times* that is dependably Tory; in reporting the first, sudden debate after the dispatch of the Anglo-

French ultimatum, for example, a special correspondent wrote, "The Prime Minister, who had had to speak from what might be called early dawn to dewy eve, carried his difficult bat."

Because I attune myself to the prose I am reading, I suppose, I was a bit put off by the tone of the *Daily Herald,* the next newspaper to my hand that morning. The *Herald* is the official Labour Party paper, and it carried a line across its front page in type twice as large as Lord Beaverbrook's: EDEN CALLS IT OFF. Its black-type lead story said with vulgar relish:

A storm of Labour cheers greeted Sir Anthony Eden when he told the Commons of the cease-fire. . . . At 6 o'clock, Sir Anthony rose to announce his major climbdown. His policy was in ruins. But his Cabinet, for the time, was intact.

What happens now to the British troops in Egypt? Nobody knows yet—except that they are unlikely to stay long.

The *Herald* editorial, boxed on the first page, said: "A squalid episode ends in a pitiable climb-down. But that cannot be the end; the British people dare not ignore the cost of Eden's folly. . . . The blood . . . spilled needlessly . . . of many human beings lies on the conscience of the war makers. . . . If the end of Eden's reckless adventure is to be the beginning of hope for peace, the destinies of our country and Commonwealth must pass—and quickly—into the hands of another abler and more faithful leader." I took this as an expression of a partisan point of view and I was, I fear, not satisfied that even the *Telegraph* was entirely free from bias.

Still puzzled, I turned to the nonpartisan *Times,* which I save for the last because there is so much to read in it. (I do not take the *Daily Sketch,* the *Daily Mail,* or the *Daily Worker* except on big race days, but I don't think they would have been of much help anyway.) While the *Times* is not a newspaper of mass circulation, the first sentence of the first paragraph and the first sentence of the second paragraph of its cease-fire editorial could have been combined, I think, to express honest mass reactions. The first paragraph began, "There was no doubt of the general relief in the House of Commons when the Prime Minister announced his news yesterday evening," and the second paragraph began, "It is difficult to draw up a balance sheet."

Leaving this ground of affirmation, the *Times* asked:

Was the whole venture, in its timing and conception, ill-advised and far too risky from the beginning? Very many, not simply among the Labour ranks, had their doubts about it. They feared that Arabs in every Arab country would see in the ultimatum and the landings—a hundred miles in Egypt—nothing more or less than a move to help Israel. Very many also regretted the affront given, through lack of consultation, to the United States and the Commonwealth countries. The terms of the ultimatum seemed unfair. The long preparatory bombing, even on carefully selected military targets, was abhorrent, no matter how necessary it was in the saving of lives. To be successful even in a narrow field, the operation had to be a *coup*. It threatened to become a long drawn out fight.

What can be said on the Government's side is that the intervention did, at any rate, stir the United Nations to action. . . . The whole Arab world might have become aflame. Now the United Nations, shaken by the Anglo-French intervention, has promised to supply a sizable force from many countries to watch over the peace between Israel and Egypt.

But the *Times* man, drawing up the difficult balance sheet, found many more linear inches of debit than of credit. "The free world was bitterly divided," he wrote. "The dangers that the war would spread could not be ignored. . . . The censure of the United Nations could be tolerated if the Anglo-French action had been manifestly sound and right. The British and French Governments could say that they acted to forestall Israeli-Egyptian fighting over the canal . . . but, in fact, the landing on the canal added to the bitterness and suspicions of critics everywhere. . . . The rashness of the Anglo-French venture will be debated many months. The British and French Governments will have many searching questions to face and many unpalatable decisions to take. But all can agree on the rightness of stopping the action now, once the immediate occasion—the danger of a long Israeli-Egyption war—was over."

One could not begrudge the man the last two words of the final sentence, although at the time he wrote, the Israelis had not consented to withdraw, so there was a good chance that the danger was not over at all. It was the United Nations, not the landing party, that eventually swayed the Israelis. But the leader writer had to end with some crumb of consolation for his readers.

After I had finished with the papers, I thought that a country is fortunate, all the same, to have a two-party national press in which there is a semblance of balance, and things are even better when there is an important third-party press to hold the ring. And things are best of all when, in addition to these, a country enjoys papers that are not reliably for any party at all, like the *Times*. Across the Channel, where all the French newspapers of large circulation supported the Government, there was a stampede to get on the bandwagon, though not on the invasion barges.

The story is less consoling now than when I wrote it. The *News Chronicle,* as I wrote earlier on, has since gone down, carrying with it some of the best newspapermen in England. The *Daily Herald* is in peril, but with a chance of surviving. The Liberal *Manchester Guardian* has changed its name to simple *Guardian* and is moving to London, where it will take the *News Chronicle's* place in the fan of opinion. This is not a true standoff, though, because the *Guardian* already had a considerable London circulation. In the field of independent Sunday newspapers, a species like viable heads detached from bodies, *The Observer,* an uncertain quantity politically, fought stingingly against Eden's policy in 1956, and suffered a severe loss in advertising. It has recovered the advertising, and maintained the prestige it gained from the battle. (Its outspokenness at least refuted the charge of dilettantism that had hurt it before.) We have nothing in the United States that corresponds in influence to the "class" Sunday newspaper, and it might be a good thing to try. *The Observer*'s reporting, incidentally, is sometimes first-class, although it too has a Crystal Ball department of experts, chiefly Central European, who have the Big Picture, written in invisible ink on the insides of their eyelids.

The next item displays formula journalism submitted to an unfair test.

The Coast Recedes

MAY 2, 1960

Newspapermen, like practitioners of any other trade, are aided by precedent. I once knew a *World* man, of the vintage of about 1910, who used to speak of "coasting" editors—fellows who could get along all right as long as they had a few familiar landfalls to guide them, like "Blonde Mourns Man She Shot," "Ragged Recluse Leaves a Million," "Bryan Says He Won't Run Again." The latest flare-up with Moscow began on lines that have become equally traditional since 1946, when the cold war began: we make a true charge and the Soviets deny it, or the Soviets make an untrue charge and we deny it. A copyreader hardly needed to interrupt his game of chess to write an appropriate headline, like the *Mirror*'s of Friday, May 6. REDS DOWN U.S. PLANE, PILOT BLACKOUT SEEN IN CAPITAL, over an Associated Press weather story with which you are probably now familiar; and an editorialist could smack out a leader without losing much time from handicapping the fourth race at Aqueduct, as, for example, from the *Mirror* of May 7:

THE WORD IS "MURDER"

Premier Khrushchev personally ordered the rocket-destruction of an unarmed U.S. aircraft which had drifted into Soviet air space, probably because its pilot became unconscious when his oxygen equipment failed. . . . Khrushchev has revealed himself and his beastly character to the full; he is a pig in human form.

The *Wall Street Journal* on the same day said: CRAFT PROBABLY SOUGHT WEATHER DATA, WAS TAKEN FOR SPY, OFFICIALS SAY PRIVATELY. (Officials always say "privately" to the *Journal* what they say publicly to the other papers; this gives it the air of being in the know.) Everbyody else followed the same line. It has become a badge of loyalty to accept the official version of such episodes; I cannot remember when any New York paper, since the demise, unlamented, of the *Daily Worker* in 1958, has ever hinted that an American defendant in an espionage trial behind the Iron Curtain might be guilty. (The *Worker,* of course, never admitted that he might not be.) The emphasis was always on the unfairness of the trial, as if in a country with an inferior judiciary system there could be no crime as charged. Moslems and Christians, in their separate chronicles, reported the Holy Wars in this way; it provides the virtue of balance, although if you read both sides you cannot tell what happened. This is normal; I have never seen a second impelled to tell the referee about a foul committed by his principal—let the so-and-so catch the other guy. And one must take care of oneself even more carefully when, as in a Holy War, there is no referee at all.

The story of the plane that Mr. Khrushchev said was shot down by a rocket went off course on Saturday afternoon, May 7, and the shoreline dropped below the horizon, leaving editors and columnists, like so many Columbuses, out at sea with no precedent to steer by. It was on that day that Khrushchev, speaking

before the Supreme Soviet, announced that Francis G.
Powers, the American pilot, was both "alive and kicking" and a prisoner, having been picked up thirteen
hundred miles inside the Soviet frontier—along with
all his charts and photographs and collection of cloak-
and-dagger properties—and that the pilot had talked.
(From dispatches published since, it appears he carried the most complete outfit of identification papers
in the records of espionage. He even had a card au-
thorizing him to buy chocolate bars in the PX.) Simultaneously, or just about, according to United Press
International, "the United States admitted . . . that the
American plane shot down in Russia last Sunday
'probably' was on an intelligence mission 'to obtain
information now concealed behind the Iron Curtain.'"
The news service added, "But, in a statement approved
by President Eisenhower, the State Department denied
Soviet Premier Khrushchev's charge that the flight was
authorized by officials in Washington. The statement
contained absolutely nothing to contradict Khrushchev's charge that the unarmed U-2 observation plane,
piloted by Francis G. Powers, a civilian, had flown
1,300 miles into Russia to spy on that country. Instead, the statement left the impression that the report
on the incident furnished to the State Department and
the White House by the National Aeronautics and
Space Administration two days ago was not entirely
accurate." The "not entirely accurate" was the neatest
understatement of the week.

The *News*, which on Friday morning, before the
coastline sank, had said, "The incident looks to us like
an urgent cue for the President to demand absolute
proof that the downed U.S. plane was military and
was violating Soviet territory," now took what I
thought a rather ungrateful attitude toward the Russians for having furnished the proof. "We're sorry
Powers' mission failed, but that is all we do regret
about this affair," it said. In the *Times*, James Reston,
less easy in his mind, wrote, "A determined argument
was made by some high officials that the United States
should concede nothing. It is the almost invariable
custom for governments to refuse to own up to in-

telligence activity of any kind. On the other hand,
some officials were reported to have argued that it
would be better to make some kind of avowal, to give
justification for what was being done, and to state that
the flight of the U-2 into Soviet territory had not been
authorized in Washington. By stressing this lack of
authorization, it was apparently contended, the good
faith of President Eisenhower would be safeguarded."
As it may be depended on to do, the *Times* covered
matters *in extenso,* offering eight columns of Khrushchev quotes, full of a kind of anticlerical sanctimony
and boasts about the rocket that he said had hit the
plane. There was also a picture of a group of anti-
aircraft rocketeers who had been awarded a unit citation for the shooting—a delicate job, since, according
to the report, they had brought the plane down from a
height of sixty-five thousand feet without damage to
the instruments it contained. The paper carried, in
addition, a long dope piece by its Soviet expert, Harry
Schwartz, attributing the excitement to Khrushchev's
need to distract his people's attention from the lack of
advertised loss leaders in Soviet department stores.

It wasn't until Monday, May 9, that the newspapers
began to adjust to the new order of things, one thing
being the State Department's contention that spying
was all right—everybody did it—and that a fellow
could be a spy and still be kind to his mother, like,
for instance, Nathan Hale. The *Herald Tribune* front
page carried in addition to the top head, U.S. PROBES
SPY FAILURE, a palliative box under a London dateline headed BRITISH ALSO SPY ON REDS; a Moscow dispatch, by Tom Lambert, telling Russian eyewitness
stories of the capture; and the first conclusive justification I had seen of our *exclusive* right to spy: U.S.
SPYING IN RUSSIA FOR DATA REDS GET HERE WITHOUT
SPYING. This was over a story by Robert Donovan,
who wrote, "On very high authority it can be reported
that the attitude of the Administration in this awkward
situation is as follows: The United States deems it vital
to its security to penetrate the secrecy of Soviet military
and scientific activities. In the nuclear age, it is imperative for this country to know, for example, whether

the Soviets are making any preparations that could be a build-up for a surprise attack. The key word here is 'could.' No one in authority believes today that the Russians will attack. Indeed, American policy is based on the contrary assumption. But in such a life-and-death matter the United States is not going to leave any more to guesses than it has to." Here, lest anybody ask "Suppose the Russians consider it imperative to know the same things?" Mr. Donovan made his point: "Because the United States is a democracy, vast amounts of strategic information are available to the Russians without the necessity for cloak-and-dagger work." All they have to do is ask the N.A.S.A. anything they want to know.

ADMISSION OF SPYING
CREATES A PRECEDENT

SUCH CLOAK-AND-DAGGER ACTIVITIES
ALWAYS PREVIOUSLY WERE DENIED

were the heads over a U.P.I. feature roundup on page three of the *Tribune*. On the opposite-editorial page, David Lawrence blamed Khrushchev for making a fuss over nothing. On the editorial page itself, Marguerite Higgins, to whom the *Trib* allows a hoydenish privilege of dissent, said, "There are problems raised also by the admission that the flight was unauthorized and that the President did not know of the plane's destruction. Thus Mr. Eisenhower has claimed that his official business is so pressing that he cannot remain more than seven days at the summit. And yet such was Mr. Eisenhower's disengagement from events that he did not even know of the presence of an American plane over Russian territory until Mr. Khrushchev announced it was shot down."

The *Tribune*'s lead editorial was grave but brave, with that clean, bronze-door-on-a-mausoleum tone that *Trib* editorials have of late assumed. "There is no obscuring the fact that the prestige of the United States has received a blow . . ." it said. "Even those who accept the absolute necessity of maintaining intelligence services to learn as much as possible about the massive military machine poised [alliteratively] against the free world by the Soviet Union must question why this particular flight . . . was made at this particular time. . . . While many Americans will be disturbed and unhappy over the equivocal position in which their government has been placed, there is no disunity here."

On the same day, Hanson Baldwin, the *Times*'s military expert, was the first to draw real matter for jubilation from the event. "The shooting down of Mr. Powers' U-2 on May 1 indicates not a Soviet lead in defensive anti-aircraft missiles, but, on the contrary, a Soviet lag," he reported, implying that our own people have progressed beyond picking off such sitting ducks. His only regret was that Powers hadn't killed himself, as "the Central Intelligency Agency . . . undoubtedly would have wanted." Reston, less cheery, began his story, "This was a sad and perplexed capital tonight, caught in a swirl of charges of clumsy administration, bad judgment, and bad faith." Editorially, the *Times* said, "The plane episode has dramatized what should have been recognized all along: the tension along the world's principal frontiers is unspeakably dangerous. It ought to be the business of the Paris conference, and of other conferences that may succeed it, to reduce that tension. If this is what the Russians want they can have it." In the afternoon, the *World-Telegram* said editorially, "Of all the crimes in human or political relations, to get caught lying is most humiliating." The idea seemed to be that if you don't get caught it's all right. The *Post,* alone of the local lot of papers, had an editorial field day: "We accept the explanation that Mr. Eisenhower was in the dark. Authorization of so provocative a flight at this juncture is inconsistent with his character; lack of such vital knowledge is consistent with his record. . . . Let the episode also give pause to those typewriter warriors who pounded out their declarations of war when the first version of the plane incident was released, and were prepared to give their all for our weather expert."

Tuesday brought more mystery, plus that gratification so dear to newspaper readers—tentative confirmation of a previous hunch. (A hunch of mine, anyway.) The *Times* quoted Mr. C. L. Johnson, designer of the high-altitude U-2, as saying that a Soviet photograph purporting to show the crashed plane was a fake; the U-2 could not have survived a sixty-five-thousand-foot fall and landed all in a bunch. The plane in the photograph was a Russian job, he said. From Mr. Johnson's testimony, I concluded that the rocket story must have been a Khrushchev invention designed to build prestige for Russian defenses, and that the rocketeers had got cheap medals. Hanson Baldwin, who had said that hitting a plane at sixty-five thousand feet indicated a lag, must have been depressed by the news that the Russians had not hit it, which leaves their range still mysterious. Walter Lippmann, who got his first crack at the mystery in that day's *Herald Tribune,* had not seen the Johnson story, because he wrote that the prime failure of the C.I.A. was its failure to learn that the Russians had a rocket capable of hitting a plane at sixty-five thousand feet, which they apparently didn't. David Lawrence, returning to the charge in the same newspaper, said that Powers was only twelve thousand feet in the air when hit, but did not divulge who told him. Twelve thousand feet, it is superfluous to say, is well within the range of ordinary Second World War anti-aircraft batteries. Lawrence also said that he had heard of accurate aerial photographs of golf balls made from a height of six miles, which seems a long way to go for the purpose.

On the same day, John W. Finney, of the *Times,* plunged into the first, and enduring, riddle of the false N.A.S.A report about the strayed weather plane, the source of our original embarrassment. The story was based on information supplied by the Air Weather Service of the Air Force, which maintains U-2s at their distant bases; the N.A.S.A., it seems, is primarily a group of physicists who only evaluate the weather data that the U-2s obtain. The Air Weather Service has not yet said where the report originated. Finney found the N.A.S.A. "still in a state of shock." "Officials who

have been involved in the contradictory statements,"
he wrote, "told today how an experienced public information officer thought he was telling the truth only
to be repudiated by another department, how one
agency issued a statement without checking with other
agencies involved, and how the State Department issued a denial without telling the National Aeronautics
and Space Administration." N.A.S.A. men whom Finney saw were desolate not only because they had been
instruments of a lie but because the agency had lost
the trust of its opposite numbers in other countries.
They said they had not known that they were being
used as a cover organization for military intelligence.
A reputation for scientific integrity is a small thing to
sacrifice in a brawl of such magnitude, however, and
it was clear to me that Finney had fallen among eggheads. In any event, his story was one of the best to
come out of the mess.

The *Journal-American* editorial on Tuesday said,
"In the world as it is today—and as it always has
been—espionage is a fact of life. . . . So let's put this
incident in the proper perspective and form up behind
President Eisenhower as he gets ready to meet Khrushchev next Monday." But in the same edition, Bob
Considine, the Hearst nominee for the world's greatest
reporter, wrote, with a rare rebelliousness, "It [the
plane] was shot down. But also shot down with the
U-2 was our reputation for fair play, integrity, rise-
above-the-sneaky-prying-scum appellation through the
world, even in the Communist countries. That's infinitely more important." I am not a Considine man,
but I think he had a moment of extrasensory percep-
tion there. And in the *Post,* Doris Fleeson, a woman
of strong mind, wrote, "Is there a moral necessity to
close ranks behind the President in a matter of this
kind? Can truth or a lie be bipartisan? Washington is
not shocked by espionage. . . . Its humiliation arises
from the manner in which the story developed, with
Presidential ignorance inflated to a pious virtue, and
fairy tales about bad weather and oxygen trouble fed
to the public."

It has not been a bad performance by the New

York press as a whole, bar the two impossible morning tabloids, and it portends, I think, a less blind
acquiescence in Papa-knows-best national policy in the
future. The most impressive performance of all came
from a source that is safe from the imputation of liberalism, a word that it usually puts between quotation
marks. The *Wall Street Journal*'s lead editorial said
last Tuesday:

Up until now it has been possible to say to the world that
what came out of the Kremlin was deceitful and untrust-
worthy but that people could depend on what they were
told by the Government of the United States. Now the
world may not be so sure that this country is any different
from any other. . . . Like the clergyman caught in noc-
turnal activities, we will no longer be able to be so self-
righteous. It is true enough that intelligence work—or
spying, if you prefer that word—is an accepted business
among nations. . . . But this particular incident is doubly
unfortunate. In the first place, it is going to be very hard
to persuade people that sending a Government plane deep
into the territory of another country to photograph its
terrain is not what the diplomats would call "provocative."
We need only imagine what the reaction of Americans
would be if we caught a Russian airplane over Chicago or
a Russian submarine in New York harbor. In the second
place, it is going to be hard to convince people hereafter
that explanations from Washington can be taken at their
face value. . . .
  So we have been caught not only in a rather provocative act but also in dissembling. The one can be explained
as a piece of bad judgment. The explanation for the other
will come harder. No one will argue, we suppose, that this
country has done anything different from what the Russians do all the time. . . . The difficulty is that we have
told others and ourselves we are different. . . . And now
the sad part is that this image, which has been one of the
strengths of America, is now sullied by our own self-
righteous zeal that led us to believe that anything we
choose to do is right.

It sounded like the beginning of wisdom.

This story, as you remember, went on and on, becoming progressively more disconcerting each time the newspapers, like an old-fashioned German band chased by a cop, tried to resume the concert. When they rallied around the piccolo tootling, "Ike didn't know," the bass drum boomed, "He *did* too know, he *did* too know," and Ike was playing it.

After denying we did it, admitting we did it, denying Ike knew we did it, admitting Ike knew we did it, saying we had a right to do it and denying we were still doing it, we dropped the subject.

But by that time all the newspaper coasting captains were seasick, and it was apparent that from now on navigation will be a required subject in Schools of Communication.

"There are no lights to guide."
—Rudyard Kipling

The next piece explains why I *love* the press.

New York Revisited

OCTOBER 29, 1955

Returning from Europe last month in time to see the fight between Archie Moore and Rocky Marciano, which was well worth the trip, I learned from the *Journal-American* of September 22, the day after the fight, that I had not been the only member of the international literary set sucked through the air lanes into the seething vortex of the fistic twister, as a *Journal-American* writer might well have said. The *J.-A.*'s coverage of the hectocataclysm ran through seven pages, including three of pictures, and on the last of these—page twenty-eight, which was the coffee-and-toothpicks course of this feast of melodrama—I spotted a headline in big black type: CAME 16,000 MILES FOR BOUT.

The *Journal-American,* like the *Herald Tribune,* is nowadays using a kind of head that you read from the bottom up, like a check in a restaurant. To find out who had come all that way, I had to shift focus to a thinner line over the big type, and this said: WORTH THE TRIP, SAYS MICHENER. Then, under the thick line but referring back to the thin line, was an identification of Michener—"World Famous Novelist and Foreign Correspondent." I tried to think of some place sixteen thousand miles from New York that the celebrated fellow could have come from, and concluded that it would have to be in Antarctica, unless he zigzagged. Desolation Island? He never gave it away, although he provided a couple of culinary clues:

I flew 16,000 miles to see the championship "go" [the quotes around "go" proved he was no mere sportswriter], and being in New York on fight night was worth every mile. The big "night" actually starts a couple of days early. You blow into Sardi's, and after eight months of rice and mutton, steak tastes wonderful. [The rice and mutton knocked out Antarctica, which I have always associated with penguin eggs and whale fritters. Whence, then, could the man have flown sixteen thousand miles?] Seated along the wall, you see old friends who catch you up on the Broadway beat. . . . Next night, you meet the fight mob at Toots Shor's, and the tempo of New York steps up. You beat your gums [Broadway-beat your gums, he probably meant] with the nation's greatest sportswriters. . . . At two in the morning, you are dancing with Rita Hayworth . . . and she likes Marciano. . . .

Then it's fight day, and New York was never more golden.

People who have never been away from the great, hungry, violent, majestic city cannot be aware how travellers coming home can love it. [When Michener went into Sardi's, he alone was hungry; in forty-eight hours he had promoted a city-wide famine.] How often in the past year you have dreamed of it . . . just like this, in the golden excitement of fight day. And then you're in Yankee Stadium. There are more than 60,000 around you, but by strange coincidence the man in the seat next to yours is Mark Robson, who made your last book into a movie. [How many miles had *he* flown?]

And suddenly you forget New York and the chatter and the news. You see an old Negro [Moore is thirty-eight, according to the *Ring Record Book;* Michener, according to *Who's Who,* is forty-eight] climb into the ring to face a marvellously tough young fellow [thirty-one] from Brockton, Mass. . . . And then you see a miracle. The old man is hit with everything but Marciano's inner soles. He falls flat so often you lose count [five times in twenty-five minutes, including one fall that the referee ruled was a slip]. . . . And you recognize Marciano as one of the greatest punchers of our age . . . a terrifying brawler, slugging the wrinkles off the face of the old man. [This is the first time I have ever seen Marciano compared to Elizabeth Arden, the millionaire wrinkle remover, and I do not think the analogy sufficiently precise. Moore has a kind of chubby face naturally, and Marciano was just slugging bumps onto it.]

Fight night in New York! You repeat to yourself that it was worth a trip of 16,000 miles, because in the past year, for you, there has been only riots, wars, revolutions, massacres, and all kinds of crazy hell.

That was all there was in his story to indicate where he had been—a place sixteen thousand air miles away where they ate mutton and rice and where there has been riots, wars, revolutions, massacres. There has been riots in Argentina, but do they eat mutton there? There is mutton in New Zealand, but has there been riots? If you flew from Buenos Aires to New York by way of New Zealand, the distance would come out nearly O.K., but where would you get the rice?

I could not share all Mr. Michener's sources of satisfaction, because there has been no massacres in my life in the past year except that of the British heavyweight Cockell by Nino Valdes, and after the *alouettes en brochette* at a little restaurant on the Rue Gomboust, and the *homard à l'américaine* with a *pilaf*

turque to soak up the sauce at another, on the Rue
Ste.-Anne, and the *araignée de mer* at the hotel in
Port-en-Bessin, and the Whitstable oysters and cold
grouse at Wilton's, in King Street, I found the food at
Sardi's rather a comedown. As for Shor's cuisine, I
would trade it for a basin (pronounced bison) of jel-
lied eels. I don't know Rita Hayworth, but if she
danced with me, she might like Marciano even better.
When I had finished reading Michener, I couldn't help
feeling that it is a pity he is a world-famous novelist
and foreign correspondent, because he would make a
hell of a boxing writer if he could just learn not to restrain himself.

New York, great hungry city, means different things
to different wandering sons, and what had made *me*
purr with anticipation as I hurtled through the ozone
on my local from Glasgow (a mere thirty-five hundred
miles away) was the thought of renewing my liaison
with the New York press. After five months of skimpy
ten-page London and Paris newspapers (among which
a twenty-page *Times* or a sixteen-page *Figaro* looms
like the twelve-story Hotel Mapes on the skyline of
Reno), I looked forward to hefting a three-hundred-
and-fifty-page New York Sunday *Times*—heavy as a
viable infant, juicy with the sapience of Arthur Krock,
and chock-full of real-estate ads and reviews of historical novels—or a seventy-two-page *Post,* stuffed
with Max Lerner and Leonard Lyons and crime
stories seasoned with psychoanalytical sociology. I
wondered if the press of that great golden magnum of
vintage urbanism had lost any of its sparkle while I
was away, but I was not truly apprehensive. Louella
Parsons, Dorothy Kilgallen, Bob Ruark, Cholly Knickerbocker, Murray Kempton, and the rest of the good
old evening-paper gang would be waiting for me down
on the Idlewild newsstands when I arrived, I reassured
myself. In the morning, I would have breakfast with
Marguerite Higgins and Orville Prescott before I
walked my dog. By that time, I would be caught up
on everything. A man who has been away for five
months, even if not amid any kind of crazy hell, has
to have some golden vision he can depend upon to

slug the wrinkles off his tired old brow when fortune
kicks him in the innersole.

The gang at Idlewild didn't let me down, exactly,
but there seemed to be a once familiar element missing from the papers as a whole. They were like curry
without chutney, or Stewart Alsop without Joseph. It
wasn't until I had read through the *Post,* the *Journal-
American,* and the *World Telegram & Sun* a second
time, while sitting on my luggage and waiting for my
wife to call for me, that I realized what wasn't there.
In the three papers, totaling a hundred and twenty-
four pages (*Post,* fifty-six; *World-Telegram* and *Journal-American,* thirty-six and thirty-two, respectively),
I had not once seen the name of Senator Joseph Mc-
Carthy. The *Journal* had quit boosting him and the
Post had quit knocking him; he appeared to be as dead
journalistically as Levi P. Morton. This was on the
afternoon of Friday, September 16, but it proved a
fair sample.

Another landmark missing from the *Journal-American* was Westbrook Pegler's rhadamanthine face, with
eyebrows fiercer than hussars' mustaches, which I had
left glowering from page three when I departed Bagh-
dad-on-the-North River last April. Checking up, I
found that Peg was still in the paper. He had simply
been decapitated and chucked over onto the opposite-
editorial page with the other faceless men, only his
byline being left to identify the torso. His stuff didn't
read as forcefully now as it did when he had his photograph, it seemed to me. He is the kind of writer who
depends a lot on mugging, and when you take his face
away, it is like stealing every third predicate. That,
however, is the way it is in this great, golden, magnificent, voracious, ineluctably ineffable cosmopolis; such
ancient landmarks as Peg's eyebrows and the Café
Lafayette disappear, and only we old-timers who have
been away notice the lacunae and sigh for the great
days before the decease of the senior William Randolph Hearst and Diamond Jim Brady—the days
when George Sokolsky on page two and Peg on page
three confronted the *Journal*'s readers every day, like
Scylla and Charybdis or the Brothers Grimm. Sock

was demugged long before I left. He and Peg are still on adjacent pages—Sock on the editorial page and Peg on opposite-editorial—but without their faces they are hard to distinguish from Fulton Lewis, Jr., and George Rothwell Brown. You might as well put a sugar sack over Marilyn Monroe. Not even Pegler, when I located him, had anything about the junior senator from Wisconsin in his column, which was datelined Rome. Peg was taking up for Ezra Pound, who, he said, was not insane enough to deserve being confined in an insane asylum by an arbitrary court ruling; what he did deserve, since he had certainly adhered to the enemy in wartime, was to be tried for treason and, if found guilty (which Peg said he was), shot. The argument, as I got it, was that it was an injustice to Pound not to shoot him, and I wondered if Pound resented it as much as Pegler.

For the rest, the *Journal* had a three-column front-page headline concerning a public character new to me: MYRT ALL SET TO COVER YANKEE GAME TONIGHT. Below, I learned that Myrt was "the N.Y. *Journal-American*'s newest sportswriter, Myrt Power, 71-year-old Buford, Ga., grandmother, who already has reached $16,000 on 'The $64,000 Question.' " Myrt was to cover the crucial American League games ahead (the pennant had not been decided yet) and the World Series. Mrs. Power wrote a good lead for a rookie: "Today's the day for Myrt. Rightly speaking, it's tonight. That's when I cover my first game as a baseball writer. . . . But, I'll tell you all about it tomorrow. What I've got to write about now is yesterday. It was so exciting I'd about like to have died." Peg, Frank Conniff, and Bob Considine, three of the most important think-writers in the Hearst empire, all started as sportswriters, too, so gosh knows where Myrt and Mich will wind up. The *Journal* also carried an across-the-page streamer, in appropriate red: IS BULGANIN "ILLNESS" START OF NEW RED SHAKEUP? The story was by Walter Trohan, long an adornment of the Chicago *Tribune,* and I was pleased to see that Walter had landed a job in a big city. Inside the paper, there was a piece of a yarn by Adela Rogers St. Johns about the assassination of an architect named Stanford White by a crazed Pittsburgh millionaire named Harry K. Thaw, and I'd about like to have died when I came to the part where it said that it happened in 1906.

The *World-Telegram*'s best-played exclusive front-page item was a story headed SLY KHRUSHCHEV OUT-WITS RIVALS and written by Ludwell Denny, the Scripps-Howard newspapers' foreign editor. I had a thrill of homecoming recognition when I saw the second line, which has remained in type, and generally in use, since Stalin's death. The adjective in the top line is varied to fit the number of headline spaces in the name of the fellow the *World-Telegram* has doing the outwitting—"Wily Malenkov," or "Cunning Beria," or "Ike-Pal Zhukov," for example. The head is proof against all contingencies except the rise of Petropav-lovsnikov, a dark horse that Hearst's International News Service is training by moonlight. The dateline of the Khrushchev story made me blink. It was "En Route from Moscow." In conjunction with another story on the same page, about a trip to Russia being made by a reporter named Andrew Tully, it indicated that the organization was now running a shuttle service through the Iron Curtain—a contrast indeed with last spring, when it was still relying largely on intuitional coverage. Mr. Tully, said the *World-Telegram,* had gone to Russia to find out how the average Russian lives. He invited readers to send him questions about anything they wanted him to find out. This appeared to me to be a fine chance for the *Journal-American* to find out about Bulganin's illness at the *World-Tele-gram*'s expense.

I could observe no short-term change in the folksy interior of the *World-Telegram,* which is the organ of New York's displaced persons (displaced from the interior of North America) and had an editorial policy designed to keep them from getting homesick: Republican, anti-labor, and suspicious of anything European. The inside pages were, however, featuring a campaign against tax evasion, which was quite a switch from circa 1938, when the Treasury Department, run by Democrats, was questioning publisher Roy Howard's inclusion of the upkeep of his yacht in his business expenses. I wondered, idly, whether this was because the Republicans were in now or because Howard had sold the yacht. Ruark, the *World-Telegram*'s fightin' hillbilly columnist, let me down by using most of his space for a reprint of an editorial that had already appeared in London in the *Daily Express,* where I might have read it myself before I boarded the plane. For a moment, my own displacement seemed hardly worthwhile.

The *Post* was having a fair day, still spreading the salve of enlightenment on the psychosomatic wounds of the People, as it had been doing when I departed. Max Lerner, its profoundest therapist, moralized over the case—new to me because of my absence from this great, traumatic country—of a young woman in Philadelphia who had died as the consequence of a criminal abortion, obtained, apparently, at the behest of her mother. Neither mother nor daughter had been to blame, Mr. Lerner argued; the culprit was the law against abortion, which made it difficult to have the operation performed properly. He got in the bit about there-but-for-the-Grace-of-God-goes-you-know-who, but somehow failed to include the let-him-cast-the-first-stone-that. It was a good, rousing Lerner piece, written all by himself and not quoted from the *News of the World* or *Horse & Hound.*

Dr. Rose Franzblau, who writes the column called "Human Relations," made me feel even more at home. An only daughter, fourteen years old, had written to Dr. Franzblau to ask what a girl fourteen could do to induce her mother to let her have a dog. Dr. Franzblau furnished a campaign plan by which the girl might overcome her mother's unexpressed resentments, taking into consideration every unconscious possibility except that the mother didn't like dogs.

Earl Wilson, the nightclub editor, reported as "Today's Best Laugh": "Henny Youngman says, 'I'm gonna invite that Marine quiz winner to my house for dinner—I wanna know what's in that stuff my wife has been cooking.' " It figured to have been a bad day for laughs.

The *Post,* I could see, was faithful to its motto:
"*Lux et Sex.*" It was streaked as evenly as bacon in
an ad with the lean of levity and the fat of *Welt-
schmerz,* a hard combination to beat for a nickel, especially when mustarded with a political policy acceptable to the majority of the city's homegrown voters:
Democratic and pro-labor. It wasn't until a month
later, when old Bernarr Macfadden, the physical-cul-
ture publisher, died, having long survived the greater
part of the fortune he made from publicizing the vis-
cera, that it occurred to me that Mrs. Dorothy Schiff,
the publisher of the *Post,* is, in a sense, Bernarr's spiritual heir. The *Post* peddles the psyche as effectively
as the old man once popularized peristalsis, and it is
much more versatile merchandise, since it furnishes an
elevated approach to prostitution, homosexuality, drug
addiction, rape, kidnapping, homicide of all kinds,
and even Walter Winchell. In addition, the paper carries almost all the Liberal syndicated national-affairs
columnists (there are only a handful, since most publishers are conservative): Robert S. Allen, Marquis
Childs, Doris Fleeson, and Thomas L. Stokes. It has
two expert needling Washington correspondents of its
own—Robert G. Spivack and William V. Shannon—
who have a whole Administration to jab without sanctioned competition from the staff of any other New
York newspaper. (*Times* fellows occasionally sneak
one in when the *Times* editorial board isn't looking,
but that hardly affects the *Post* monopoly.) The only
missing ingredient is news, but that, in this great,
golden, incurious city is to be found only in the two
morning papers of least circulation—the *Times* and
the *Herald Tribune*—and the *Tribune,* like the book-
stores that install phonograph-record departments, is
engaged in a furious search for more salable forms of
merchandise.

The *Post* of September 16 had nobody in Russia,
but it had made a telephone call to the Kremlin to
inquire about the reputedly ailing Bulganin. (Another
chance the *Journal* had passed up; it could have offered to share the cost of the phone call.) "Such is the
current status of sweetness, light, and transatlantic

communications, we got through to Premier Bulganin's office," the *Post* reported. A headline recorded its findings: NOT VERY ILL, BULGANIN OFFICE TELLS POST BY PHONE.

I felt as if I had never been away from the great, hungry, violent, majestic city and its afternoon newspapers, except that I hungered to know what had become of Senator McCarthy and those two young fellows who used to work for him.

That's one good point about the New York press: the papers that survive never change much, or at least never much in a period of less than 50 years. It gives life continuity: you have been away, but the good ole East River, and the good ole North River, and the good ole Harlem River, they just keep oozing along, like old Cholly Knickerbocker, and ole Sokolsky, and ole Dave Lawrence, and them others. That was 1955, but nothing much has changed since—or sence, if I affect *le genre* Scripps-Howard. Peg and Sock have got their faces out of hock, or wherever they was in 1955, but they ain't scarin' people like they useta.

I hope them fellas never die. I couldn't get along without them.

8
Look
What's
Happened

Potemkin Rides Again

APRIL 29, 1961

I was put wise only recently—by *The Blue Book* of the John Birch Society—to the true purpose of the first Soviet sputnik, in 1957. "The most important ultimate effect of Sputnik, as planned by the Soviets," according to *The Blue Book,* which is the Society's Koran, was to scare us into "getting rid of ever larger sums of American money, as wastefully, as possible," for defense and education, which would bring a rise in taxes, which would bust down the economy and lead to federal control of education, which *is* Communism. Despite this warning, though, I must admit I was taken in by the newspaper headlines that on April 12 celebrated Major Yuri Gagarin's voyage into space, for they made me think that it would be mighty nice if we could get somebody up there who could describe his experiences in English, and this, of course, was precisely the kind of reaction that the Russians were aiming at. My first misgivings were aroused by a story in the *Daily News* on April 13, headed: SPACE IDOL UNMASKED AS THE SON OF CZARIST.

"Russia's greatest hero since Lenin, spaceman Yuri (George) Gagarin, who according to the Commies is the son of a humble Russian carpenter and a product of the superior Soviet state schools, is actually the grandson of a Russian prince who was shot by the Bolsheviks," the story said. "Gagarin, whose father was also a prince, was ostracized by the Communist Party because of his blue blood. He was chosen for the space flight because he was not too highly regarded as an officer and if he did not make it he would not be missed, the *News* was informed on high authority yesterday." The high authority turned out to be a White Russian who lived on East Eighty-First Street and had left Russia in the thirties, but the story bore every evidence of truth, because it illustrated the fiend-

ish efficiency of the Commie demons: if they were
going to lose a costly space capsule anyway, they
would at least salvage the price of the bullet they
would otherwise have had to fire into the back of the
Czarist rat's neck. Little economies like that are what
build financial empires. I could not help reflecting for
a moment that with a blue-blooded Gagarin now en-
sconced as Russia's greatest hero since Lenin, the
leaders of the world conspiracy to raise the level of
education in the United States might have outsmarted
themselves. Orphaned and grandorphaned by the firing
squad, and barely escaped himself from an ostensible
plot to get rid of him, the Prince might turn against
them. He would make an attractive head of a Back
to the Freedom of Ivan the Terrible Society, and it
might have proved cheaper to dispose of him the old
way, even if the bullet had cost a kopeck. A couple of
days later, all the newspapers carried the unmasked
Czarist's denial of his identity, but his very insistence,
as quoted by the *Times,* confirmed his terror: "My parents were poor peasants before the revolution, and
the older generation, my grandfather and grandmother,
were also poor peasants." Wouldn't a man at ease in
his mind have admitted to at least a fourth-class post-
master somewhere in his ancestry? The parents attributed to him by captions on newsphotos taken during
his official reception looked to me suspiciously like
character actors I have been seeing in Soviet films
since 1929. In the photographed clinches, they were
clutching him hard, like Honored Plainclothes Operatives of the Soviet Union keeping him under twenty-
four-hour surveillance.

Despite my pessimism about the Prince's future
after the unmasking, knowing who he was helped me
identify with him and share the pleasures he described
so enchantingly in the newspapers of April 14. Aware
that he was a clean American-oriented boy, like the
U-2 pilot, I did not feel the same compunctions as
William V. Shannon, who wrote in the *Post,* "Mankind can draw no pride and no solace from the
achievement of a totalitarian system that dwarfs and
enslaves man." It occurred to me that mankind has

been getting a lot of fun for the last ten thousand years out of the wheel, which was invented in totalitarian Assyria, and beer, which was first made in totalitarian Babylonia. Actually, a "first," in the long run, means only that somebody else has done your homework for you. Nobody remembers the name of the first poet, but his work opened the way for Allen Ginsberg. "Fate has made us the trustee of mankind's freedom," Mr. Shannon wrote, but, leaving my share of it with the proprietor of the Palace Bar & Grill to hold for me while I was away, I traveled vicariously with Yuri in his spaceship as happily as ever I traveled with Tom Sawyer in his balloon.

"When you go orbiting around the earth, says Yuri A. Gagarin, you float above your chair in the space-ship. The sun blazes 'tens of times brighter than here on earth.' The earth's sunny face is separated from the black void by a band of delicate blue." This was from an A.P. story by Preston Grover, in Moscow. Else-where I read, "One's legs, arms, weigh nothing. Ob-jects float in the cabin. Neither did I myself sit in the chair . . . but hung in midair. While in the state of weightlessness, I ate and drank [eat and grow weight-less], and everything occurred just as it does here on earth. I even worked in that condition, jotting down my observations. My handwriting did not change, al-though the hand does not weigh anything. Only I had to hold the notebook. Otherwise it would float away. I maintained communications over different channels and tapped the telegraph key." This has the grip of Gulliver or Crusoe, plus Tom Swift. It is the magic-carpet dream that the airplane, with its noises and ghastly lunch trays, has never more than partially gratified. It recalled Penrod Schofield's reverie of float-ing weightlessly above the parade while Marjorie Jones, like Mrs. Gagarin, remained at ground level and suffered. Penrod, in his dream, had eliminated the capsule—he just floated. But science will catch up to him someday.

Then the return to weight, with the return to earth. The teacher's voice tells Penrod where he is. "The transition from weightlessness to gravitation, to the appearance of the force of gravity, is smooth. One's legs and arms feel as before, as during weightlessness, but again acquire weight. And I no longer hovered over the chair, but eased myself into it."

And here, for the color, I quote from poor Prince Gagarin as reported in the *Times*. They could execute him, he seemed to me to be saying, but they could never take away the glory he had seen: "I could see the daytime side of the earth very well. . . . The shores of the continents, islands, important rivers, great water surfaces, wrinkles and localities were clearly distinguishable. While flying over Soviet territory, I saw perfectly great squares of collective farms. It was possible to distinguish between plowed land and grassland. From a spaceship, visibility is, of course, not so good as from a plane, but it is still good, and even very good. During the flight, I was able, for the first time, to see with my own eyes the spherical shape of the earth. You can see it when you look at the horizon. The view of the horizon was different up there and very beautiful. You can see a beautiful transition from the bright surface of the earth to the completely dark sky, in which the stars are visible. This transition is very subtle. It is as though a film ringed the earth. It is of a delicate blue color. This change from the blue to the dark is very gradual and lovely. It is difficult to render it in words. And when I emerged from the shadow of the earth, the horizon looked different. There was a bright orange strip along it, which again passed into a blue hue and once again into a dense black color. I did not see the moon. In space the sun is shining tens of times brighter than on earth. I could see stars very well. They were bright and distinct. The whole picture of the sky had more contrast than when it is seen from the earth."

By the time I came down from space with Yuri, I had contracted an invisible homesickness for it. It was indispensable to me, and I sympathized with Shannon and others like him, who wanted to do something about it, at whatever cost. (Shannon, falling into the Soviet trap, wound up his piece with an adjuration to President Kennedy to start spending in order to close

the space gap right away. He has apparently not read
the "Blue Book." First thing he knows, his children
will be victims of free higher education.) When I read,
in the *Herald Tribune* on Saturday morning, a United
Press story headed $40 BILLION COULD SPEED US TO
MOON, I felt the price was moderate. The *Trib* said
that a top space official had made the estimate: "He
said the nation must decide whether the results would
justify the costs." The $40,000,000,000, I thought,
might be raised in the form of a gradual surtax, with
the graduation based on patriotism as well as income;
that is, a fellow who asserted his patriotism every day
would have to pay more than one who just left it to
be inferred, and a fellow who was always blowing
about it, like William Randolph Hearst, Jr., for example, would have to pay still more. I had forgotten,
in my *engouement,* the John Birch doctrine that a
true patriot is a man who does not want to see the
country wrecked, that taxes wreck the country, and
that the best patriot of all, therefore, is the one who
wants to pay the least taxes. When I remembered, I
found myself in a quandary. I certainly didn't want us
to collapse economically, so that Mr. Welch would
have to go back to the candy business, but I did want
to get a rocket-railway going, so that I could hitch
a ride.

My dilemma was solved by an elder statesman of
journalism whose intelligence and reliability I have
never underestimated: David Lawrence. In his syndicated column, "Today in World Affairs," in last
Monday's *Herald Tribune,* Mr. Lawrence got to the
nub with the headline REDS' SECRECY RAISES QUERY:
DID GAGARIN REALLY ORBIT? "Was the Soviet stunt
in outer space, as announced officially from Moscow,
a hoax?" Mr. Lawrence demanded. "Granted that
something went around the earth, was a man really in
it, or did the astronaut merely make a separate flight
similar to that which an American airman, Joseph Albert Walker, recently made in an X-15 rocket plane at
an altitude of 32 miles? These questions are being
asked by scientists because there are some obvious dis-

crepancies in the boastful account of his trip given by
Major Yuri Gagarin."

From anybody but Mr. Lawrence I would have considered the question captious and perhaps niggling, sug-
gestive of a sore loser, but I saw that the elder statesman had just saved his country. If the Russians had
never got a man into space, we would save $40,000,-
000,000, because there would be nothing to catch up
to. That would save our civilization from collapsing,
and us from having to get educated.

"It probably is true that the Russians sent a satellite
around the earth in ninety minutes," Mr. Lawrence
went on. "America has done this too. It is also probably true that Maj. Gagarin went high into the air.
But whether he traveled around the earth as claimed,
or merely achieved a high altitude in the air, remains
an unsolved mystery."

"Potemkin rides again!" I exclaimed when I finished
this, and, looking back with a fresh eye on the news
stories and photographs from Moscow in the past five
days, I remembered that the "ecstatic crowds" had
looked highly balletistic. As for Maj. Gagarin's putative parents, they looked to me more than ever like
cops, and the early pictures of the major, in his flying
helmet, were pretty obviously 1927 shots of Charles
Lindbergh—who, come to think of it, may not have
flown to Paris, either, but just waited on top of the
Eiffel Tower on a dark night and then slid down a
slack wire in a toy airplane.

The only one of the "obvious discrepancies" Mr.
Lawrence cites that I'd like to quibble with him about
is his objection to the False Yuri's visual claims. "Can
the human eye really see 200 miles away through
portholes or 'slits'?" Mr. Lawrence challenges. "It
might distinguish large formations such as the lines on
the moon, but it seems incredible that Maj. Gagarin
could have seen anything as relatively small as mead-
ows or fields such as he described." I would remind
Mr. Lawrence, first, that the glass in the portholes
may have been ground to a prescription, like a Texas
windshield, and, second, that last year, during the fuss
over the U-2 reconnaissance flight, he himself said

that the Air Force had a camera that could take a
photograph of a golf ball from a height of six miles,
which I said was a long way to go for the purpose.
You can get roughly 49 golf balls into a square foot.
A one-acre plowed (or unplowed) field has 43,560
square feet. It is therefore 2,134,440 times as visible
as a golf ball, while the major was a mere 31.17 times
as far away as the golf-ball photographer.

We have changed an old saying in America. The
way we say it now is "If you can't beat them, say they
didn't do it."

The Candy Kid

MAY 20, 1961

In 1922, when I was eighteen and it was new, I
read James Elroy Flecker's play about Hassan, the
confectioner of Baghdad, and it became one of my
clandestine addictions, like my taste for Atkinson's
Doncaster Toffee. It has a sucrose, glucose, dextrose
quality, like warm spun sugar twining itself around the
aorta. Hassan, its protagonist, through a chance encounter with the Caliph Haroun al-Raschid, is removed
from the humble but cozy purlieus of his shop to the
world of affairs of state. At first the transposition
pleases him. "For all these years I have been a humble man, of soft and kindly disposition—such a man
as the world and a woman hate," says he. "But now I
shall never again be the fool of my fellows." Afterward, though, failing to soften the Caliph's line on
capital punishment, he is glad to retire, and withdraws
from public life as a pilgrim, marching offstage singing, in chorus with the rest of the caravan, "We take
the Golden Road to Samarkand."

For Hassan's sake, I was predisposed in favor of
Robert H. W. Welch, Jr., founder of the John Birch
Society and author of its Koran, *The Blue Book*
(copyright Robert Welch, 1959). Mr. Welch had an

early life much like that of my older friend. He was, before he became an author, a candymaker in Cambridge, Mass. The only other American public man I can think of with an equally mellifluent background is Adolf A. Berle, Jr., who was chairman of the board of the American Molasses Company. But whereas Hassan, squatting among his sugar kettles, used to write poetry, Mr. Welch, by his own account, read world history. And while the peppermint popped and the popsicles purred, he became so impressed by the analogies he discovered in his reading that, like Mohammed, he heard a Voice saying to him, "Recite." Accordingly, he summoned a number of disciples to meet him at a hotel in Indianapolis, where there are always rooms (except during auto-race week), on December 8, 1958. *The Blue Book* is, its author explains, a record of what he said at the ensuing meeting, as fraught with consequences as a chocolate bar with peanuts. Only eleven disciples attended, leaving him one short of the conventional complement, but they represented eight states. It is inspiring to think of that seminal meeting, in a hotel banquet suite, perhaps named for one of the characters of James Whitcomb Riley, the Hoosier laureate—the Little Orphan Annie Room. The Wise Men from afar sit one knee over the other around the manger of the new truth, and Mr. Welch tells them: The Gobble-uns'll git you ef you don't watch out!

"With short breaks for coffee, for luncheons, and for brief discussions in between sections of the presentation, it required two whole days to set forth the background, methods, and purposes of the John Birch Society. The pages that follow are simply a transcript, practically verbatim, of that presentation," Mr. Welch reports. "I personally have been studying the problem [of Communism] increasingly for about nine years," he also told the Original Eleven, "and practically full time for the past three years. And entirely without pride, but in simple thankfulness, let me point out that a lifetime of business experience should have made it easier for me to see the falsity of the economic theories on which Communism is supposedly based, more readily, than might some scholar coming into that study from the academic cloisters; while a lifetime of interest in things academic, especially world history, should have given me an advantage over many businessmen in more rapidly seeing the sophistries in dialectic materialism."

His world history is Neo-Spenglerian, although, he concedes, "there is certainly more Welch than there is Spengler" in it, and he has contributed not a few new details. It was Darius and not Cyrus who, according to Mr. Welch, overthrew the "Neo-Babylonian civilization"; Greek colonists conquered Italy, founded Rome, and "developed Roman civilization"; and the Roman Empire of the West "started dying from the cancer of collectivism from the time Diocletian imposed on it his New Deal." The notion of conventional historians like Rostovtzeff and Burckhardt has been that the Roman economy hit the skids a century and a half earlier, and that Diocletian, poor man, was merely trying to pick up the pieces. One of his measures was a system of price controls, and this probably has caused Mr. Welch to confuse him with Franklin D. Roosevelt. The theory that Greece conquered Rome has not yet become dogma, either, but it may; it is in line with the discovery that the South won the Civil War after Sherman's Flight to the Sea.

"Basically, when you dig through the chaff and the dressing in Spengler enough to get at his thought, he held that a societal development which we ordinarily class as a civilization is an organic culture which goes through a life cycle just the same as any of the individual organisms which we see whole and with which we are more familiar." Western Europe reached its high point in the second half of the nineteenth century, Mr. Welch holds, and is now dying of a "collectivist cancer" that has invaded *us*. We must excise it —a herculean task. His prose abounds in figures of speech based on cancer and cardiac afflictions, which should be impressive to a public of predominantly elderly executives. (Welch himself is 61.)

Theories, however, are less his concern than facts— his eye deciphers surface appearances as easily as it does the crème fondant within the walnut imperial. For example, he says of one nation not commonly detected: "And gentlemen, any idea that Norway is not, for all practical purposes, now in Communist hands . . . is in my opinion as unrealistic as the thought that Kwame Nkrumah of Ghana is a Democrat." (The Norwegian Storting, or Parliament, has one Communist among its 150 members.)

"Syria, Lebanon, Egypt, Libya, Tunisia, Algeria, Morocco" are places where the Communists "either already have control, however disguised, or are rapidly acquiring control." Nehru, Nasser, and Sukarno are Communists, like Gen. Eisenhower.

"The Communists are now in complete control of Bolivia and Venezuela." The only Latin American governments Welch endorsed in 1958 were Paraguay, Nicaragua, the Dominican Republic, and Batista's Cuba, all dictatorships. Batista has now, of course, gone down the drain—an incalculable loss to Western civilization. Hawaii, Mr. Welch revealed, was Communist through and through. Since its admission as a state, the poison has, presumably, reached our vitals.

"The whole slogan of 'civil rights,' as used to make trouble in the South today, is an exact parallel to the slogan of 'agrarian reform' which they [you are expected to know by this time who "they" always are] used in China." Discovering the points at which the John Birch line makes fast to those of other kindred revelations is a continual beguilement as the reader of *The Blue Book* goes along. Here it hitches with the White Supremacists. A bit farther on, declaring the Algerian war a Communist creation, it ties on to the *colons*.

Our troubles, however, are of our own making. "The first great break for the Communist conspiracy came in 1933, with our formal recognition of Stalin's regime. At that time the Russian government was staying alive financially from week to week by methods which, in the case of individuals, would be called check-kiting." (At the moment, as I recall, we were pretty broke ourselves. The banks stayed closed until Roosevelt got them open again, and Al Smith and the *Daily News*

advocated recognition of the U.S.S.R. as a method of
reviving *us*.) "Our recognition tremendously increased
their prestige and credit, at home and with other nations. It saved them from financial collapse." What
good it would do the Russian Government, if broke,
to increase its credit at home, in Russia, where nobody had any money, is one of *The Blue Book*'s minor
enigmas.

In Asia, where we are also out of luck, "our government prevented Chiang Kai-shek's troops from
getting even ammunition," while the Russians gave the
Reds "tremendous stockpiles of Japanese arms." ("The
primary cause of the defeat of the Chinese Nationalist
Army was the military aggressiveness of the Chinese
Communist forces, and sound tactics, which were
based on the capabilities and limitations of the Red
military. Communist victory was achieved without the
extensive use of modern, large-calibre weapons, motor
transport or aircraft, but by sound, aggressive tactics
on the ground."—Lieutenant Colonel Robert B. Rigg,
a United States military observer, in *Red China's
Fighting Hordes*.)

The chief weapon of the Communists in thus mag-
goting the world outside our borders has been treachery, not science. They have never, for example, *built*
an atomic bomb: "Their agents had simply walked
off from our plants with the necessary separate parts,
which had then been assembled in Russia, and ex-
ploded whenever it best suited the Soviets' pretenses."
In the light of this fact, all the pother about disarmament conferences is superfluous. All we have to do to
disarm the Russians is to install a proper security system in our own plants. (When they walked off with
the parts of our heavy-rocket booster, they might at
least have left us the plans.)

And now that they are working up on us—they've
got Hawaii already, remember, with two Red senators
on Capitol Hill—they have three possible courses.
"One would be, through a sufficient amount of infiltration and propaganda, to disguise Communism as
just another political party." When I reached this
point, I peeked ahead to see *which* party was to be

the Trojan donkey. But Mr. Welch had written, "We
do not anticipate that development." Another route to
the consummation of conquest "would be by foment-
ing internal civil war in this country, and aiding the
Communist side in that war with all necessary military
might," as an outside power might do in, say, Cuba.
But he didn't anticipate that, either, although, he said,
one never could tell. The third method, "which is far
more in accordance with Lenin's long-range strategy,"
is the "one which they are clearly relying on most
heavily." This, on which they are already launched
with gratifyingly fearful results, is to take over the
government by a process so gradual and insidious that
they will have us in the bag before we know it. One
step is to lure us deeper and deeper into the United
Nations, which is a thinly disguised branch of the
Soviet Government itself, "until one day we shall
gradually realize that we are already just a part of a
worldwide government ruled by the Kremlin, with the
police-state features of that government rapidly closing in on ourselves. But another part of the plan is the
conversion of the United States into a socialist nation,
quite similar to Russia itself in its economy and political outlook. . . . The best way to explain the aim
here is simply to quote the directive under which some
of the very largest American foundations have secretly
but visibly been working for years. This directive is
'so to change the economic and political structure of
the United States that it can be comfortably merged
with Soviet Russia.' "

Here Mr. Welch, like Mohammed in most of the
Koran, omits the source of his quotation. In the Prophet's case, it is always understood to be God. At this
point, with Asia gone under altogether, Europe gone
under (all but Spain and Portugal), South America
gone under (all but Paraguay), Africa gone under (all
but the Union), us going (all but Arizona), the reader
might well expect, as I did, a call to a preventive war,
or at least the setting up of a force, entirely commanded by admirals called back from retirement,
that would put the skulking devils in their place. This
could be done in three steps. One, we stop them from

snitching any more bomb parts. Two, we blockade
them and starve them out. Three, we send them only
stale surplus chocolate bars to eat until they say
"Uncle" ("*Dyadya*"). I can imagine the Eleven Disciples squirming on their hotel chairs in the Claypool,
hardly able to hold themselves down as they waited
the slogan cry "Out cutlasses and board!"

But, Welch warns, *this is the trap they planned for
us*. "Although our danger remains almost entirely internal, from Communist influences right in our midst
and treason right in our government, the American
people are being persuaded that our danger is from
the outside, is from Russian military superiority."
What we have to do, then, is *not* spend money on
defense, *not* pay taxes, but balance the budget at zero,
stultify central government, defend states' rights, stop
federal aid to education (it leads to thought control),
pay no attention to talk about the horrors of war,
since we won't have any arms anyway, and, above all,
derecognize Russia and it will blow away. To make
the juju stronger, we are to abandon foreign aid, abol-
ish the income tax, and "win that battle [against Communism, presumably] by alertness, by determination,
by courage, by an energizing realization of the danger,
if we can; but let's win it, even with our lives, if
the time comes when we must." (Without spending
money.) It sounds like a program for eating your
jelly beans and having them, or ruling the skies with
obsolete airplanes. It also sounds like the program of
turning a back on the world devised for seventeenth-
century Japan by the Tokugawa Shogun Iyemitsu.
"Don't look and it will go away" was the Tokugawas'
prescription, but the outside world didn't, and when
Japan looked again, centuries later, she found herself
in a most humiliating position. (In the interim, 80
percent of her people had lived in fairly continuous
hunger, which forced them to the regular practice of
infanticide to keep the population down.) The Birch
creed should, I would think, tickle the pants off any
Russian official in his right mind, for its essence is
unilateral disarmament through permitted obsoles-

cence, a breakup of federal authority, and a withdrawal from the international field.

One of the entrancing episodes of the John Birch epopee, for me, was the behavior of Major General Edwin A. Walker, supposedly a fire-eater, who had John Birch tracts, which are essentially pacifist, passed out to his men. I wondered whether he had read them. The obsession of ubiquitous treachery, moreover, is exactly what will make a soldier soonest take off. A division convinced of the prevalence of treason all the way back to base will scatter at the first shot.

When the modern Hassan reaches the chapter of his revelation in which he discusses positive measures against the "worldwide Communist conspiracy" ("And so, let's Act"), he is less impressive than when he is evoking the dangers that hedge us round. As an initial move toward breaking Marx's back, he would establish reading rooms, "somewhat similar to the Christian Science reading rooms," where the writings of Robert Welch would be available. The society's publications "should be put in barbershops, from which we obtained firm written promises to welcome these publications and keep them on the reading tables." Members of the society should listen to the broadcasts of Fulton Lewis, Jr. And everybody should write letters for worthy causes like withdrawal of recognition from Russia and the repeal of the income tax. Above all, there should be "exposure" of Communists, by publication.

"Let's make what we are talking about clearer by an illustration. There is the head of one of the great educational institutions in the East (not Harvard, incidentally) whom at least some of us believe to be a Communist. Even with a hundred thousand dollars to hire sleuths to keep him and his present contacts under constant surveillance for a while, and to retrace every detail of his past history, I doubt if we could prove it on him. But—with just five thousand dollars to pay for the proper amount of careful research . . . I believe we could get all the material needed for quite a shock. . . . We would run in the magazine an article consisting entirely of questions to this man, which would be devastating in their implications. The question technique, when skillfully used in this way, is mean and dirty. But the Communists we are after are meaner and dirtier, and too slippery for you to put your fingers on in the ordinary way—no matter how much they look and act like prosperous members of the local Rotary Club."

The disproportion between the magnitude of the evil discovered everywhere and the insignificance of the remedies proposed makes Birchism a demoniac religion. The Birchist, like man before the invention of fire, wanders helpless among malignant forces, his only consolation inner knowledge of how terrible things are, his only protection an amulet in the form of a "Blue Book," his only weapon a postage stamp. His chiefest satisfaction is his conviction that his neighbor will perish, and that he will probably deserve to. "Communist" for the Birchist, the reader gathers after the first page or so of the book, means anybody who approves of paying taxes, national defense, public education, civil rights, the United Nations, labor unions, or poetry since Tennyson. There is *no* politican in whom Welch sees hope; even Barry Goldwater is a softhearted sap. And so it is true, for him, that there are "Communists" everywhere. Socialists, in the penumbra of the weird world Welch inhabits, *are* Communists; Roosevelt and, save the mark, Woodrow Wilson strengthened central government, so *were* Socialists, so Communists. It is an ugly doctrine, which inhibits every effort to outperform our rivals that the effort will end in betrayal. Taken seriously, it could be more destructive than the nerve gas that all up-to-date chemical-warfare branches are now supposed to possess, which paralyzes the will to resist. Only this gas, instead of being carried over borders by I.C.B. missiles, is a native product, for home consumption, like cocoanut bars.

A Touch of Wall Street

NOVEMBER 25, 1961

Between 1918, when Oswald Garrison Villard, a reforming liberal millionaire, sold the New York *Evening Post* to Thomas W. Lamont,, a Morgan partner, and 1933, when the Curtis Publishing Company, which had meanwhile acquired it, sold it to J. David Stern, a newspaper-jobber, as salvage, the *Evening Post* was known almost exclusively as a Wall Street paper. With the United States in the First World War, 1918 was a bad sales year for liberalism, whereas 1933 marked an all-time low in peddling stocks. Stern steered the paper into the full New Deal tide and picked up circulation, if not much cash. In 1939, he sold the *Post* to George Backer, a liberal *with* cash, and faded with a small profit. Continuing in the New Deal tideway, Backer and his wife, the former Dorothy Schiff, jettisoned the *Post*'s stock-market reports in 1941, when public interest in Wall Street was still faint. This was an important economy, because stock tables are costly, necessitating not only the employment of a horde of men called tabulators, who keep track of the changing quotations, but a wild amount of typesetting. (The Associated Press now does the tabulation, on a cost-sharing basis, for all the New York newspapers except the *World-Telegram* and the *Journal-American,* but the type still has to be set in the individual plants.) There were still five competing evening newspapers in 1941, and three of them continued to carry stock tables. The threat to the *Post* on the liberal side of the street, though, was *PM,* which did not carry them, and which folded (in its terminal form as the *Star*) in 1949. The papers that ran the stock prices were the *Journal-American,* the *World-Telegram,* and the *Sun,* of which the second engulfed the third in 1950.

That left three evening papers, with Miss Schiff (by now divorced from Mr. Backer) in full control of the

Post, which was still without stock-market tables. The
Post must have figured that its readers were unlikely
to own stocks, and that any who did could afford to
buy a second paper. With the return of the public to
the market in the last few years, however, everything
changed. Schoolteachers and bartenders were buying
stocks now, as they did in the twenties, and barbers
who had failed in thirty years to beat the races had
become confident that they could solve a murkier
mystery. Wall Street men say that 1960 initiated a
new vulgarization, with the volume of over-the-coun-
ter trading almost equaling that on the big boards.
The minor stocks proved to be the petty punters' favorites. The *Post* had acquired a white-collar subcapi-
talist readership that even a decade ago was still
shuddering at the memory of 1929. Now the tips of
these readers' collars began to sprout buttons, and the
paper found the lack of stock tables a handicap so
serious that a month ago it restored them.

The American newspaper industry has become a
series of local elimination tournaments, like Golden
Gloves boxing, and the return of the tables boosts the
Post's chances of being one of the two New York
finalists, because its rivals, the *Journal-American* and
the *World-Telegram* and encysted *Sun,* are so alike in
tone and appeal that either one could disappear without inconvenience to its readers, who would shift over
to the other as semiconsciously as they change trains
on their way to their suburban nests. This applies also
to the contributors most likely to survive a merger;
George Sokolsky stepped off the *Sun* and onto the
Journal-American in 1950 and, in a couple of days,
looked as natural as if he had been born there. He
found Westbrook Pegler, who had moved from the
World-Telegram, already settled in. Inez Robb, a coyly
cantankerous lady columnist, made the reverse journey from the *Journal-American* to the *World-Telly,*
and with as little trauma as if she'd lived *there* all her
life.

A quick survey of the *World-Telegram* and *Journal-
American* of a week ago Monday will illustrate their
similarity. That day, the *Telly* carried on its first page

an eight-column-wide panegyric of Major General
Edwin A. Walker, the corn-fed Massu who recently
resigned from the Army because he was not allowed
to preach the John Birch line to his captive audience
of conscripts. "This situation puzzles many Americans," the panegyrist, Jim G. Lucas, wrote. (Lucas is
the chap who ten years ago discovered an army of six
million Chinese Nationalist guerrillas on the mainland
of China. They were dispersed by Dean Acheson.) He
went on: "Just what, they ask, was wrong with Gen.
Walker's brand of anti-communism and right about
the Pentagon's, or vice versa? Why should Americans
fall out about something on which we all should agree?
. . . Gen. Walker's pro-blue plan was based on the
idea that a major threat to our existence is communism
at home. Prominent Americans like Harry Truman,
Dean Acheson, and Eleanor Roosevelt, he told a
P.T.A. meeting in Germany, are 'pink.' "

Far down in the runover, on page nineteen, Lucas
conceded that there were those who disagreed with the
general. On page three, "Lawrence Fertig, outstanding
economist and special writer for the *World-Telegram*
and other Scripps-Howard newspapers," revealed "how
U.S. inflationary policies year after year undermined
the dollar," and he was not finished even then; on
page twenty-five, an outstanding guest economist reviewed Mr. Fertig's book *Prosperity Through Freedom* (cut federal tinkering, furnish incentive). On the
same day, Pegler, in the *Journal-American,* had one
of his bluff, hearty, humorous bits: "These days you
hear nothing but the symphony, the opera and the
ballet, a lot of beefy Russian tomatoes bouncing
around like a bunch of elephants. . . . There comes a
time when a free-born American citizen gets darn
good and sore the way those culture-bums push clean-
living, God-fearing, baby-having Americans around
shoving culture at us." The lead editorial that day expressed fearless disapproval of rape and stomping
women to death, a stand supported by a cartoon captioned "Coddled Delinquent" and showing a Latin
American type with a cigarette in one hand and a

knife in the other reclining on cushions labeled "Soft Youth Agencies" and "Soft Courts."

Both papers have congealed in a mold cast by the Know-Nothing and Native American editors of the 1850's—anti-foreign, anti-intellectual, anti–poor people (the poorhouse-master of Newburgh, New York, is one of their culture heroes), anti-government (except for J. Edgar Hoover), and, particularly in the case of the *Telly,* savagely anti–New York City. (A good proportion of the *Telegram*'s readers are commuters who get lost if they stray from the direct path between their offices and Grand Central, and the *Telly,* whose management is itself a stray from the sticks, exacerbates their resentment of the yeasty metropolis. The *World-Telegram* is Scripps-Howard's New York "show window," and it looks like a J. C. Penney store in Bergdorf Goodman territory.)

In contrast to both, the *Post* is the expression of autochthonous New York, which is more an extension of Europe than of Muscatine, Iowa. The paper is warm, shrewd, pretentious, and insecure, like a first-generation Phi Beta Kappa student at Hunter College. Its advice-to-the-lovelorn columnist, or nearest approach to one, is a severe lady psychologist who invariably exposes the unworthy motivation of her correspondents. Its general-utility switch-hitter columnist is Max Lerner, a reformed university professor who is a frequent recidivist. "The life-history of a call girl is usually the life-history of a psychic drive that has turned sex away from love toward destructive purposes," Dr. Lerner will write one day, and the next he will be explaining the linguistic basis of Ceylonese political dissension. Mrs. Franklin D. Roosevelt is the *Post*'s pinup girl, and Adlai Stevenson is its equivalent of the other papers' J. Edgar. When juveniles are delinquent in the *Post,* it is because their parents sometimes forgot to leave a night light burning, and boys stomp on women because there are too few basketball courts in the slums.

It is hard to imagine a *Post* reader buying the *Journal-American* or the *World-Telegram* except to look up the price of a stock, and now that the *Post*

has its own financial section, there will be no reason
to stray. Since I have consistently found in the paper,
besides a daily ration of amusement, an expressed—
and sometimes well-expressed—concern for values
I can recognize, I was glad to see it strengthen its
hand with the stock tables. (Where, without the
Post, would I go to learn that *tout comprendre, c'est
tout pardonner?* I can hardly imagine Dorothy Kilgallen's writing, "The call girl is likely to have been
rejected by one or both parents, and feels unwanted,
unloved, and unworthy of being wanted or loved.")

On November 6, however, I received a letter from
a professional zoologist named Sam B. McDowell, a
resident of the Bronx, that filled me with disquiet.
Mr. McDowell said he had been following the press
coverage of the milk strike, which had then been on
for a while, and hoped I would clarify some points
for him:

One point is the meaning of the word *"featherbedding."*
I meet this word quite frequently, but its use surprises me
every time. At first I thought it referred to making the
owner (or stockholders) pay for unnecessary employees,
but when I used the word in conversation to describe a
management that invests the stockholders' money in salaries for underworked executives, my friends all pointed
out to me that I was misusing the word. Recently, the milk
companies have explained that it would be improper to
install time clocks in milk wagons to record employees'
overtime because this would lead to featherbedding. I had
always thought the time clock was an employer's weapon
against featherbedding, and editorials in various New York
papers had confirmed me in my wrongheadedness. Some
explanation of this new aspect of featherbedding seemed
a reasonable expectation from these same editorial pages,
but a careful study of the *Herald Tribune, World-Telegram
& Sun,* and *Post-Home News* * revealed not a word of

---

* The *Post* quite a long while ago absorbed a *journal du
faubourg* called the *Bronx Home News,* which it has digested
so thoroughly that the name, unlike the *"& Sun"* that resembles a spot of jam on the *World-Telegram*'s chin, does not
appear on its face at all.

comment on what appears to be an important discovery: automation in the form of time clocks leads to featherbedding, the vice that automation strives to combat. (The above papers are my daily choice of reading because I am of Scotch extraction and I seem to get so many papers for the price of three.)

Another point is the complaint on the November 2nd editorial page of the *Trib* that the public isn't sufficiently aroused about the strike. This surprised me, because I had always thought it the job of editorial writers to arouse me, and until that date I had found nothing about the strike on the editorial page of the *Tribune*.

A third point is the unexpected similarity of editorial comment on the strike in the *Trib* and the *Post*. Just recently, the *Post* installed a market-quotations page, and already it is assuming a mature, well-balanced, and wishy-washy attitude.

Mr. McDowell's letter recalled to me a peril inherent in the new situation. The mechanics of a financial section are so dear that in order to maintain it a paper must in a brief period dig up a large volume of financial advertising. There are few newspapers, however immune to direct suasion, that do not in time become subject to an osmotic absorption of a whole class of advertisers' sociological pigmentation. I trembled for the *Post*.

The milk strike, meanwhile, went on, hell-bent for election. I had not paid much attention to it, because the day on which I received Mr. McDowell's communication was my first in the city since the strike began. I thought, though, in my childish way, that if I were watching a broad-jump competition in which one man rejected the use of a tape measure, I should suspect *his* motives first, and if he lay down in the pit and kicked his heels and refused to continue, I should blame *him* for the interruption of the event rather than the guy who called for the tape. (When I first went to work for wages, I found the notion of a time clock abhorrent, because I intended to come late and leave early, and also to work out the past performances over coffee at the Waldorf

Lunch on the Providence *Journal* Company's time.
Only a sharp conviction that I was being rooked
would have led me to ask for a mechanical check.)
I could find nothing on any editorial page during the
strike to confirm this primitive inference. Under the
heading MILK STRIKE ENDS AT LAST, the *Mirror,* on
Tuesday, recorded solemnly and without comment,
"The Teamsters wanted the time clocks installed in
delivery trucks so the drivers could be paid for all
hours actually worked. The dealers contended this
would lead to featherbedding." The lead on the story
read, "The milk strike which had drastically cut the
city's supplies for two weeks ended suddenly last
night when both sides in the lengthy wrangle agreed
to take their main point of dispute—the time-clock
issue—to arbitration."

I suspected even more strongly that McDowell and
I were aberrant when, that afternoon, I read in the
Post a column by James A. Wechsler, the editor, that
began, "For many long years organized labor has
viewed itself as the target of a conspiracy by the
'capitalist press.' " This is no longer so, Mr. Wechsler
assured us; the press is impartial. Then he made
some remarks about a book he had read, gave the
Carpenters Union the back of his hand in passing
("that benighted, restricted club"), and teed off on
Jimmy Hoffa before getting to the part that interested me: "For 14 days New York was plagued by a
milk strike run by the Teamsters Union. [*Not,* as I
have pointed out before, in connection with other instances of writing about strikes, "run by the union
and the employers, neither of whom would yield."]
The ostensible reason for prolongation of the conflict
lay in such marginal questions as the use of time
clocks." To a man driving a heavy milk truck on a
slippery hill, the question whether he is doing it on
unpaid overtime isn't marginal at all. Wechsler was
all for arbitration, although he didn't say by whom;
the old gag about the arbitrator "to be agreed upon
by both parties" can easily double the wrangle. (On
the border between Israel and the Arab states, where
an officer of the United Nations Truce Supervision

Organization is the third party to every inquiry into a border incident, his is always the casting vote, and the losing party has never yet concurred in his findings or honored his ruling.)

Wechsler then took another smack at Hoffa, the head of the national Teamsters Union, which includes the local that wanted the time clocks, and went on to tell labor what its real concern should be. "The great unsettled questions," Mr. Wechsler wrote, "are how labor can achieve an identity with the unorganized consumer; how it can use its resources to aid the most backward, underprivileged areas of our society —such as the migrants; how it can conquer discrimination in its own house; how it can devise creative formulae for dealing with the problems of automation; how it can speak without sounding like an affluent vested interest; how it can regain a spirit of social idealism now limited to a few." He did not say that the manufacturer should achieve an identity with the unorganized consumer and put some roast beef in the roast-beef hash, or that the farmer should use his resources to aid the migrants he hires, or that employers should cut down on discrimination in hiring, or that affluent vested interests should learn to speak as if *they* weren't affluent vested interests.

Edified, I turned, next day, to the new financial section, where I found Sylvia Porter, one of my favorites all through the years when we *Post* readers understood among ourselves that we were modest folk. The running head on her column, "Your Dollar," was a measure of my usual circumstances. If she had raised it to "Your Dollar and a Half," she would have priced me out of her market. A substitute for the fulminating investment counselors in other papers, who spoke of megatons of money, Miss Porter used to warn her faithful not to forget that a proportion of the occasional maid's four-hour fee was tax-deductible if the dinner guest was a prospective customer for the host's line of homemade fudge. Reading her, I used to feel that destitution was no disgrace. "Tax Tactics," the headline over her column on November 8, bespoke another consoling list of humble dodges short of criminal, and I plunged into it hoping to find out how to save 95 cents. I was in for a shock. Miss Porter, once Everyman's helpmeet, began, "Throughout the past 18 months, a recurring discussion we've had with our broker has been about selling three stocks which we bought years ago and on which we have accumulated a fat percentage of paper profits." It shook me. I had no recollection of Sylvia's having invested years ago, and that she had done so successfully and without touting me on seemed a betrayal. "We have not disagreed with the broker that the stocks are probably over-priced now," she went on, "and that there are more attractive investments for us. But whenever we have come up against a decision on sale, my husband"—here I realized that the "we" was not editorial—"particularly has been reluctant to cash in and pay a capital gains tax of 25 per cent on so large a part of our nestegg." This revealed a hitherto unsuspected streak of greed in Miss Porter's character; she was beginning, I feared, to sound a bit like an affluent vested interest.

From that point on, Miss Porter got sorrier for herself and her husband and all other successful investors. "The New York Stock Exchange this afternoon is releasing the results of an independent study which underlines dramatically the extent to which a reduction in the capital gains tax rate would impel investors to unlock their portfolios and, by so doing, hand over a bigger chunk of taxes to the Treasury on their profits as well as get cash for reinvestment in ventures that would stimulate the economy's expansion," she wrote. This unprejudiced survey showed, my old dollar-scrimper went on to say, that if the government cut the rate to 20 percent, a lot more people would consent to accept their 80 percent, and that at 12½ percent still more would consent to pocket their winnings. That sounded like Heywood Broun's story of how he asked William O. McGeehan whether he preferred to work for $50 a week or $55. It occurred to me that if the government earnestly desired to get the boodle in, it could threaten to raise the rate on capital gains next year to parity with the rate on money you work for, or even to raise it to 30 percent, and the money would come tumbling in like the rain in Spain. Actually, a rumored rise to 25.01 would do the trick, and I believe that a few years ago the *Post* might have thought of that. If the trend continues, I expect to see the *Post* publishing the point spread on polo games.

Meanwhile, I have had another letter from McDowell, who now reveals a bias sucked in with his Ph.D.:

I am not connected with the Teamsters Union, the dairy industry, or the press [he writes]. I am not unprejudiced, however; my heart is entirely with the man who brings me the milk and against the company that receives my cheque (when necessary). I also note that at about 11 o'clock the night before the strike the milkman brought us a full delivery of milk because he might be on strike the next day; during the heavy snows last winter the milk drivers were the first to resume deliveries under particularly trying circumstances. (Our apartment house is at the top of a hill so steep that we all wait half an hour for a bus rather than walk up the five blocks of mountain slope from the Yankee Stadium subway station. The milk trucks were surmounting this height a day before the buses and several days before the newspaper delivery trucks.) I don't know whether our milkman delivered milk above and beyond the call of duty to everyone on his route, or just to families (such as mine) with small children; I certainly hope he received his full overtime pay. I just can't convince myself that our milkman is a grasping labor racketeer.

The milk company is something else again. My understanding of the new law is that the companies are no longer required to date their milk, but they are permitted to date it if they wish. Our company does not so wish. I don't think they refrain from dating milk out of any desire to foist stale milk on their customers; it is probably a matter of principle and they fear milk-dating might beget featherbedding.

Another point for your clarification has come up since my last letter to you. The real reason the companies oppose time clocks was contained in a story at the top of the *Herald Tribune* the morning after the strike ended. Some of the companies fear they will be in a bad competitive position if a fair account of overtime is kept, because some union locals may not press the smaller distributors for overtime pay. I gather that there is not enough union featherbedding to please the employers, and that the strike might have been avoided if some of the locals hadn't absorbed *Trib* editorials about not killing the goose that lays the golden eggs.

Confusedly yours,
Sam McDowell.

He sounds like a dangerous character.

9
Then
and
Now

Of Yesteryear—I

NOVEMBER 7, 1953

Along about last January 20, when the present era was beginning—IKE HEADS PARADE OF HAPPY NEW ERA, a *World-Telegram & Sun* headline phrased it—I got to thinking about the beginning of the immediately previous era, which had started with the inauguration of Franklin D. Roosevelt on March 4, 1933, and lasted for nineteen years, ten months, and a couple of weeks, during which time I had grown that much older. In 1933, I was a reporter on the *World-Telegram,* which had not yet become the *World-Telegram & Sun*, because there was still a *Sun*, with a circulation of 301,500 undaunted Republicans. The *World-Telegram* itself had a circulation of 403,100. The *Journal* had not yet become the *Journal-American,* but aside from that it was just about what it is today; even its circulation was almost the same: 632,300 then and 620,500 now, if you figure it on a six-day-a-week basis. The *Post* was called the *Evening Post* and was a dignified paper of standard size instead of the tabloid it is at present. It was known as "the Wall Street paper" and was more conservative than the *Sun*.

During those days of domestic discomfiture, the *Evening Post* gave most of its first page to foreign news. All through the winter and spring of 1933 it ran a succession of superb long stories by the late H. R. Knickerbocker out of Germany, where the Nazis were inaugurating their own new era with a brutality that readers found it hard to credit. As one looks back over Knickerbocker's dispatches, it is difficult to recapture the mood in which we read them; no longer incredulous, we are no longer moved. So much worse was to come that in retrospect the beatings and window-breakings seem merely benign symptoms. The *Evening Post* also had a great sports

429

columnist named Westbrook Pegler, who made occasional forays into the news field for subjects to be funny about. The practice proved habit-forming. And the paper had a trio of notable critics: William Soskin, John Mason Brown, and Oscar Thompson, in the fields of belles-lettres, the theater and music, respectively. Most striking of all its features, however, was a financial section that was a newspaper in itself, with the fastest and most comprehensive market coverage to be found anywhere. As the volume of stock transactions declined, this section, which was expensive to maintain, became a pure liability, but the *Evening Post*'s proprietor, Cyrus H. K. Curtis, of Philadelphia, hated to kill it off. It was like making the decision to hand over the vest of a suit to a tailor so he can patch the pants. Curtis, who was a proud and rich man, died without making it. His paper had a policy of keeping all news of financial calamity inside the financial section, and it was not until March 3, the day before the new governor, Herbert H. Lehman, closed all the banks in New York State for two days, that the *Evening Post* conceded the Depression had become a matter of general news interest. For all its imposing exterior—it looked like an evening New York *Times*—the *Evening Post* had a circulation of only ninety-one thousand. It therefore appeared by far the least viable of the four evening papers.

My personal memory of that March 4 is that I spent it in the outer office of the New York Clearing House Association, at 77 Cedar Street, in company with representatives of the three other evening papers, the five mornings (there was still an *American* then, in addition to the *Times,* the *Herald Tribune,* the *News,* and the *Mirror*), the three press associations, and probably, although I am no longer sure of this, the *Daily Worker,* the Brooklyn *Eagle,* the *Morning Telegraph,* the *Daily Racing Form,* and the entire foreign-language press. We were all waiting for a man named Mortimer N. Buckner, who was then president of the Clearing House, to announce the authorization of scrip money. The scrip was to be backed by all the member banks of the Clearing

House, and was to replace ordinary money, which was rapidly disappearing from circulation.

March 4, 1933, fell on a Saturday, and if the five-day week had then obtained, Governor Lehman would not have had to mar Inauguration Day by declaring his moratorium; he could have waited until Monday morning. But banks stayed open then from nine to one on Saturdays, and at the rate depositors were asking for their cash there might have been riots had they opened that morning. The other reporters and I waited on hard wooden benches in what I remember as a colonial interior painted a sick beige. When we got the word from Mr. Buckner, we were to sprint to telephones and notify our offices.

The substitution of one kind of money for another had only the most academic interest for a Scripps-Howard reporter in those days, but it was the sort of story city editors hate to miss, and jobs were hard to come by in 1933. So I remained tensely at the Clearing House while the afternoon dragged on. Delegations of reporters knocked at Mr. Buckner's door every fifteen minutes or so and got shooed away. When the time for the last edition had passed, I phoned my office and was told to hang around for as long as there was a chance of catching any papers at all with a replate. Finally, I extracted permission to go home, and went, leaving the morning-paper boys to keep the deathwatch.

Next day, when I was off, Mr. Buckner announced that the scrip would be issued, but it never was. The new Administration printed a lot of new money instead. The banks reopened, confidence revived, and I haven't had occasion to visit the New York Clearing House since. (The American Bank Note Company, of Hunts Point, in the Bronx, actually printed about 50 tons of scrip, with an aggregate face value of around $50,000,000, but the Clearing House Association, which footed the bill, subsequently ordered it all destroyed.)

Thinking back to Mortimer N. Buckner Day, as I have always privately tabbed that Saturday, I got the idea that it might be fun to look into the files of the newspapers of that distant epoch and see how much the New York daily press has changed.

The *World-Telegram,* rather naturally, was the one I looked at first. Certain features of the first page were familiar when, in the Public Library newspaper annex, I opened the bound volume for March, 1933. The Index, the Hialeah Results, and the Weather Report at the bottom of the page, and the Scripps-Howard lighthouse in the upper left-hand corner were all very much what they are now. But the tone of the paper seemed to have changed—I mean, I suppose, that the tone of the *World-Telegram* seems to have changed since. On March 1, for example, there was this four-column headline over a feature story on the first page: THOUSANDS OF WOMEN PAID LESS THAN $4 A WEEK; MANY SLEEP IN SUBWAYS SO THEY CAN BUY FOOD. The story was by a fellow named E. K. Titus, whom I remembered as a long, lean type with a kind of undernourished look himself. "The drive against starvation wages which are forcing New York City women and children down to the pay level of the Chinese coolie gained headway today as fifty important organizations got behind Governor Lehman's campaign for a minimum wage," Titus's story began. It was part of a series directed against a free, competitive labor market—one that the *World-Telegram* favored even then, however, for its own reporters and copyreaders. Another *World-Telegram* first-page head read: LAGUARDIA ASKS BANK DICTATORS. The future mayor was still a Republican congressman then, and he wanted "a Congressional committee with virtually dictatorial power over banking legislation for the remainder of the session" to stop the wave of bank moratoria that was sweeping the country. HOUSE PASSES DEBTOR'S RELIEF was the head over a Washington dispatch in the *W.-T.* about a bill that would "lift the load of the debt-burdened farmers who in many states have resorted to force in order to save their homes from foreclosure." A shirt-tail at the end of this story bore the caption "Mortgage Moratorium Is Passed in Senate."

There were two more stories that evoked the mood of the old G.O.P., or antepenultimate, era for me. One was headed: WHITNEY QUESTIONED ON POOL PRICE FIXING; MORGAN MAY TESTIFY. The Whitney referred to was Richard, president of the New York Stock Exchange; the Morgan, of course, was J. P.; and the questioning was done by a Senate subcommittee. Congressional committees then were investigating a better class of people. The other story, which was headed DIVES IN BLAZING FURNACE, CRYING "SO LONG, HERE I GO," told about a worker at a city incinerator who had "worried over making both ends meet on his $30 weekly salary." He had a wife and five children, friends at the incinerator explained.

On the editorial page of the same issue was a cartoon by Rollin Kirby showing a bulgy Mr. Hoover, with his suitcase packed, waving an admonitory forefinger at "G.O.P.," portrayed as a bulbous old gout sufferer in an armchair. "Don't You Try Any New-Fangled Ideas" was Mr. Hoover's valedictory warning to the old boy. In all editions since about 1936, the *Telly* has been worshiping Mr. Hoover as an elder statesman.

In the lead editorial, headed ALFRED E. SMITH'S ADVICE, I expected to find some of that good, Conservative horse sense that the *World-Telegram* now affects. I read that Mr. Smith at a hearing in Washington had advocated "a quick increase in public construction," anathema to the *World-Telegram* in its present phase, and I also found that the paper agreed with Mr. Smith and even expressed the belief that public works alone would not be enough. "The other major point in the Smith program," the editorialist wrote, "besides a debt moratorium and tariff reduction, was recognition of Russia. . . . Russia is the only place we can get a large foreign market quickly for much of our surplus production—and a market which has the unusual distinction in these times of never defaulting in its trade payments. Immediate recognition of Russia is essential not only to revive business but to prevent spread of the Far Eastern war and preserve the peace treaties." I had not remembered that either Mr. Smith

or the *World-Telegram* had been so set on resuming
relations with the Kremlin; newspaper readers have
for years been conditioned to think of that step as a
New Deal error. It may be lucky for the Happy War-
rior that he is no longer with us. Some senator or
other would have had him on television for sure.

Another editorial that I couldn't remember having
read before was titled simply "Frances Perkins." "No
better news has come from Cabinet-making councils
than the appointment of Frances Perkins as Secretary
of Labor," this one began, and continued, "Under
Secretary Doak, politics has further clogged the Department's inefficient machinery. When Miss Perkins
puts her hand on the throttle, this condition will change.
She is a skilled sociologist, not a politician. . . . Every
working man and woman in the country should rejoice
in Miss Perkins' appointment to the Cabinet."

Dazed by this unremembered aspect of my old paper, I stared through a haze at a column on the editorial page called "The Liberal Viewpoint," by Dr.
Harry Elmer Barnes. Dr. Barnes as of March 1, 1933,
was bemoaning the resignation of a fellow-liberal, Professor William Zebina Ripley, from Harvard—"an irreparable blow to university instruction in this country," Dr. Barnes called it. This Professor Ripley, he
stated, had written a book called *Main Street and Wall
Street,* which "showed how the mass of stockholders
in modern corporations, particularly in holding companies, are ignored, bamboozled, or hoodwinked by
powerful insiders who actually control the doings of
the concern." I had no doubt at all about how that
kind of talk would be regarded by the same paper in
this era. "Liberal" is a suspect term on the *World-
Telegram* now.

On the next day, March 2, the *World-Telegram*'s
editorial cartoon, by Talburt, showed the Republican
elephant dressed as a tramp and sprawled on a park
bench under a tree while the Democratic donkey and
a couple of human colleagues, visible through an office
window, struggled with a stack of papers marked
"Work" and "Trouble," and a telephone rang "Worries." The caption was "Hallelujah—I'm a Bum!"

There was a hint of optimism on the *World-Tele-gram*'s front page on March 3. It was in a story by Wesley Price, now an editor of the *Saturday Evening Post,* and the headlines over it read:

BANKERS MOVE
TO EASE STRAIN

RAISE TIME AND DEMAND DEPOSIT,
REDISCOUNT AND MONEY RATES

ALL MARKETS SHOW GAINS

NO NEED SEEN FOR MORATORIUM
IN NEW YORK

Under this, Price wrote, "New York bankers, confident they would not have to ask for moratorium relief, acted today to relieve the pressure of banking difficulties in other states."

That day's editorial cartoon, by Talburt again, showed a vast and blowzy bride, holding a few stringy flowers and attended by a number of hideous brats, standing beside a poor little Democratic donkey in a morning coat. The donkey held a scroll marked "Marriage License," and the bride was labeled "The Deficit." The Republican elephant, in a plug hat this time, was in retreat through an ogival doorway (the scene was a chapel), and in his hip pocket was a scroll marked "Divorce Papers." The caption of the cartoon was "The Girl He Left Behind Him!" It was a belittling picture of the heritage bequeathed to the as yet unchristened eggheads by the party of wise management, I thought, particularly as there had been no heavy defense expenditures to explain the bride's condition. In 1933, we enjoyed approximate military parity with Uruguay.

The head over one of the editorials, however, indicated to me that the *World-Telegram* even then had been Anti-Spy, just as, I remembered, it had been Anti-Swimming-in-Polluted-Waters. ESPIONAGE GOING OUT, the editorial was headed, and I started the piece with confidence, feeling that here, at last, was a direct

link with the *World-Telegram & Sun*. But I discovered
that espionage apparently meant something different
then. "Congress has outlawed wire-tapping as a means
of enforcing prohibition," the editorial started off,
"and Michigan has dismissed its stool-pigeon case
against William Z. Foster and seventeen others. It begins to look as if the country is awakening to the
shame of espionage. The Congressional ban on wire-
tapping as a means of obtaining evidence is a merited
reversal of the 5–4 Supreme Court decision of several
years ago upholding the practice. . . . Government
snoopers and agents provocateurs can never do anything but defeat the principles of law and order they
profess to serve." This struck me as such rank heresy
that I hoped nobody had spotted me reading it. I
looked anxiously at a man who was sitting at my el-
bow, but he was safely buried in a study of old race
charts in the *Morning Telegraph*. Only the other day,
I read an editorial in the *World-Telegram & Sun* in
which the writer wanted to re-legalize wiretapping and
then retry a woman whose case had been thrown out
of court because the evidence against her had been
obtained that way.

The *World-Telegram* editorial that got the biggest
play on March 3, 1933, though, was three columns
wide and bore the title "There Is a Cure." "Restore
buying power," it read. "This is the one cure for the
depression upon which all agree. . . . There is only
one direct and quick way to get it. That is through
wages. Somehow payrolls must be increased so that
money will flow again from the worker to the mer-
chant, to the manufacturer, to the banker and continue to circulate." I remembered as I read these
words that our wages had been cut 10 percent a few
months before the editorial was printed and another
10 percent shortly afterward.

But the *World-Telegram* for March 4 was the one
I really wanted to see again, and now I had reached
it. There was an eight-column streamer across the top
of page one: READY FOR WARTIME POWER—PRES.
ROOSEVELT. A long account of the inaugural speech
dropped away from this line at the right-hand side of

the paper. The story was by the late Raymond Clapper, of the United Press, who led off, "Franklin D. Roosevelt became President of the United States today with a demand for adequate but sound currency, an excoriation of the 'money changers,' and a promise that he might have to adopt wartime measures to combat the financial crisis now enveloping the nation." Clapper didn't work into his lead one line of that speech that nobody has forgotten: the one that went, "The only thing we have to fear is fear itself." But it ran in the text, on page five.

The left-hand side of the front page was given over to the local situation. SHUT BANKS HERE 2 DAYS was the headline, and the principal story depending from it bore the subheads:

GOVERNOR MOVES
TO RESERVE CASH

EXCHANGES CLOSE

HEAVY WITHDRAWALS FROM OUT OF
TOWN FORCE DECREE AS DEFENSIVE
MEASURE—FORTY-SEVEN STATES
HAVE RESTRICTIONS

(The only state in which the banks hadn't closed, according to this story, was Delaware.) It was neat makeup—banks closed on the left, Roosevelt inaugurated on the right, and in the center a big picture of Mr. Hoover and Mr. Roosevelt riding together to the inauguration. The bank story, again by Price, evoked a new hope. "In banking circles a belief existed that Clearing House certificates might be issued if New York business is hampered unduly by lack of ordinary banking facilities," he wrote. "This would enable bank customers to deposit and draw checks but not to get cash. (It wouldn't have done me any good in that case, since I had no bank account. I think, though, that Price was wrong and that the stuff was intended for general circulation.) "Mortimer Buckner, president of the New York Clearing House Association, said that the Committee was working on a plan he would not disclose. An announcement is expected by tonight." That was the announcement I had waited for.

The human side of the story, as editors like to call it, was written by William D. O'Brien, a confirmed rewrite man, to whom the outside world was ever a place of romance because for years he had known it only by hearsay.

CROWDS FLOCK
TO SHUT BANKS

GRAND CENTRAL ZONE BLOCKED
FOR A TIME—THRONGS ARE ORDERLY

the headlines over the human side of the story read. "The tingling news—'the banks are closed'— spread fleetly today to all parts of the city," O'Brien wrote, brightly as always, "breaking down, in the streets, in trains, in all public places, those common barriers of silence that separate aloof individuals in compact crowds, making for free gossip and silent, grim parades to bank buildings 'just to make sure.' Depositors arrived early in front of the Bowery Savings Bank in the bustling Grand Central Zone, massing on the steps at 110 East 42nd St., crowding, five hundred of them, along the sidewalks. . . ." After that, O'Brien had a clutch of cheerful anecdotes, spilling over onto page twelve, which, I saw from the heads on other yarns there, had been set aside as the Human Page for the day: CROWDS KEPT IN GOOD HUMOR BY POLICEMEN, GOOD HUMOR MARKS CRISIS, BUSINESS AS USUAL IN CHAIN GROCERIES, WOMEN TREAT HOLIDAY AS JOKE, and BARTERER PUTS HIS HOPE IN HENS.

Price's bank-closing story ran over onto page six, which was a kind of Hot Dope Page: DOLLAR TRADING, CHECK CASHING HALT IN EUROPE; ONLY DELAWARE IS UNAFFECTED; ILLINOIS CLOSES; TREASURY TALKS ON BANKS GO ON TILL NEAR DAWN; WESTERN UNION AND POSTAL LIMIT ALL MONEY ORDERS TO $100 IN U.S. The lead editorial began, "President Roosevelt holds the hope of the nation and of the world," and continued, "No longer is the cry heard that government should keep its hands off and allow rugged individualism to find a way. Three years of that has led us deeper in the hole. Now the plea is for government action."

The member of the *World-Telegram* staff most distrustful of the new President was Heywood Broun, who suspected Mr. Roosevelt of being a booby trap set by the Conservative wing of the Democratic Party. "I'd rather be right than Roosevelt," Broun had written from the Democratic Convention the previous summer. "And if I just had to be a Democrat, why then I'd be Al Smith." Broun, who had conferred its only distinction on the Scripps-Howard not-yet-hyphenated *Telegram* by accepting a handsome offer to join it in 1928, had had star billing there ever since. Of all the agreeable wits who wrote first-person columns in the twenties, Broun alone had changed and grown with the times, and by 1933 he was the only important practitioner of personal journalism in the city, outside of the gossip columns and the sports pages. The internal change in one who had been principally renowned as a civilized funnyman began with the Sacco-Vanzetti case, over which he quarreled with the *World,* where he had achieved his greatest fame. The quarrel sputtered on until Broun wrote an article in the *Nation* in which he said, "There ought to be a place in New York City for a liberal newspaper. . . . The *World* . . . is at best on the outer rim of the target. . . . Perhaps the first thing needed for a liberal newspaper is capital, but even more important is courage."

The *World,* terming this disloyalty, fired him, presumably to prove its Liberalism, and the *Telegram,* anxious to catch on as *any* kind of newspaper, hired him. His new employers indulged him until the *World* disappeared, leaving him with no place to take his white plume if he got mad again. By November, 1933, Broun was to be disillusioned with Smith. "Good-by, Al; take care of yourself," he would write. ". . . Al Smith has come out lock and stock and barrel for

Grover Cleveland." Concurrently, his opinion of the new President was to rise, and Broun's employers' opinion of Broun to decline, until 1939, when the columnist was to separate from the *World-Telegram* in much the same way he had left the *World*. By that time, the *World-Telegram* had a personal journalist to its own measure in Westbrook Pegler.

But in 1933, Talburt's editorial-page cartoon showed his donkey, this time wearing a bellhop's uniform, leading a traveler labeled "F.D.R." into a hotel room numbered 33 and completely unfurnished except for a bed marked "The Presidency." The bed had broken slats and springs, a burst mattress labeled "Banking Troubles," and a pillow stuffed with bricks and identified as "The Depression." Atop the mattress were strewn a cactus plant marked "War Debts" and a few spiked planks labeled "Taxes" and "Farm Problem." "I Hope You Find Everything O.K., Sir!" the bellhop was saying to F.D.R. The caption on the cartoon was "Not Exactly a Bed of Roses!" This brought to mind a cartoon I saw in the *World-Telegram & Sun* on the day of Gen. Eisenhower's inauguration. It showed a tiny man, who might have represented either Mr. American Citizen or the publisher of the *World-Telegram & Sun* driving a pair of goggle-eyed pygmy elephants hitched to a kind of circus wagon, marked "Eisenhower–Nixon Inaugural." The circus wagon contained, besides the driver, a big fat scroll labeled "The Hopes and Prayers of an Admiring Nation." The donkey, by now no bigger than a rabbit but, as usual, in human clothes, stood down at the bottom of the picture waving his hat in salute. The cartoon was by the same Mr. Talburt.

The *Evening Post* for March 4, 1933, contained a pre-inauguration story from Washington by Pegler—on the sports page. Pegler's photograph, at the head of his column, had him looking more like Buster Keaton than like Boris Karloff, as he does in the one he uses now. His dispatch read, in part:

Solemn days this capital has seen before, but never in our

time have the people been as twitchy and jerky as they were this morning, the last day of Mr. Hoover's unhappy Presidency. . . . There was a general sense that the court-plaster and chewing-gum expedients by which it had been hoped to keep the banks stuck together at the eaves and corners until Mr. Roosevelt could take over would barely last, if that.

Everyone was discussing money, and the fact that the local newspapers were whispering the story down and playing up items about two-headed calves and the first robin only aggravated the anxiety, suggesting that the news might be so sad that they didn't have the heart to tell it. . . . This was a sort of war feeling that pervaded the capital on the eve of the new deal, but with the agonizing difference that nobody could quite make out who the enemy might be. . . .

Mr. Hoover's exit from Washington recalls the brisk, informal departure of Jack Dempsey from Shelby, Mont., when the fight was over. As the decision was given by Mr. Dempsey's own roommate, Dempsey hopped over the ropes and was last seen legging it over the baked clay plain alone, with a bath towel streaming from his shoulders, toward an engine which stood on a siding, ready to go.

Pegler also quoted a Washington correspondent who said to him, "Do you see that low, fat, gray building with the turtleback roof over there? That is our town depot, and Mr. Hoover's train is going to be waiting for him right there. And as soon as Mr. Hoover makes absolutely certain that Frank is President, with no chance of any kickback, he is going to split a neat crack in the atmosphere, making for that train. Mr. Hoover aims to leave town with a minimum of delay. I don't think he likes our little city. He had terrible luck here."

Pegler's was the only unsympathetic voice on the *Evening Post,* which ran an editorial that enshrined Mr. Hoover among the martyrs of history who died with their boots on and their teeth clamped on the ankle of outrageous fortune. Commenting on Mr.

Roosevelt's inaugural address, the *Evening Post,* while conceding that it was an "effective speech," said proudly, "There was lacking the electric thrill of Calvin Coolidge's definite pronouncement: 'I do not favor a soldier's bonus.' " A letter to the editor said, "Now that moratoriums are in fashion, I suggest one on all photographs of the Roosevelt family for 30 days, beginning March 6, 1933."

Not much more remains of that *Post* than of the *Sun,* which survives only as a name on the front page of the *World-Telegram & Sun,* like the end of a goldfish's tail protruding from a cat's mouth. A line on the editorial page, "Founded by Alexander Hamilton in 1801," is about all that the present *Post* and the old *Evening Post* have in common. That is not amazing, because the paper has changed hands—and political parties. The unbending Mr. Curtis died not long after Mr. Hoover split his crack in the atmosphere, and his heirs sold the paper down the river to a New Deal Democrat, J. David Stern. Stern got its circulation up to a quarter of a million and then sold it, in 1939, to Mr. and Mrs. George Backer. Under its present owner, Dorothy Schiff, who was then Mrs. Backer, the circulation has climbed to 389,000 on the five good days of the week, or 367,000 reckoned on the old six-day basis, which is the only fair one for comparing 1933 and 1953 circulations. The tabloid *Post* has no financial section except a daily column by Sylvia Porter, and it was, as everyone probably knows, the only New York paper that supported Adlai Stevenson in the last presidential campaign.

· The *World-Telegram,* however, has changed just as much without being sold even once. On Mortimer N. Buckner Day, when they were separate papers, the *World-Telegram* and the *Sun* had an aggregate circulation of 704,698, but the *World-Telegram & Sun* musters something less than half a million (again on a six-day basis). Practically all the survivors of the little band who used to read the *Evening Post* must be included among the readers of the *W.-T.&S.* Now they would feel at home there. And it is a fair assumption that a lot of the old *World-Telegram* readers who followed Heywood Broun and the "Liberal Viewpoint" in its pages now take the *Post*. Between the beginning of one era and the beginning of the next, the *Post* and the *World-Telegram* have swapped sides.

Of Yesteryear—II

NOVEMBER 14, 1953

In the first week of March, 1933, when the banks closed in 47 states and Franklin D. Roosevelt was inaugurated President, the late William Randolph Hearst's *Evening Journal* offered, to readers only, a magic spell for exorcising the Depression. Before voicing this incantation, the would-be magician had to find and recognize, from a photograph published in the *Journal,* a youngish blonde called King Kong's Beauty. (A picture called *King Kong* was opening at both Radio City theaters simultaneously.) "You MUST have a current copy of the *Evening Journal* in your hand when you approach the girl you believe to be King Kong's Beauty," a box on the first page advised persons setting out on the quest. "Do not grab her but simply say: 'You are King Kong's Beauty, for whose capture the Radio City theatres offer a reward of $100.' "

Each afternoon, the *Journal* carried a picture of King Kong's Beauty, her captor of the previous day, and somebody from the Radio City Music Hall presenting the money to the lucky man or woman. The search for King Kong's Beauty afforded employment to many thousands of people who had no jobs, and at a much cheaper rate than subsequent government schemes of made work. At the same time, it kept them from bothering erstwhile employers, who now had no jobs to give them anyway. Concurrently, it called to the attention of those people who were not yet strapped the fact that a picture entitled *King Kong* was opening at Radio City. Along with the King Kong's Beauty story, the *Journal* regularly carried a half-page or full-page ad for *King Kong,* which helped the *Journal* survive the Depression itself. Altogether, the King Kong stunt was an example of the enlightened paternalism that has always marked the *Journal*'s relations with its public. The paper rounded out its service to its readers by offering the winner a chance to invest his $100 at a high rate of interest—a piece of munificence that was, in fact, available even to readers who hadn't caught King Kong's Beauty. The *Journal* made known this opportunity in a large, friendly house ad showing a hearty, cheerful, white-haired codger, obviously unaffected by the precarious times, and bearing in heavy headline type the legend:

IN THE AUTUMN OF LIFE
FREE FROM ALL WORRIES

I INVESTED WISELY IN HEARST 7%
SHARES; YOU CAN DO THE SAME BY
PAYING ONLY $1 PER SHARE
MONTHLY

HEARST CONSOLIDATED NEWSPAPERS, INC.

By investing in "the greatest publishing enterprise the world has ever known," the ad went on, the old party in the picture had placed himself beyond the baleful influence of the economic cycle. Taken together, the King Kong contest and Hearst Consolidated Newspapers' 7 percent preferred stock offered a full program for recovery. A Gimbels advertisement in the same issue (March 9) that carried word of the 7 percent bonanza reminded the public, "If there was ever a time when it was important to keep up appearances this is it!" and offered men's broadcloth shirts at 69 cents.

I came across these advertisements in the course of looking back in the files to see what the various members of the New York daily press were up to at the opening of the last political era; I thought it might be interesting to observe what changes twenty years and the opening of a new political era have brought about. I couldn't help reflecting that the old codger in the *Journal* might have appeared a trifle less cheerful if he had known that his stock was destined to pass three successive quarterly dividends in 1938, just when he might be needing some autumnal eating money.

With a few exceptions, such as the stock advertisement, which has been discontinued on the advice of counsel, the *Journal* then was much like the *Journal-American* now. (It assimilated Hearst's morning paper, the *American,* in 1937.) At least, the samples in the files don't produce any shock of nonrecognition, as do many 1933 copies of two of the city's other evening papers, the *World-Telegram* and the *Evening Post.* In those days, the *Post* was undiscourageably Republican, and the *World-Telegram* was scrabbling desperately to hold the Liberal readership of the *World* and the *Evening World,* which it had bought out two years earlier. Editorially, it proclaimed the inadequacy of individual enterprise to pull the country out of its slump. Republican foreign policy, William Philip Simms, its expert in that department, declared, "has proved an almost 100% failure." The *Sun,* hardly less Republican than the *Post* in 1933, has now disappeared except for its name, which dangles, in diminished type, below the *World-Telegram*'s, like a scalp from an Indian's belt. In 1933, the *Post* and the *Sun,* rather than the *Telegram* and the *Sun,* would have seemed the logical pair for a merger.

My researches also brought to light an illustration of the artistic continuity that links the old *Journal* and today's *Journal-American.* Back in 1933, the *Journal* published an intimate report on Fay Wray, the female star of *King Kong,* by Rose Pelswick, who was its motion-picture editor then and has the same job on the combined paper today. Miss Wray, Miss Pelswick disclosed, "uses a different perfume in each picture, insisting she'd be confused in her characterization if she duplicated one." This reminded me of a story I had read not long ago in the *Journal-American,* by Louella Parsons. In 1933, Miss Parsons wrote for the *American,* the *Journal*'s morning running mate. (Miss

Parsons and Miss Pelswick both write for the *Journal-American* now.) "An electric something which projects the essence of sex appeal makes Marilyn Monroe tops among Hollywood's current glamor queens," Miss Parsons announced in her recent essay. "Why, you may ask, when there are so many more beautiful girls than Marilyn, and certainly more talented ones as actresses? I was at a party a few weeks ago, when Marilyn walked into the room. It was a gay social event and the room was filled with famous Hollywood beauties and great stars. Yet the moment Marilyn entered the scene, all conversation stopped and the eyes of everyone, men and women alike, were riveted on her. She wore a dress that fitted her skin tight, and I might add, it was obvious she wore nothing but her skin under it." The principle of the two stories is the same; both give the Hearst public the inside line on the motion-picture industry—inside Miss Wray's mind and inside Miss Monroe's dress.

Society news written in a dashing manner is another Hearst specialty that has carried over from the *Journal* to the *Journal-American*. In 1933, two *Journal* columnists divided the glory that has now descended upon the single head of Igor Cassini, the current Cholly Knickerbocker. Their pseudonyms were Mme. Flutterbye and Billy Benedick. One of the most moving excerpts I jotted down from the *Journal*'s chronicle of those stirring days was Mme. Flutterbye's: "The Wideners are sensible people and they refuse to be stampeded by the closing of the banks." Billy Benedick also contributed many an anecdote of intrepidity, about fellows who borrowed money from the butler so they could take a taxi to the Colony, where they could sign the check—things like that. Benedick, in real life Baron George Wrangel, lost his job, but he has since gained a new pseudonymous vogue as the model for the Man in the Hathaway Shirt. Maury Paul, the most celebrated in the long family line of Cholly Knickerbockers, was alive then, but his column, like Miss Parsons's, ran in the *American*. When that paper folded, Cholly moved to the *Journal-American*, and Mme. Flutterbye and Billy had to go. The present

Cholly covers a lot more ground than Mme. Flutter-bye and Billy Benedick ever did in tandem. He sometimes gets more movie names into his column than Miss Parsons gets into hers, and he is also an authority on foreign and domestic politics, as well as an expert in the *roman à clef,* of which the following is a typical specimen: "The open secret in the Surf and Bath Club set in Miami Beach concerns the wife of an important Detroit executive who had a boy friend she was keeping in style. Even bought him clothes, etc. But recently they had a spat and he turned up at a big charity party in Miami with a cute blonde. This enraged Madame to such a point that next day she went and got all the clothes she gave him—even went to the dry cleaners and got his suits out of there—and scissored them into little pieces. The topper is that the boy friend notified his insurance company, and now they are trying to get back the money for the clothes from her! And she'll have to pay the thousand-odd bucks rather than have her husband find out about it!"

In international affairs, Igor-Cholly is a staunch royalist: "One story that has been circulating in the fashionable drawing rooms of Europe and is now being repeated here is that young King Baudoin of Belgium is madly in love with his beautiful stepmother, the Princess de Rethy. That is a vicious and false story spread by the Belgian Socialists, those dear cousins of the Communists, who would like to overthrow the Monarchy. True, King Baudoin is a very badly advised young man. . . . The young king . . . is profoundly attached to his stepmother, but it's a son's devotion, not that of a man in love. The Princess de Rethy is one of the most maligned women in Europe. She has been a wonderful wife and companion to Leopold and her influence over King Baudoin is anything but 'sinister,' as her enemies in Belgium describe it." On the question of morals, Cholly is a fearless fellow, taking a bold stand on the controversial issues of the day: "I'm not a Mickey Jelke fan, but I was on his side when I read an interview with Pat Ward, the call-girl who sent him to prison, in which Miss Ward states that she thinks the judge was very lenient in sentencing Mickey from 3-to-6 years in the penitentiary. What gall that call-girl has! By all standards she should be in jail with Jelke."

Mme. Flutterbye and Billy Benedick were not the only propagandists for the stiff upper lip during the days when the banks were closed and money was scarce unless you could find King Kong's Beauty. Dorothy Kilgallen, fresh back from Mr. Roosevelt's inauguration—it took place on Saturday, March 4, when the banks in 47 states had been ordered closed —contributed a column of cheer to the *Journal* of March 7. The head over Miss Kilgallen's story read: HYSTERIA GONE, WIVES WAITING SCRIP INCOME. (The scrip referred to was a kind of ersatz money that was being printed under the auspices of the New York Clearing House Association. It was to be circulated in case the real stuff remained a long time in official protective custody.) "Not since World War days, when they knitted socks, rolled bandages, ate brown bread, and economized on sugar, have the women of America so enjoyed themselves as during the present 'bank holiday,'" Miss Kilgallen reported. In Washington, her assignment had been to tail Frances Perkins, who had been named by Mr. Roosevelt to be his Secretary of Labor—the first woman Cabinet member in the history of the United States. Miss Kilgallen gave Miss Perkins a standard treatment reserved for Hollywood starlets—No. 3-A, Just a Homebody. MISS PERKINS PACKS SIMPLE GOWN FOR INAUGURAL BALL was the headline over another Kilgallen dispatch.

At the Eisenhower inauguration, Miss Kilgallen covered Mrs. Eisenhower with unaging enthusiasm. "'America's sweetheart' is a corny phrase," she wrote, in one of her more moderate raptures, "but Mrs. Dwight D. Eisenhower, standing on the threshold of the White House, rates it more completely than any woman since Mary Pickford had long curls."

In 1933, a cartoonist-poet named Nelson Harding, who was then an institution on the *Journal,* maintained the note of optimism with an allegorical drawing a day. My favorite, on March 7, showed the ship of state, carefully labeled "United States of America,"

listing above an area marked "Stagnation Shallows."
Two tugboats were steaming to her aid, one marked
"F. D. Roosevelt" and the other "Confidence." The
F. D. Roosevelt flew a flag bearing the word "Action."
The poem part went like this:

> At last the rescue fleet has come
> And it is well commanded.
> The giant ship is not a wreck
> But on the shallows stranded.
> The sturdy tugs are on the job
> And with united towing
> They'll float her on the rising tide
> With sailing whistles blowing.

On some days, Mr. Harding also did a stint in prose,
under the heading "In Other Words." One fair sample
ran, "Ogden Mills will retire as Secretary of the Deficit. He'll leave all the books and a lot of black ink
that hasn't been used."

Arthur Brisbane, the mighty thinker who could find
things to worry about in the best of times, offered a
granitic form of reassurance during the preliminary
phases of the storm. Brisbane's column appeared each
day on the front page of the *American,* but he often
made speeches, and these were quoted in the *Journal,*
the result being that both papers enjoyed the advantage of his inspirational sapience. The kind of thing
that would worry Brisbane, even during a World Series, was the number of eggs produced by a female
codfish. According to Brisbane, it was millions. Then
he would multiply the number of eggs by the number
of codfish, and point out that nature, which he always
spelled with a capital "N," had thoughtfully provided
a number of oöphagous fellow-creatures who kept the
codfish population of the world within bounds. But
what would happen if these monitors suddenly lost
their appetite for eggs, he would ask. The world, within
eleven months, fourteen days, and a number of hours
that he ventured only to approximate, since he hadn't
gone into the problem deeply, would turn into one
vast uncooked codfish ball, with only the top of Mount

Everest and possibly a small portion of San Simeon protruding from a limitless sea of cod-liver oil. The *American*'s motto was "A Paper for People Who Think," and on days when Brisbane wrote a column about codfish eggs the pages would drop from hundreds of thousands of nerveless fingers and flutter wraithlike to the floor.

But when the going was tough, Brisbane provided erudite solace. U.S. MUST MEET CRISIS, SAYS BRISBANE, a headline in the *Journal* proclaimed on March 3, the day before Roosevelt's inauguration. "Europe survived the 100-years War, the 30-years War, the 7-years War and the Black Death," the Sage had told a California audience, the *Journal* reported. He thought we had a chance to get by.

A March, 1933, *American Weekly*—the *Weekly*, a Sunday supplement to the *American*, survived the merger and is now distributed with the Sunday *Journal-American*—carried a smashing scientific feature in the true Brisbane tradition, entitled "Why Intelligent Parents Ought to Have Intelligent Children; Interesting Experiments with Rats Seem to Settle the Long-Standing Scientific Dispute as to Whether Highly Developed Brains Can Be Inherited and If 'Dumb' Couples Are Likely to Have Rather Stupid Children." The *Weekly*'s preoccupation with science has continued right through the years. It made a big thing recently of *The Story of My Life*, by Christine Jorgensen, the G.I. who became a woman, according to her or him, or who, according to the *Post*, didn't.

Among the *Weekly*'s other features during the troubles were "How the Mysterious Mayans Made War," "Played Suicide Role at the Theatre—Kills Herself Same Way" (a story about a Parisian actress), "Chorus Girls Too Innocent and Trustful?" (three of them were suing men for breach of promise), "Jilted the English Earl for a Plain American," and one with a topical slant, "Prosperous Times for Professional Beggars—How the Depression Has Made It Easy for Tramps and Panhandlers to Impose on Charitably Inclined Men and Women, and the Tricks and Devices Which Stir Sympathy." All in all, a good display of the standard Hearst commodities: blood, money, and sex.

In addition to Brisbane, Miss Parsons, and Cholly Knickerbocker, the *American* enjoyed the services of Damon Runyon, Robert L. Ripley, and a celebrated stylist named O. O. McIntyre. McIntyre's style is hard to convey without quotation. A bank-holiday sample was "All my life I've wanted to walk barefoot over a big lawn after a shower. Watching Lupe Velez gives me the ork-orks. But I go womp watching that tasty tornado, Mae West." The *American* also had a peculiarly pretentious opposite-editorial page, which was split into columns of essays by an improbable assortment of writers, some celebrated only within the Hearst world. Aldous Huxley, Bertrand Russell, Gobind Behari Lal, Adela Rogers St. Johns, Agnes Smith, Bruno Lessing, and G. K. Chesterton were among the bylines during the first week of March, 1933. But the page was haunted by an endemic dullness, as a swamp is by malaria. Regardless of bylines, all the offerings limped; perhaps literary agents sent pieces there only after every other market had failed. The *American* was William Randolph Hearst's lone attempt at a newspaper for the elite, but it never got anywhere except on Sunday, when it had the *Weekly* and the colored funnies to pull it along. In 1937, when the bankers' representatives took over the administration of the old gentleman's empire, they jettisoned the *American,* along with his stained glass and his Egyptian knickknacks.

The *Journal* for March 2, 1933, carried a signed editorial by Claude G. Bowers, its political columnist, which I don't think would be likely to get into the *Journal-American* now. A warm-over of testimony Alfred E. Smith had given before a Senate committee in Washington a few days earlier, it read, in part, "Alfred E. Smith said some good things before the Senate committee in Washington, but nothing that was said was better put than his views on the recognition of Russia. This is long overdue." What Smith had said was "We ought to recognize Russia. . . . There is no use in trading with them under cover. . . . I do not believe in being against them just because they have a form of government that we do not like." But such divergences from the *Journal-American*'s present policy are the exception. The general feeling I got from the file of old *Journals* was the one I now experience when I read an accumulation of several days' *Journal-Americans*—that of entering a self-contained world which has little relevance to the one outside but which has its own constants: gossip, xenophobia, the movies, and a continual Byzantine-palace struggle for precedence among byliners. In 1933, the beg news of the day was that everybody was broke, and the big question was what we were going to do about it. But in reading the *Journal* for the first three days of that strange March, one gets no sense that the country, and particularly the City of New York, was traversing unique times. The villain for the *Journal*—and also for the *American*—was England. The *American* carried an expository series headed DO THE BRITISH CONTROL AMERICAN PRICE LEVELS? According to the author, they did, for England's benefit. Both papers agreed that cheap foreign goods and high taxes were the chief enemies of prosperity, although imports were at a dead stop and every day found fewer people who had to pay any income tax at all.

Once the banks closed, however, the Hearst papers erupted good cheer, as obviously ordered up as their previous impassivity. The performance, viewed now in cold type on crumbling paper, reminded me of the way the Russians at the Olympic Games in Helsinki a couple of years ago all frowned and smiled in unison. In the forty-first month after the stock-market crash, the *World-Telegram*'s purpose seemed to be to arouse its readers and the *Sun*'s and *Evening Post*'s mission one of reassurance. The Hearst papers, though, simply tried to distract their readers from what was going on. When it came to the treatment of foreign news, they gave the rising Hitler better than the benefit of the doubt—they expressed no doubt whatever. HITLER "FIRING SQUAD" GIVEN POWER TO END GERMAN RED PLOTS was the *American*'s headline over the story of events that the *Times* summarized as:

HITLER SUSPENDS
REICH GUARANTEES;
LEFT PRESS BANNED

EMERGENCY DECREE TO COMBAT
"COMMUNIST TERROR" VOIDS
CONSTITUTIONAL SAFEGUARDS

The decree, according to Charles Flick, the Hearst correspondent, simply followed "the revelation of an alleged Communist plot." On the other hand, Frederick Birchall, the *Times* man, reported, "Nothing is being left unsaid and undone to arouse a wave of popular hysteria in advance of Sunday's elections." Mr. Brisbane wrote, oracularly, "Soon the world will know whether Hitler is another Mussolini or another Rienzi," by which he presumably meant a success or a flop, since Mussolini was a Hearst idol and contributor. Il Duce wrote, or at least signed, weekly articles for the Sunday *American,* as, for that matter, did David Lloyd George and Mrs. Franklin D. Roosevelt.

Then as now the *Journal* attached much value to clerical opinion. On March 6, it recorded the verdict on President Roosevelt's inaugural speech reached by Father Charles E. Coughlin, a Roman Catholic priest famous at the time as the Radio Priest of Royal Oak, Michigan. COUGHLIN PUTS F.D.R. AHEAD OF LINCOLN, the headline said. In these unregenerate days, the *Journal-American* retains a feature preacher, Bishop Fulton Sheen, whose column appears on the editorial page every Saturday. "It is what comes out of a man's heart that defiles him," the bishop wrote in the course of one typical workout, "for out of the heart come evil thoughts, murders, adulteries, fornications, theft, false witnesses, blasphemies." The catalogue read like the first page of the *Journal-American* on a good news day. Across from the Bishop, Joseph Whitney, psychologist, discussed the probable psychosomatic etiology of the common cold in "The Mirror of Your Mind," a regular *Journal-American* feature. There must be something for everybody in a well-balanced paper.

While in most respects the *Journal-American* has not changed at all, since the recent inauguration it has seemed as if the paper might even unchange a change. There was a notable difference between the *Journal* of 1933, in which a cartoonist was allowed to link Roosevelt with Confidence, and the *Journal-American* during the last years of Roosevelt's Administration and the whole of Truman's. In this latter period, the *Journal-American* assembled a crew of professional Roosevelt and Truman haters, who filled so many columns with their copy that at one time they threatened to shove Hollywood back onto the amusement page. The stridency of their outcries has necessarily diminished in the course of the past year, but the old haters are still there, bearing up as best they can under the circumstances. The first of them to be tapped by Hearst —and to my perhaps nostalgic taste the most talented —was Westbrook Pegler, who brought his hypnotic eyebrows from the *World-Telegram* to a double column on the *Journal-American*'s page three late in the third Roosevelt Administration. (This was the same Pegler who, when he was a sportswriter on the old *Evening Post,* did such a rollicking yarn about Herbert Hoover's hasty exit from Washington on March 4, 1933; but he had changed a lot in the interim.) In November, 1948, after the election of Truman, Pegler announced that the American Republic was done for, and confirmed this diagnosis on October 3, 1950, when he wrote, "The awful truth seems to be that the republic is dead."

But what really died in 1950—or, to be more accurate, decided to acknowledge its decease—was the *Sun.* From the *Sun* to the *Journal-American,* like Aeneas fleeing burning Troy, hastened George Sokolsky, and, setting up his face and his column on page two, he became a kind of Scylla to Peg's Charybdis. Not long ago, Sokolsky took out after the concept ("Mrs. Eleanor Roosevelt has been its principal advocate") embodied in Article 10 of the United Nations Covenant on Human Rights—the one about the right of everyone to adequate food, clothing, and housing. "How can anyone decide what is adequate about food, for instance?" he demanded whimsically. "There is a young lady with plenty of money who eats Melba toast, grapefruit, and drinks black coffee to keep her figure. Is she to be forced to eat a specific number of calories a day to satisfy the United Nations?" This puts the whole problem of famine in a far more encouraging light. People don't starve; they diet themselves to death. "Who knows really what a high standard of life is?" he continued. "Can everything be measured by the consumption of butter or are there a few spiritual values such as peace of mind?" This posed an old question in a new form; instead of "Guns or butter?" the quandary now is "Peace of mind or butter?" I had got well into Louis Sobol's column on the next page ("Barbara eying old flame") before it occurred to me that I prefer peace of mind *and* butter. In 1933, Sobol's column used to be called "The Voice of Broadway," but now the Voice is Miss Kilgallen's and the Sobol area, on the opposite-editorial page, is called "New York Cavalcade." As you can see, some things have changed.

Neap tide on the *Journal-American* arrived in October, 1950, when Fulton Lewis, Jr., a radio commentator of conservative sponsorship, was installed on page one, along with his face; it had got so when you saw a photograph in the paper, you could no longer safely assume it was that of a movie actor. Lewis was rapidly shuffled back in the pack, as the racing-chart makers say, but Peg and Sock stayed up front hating Harry Truman until he retired undefeated. Pegler's column does not appear with its old regularity in the *Journal-American* anymore, and when it does appear, he is usually hating Eisenhower Republicans or people who haven't been around for a long time, like Harry Hopkins. To function, Pegler has to oppose, and William Randolph Hearst, Jr., the *Journal-American*'s publisher, has not yet decided whether to go in for opposition. Sokolsky, demugged, has been moved to the editorial page, where he performs on the right-hand side of the main cartoon, in a column of double width. But the editorials, on the left of the cartoon, are in type twice as large and in a column of triple width, as if to emphasize his subordination. Lewis and a number of his colleagues on the same rung of the ladder are scrounged down into two columns under the cartoon, and since there isn't enough room for all of them, none makes it more than three times a week.

Lewis and his neighbors in the basement aren't very happy about the Administration. "The shadow of what happened to Herbert Hoover back in 1930 hangs today like a threat over the hopes of General Eisenhower in 1954," one of them, named George Rothwell Brown, wrote hardly three months after the President was inaugurated. The tone of the editorials themselves has been slightly more indulgent, but the boys under the cartoon sometimes remind me of a pack of beagles without a rabbit.

Of Yesteryear—III

NOVEMBER 21, 1953

New York is uniquely fortunate among American cities in having two tolerably good morning newspapers—the *Times* and the *Herald Tribune*. Editorially, neither is outstandingly brave or perspicacious, but both pay for and publish a considerable quantity of good reporting. This means that they do not buy their out-of-town coverage entirely from press associations and then tailor it to their individual tastes with scissors and headlines; they maintain staffs of correspondents abroad and in Washington, and send men farther than the ends of the subway lines to cover stories within the United States. I don't believe that they tell these employees what to find, although it is possible that they sometimes reject their findings. (I purposely refrain from any subtler considerations, such as the possible desire of some reporters to make their stories conform to what they surmise to be the paper's point of view.) These may seem modest claims to distinction in a country that is supposed to have a ring-tailed

Argus of a press, but there is no other city in the United States with two papers that can make them.

A while back, I was looking through the files of New York's daily papers of twenty years ago to see what the press was up to then; March 4, 1933, when Franklin D. Roosevelt was first inaugurated President, marked the beginning of a political era that ended in January of this year, and I thought it might be interesting to make a few then-and-now comparisons. In March, 1933, the city had for its morning reading the *Times* and *Herald Tribune,* plus a Hearstian absurdity called the New York *American,* which has perished, and two giant tabloids, the *Mirror* and the *News,* which have, to understate the case, survived. Until two years before, the city had possessed what now seems the astronomical number of *three* real morning newspapers. The cessation of the *World* in February, 1931, ended that unbelievable age. In 1933, it survived only as the first name on the masthead of the *World-Telegram,* like the remains of a holstein on the cowcatcher of a locomotive.

At the opening of the Democratic fifth of a century, the *Times* had a quantitative edge on the *Herald Tribune*: a bigger staff, more pages, more stories, more news, about 40 percent more circulation, and a whale of a lot more advertising. It still holds this lead—in fact, it has increased its lead. The *Tribune* has lost about six thousand readers in the intervening twenty years, whereas the *Times* has picked up about thirty-five thousand. In 1933, the *Times* was counted Democratic and the *Herald Tribune* Republican, a circumstance that guaranteed to each a hard core of readers safe from the lures of its rival. This left the large mass of political skeptics to be wooed by the *Herald Tribune* with whimsey, then its stock in trade, and by the *Times* with a greater bulk of news.

There has since been a change. The *Times* supported the Republican candidate in three of the last four presidential elections—Willkie in 1940, Dewey in 1948, and Eisenhower in 1952. It chose Roosevelt in 1944 because there was a war on. In time of peace, therefore, it may be counted as Republican as Catta-

raugus County. The *Times* was not without editorial
reservations about Franklin D. Roosevelt even in 1933.
"Time will show whether his genial personality has the
necessary admixture of cold steel," it editorialized on
the morning of his inauguration. And a couple of mornings earlier it had observed, "The need of the times
is not a novel panacea but more courageous leadership along a path well charted by experience." The
Times thought that the national deficit of $5,000,000,-
000 had undermined public confidence; a balanced
budget, sound currency, and a lower tariff were its
prescription. (The Hearst papers, also in favor of
Roosevelt with reservations, thought what the country
needed was a *higher* tariff.) But Arthur Krock, the
Times's chief Washington correspondent, then in the
sanguine flush of middle middle age, burbled with
optimism. The head over a typical Krock effusion on
March 3 began, ROOSEVELT ARRIVAL HEARTENS CAPI-
TAL, and went on:

SPIRIT OF COOPERATION AND
HOPE PERVADES CITY AS
"NEW DEAL" NEARS

REPUBLICANS ARE HELPING

HOOVER CABINET "STANDS BY"——ENVOYS
OF FOREIGN NATIONS JOIN
IN OPTIMISM

WAITING FOR LEADERSHIP

WASHINGTON FEELS THAT A PRESIDENT
IN HARMONY WITH CONGRESS
IS A NATIONAL NEED

Mr. Krock led off:

When Franklin D. Roosevelt reached Washington tonight,
to spend his last day and a half before becoming President, he found himself in an atmosphere of cooperation
and anticipation of the leadership for which the capital has
been clamoring for two years.

While conditions in the country and the rest of the world are grave, and citizens elsewhere, it appears, are inclined to shake their heads sympathetically over the magnitude of the task Mr. Roosevelt is to assume, the mood of Washington is different. It is distinctly hopeful. It welcomes the "new deal" even though it is not sure what the new deal is going to be. . . . Perhaps the happiest group of all over the imminence of a functioning government is the diplomatic corps. For two years it has been marking time in most matters.

For the *Herald Tribune,* the situation was moist with tragedy. Fate had been against Mr. Hoover, an editorial pointed out; at the beginning of his Administration, he had been insufficiently favored with adversity, underendowed with afflictions. "As between taking office at the peak of prosperity, as did Mr. Hoover, and starting in an hour of complete gloom, as does Mr. Roosevelt, every practical consideration favors the latter," the editorialist wrote. Mr. Hoover has struggled nobly against this initial handicap, the writer continued, but the effort had proved too great. Just as he had succeeded in eradicating the last traces of debilitating solvency, Election Day caught up with him. Mr. Roosevelt was reaping the benefits of Mr. Hoover's labors. The new President was setting out in a condition of enviable destitution. Walter Lippmann, in his column, "Today and Tomorrow," which has lasted in the *Herald Tribune* through twenty years of what were then tomorrows, ascribed the failure of Mr. Hoover's Administration to its refusal to take the Depression seriously while it still had control of Congress, and its loss of influence over Congress by the time it did begin to take the Depression seriously. "Certainly it is true that once Congress ceases to respect and obey the President, it is almost impossible to restore the President's authority," Mr. Lippmann said.

The *Times* was less sympathetic. "All of the political blueprints which Mr. Hoover prepared in advance for his Presidency were drawn to the grand scale of prosperity," it stated editorially. "That he expected it to continue and even to swell into a greater diapason of complacent pride can hardly be doubted. His campaign speeches in 1928 and the large plans which he took with him into the White House are sufficient evidence on this point. The result was that when prosperity shrivelled and crumbled in his hand, all his calculations were out. . . . There was something heroic about his posture, but to many it appeared sadly like that of a modern Laocoön, caught in the coils of business disaster, and with the serpent of frustrated hopes and unfulfilled predictions and broken campaign promises sinking its fangs into his side."

Whether Mr. Hoover was a victim of prosperity or of snakebite, it was a subtle malaise that my friend Colonel John R. Stingo would call a *lapsus pecuniae,* or shortage of tease, that weighed more heavily on the public mind than his departure. On March 1, F.P.A. wrote in his column, "The Conning Tower," in the *Herald Tribune,* "Most of us today are worrying along on last year's sackcloth."

The principal headline on the first page of the *Herald Tribune* of March 1 was over the story by John Elliott, the paper's Berlin correspondent. HITLER IMPOSES IRON RULE, ABROGATES CIVIC RIGHTS, JAILS 100 REICHSTAG REDS, it read, and two long banks depended from it:

> HINDENBURG SIGNS DECREE ABETTING
> FASCIST DICTATORSHIP, GAGGING
> PRESS AND SUPERVISING STATES

> NAZI SPOKESMAN ADMITS BRUTALITY OF
> LAWS, DECLARES COMMUNISTS PLOT
> PROLETARIAN REVOLUTION

This was not as bad as it sounded, a *Herald Tribune* editorial explained the next morning. "If the spectacle that the Hitler Government is making of Germany at this moment were being presented in any other European capital, in any country less heavily ballasted with common sense and less passionately devoted to unity and order, the onlooker would be. more than justified in expecting a violent popular eruption," the editorialist conceded, but Germany, he was confident, would remain placid.

The same morning, the *Tribune* carried three dignified front-page headline references to the imminent change of Administration in Washington. They were, from left to right, MISS PERKINS, WALSH, ROPER FILL CABINET, TIDE OF VISITORS IN CAPITAL NEARS 250,000 PEAK, and HOOVER FRIENDS PLAN GREETING ON BOTH COASTS—the last concerning the outgoing President's intended trip from New York to the Pacific Coast by ship. (He changed his mind and went by train.)

That issue of the *Tribune* also carried a story, under the headline "SHORN LAMB" LAYS LOSSES TO NATIONAL CITY, which told of testimony before the Senate Banking and Currency Committee by a man named Edgar D. Brown, of Pottsville, Pennsylvania. Mr. Brown had said that on the advice of salesmen for the National City Company, an investment affiliate of the National City Bank, he had put $250,000 into foreign bonds and domestic stocks and was now living on an allowance from what he called "the poor board." Mr. Brown had referred to himself as "a shorn lamb." The headline value of the title must have impressed the copy desk of the *Times,* too, for on the first page of that paper appeared the head "SHORN LAMB" TELLS SENATORS OF LOSS. Mr. Brown, according to the *Times,* testified before the committee that he had felt twinges after buying the stocks. But when he told the National City Company early in 1929, before the market crash, that he wanted to sell them, he was, in his own words, "placed in the position of one who was about to put his own mother out of house. As soon as I had communicated my plans, I was surrounded by every salesman in the house and told that to sell would be a very foolish thing to do."

On its front page that day, the *Times,* with a traditional fondness for balanced makeup, had two two-column heads—one on former Governor Smith, who had been giving his views on the economic situation to a Senate subcommittee, and the other on the "slackened" advance of two Japanese armies in an undeclared war that was raging in North China. (The "slackening" was to be followed in a few days by the complete collapse of the defenders. "Slacken" is an ominous word in a military headline.) Great Britain had placed an embargo on the sale of arms to the Japanese, who were already fully equipped, and to the Chinese, who weren't, but Russia, according to a front-page box partway down the second column of the *Times,* was "said to be sending big arms supplies to China." To the retrospective eye, a curious feature of this benevolence is that the recipient, as head of the Chinese Government, was Chiang Kai-shek.

The *Times* thought the Chinese and Smith stories hotter than its Berlin report from Frederick T. Birchall, a former acting managing editor of the paper, who was establishing himself as a memorable foreign correspondent, but it gave Birchall a good one-column top: HITLER SUSPENDS REICH GUARANTEES; LEFT PRESS BANNED. "Last night's fire, which rendered the Reichstag building untenable for at least a year, has provided the expected basis for measures of repression throughout the Reich unprecedented save in time of war or revolution," Birchall wrote. "Nothing is being left unsaid and undone to arouse a wave of popular hysteria in advance of Sunday's elections." (This appeared on a Wednesday.) Although the Communists were accused of setting the fire, the correspondent noted, it was made the pretext for an attack on all German newspapers having the faintest tinge of Liberalism.

On the matter of Russia, Walter Duranty, in a long dispatch on page eleven of the *Times,* wrote, "Recent decrees bristle with words like 'mercilessly' or 'without pity,' and the Bolsheviki believe themselves no less bound by duty to 'smite and spare not' than the soldiers of Allah, who offered unbelievers the choice between the Koran and the sword." Duranty was not strictly fair to the soldiers of Allah, who were usually willing to allow Christians to survive as taxable second-class citizens. " 'In the name of humanity and socialism,' or 'in the name of Allah and his Prophet' may differ in form, but they are identical in fact," Duranty went on, "and since Torquemada burned the bodies of heretics to save their souls there has been no form of human action so ruthless as that which has been inspired by idealistic and altruistic motives." Things were tough all over.

Of the remaining headlines on the *Times*'s front page, one was devoted to a story on the impending change in Washington, another to a bill to cut the salaries of New York State employees, and a third to the prospect of "debt talks" with Great Britain, which was held to be unlikely; the debts were those dating from the First World War. Mr. Krock, writing about them, quoted Neville Chamberlain, then Chancellor of the Exchequer, as advocating "cancellation as the best course for this creditor nation." A two-column box in the middle of the page, right under the date, accentuated the balance of the makeup—2-1-2-1-2—in mute contrast to the imbalance of the national finances. HOUSE HELD SURE TO PASS BANKRUPTCY BILL, this box was headed, and the story beneath it read, in part, "According to Democratic leaders, Mr. Roosevelt has made it clear that he desires to see the bankruptcy act amended to prevent unjustified receiverships before he enters upon his duties as President. They represented him as saying that the present situation is such as to make wise the enactment of such a law to protect railroads and corporations which might be suffering temporarily from being thrown hastily into destructive receiverships." It is a forgotten portrait— Roosevelt the corporation coddler.

It was not until the reader got back to page five in the *Times* that March 1, and a lot farther back in the *Herald Tribune,* that he might have begun to suspect something was going a bit queer with our banking system. In the *Herald Tribune*'s case, this was perhaps natural, for after Mr. Hoover's defeat a mere national dearth of tease may have seemed a redundant misfortune, unworthy of notice on its own account —like missing the last limousine after your best friend's funeral and having to walk to the bus stop. But the *Times,* I suspect, just didn't want to put too many ideas in the heads of too many depositors, although, of course, it didn't feel that it was ethical to ignore the situation completely. MORE STATES MOVE TO PRO-TECT BANKS, a *Times* headline over a roundup of dispatches on the subject read. (In those days, "protect" was a nice way of saying "close.") Governor Ruby Laffoon had designated March 1, 2, 3, and 4 as "days of thanksgiving in the State of Kentucky," making them legal holidays, on which the banks would not have to open. Tennessee was enjoying a holiday, too, and "curbs were spreading" in Indiana and Arkansas and Ohio. Michigan was shut tight as a drum already, and the Commercial National Bank of Washington, D.C., had beaten the gun by simply going into the hands of a receiver. The Bureau of Internal Revenue had announced that no holiday would be allowed in filing income-tax returns but said it would accept checks on banks that were temporarily in repose. "The check will be collected later or in case of failure to collect it will have to be made good by the taxpayer," it was consolingly explained.

A helpful suggestion was contained in a short cable story to the *Times* from Havana: "Military censors this afternoon issued orders to all the newspapers published on the island forbidding them to publish dispatches which have any reference to the banking situation in various parts of the United States, particularly news regarding banks in New York. The Senate investigation now under way in Washington and the bank moratoriums in some states have focussed the attention of the Cuban public on American banks, and it is thought that financial circles here sought the censorship, since some United States banks have branches in Havana."

In the absence of a similar order in New York, the papers continued to print the stories in places where the editors hoped nobody would get excited about them. The only hopeful note on page five of the *Times* was the headline BRITISH CONFIDENT OF OUR STABILITY. The British Government, the dispatch under this noted, was supporting the dollar by liberal purchases, and "responsible quarters" considered the position of the New York banks—which Governor

Herbert Lehman was to close three days later—"extremely liquid."

Saks Fifth Avenue, as confident as London, advertised a new woman's hat named Pinch Punch II, at $10.50, which it described as "a new version of Saks Fifth Avenue's Pinch Punch—the famous slouch hat with the nonchalant *dégagé* air. Made with the higher pointed crown so very definitely nineteen thirty-three." On the following Sunday, after the New York banks had closed, 23 leading New York department stores, including Saks, took space for a joint advertisement in all the city's papers urging customers to use their charge accounts "Business is based on faith and credit," the stores chorused. "We have not lost our faith in our customers. You have not lost your credit with us." Nonchalant and *dégagé* was the way to be.

The *Times* handled the matter of bank protection with increasing discretion as the first week of March wore on. The story made page eight on March 2, with BANKS PROTECTED IN 5 MORE STATES (they were California, Oklahoma, Alabama, Louisiana, and Mississippi), and page nine on March 3, with 8 STATES IN WEST DECLARE HOLIDAYS (Texas, Oregon, Arizona, Idaho, Washington, Utah, Nevada, and Wisconsin). On both these days, the *Herald Tribune* ran the banking story on page nineteen, in its financial section. Under the circumstances, as noted shortly after the bank closings by Robert Benchley, my distinguished predecessor in this department, "Readers of the *Herald Tribune* . . . must have had a strange sense of uneasiness on reading on page one, in the lead to Theodore C. Wallen's pre-Inaugural story, the following mysterious sentence: 'In an air of suspense seldom, if ever, felt in peace times, Franklin D. Roosevelt arrived last night, amid cheering throngs, to assume the Presidency of the United States at an acute stage of the depression.' What acute stage was that? What depression?"

When Governor Lehman did close the New York banks, he issued his proclamation at 4:20 A.M. on March 4, Inauguration Day. (It was a Saturday, but banks would normally have been open for half a day.) This was too late for the *Herald Tribune*'s late-city edition, so it was a second-day story by the time the *Tribune* could print it. The *Times* had the story that day, though, in a special 5 A.M. edition. After that, as Mr. Benchley wisely and savagely noted, the newspapers "just decided that the thing to do was to bolster, bolster, bolster, like good morale builder-uppers, with the result that they very nearly dissipated the good impression that the new administration had made and gave the public cause to believe that things were in the hands of the radio announcers and fortune-tellers. Two more days of cherry-ho, followed the next minute by hory-cheer, and there *would* have been a panic."

Newspapers were shot full of stories of cheery-ho all through the Depression. On the *World-Telegram,* where, as a reporter, I had an assignment to write a funny story a day during that period, we used to mix cheery-ho with an article known to the trade as stark tragedy, and run them in effective juxtaposition. Sometimes I used to do my funny story in the morning and a stark tragedy in the afternoon—or perhaps two stark tragedies, one to be held overnight for use in the early editions. Stark tragedy has excellent keeping qualities.

No stark tragedy I ever did seems as awful to me now as a small item of what was evidently meant for cheery-ho that I noticed during my researches on page nineteen of the *Times* of March 3, 1933. It was about a neat trick the police of Mount Kisco had hit upon for feeding homeless men who applied for lodging in the new village jail.

PARTY TITBITS FEED
HOMELESS IN JAIL

HORS D'OEUVRES AND LADY FINGERS,
"LEFT-OVERS," RELISHED BY
MOUNT KISCO VAGRANTS

Since last October, when the new village hall and jail were opened, the jail has been used as a lodging house for the homeless. Fifteen to twenty men sleep in the jail each night, the police said. [Mount Kisco is a prosperous village in Westchester, where in the twenties, or in the forties and fifties, you wouldn't find one homeless man in an ordinary week.] Chief of Police William McCall said that the food problem had been solved by attuning the appetites of the homeless men to the social life of the Village.

A few days ago the remains of a church social provided a dinner of cream puffs, tomato salad, lady fingers and melted ice cream. In several instances, the police said, enough food had been received to provide breakfast also. As a result the jail inmates have learned to relish hors d'oeuvres, sandwiches and assorted biscuits.

Reading this, I had the taste of the last Hoover days in my mouth—cream puffs turned sour and ladyfingers gone stale.

After the weekend of March 4–5, the character of history and newspapering changed. The bank holiday itself was a symbol, like the bursting of an abscess, or the moment the fever patient breaks into a sweat. The Roosevelt inauguration, at which the new President made the speech about nothing to fear but fear, was another. The victory of the Nazis in the Reichstag elections of Sunday, March 5, was a third. Hitler had been invited to power by Hindenburg the previous January, but he hadn't had a majority of elected deputies behind him. "Just as two and two make four, so suppression and intimidation have produced a Nazi–Nationalist triumph," Birchall wrote in the *Times*. "The rest of the world may now accept the fact of ultra-Nationalist domination of the Reich and Prussia for a prolonged period with whatever results may entail." Notwithstanding the suppression and intimidation, the Nazis and the Nationalists had only 52 percent of the popular vote and 52 percent of the seats, a fact curious to recall in view of the monolithic aspect Germany assumed within another couple of years. Birchall understood the Germans.

Nothing was ever the same again. So many things happened in Europe and in Washington and, within a decade, to us in the Far East that the day of cherry-ho and hory-cheer, and even stark tragedy, passed on. Space was tight. The change affected the *Herald Tribune* more than it did the *Times*. When it took place, the papers looked alike. The *Herald Tribune* was a standard-size newspaper, favoring a studiously balanced makeup. (Standard then meant seventeen inches wide; now the *Times* is sixteen, the *Tribune* fifteen.) The *Tribune's* heads had multiple banks, like the *Times's*. Its stories were often long. This is because, with a smaller staff than the *Times's*, the *Tribune's* city desk covered fewer assignments, so the readers usually got a lot more good writing on the ones the *Tribune* did cover. In a period of low salaries, writing is the cheapest commodity with which one can fill a newspaper, and if the writing is good, it is almost as salable as news. The *Tribune* then had a staff that provided a fairly continuous stream of mild amusement and melancholy. It was a paper not particularly adapted to reading on a crowded, jolting subway but perfect for the ride in from Greenwich or Chappaqua.

In March, 1933, this Silver Age of the *Herald Tribune*—so called because of its gently elegiac quality and because a man on the paper could carry away his pay in quarters without making a bulge in his pants pocket—was already drawing to an end. The crush of national and international news was taking the shine off even the most wryly humorous interviews with centenarians, and it had become apparent that eccentric sculptors were not the only people who got dispossessed. The sumultaneous outbreak of the New Deal and the Third Reich supplied the finishing touch. The paper retained the regular features that gave it personality for its readers: Lippmann; F.P.A.; Mark Sullivan, the deadpan political commentator; W. O. McGeehan, the illustrious sports columnist; Lewis Gannett, the readable and sagacious book reviewer; and the cartoons of H. T. Webster, that incomparable humorist of suburbia. Now these were no longer enough, and under the pressure of new conditions the *Herald Tribune* became a world newspaper, meeting the *Times* on equal terms everywhere and frequently beating the daylights out of it. It also developed syndicated pontification into an industry ranking in gross annual take midway between caramel popcorn and the pari-mutuels. With first Dorothy Thompson and then the Alsop brothers joining Lippmann in wringing secrets from the Fates at so much a syndicated wring, while first Sullivan and then David Lawrence lay moaning in the scuppers at so much a syndicated moan, the *Tribune* sailed through the storm. But after last January 20, when the New Deal went the way of the Third Reich, the *Herald Tribune* and the *Times* have found themselves in the same relative positions as in March, 1933. The positions are the same tactically, too, with the *Tribune* using a lot of features to divert attention from its less extensive news coverage, like a boxer using 16-ounce sparring gloves to hide his face. (The trouble with this is that he loses hitting power.) But there has been one important change: the change, noted earlier, in the *Times*'s political flavor. When both stores sell strawberry ice cream exclusively, the only problem that interests the customer is where he gets the larger scoop.

Of Yesteryear—IV

NOVEMBER 28, 1953

On March 3, 1933, the day before the inauguration of Franklin D. Roosevelt as President of the United States, it might easily have been argued that the *Daily News* was the best newspaper in New York. This was a conclusion I reached recently when I was going through the files of the city's daily papers of twenty years ago to see how the press then, at the beginning of one political era, stacked up with the press of today, at the beginning—more or less—of another. During the three weeks before that March 3, numerous states had declared what were in those times gaily termed bank holidays, or else had stringently limited the amounts depositors might withdraw from their accounts. By March 3, 24 states and the District of Columbia had taken one or the other of these so-called protective measures. But the New York papers had consistently ignored such tidings or had printed them as inconspicuously as possible. This was a policy designed to assuage the fears of depositors, although, naturally, it didn't. The run on New York banks grew so fast that on the morning of Inauguration Day, the new governor, Herbert H. Lehman, had to close the banks here, too. The *News* gave its readers at least a twenty-four-hour scoop on the news that there was a banking crisis of national proportions.

On that March 3, it carried on pages three, four, and five (page three of a tabloid is equivalent to the right-hand side of page one of a standard newspaper) a summary of the situation in each of the states affected. To this it added a survey of the smitten states, made by telephone, which reported "exactly what people do when the banks close, or restrict payment of savings on deposit." The *News*'s roundup story bore the headline 24 STATES HIT IN BANK CRISIS BUT CARRY ON, and began:

Twenty-four States yesterday decided to continue bank holidays, to declare new bank moratoria, or to grant bankers permission to restrict withdrawal of cash from their institutions to a total of around 5 per cent or took steps to make bank moratoria legal. . . . Bankers declared that heavy withdrawals in recent weeks by nervous depositors who had no reasons for worry about the safety of their money forced these States to act in order to protect the structure of their credit system. In plain language, that means the people of the States and the District pulled their money out of the banks and stuck it in the sock at home, forcing an unnecessary banking crisis. . . .

The spread of the banking moratoria arrangements to the nine new States—New Jersey, Oregon, Nevada, Arizona, Texas, Idaho, Utah, Washington, and Wisconsin—caused concern that banking restrictions might even be imposed in New York, the biggest and most powerful financial center in the country. Reassurance that this would not occur came from various institutions.

Discussion in Wall Street bubbled about the statement of Ambassador and former Secretary of the Treasury Andrew Mellon. He called the present situation a good thing for the future when he said, "American banking will benefit by the reforms which undoubtedly will come as a result of the difficulties through which we are passing."

Comment on the statement called attention to the fact that there is only actually about $6,500,000,000 in genuine existing cash—money you can touch—in the United States today. Yet through our banking credit system we are doing business on the basis of about $46,000,000,000—there is that much on paper in bankbooks and credits. That leaves $39,500,000,000 of fictitious money, a leading banker pointed out, and when the door is closed and locked on this money by a so-called holiday of the banking credit system, there is a money shortage.

Wall Street expressed the belief that in view of this condition, and obvious need for reforms in banks of the South and West, the new Roosevelt administration will act immediately to cure the financially sick States. . . . The lack of cash money for necessaries of life in affected States will force a quick, decisive stroke, it was said in offices of the leading financiers.

Any one of the million and a half readers of the *News* who went this far with the story, which was under his nose as he opened the paper on the subway, was better informed than a *Times* or *Herald Tribune* reader on the same day could have been without an excursion into the financial page and a determined exercise of his powers of deduction. Position and wording reflected the editorial skill of the late Captain Joseph Medill Patterson, the founder of the *News,* who had a gift of putting complex propositions in simple words. The drawback that accompanies this gift is a tendency to believe that all complex propositions are basically simple. But Patterson had not yet fallen victim to his own talent.

On page four of the *News,* under the page-wide streamer 24 STATES CARRY ON IN BANK CRISIS was the result of the telephone survey, which started with the city of Detroit, "where the banks haven't been paying a cent more than 5 percent to anybody since they closed on Feb. 10 for the three-day Lincoln's birthday weekend." Out there, the *News* said, "Most downtown businessmen carry their lunch to work. Lots of clerks have dug up bicycles from cellars and are riding to work. One crowd of stenographers is roller skating to work and very cheerful about it. That's because street cars and buses and taxicabs refuse to ride anybody for anything except cash. . . . One businessman famous for having one of the best cellars in Detroit [prohibition was still in effect, of course] is trading Scotch by the bottle to people who have food to give in exchange. . . . A lot of people are going back to the farm. Others are taking what cash they have and going across to Windsor in Canada and putting it in safe-deposit vaults there. . . . 'So far as I know,' the Detroiter at the other end of the telephone connection was talking, 'nobody's starving. The welfare agencies still seem to be supplying the hungry. There has been no rioting or other trouble.' "

The *News* carried with its survey a map showing "Where Bank Shoes Pinch in U.S." and a table showing "Bank Situation of 24 States As Seen at a Glance." By the time the reader reached page five, if he got that far, he had an appropriate perspective for the top line, BANKS HERE SOLID, OFFICIALS SAY.

The day's lone editorial began with a statement calculated to terrify Captain Patterson's cousin, Colonel Robert Rutherford McCormick, publisher of the Chicago *Tribune:*

A revolution is going on in this country. It is a bloodless revolution, and promises to remain bloodless to the end. But it is a revolution just the same, meaning that it is an overturn of old values, an overthrow of former leaders, an upthrust of new forces and new ideas. Just now, the revolution is hitting the 18,000 banks which have survived the last three years of depression. The bank moratorium idea has spread to twenty-four States at this writing, in one form or another. We think it is a good idea. . . . As we've said before, we are in favor of inflating the currency; increasing the amount of actual money. But inflation will take time. This situation demands quick action.

The quick action which we think is indicated now—though we wouldn't think so in times less serious than these—is Government guaranty of all bank deposits. That is a desperate measure, true; a measure which savors of Socialism and which might conceivably prove too much for even the Government to accomplish. But what other agency or combination of agencies can stabilize the banking situation and restore nation-wide confidence in the banks? There is none. . . .

We believe it would be an act of profound statesmanship for Mr. Roosevelt to call a special session of Congress as soon as physically possible after his inauguration tomorrow, and urge a Government guaranty of bank deposits as a piece of indispensable emergency legislation. In a revolution, time is of the essence; and a step that would save the situation one day or week may be too mild the next day or week.

Captain Patterson had left the Socialist Party in 1910, a decade before he came to New York to found the *News*, but it was evident that if he was going to be compelled to return to Socialism, he preferred the leaping to the creeping kind. (Only a few days before, Alfred E. Smith, a Conservative saint in present-day editorial reminiscence, had recommended the nationalization and consolidation of the railroads, the airlines, trucking, and long-distance buses.) The *News's* editorial cartoon for March 3, by the C. D. Batchelor who still supplies the house, showed a liner labeled "Ship of State" hauling a hermaphrodite brig, "The Banks," off a shoal by means of a double cable, "Guarantee of Bank Deposits." (The *Journal*, in the same week, had the Ship of State *on* a shoal, and a tug named "F. D. Roosevelt" coming to pull her off.) The "Inquiring Photographer," a *News* editorial-page fixture, which the paper in recent years has spelled "Fotographer," has asked six men, "On what salary can one support a family in reasonable comfort and security?" The answers ranged from $25,

for a family of two, to $50, which according to one
interviewer was enough for six but which another
thought was just about right for four. The best, or at
least the most optimistic, manager interviewed thought
he could make do for his family of five on $35.

The "Voice of the People" section included a prophetic letter, signed Reynold Friuli, that read, "Once
more fearless Japan defies the whole white race. On
guard, Uncle Sam. Japan sometimes attacks without
troubling to declare war. Remember how Japan jumped
on Russia overnight in 1904?" Another letter con-
gratulated the *News* on giving a free trip to New York
to a Florida woman named Mrs. W. F. Cross, who
was credited with striking away the gun arm of Giu-
seppe Zangara, the assassin who had fired at Franklin
D. Roosevelt in Miami that winter. Mrs. Cross's experiences in New York—and, later, in Washington—
were reported for *News* readers by Doris Fleeson, now
a *Post* syndicated columnist. Miss Fleeson's story that
morning began, "Snow-starved Mrs. W. F. Cross of
sunny Miami awoke yesterday morning to a treat that
her New York host, the *News,* couldn't have provided
for her no matter how hard it tried." It had snowed.
In 1950, John O'Donnell, a *News* political columnist,
was to complain, "The gods of assassination are all on
the side of the Democrats." A pair of assassins had
failed to kill Harry S. Truman.

One of the summaries in "The News in Tabloid,"
a daily digest of stories that the *News* has since discontinued, was "En Route Washington—Senator
Walsh, Attorney-General designate in Roosevelt Cabinet, dies of heart attack on train." The senator, aged
73, had been returning with his bride from their wedding in Havana. Another was "New York specialists,
commenting on Senator Walsh's death, assert marriage
is dangerous for men over 70." The latter was the
kind of follow-up that helped build the *News*'s circulation. The Sunday *News* that week had a longer
story, headed WALSH DEATH A WARNING TO ELDERLY
BRIDEGROOMS?

The *News* family of comic-strip characters was already near full strength in March, 1933. The Gumps,

Little Orphan Annie, Smitty, Harold Teen, Winnie Winkle, Dick Tracy, and the inhabitants of Gasoline Alley, none looking a day younger than they do in 1953, were walking through their respective Punch-and-Judy shows. Moon Mullins and Kayo and Willie and Mamie and the Plushbottoms were taking their lumps in the near neighborhood of the sports page. The *News* also carried an old *World* favorite—"Mutt and Jeff," by Bud Fisher—but "Terry and the Pirates" and "Smilin' Jack" were as yet unborn. A quality most of these early *News* comics had in common was a harsh ugliness, which pre-Patterson newspaper artists had avoided. The aim of the older comic strips—from "Happy Hooligan" to "Mr. and Mrs."—had been to make the reader laugh, but of the *News* comics only "Moon Mullins" adhered to this tradition. The others were, and are, a mixture of nightmare and soap opera, in which the characters have severe and asymmetrical faces (like the face of the old Captain himself), and are continually engaged in trying to overreach their fellows. An odd thing about these *News* comics is that after looking at a sufficient number of the impossible mugs in them you begin to see similar faces on people's necks all over town.

Paul Gallico, then the sports editor, was trumpeting the glories of the Golden Gloves boxing tournament, the *News*'s annual slaughter of the innocents by the innocents and for the promotion department. Gus Lesnevich, destined to be a light-heavyweight champion of the world, was in the field, and so were a couple of thousand lads destined merely to suffer from mild concussions of varying duration. The potent features—"Embarrassing Moments," "The Correct Thing," "Bright Sayings of Children," Antoinette Donnelly's beauty hints, Doris Blake's advice to the lovelorn, the "Real Life Story"—were already in full swing. The Captain was not the first to realize that scandal, crime, and messy disasters sell newspapers, and that lavish illustration helps, and he exploited both these immemorial truths. But he also knew that most people are constantly embarrassed, never sure of themselves, silly about children, worried about blackheads, mixed up about their sex lives, and eager for reassurance. Here, I think, lay one of his chief advantages over his competitors in the field of vulgar journalism. To his emphasis on such matters he added a show of down-to-earth American radicalism in his editorial approach, and by 1933 this quality distinguished the *News* from the Hearst sheets, which between 1895 and 1906 had been fake-radical, too. Hearst had also come to New York as the champion of the common man, but he had quit pretending. How much this editorial approach, typified by the "revolution" editorial, helped the *News* is debatable, but it is hard to believe that it hurt. Starting from scratch in 1919, Patterson built up the circulation to two million by 1941, when he broke with Roosevelt, and to just under two and a quarter million in 1946, when he died. This would indicate that "The Correct Thing" and the Golden Gloves have more to do with its success than any brand of editorial policy.

Even in 1933, the *News* was difficult in the matter of foreign policy. The principal objects of its scorn on March 1 that year were Mr. Hoover, the President for three more days; his Secretary of State, Henry L. Stimson; and a Chinese general of the period named Chiang Kai-shek. The *News* was against helping this Celestial in any way. "The chief reason why 65,000,-000 native Japs seem able to take whatever they want from 400,000,000-plus Chinese," the editorialist wrote, "is to be found, in our opinion, in the refusal of Gen. Chiang Kai-shek, Nanking commander-in-chief, to send soldiers to Jehol, on the ground that the northern Chinese generals probably would not obey Chiang's orders. It's a repetition of Chiang's refusal to help the Chinese Nineteenth Route Army from Canton when it was making its gallant stand outside Shanghai last year. If China will not unite, what possible sense or gain can there be in our trying to help China with notes, boycotts, embargoes?"

The British, the *News* felt, were more realistic; they were going to let the Japanese ramble on. "This historic piece of British diplomacy makes the Hoover-Stimson diplomacy look sicker than it ever looked before, which is saying something," the *News* declared. "It shows us up as the only nation which really takes the League of Nations pacifists and debaters seriously —and we don't even belong to the League." (The *News* now wants to dissolve the United Nations.) "It is said that Cordell Hull, incoming Secretary of State, has learned his Far East policy at the feet of Henry L. Stimson. We'd like to suggest that Mr. Hull now forget those lessons, and devote all the time he can to a study of the policies and methods of Sir John Simon." Sir John's policies—or, at least, an extension of them— were to culminate in the sinking of the *Repulse* and the *Prince of Wales,* the fall of Singapore, and German bombs on London. As additional indication that no grievances are new, there was in the "Voice of the People" for March 1 a letter that began, "Congratulations to Congress for having defeated Mr. Hoover's attempt to cut the strength of the Marine Corps still further."

On March 2, the *News*'s attack shifted to "the 181-cent dollar"; it didn't like this any better than the 59-cent dollar it has been hollering about lately:

As inflation of the currency comes to look more and more inevitable, not to mention desirable, the protests of opponents of inflation grow louder and funnier [the *News* said editorially that day]. Al Smith, appearing before the Senate Committee on Economics to state his prescription for better times, tries to dismiss inflation with this remark: "It is just like giving a sick man a shot in the arm of something that goes on for a little while, and when it dies out he must get another one."

It seems to us the answer to this is that a shot in the arm is exactly what a sick man sometimes needs to keep him from passing away altogether. The man under discussion is sick and growing sicker, what with the bank moratorium idea spreading from State to State, commodity prices and stock prices still feeble, and unemployment still on the rise according to reports usually considered reliable.

Howard C. Sykes, President of the New York Curb Exchange, protests against currency inflation in this language: "Inflation, if resorted to for the seemingly expeditious purpose of increasing the supply of money in public hands and stimulating purchases, would have the immediate effect of lowering the buying power of all money."

Isn't that just what we want in our present condition? Haven't economists and financiers been screaming for months that our chief trouble is too low prices, meaning too high-priced dollars

An inkling of just how costly the dollar has come to be, and one answer to the anti-inflationists, is to be found in a remark made a few days ago by President U. G. Stockwell of the New York State Association of Real Estate Boards. Mr. Stockwell wasn't arguing for inflation, but he did drop these words: "Today the dollar will buy more of practically everything except interest and taxes. According to Prof. Fisher of Yale, the purchasing power of the dollar based upon the wholesale market price of 200 representative commodities was 181 cents on Feb. 8, 1933, as compared to 100 cents in 1926."

When the dollar reaches 181 cents, is it any wonder that we are crippled financially; that business can't get started; that we all go in for dodging debts or selling one another out in a mad scramble to keep or get our hooks on as many dollars as we can?

The Batchelor cartoon for the day showed a nude, bloated, bald, middle-aged man marked "Wall Street" standing under a shower bath labeled "Senate Investigation" while a debonair, know-the-score type, fully clothed, looked on without sympathy and without a label on him. The dialogue:

"Br-r-r, this is t-t-terrible."

"Aw, you'll be all the better for it when you come out."

"Yes, b-b-but when w-w-will I get out?"

"Voice of the People" contained a letter ending, "The real reason for cheap contracts and cheap labor is that so many bankers will not loan money to contractors until assured that low wages will be paid."

But on March 4, the *News*'s editorialist was happy, although the front page carried the news of Governor

Lehman's ptroclamation closing the banks. (The *News*
on the previous day had called the moratoria a good
idea, anyway.) The editorial, headed THE NEW PRESI-
DENT AND THE NEW DEAL, began:

Four years ago today, Herbert Hoover took office as President. Mr. Hoover entered the White House on the high
tide of the greatest era of prosperity the country ever saw;
an era which at that time seemed to promise to be endless.

Frank Roosevelt takes office today; and Mr. Roosevelt
enters the White House when the country is at what we
hope is the bottom of the worst depression it has ever
suffered.

So the pendulum swings. If the pendulum continues to
swing as it always has done, Mr. Roosevelt will go out of
office four or eight years from now with the country and
all of us in better shape. Here's hoping.

Batchelor contributed a cartoon of an idealized
F.D.R. being greeted with a handshake by Miss Columbia, wearing a new girdle under her slithery robes
and simpering like all getout. (It was the same female
figure that he frequently makes into a siren labeled
"World War II" or "World War III" by substituting a
death's-head for the fleshed face.) The dialogue:

"Pleased t'meet cha."
"Same here."

The "Inquiring Photographer" had asked six
New Yorkers: "Do you still read the stock-market
quotations?" They had told him off properly.

In the account of the inauguration, in the paper of
Sunday, March 5, the new President was ushered in
with a wild paean by John O'Donnell, which began,
"Franklin Delano Roosevelt took over the guidance of
a stricken nation today with a cry of 'Courage' to millions of distressed citizens and a promise that he
would assume the powers of a war President if such a
step is necessary to conquer the forces of depression.
In a vibrant voice that challenged the sombre gray of
the Washington sky, the man who a minute before had

succeeded Herbert Clark Hoover as President of the United States pronounced the most important inaugural address that America has heard since Abraham Lincoln took his second oath of office." A dozen years later, O'Donnell was likening Roosevelt's grave to Benedict Arnold's.

The March 5 city color story on the bank holiday, by Fred Pasley, was headed GOTHAM NURSES $5 AVERAGE ROLL IN BANK FAMINE, and began cheerily, like its prototypes in other papers, "East Side, West Side, all around the town, New York City started putting it on the cuff yesterday, as the bum and the banker, the man in the street and the man in the limousine, became economic equals due to Gov. Lehman's unexpected moratorium."

A couple of items in "The News in Tabloid" showed that the paper had not allowed the crisis to smother its usual preoccupations completely. Readers were advised that on page forty-one they would find SHOWGIRL WITHOUT CASH MUST SERVE TWO DAYS IN JAIL FOR INTOXICATION UNLESS FRIENDS PAY HER $5 FINE, and, on page fifty-nine, YOUTH, 16, SLAYS MOTHER HE SAYS HAD TOO MANY MEN VISITORS.

The Red Menace did not figure until page twenty-two, and then it was treated without apparent trepidation, although there seem to have been a lot more communists in evidence then than now. 10,000 HEAR SPEAKERS WITHOUT CHECK DEMAND A "RED HOLIDAY," the headline read over a photograph of "ten thousand Reds as they took possession of Union Square yesterday."

The comrades, male and female, began to gather at 11 A.M., singing the "Internationale" and waving banners [the *News* man reported]. One read: "President Roosevelt —Don't play with death. We demand relief. Our children must not starve!" . . . Staged as a counter-demonstration to the Roosevelt inaugural, the affair was disappointing to its sponsors and a surprise to police, who had made elaborate preparations to cope with disorder.

At 1 P.M. the demonstrators dispersed in parade formation [a good bit of descriptive writing, even if unconscious] and several thousand shouting and singing men, women, and children marched uptown to the State Labor Department offices on E. 28th St. and back to the 14th St. open air forum.

An A.P. dispatch dated March 4 and run as a shirt-tail to the above read, "Thousands of unemployed marched through the Chicago Loop at noon today, waving red flags and singing the 'Internationale' as they paused for a demonstration before City Hall. 'We want cash relief!' was the cry, shouted again and again, in cadence, while police escorts opened a way for them through crowded streets. . . . For the most part the marchers proceeded in orderly fashion."

The senior William Randolph Hearst's *Daily Mirror* seemed no more alarmed by these activities than the *News.* The *Mirror,* launched in frank imitation of the *News* but without the cynical genius of the ex-Socialist Captain at its helm, had, despite its inferiority, attained the second-largest morning circulation in the city. In addition to the *News,* it competed chiefly with Mr. Hearst's own New York *American,* which it drove out of business in 1937. (The *Mirror*'s 1933 circulation, 569,000, plus the *American*'s 343,000, add up roughly to the *Mirror*'s today—892,000. Mr. Hearst's competition with himself was an example of his celebrated astuteness.) AN INCURABLE CASE OF THE SHIVERS was the *Mirror*'s heading over a March 4 editorial making fun of Bainbridge Colby, Secretary of State under Woodrow Wilson, who had come out in opposition to recognition of Soviet Russia. "Just how our refusal to recognize Russia serves as a defense Mr. Colby does not make clear," the *Mirror* said. "Mr. Colby is still shivering. Too bad." Nor were the *Mirror*'s views of the outgoing Administration more indulgent than those of the *News.* "[Hoover] had been presented to the American people as a great administrator and a deep student of economics," a *Mirror* editorial recalled. "How, then, will history judge his failure, with all the sources of information open to him, to recognize the speculative frenzy for what it was, and to see the dangers that lurked behind a false prosperity? . . . Did he, or members of his Cabinet, give support and encouragement, direct or indirect, to financial interests now revealed as having victimized the American public through the promotion of securities of fictitious value? In any event Mr. Hoover retires to private life a somewhat tragic figure. Denied by the electorate a chance for vindication, he must, for the present at least, take a place in the list of the lesser Presidents."

Nick Kenny, the *Mirror*'s poet laureate then as now, contributed a rousing sociological epic:

> Your streets are full of beaten men
>   Of every class and rank,
> The only way to beat this thing
>   Is get in back of Frank!
>
> The Army of the Unemployed
>   Increases every day,
> And fans to white hot flame the spark
>   On which the Reds can play!
>
> For idle minds are often apt
>   To get distorted view,
> And idle hearts too often drink
>   The devil's poison brew!
>
> Men are most happy when at work,
>   Their hearts are full of song,
> So put them back, you industries,
>   To work, where they belong!

Against "Dick Tracy" and his allies on the *News,* the *Mirror* had aligned a side of comics that included "Joe Palooka," "Tailspin Tommy," "Tarzan of the Apes," "Fritzi Ritz," and "Mickey Mouse"; but "Li'l Abner" and "Steve Canyon" were still in the womb of the future. Dan Parker, in his sports column, had inaugurated his policy of biting the promotorial hand that fed a considerable number of his Hearst colleagues. "Washington Merry-Go-Round" carried the joint byline of Drew Pearson and Robert S. Allen.

Walter Winchell ran deeper inside the paper than he does now and, along with his obstetrical announcements, was conducting a crusade against bankers. ("Why not banksters?" and "They locked up the banks instead of the bankers!") In opposition to the *News*'s "The Correct Thing," the *Mirror* ran "Modern Etiquette." ("Is it proper, when shaking hands, to hold the hand high, at about chin level?" "Ans. No, this is affectation. The hand should be just above the waist line.")

Through the week following the most important inaugural address since Lincoln's second, the *News* got progressively more enthusiastic about Mr. Roosevelt. On Monday, March 6, the Batchelor cartoon showed "F.D.R." as a top sergeant, wearing the puttees and high collar of the First World War, calling "Comp'nee, *'tenshun.*" Lined up before him were Privates Banks, Newspapers, Railroads, Labor, Manufacturer, Farmer, Retailer, and Illegible. The caption was "The New Top Kick." That day's editorial, headed A PLEDGE TO SUPPORT ROOSEVELT, started: "This newspaper now pledges itself to support the policies of President Franklin D. Roosevelt for a period of at least one year from today; longer, if circumstances warrant." (The pledge was kept for considerably longer than the minimum period.) "It is no small sacrifice for a newspaper to make the pledge that is made above. One of an editor's chief prerogatives in a free-press nation is his right to tell everyone, from the President down, how to act, and, on occasion, where to head in. . . . But these times are anything but normal."

Then Captain Patterson exercised his free-press-nation prerogative to tell Mr. Roosevelt how to act about foreign affairs: "As for our foreign policy, the skies are pretty dark—two wars going on in South America (Bolivia vs. Paraguay, Peru vs. Colombia), a war between China and Japan in the Far East, ominous rumblings from Europe as Hitler's power increases. With none of these conflicts has the United States any legitimate concern. And the last thing Mr.

Roosevelt can desire for this country, we are certain, is a war at this time. We're confident that he knows how the land lies, and that he will force the State Department to steer clear of meddlesome, provocative policies." It was one of the Captain's glorious over-simplifications. If you don't "desire" war, you refrain from meddling or provoking, and if you refrain from meddling and provoking, war will never be necessary. It was the issue on which the *News* and Roosevelt were to split.

By Tuesday, the *News* was hailing "The Dictatorship of Roosevelt." "A lot of us have been asking for a dictator," its editorial led off. "Now we have one." (The editorial was illustrated by a picture of Mussolini giving the Fascist salute, over the caption "We've elected one of these." This was a mixture of projection and flattery.) "Dictators have been necessary from time to time throughout history. . . . Fortunately, we seem to have turned over the power and the authority to the right man. Mr. Roosevelt, in his first two days as President, has shown tremendous skill, great courage, swift decisiveness."

In 1933, the *News* and *Mirror* had a combined daily circulation of almost 2,000,000—1,411,000 and 569,000, respectively. The three other morning papers —the *Times,* the *Herald Tribune,* and the *American* had an aggregate circulation of a little over a million. All four evening newspapers—the *World-Telegram,* the *Journal,* the *Evening Post,* and the *Sun*—mustered a total of 1,428,000 readers. And the *News* had almost precisely as much circulation as the three Hearst entries combined. It was the dawn time of the Tabloid Epoch.

10
Press
People

The Man Who
Changed the Rules

SEPTEMBER 8, 1951

The New York daily newspapers' treatment of William Randolph Hearst's death, at the age of eighty-eight, reflected a considerable difference of opinion not only about Mr. Hearst but about how much space he was worth. In the columns of the *Journal-American* and *Mirror,* both Hearst papers, the funeral ululations are still reverberating as I write, nearly two weeks after the *Journal-American*'s eight-column black banner head in 172-point type reading, W. R. HEARST DEAD, apprised the public of the news on the afternoon of Tuesday, August 14. The *Journal-American* ran a full-page editorial, tricked out with all the mortuary embellishments of the printing trade. It started off:

The world has lost a colossus. William Randolph Hearst has passed into history.

He was the last of the dauntless pioneers, the last of the indomitable individualists. . . .

Such a man as he, who became a legend within his lifetime, we shall not see again.

Only he withstood a regimentation and socialization which overwhelmed and obliterated so many of his able and powerful contemporaries, until he remained the sole surviving giant tree where once had been a forest of titanic men.

There was also a biography, running to about 15 standard columns, which began:

Out of the incredible vigor of his mind and body William Randolph Hearst wrought, in more than a half century of sustained effort, the mightiest publishing venture the world has known. . . .

The greatest inheritance Mr. Hearst received from his mining-statesman father and his beloved mother was not measured in gold [his inheritance was, in fact, estimated at only about $30,000,000] but in the bequest of an ineradicable faith in America.

Soon the eulogy of the departed turned to a reassurance of the solidity of the mighty publishing venture he had left behind:

For Mr. Hearst so contrived his enterprises, and so caused them to be buttressed against all contingencies, that no man's passing—not even his own—could shake their strength or swerve them from their course, which is the service of the American people. . . .

His chain of newspapers stretch along the Atlantic and Pacific seaboards and thrive in the great industrial centers of the Middle West.

His magazines, representing the cream of fiction, fashion, articles, and specialized information, blanket the nation and even extend into Great Britain, as separate publishing enterprises there.

In addition there are the worldwide network of news wires, the tremendous feature service, radio stations, land and mine holdings, a separate philanthropic organization, and a priceless art collection.

These activities may be grouped under the general title of the Hearst Organization.

The obituary, which for a column or so at this point read more like a stock prospectus, then enumerated the newspapers (sixteen daily, two Sunday only), the services (one news and one photo), and the magazines (nine). After that, it got back to Mr. Hearst.

The *Mirror,* a sister unit in the "mightiest publishing venture the world has known," used the same biography on Wednesday. James Padgitt, of the International News Service, which is a part of the mightiest publishing venture, wrote the lead news story in the *Mirror,* in which he recorded a phenomenon unreported by other correspondents in Beverly Hills, California, where Mr. Hearst died. "The people stood in stunned silence in realization of their loss," Mr. Padgitt stated.

The *Times, Herald Tribune, News, World-Telegram & Sun,* and *Post* took the event more calmly. The difference in tone was exemplified the following Sunday by the *Herald Tribune*'s treatment of a statement by William Randolph Hearst, Jr., second of the publisher's five sons, speaking for himself and his brothers. The statement had originally appeared in both the *Journal* and the *Mirror* and read, in part, "Will you please convey to the readers of the Hearst newspapers our pledge to continue to operate our father's publications as he guided us, and our determination to carry on in the tradition of his life which was dedicated to the service of America and the best interests of the American people." The *Tribune* man, Ralph Chapman, reviewing the week's news, translated this to read, "Continuance of the sensational journalistic practices established by their father was pledged by the sons of William Randolph Hearst."

The *World-Telegram,* which ranks second to the *Journal-American* in afternoon circulation, and the *News,* whose only competition in the morning tabloid field comes from the *Mirror,* showed a tendency, I thought, to underplay Mr. Hearst. The motivations of publishers in dealing with other publishers in such circumstances are ambivalent: a desire to respect a competitor's sorrow coincides with a wish to give it the minimum of publicity. The *World-Telegram,* which is part of another mighty journalistic venture, the Scripps-Howard newspapers, confirmed the *Journal-American*'s identification of Mr. Hearst as a colossus —"Men both blessed and cursed the towering colossus of journalism," one of its writers declared in a sketch of Mr. Hearst's career. "A man praised and execrated, in equal measure, to a greater extent, perhaps, than any other notable figure of his times," the piece went on. "Equal measure," it seemed to me, was giving the defunct an edge in the scoring.

The *World-Telegram* held Mr. Hearst down to a

couple of columns on the afternoon of his death. On the following day, it printed a message to the bereaved family from Roy W. Howard, president of Scripps-Howard, who is the *Telegram*'s own small colossus. "No man in history has had a greater impact on American journalism or contributed more to its sturdiness or devoted himself more unceasingly to making it the nerve center of American patriotism," Mr. Howard wrote. An editorial in the same issue said, "William Randolph Hearst was one of the most controversial figures of our times, and he left a vast imprint on journalism and American life." There was no attempt to define the imprint.

The *News* didn't use the word "colossus" once, and wound up its obituary with a quote from Allan Nevins, a historian at Columbia, that I thought underrated Mr. Hearst: "His importance has lain in the huge scale of his operations, and though he hardly ranks as a great innovator—his sensationalism imitated Pulitzer's, while E. W. Scripps preceded him in forming a newspaper chain—the Hearst methods have profoundly influenced American journalism." His innovation, as I intend to point out later, was one of means rather than method, and far transcended Pulitzer's. On the same page as the obit appeared a reminder of why the *News* didn't consider Mr. Hearst quite in the colossus class. This was a message from Colonel Robert R. McCormick, editor and publisher of the Chicago *Tribune* and overlord of the *News,* to William Randolph Hearst, Jr. Around the *News,* obit writers don't have to be told who is a colossus. "My sincere sympathy to you in the loss of your father, news of whose death reached me over the radio," Colonel McCormick had wired. "His life up to the moment of his passing was devoted to the interests of his country and humanity." It was well for Colonel McCormick's disposition, I thought, that he had learned the news from the radio and not from the editorial page of a Hearst paper. Colonel McCormick knows who is the last of the dauntless pioneers, the sole surviving giant tree, and so does every man jack who works for him.

The three colossi have been as one politically, even

while they scrabbled against each other like Algerian
shoeshine boys for circulation coppers. In the case of
the *Herald Tribune* and the *Post,* however, neither
political affinity nor the considerations of circulation
was a matter of concern, and yet their stories were disappointing. The *Tribune's* obit treated the late publisher simply as a whacking success, even if a bit of
an oddity. "An extraordinary newspaper talent combined with a consuming ambition for power were the
principal factors in shaping the career of William Randolph Hearst," the biography began. ". . . Mr. Hearst
never permitted anyone to call him by his first name.
To his employees he was known simply as 'The Chief.'
He wielded an iron hand over all of them, treating
them with utter cynicism, if not contempt." (The fellows who wrote about him in the Hearst papers invariably remembered him as a lovable character.)
Editorially, the *Tribune* said, "The strange, erratic,
and powerful genius of William Randolph Hearst has
colored the American political journalistic scene for
so many decades that it is difficult now to realize that
it has been extinguished at last. About the genius there
has never been any doubt. About the uses to which he
put it there has been constant and usually impassioned
controversy throughout the more than half a century
in which he held place on the national stage."

The *Post,* describing Hearst as "fabulous," showed
its fearlessness by recalling that he had left Harvard
by request in his senior year "after he had sent chamber pots, unsuitably inscribed, to his instructors."
(The *Telegram* referred to this incident as a "campus
prank," while the ruggeder *News* called it a "ribald
joke.") The *Post* also alluded to a report that he had
once asked his wife for a divorce so that he could
marry Marion Davies, in whose residence the old man
died. (All the newspapers persisted in referring to it
as his house, but there was an understandable confusion. It was Miss Davies's house originally, but she
deeded it to him, and then he deeded it back to her.)

Where all the papers I have quoted from so far fell
down, I thought, was in the way they treated the story
of Hearst as a closed episode, and an unqualified suc-

cess story, at that. Moreover, they failed to bring out
what seems almost certain to be, in the light of history,
the most significant aspect of his career. It occurs to
me that what is really important about Hearst is not
whether or not he was a great newspaperman, or a
talented and cynical amateur, or a great humanitarian,
or a genius, or a liberal, or a reactionary; he could
have been any of these, but I believe that as the years
pass he will be remembered primarily as the man who
introduced the use of big money into the newspaper
business. It was only in the *Times* that I found what
seemed to me to be adequate coverage of Mr. Hearst's
prodigal, and not always successful, use of money to
buy his way to the top. In fact, the *Times,* in its various departments, carried off all the honors of the campaign. For one thing, its lead story, by one of its own
correspondents, Gladwin Hill, was naturally better
than the press-association leads in other papers. Press-
association stories are written for a theoretical average subscribing newspaper in a small city and consequently have to explain a story before they tell it.
Hill stuck close to the Beverly Hills angle of the story:
the publisher's apparent degree of control of the editorial policy of his mighty venture up to his death
(more than you might think, according to Mr. Hill),
the reported presence of Miss Davies as well as of the
Hearst sons at the bedside, the seeming confusion in
the Hearst organization in the hours following his
death. The confusion must have been considerably
augmented, later, by the report from Beverly Hills
that the colossus and Miss Davies had drawn up an
agreement vesting control of the Hearst Corporation
in Miss Davies. The administrators of the Hearst
estate, in the *Journal-American* of August 27, stated,
however, "This so-called agreement dated Nov. 5,
1950, was never executed and for this and many other
reasons has no more effect than if it never existed."
The question is, presumably, to be left to the courts.
The *Times*'s long, unsigned biography of Hearst,
measured and occasionally wry, led off, "At the height
of his career, William Randolph Hearst was one of
the world's wealthiest and most powerful newspaper

owners. . . . At the peak of his influence he engendered the heat of controversy more than any other American." Here it was at least implied that the height and the peak were past. There had not, in fact, been much controversy about Hearst for the last thirty years—nothing, that is, to compare with the controversy over Franklin D. Roosevelt or Harry S. Truman. And even at the height of his career he was never able to demonstrate the power he claimed. "Actually, few persons ever succeeded in picking the lock of his character to discover the demarcation line between self-interest and public interest," the *Times* obituarist continued. "He often expressed the belief that his mind was the same as the collective mind of the American people, a belief that the American people did not always share."

The *Times*'s three best stories on the subject were deep inside the paper—one, on the financial history of Hearst's corporations, by Burton Crane; another, on Hearst's adventures in New York City real estate, by Lee E. Cooper; and a third, unsigned, on his self-invited misfortunes as an art collector. Crane's piece, particularly, seemed to me to get near the nub of the Hearst story. All the other newspaper approaches to Hearst, friendly or objective, assumed that he was, materially, a tremendous and continuing success, however "controversial" his character and policies may have been. (Most comments on these "controversial" aspects were astonishingly guarded, by the way, far more so than they would have been seven, or twenty, or thirty years ago. Hearst's chauvinism had by the time of his death made him a kind of sacred symbol, like Senator McCarthy.) There were, it is true, in some of the papers other than the *Times,* respectful allusions to Hearst's financial difficulties, owing to the Depression, a circumstance beyond even colossal control—difficulties from which the publisher had somehow escaped. "It was World War II, ironically, which put many of Mr. Hearst's tottering enterprises back on their feet," the *Tribune* said. "By mid-1945 every unit in the Hearst empire was making money again." There was left an implication that every unit still was.

Crane's financial history, based on fact easily accessible to every newspaper, cast considerable doubt upon this implication. Crane made it obvious that while no lay mind could be expected to comprehend the intricacies of Hearst's financial operations, there is plenty of evidence—watered stock, reorganizations, forced sales of property, and the like—that the business structure the publisher set up was and is not exactly in the same class as, say, General Motors or A.T.&T. "The story of the newspaper empire of William Randolph Hearst," Crane began, "is the story of a man who started with an inherited gold-mining fortune and accumulated more newspapers, radio stations, news services, and real estate than probably any other man had ever owned. But he never wanted to let anything go. It is also the story of a man who, for the last fourteen years of his life, seldom enjoyed more than nominal control of the dominion that bore his name." By 1924, long before the Depression, Hearst "was pressed for ready cash," Crane went on. "His properties were costing him more than they were bringing in." (But there was the inherited $30,000,000, largely in mines that were throwing off money steadily. What would have happened to the mightiest publishing venture without this steady support from the Hearst underground is problematical.) So a magazine holding company, known as Hearst Magazines, was formed in 1927 and a newspaper holding company, known as Hearst Consolidated Publications, in 1930. Hearst Consolidated Publications gave Mr. Hearst, through a third holding company, a note for $50,000,000 and all the common stock, and then paid off the note with the receipts from preferred stock, "sold at $25 a share with the aid of a great stock-selling campaign in Hearst papers," to quote Mr. Crane. "They inveighed strongly against spurious stock deals," he added.

Crane noted that in 1935, after Hearst had pocketed the fifty million, *Fortune* appraised the publisher's gross assets at $220,000,000 and his net worth at $142,000,000. "In view of what happened in the years immediately following, this appears to have been something of an overstatement," Crane remarked. He then listed the principal Hearst "holdings" (so tenuously, yet so ostentatiously, held) in 1935, and described the legal apparatus whereby they were manipulated. "But apparently all was not so rosy as it seemed," Crane wrote. "In 1935 American Newspapers, Inc. [Hearst's principal holding company], sold its newspapers in Baltimore, Atlanta, and San Antonio to Consolidated [in which the public held the $50,000,000 of preferred] for $8,000,000 . . . despite the fact that the three papers had lost $550,000 in 1934. This transaction was later questioned in a stockholders' suit. There was considerable water in the Hearst structure. . . . When a registration statement was filed by Consolidated in 1936, the company revealed that, between 1924 and 1930, it had written up the value of tangible assets by $4,490,863 and of intangibles by $58,261,-820. . . . The attempt to hold on to everything for the sake of mere size proved unsuccessful. . . . Mr. Hearst held more than 2,000,000 acres of real estate and most of it yielded nothing."

So a corporate dictator, Clarence John Shearn, was named by a group of Hearst's creditors in 1937 and, as Crane put it, "set to work to clean up some of the mess. He immediately withdrew . . . some projected financing, because the Securities and Exchange Commission demanded additional information that the Hearst interests would have been embarrassed to reveal." Shearn, according to Crane, jettisoned five newspapers, a news service, and seven radio stations. But troubles continued to pile up. Hearst-Brisbane Properties, Inc., a New York real-estate corporation, ducked under the ropes, taking advantage of a mortgage moratorium. Hearst Magazines passed to the control of the Chase National Bank. Hearst's salary from Consolidated was cut from $500,000 to $100,000 a year. The dividends of the fifty thousand holders of preferred stock were cut from $1.75 a share to nothing at all. Harry Chandler, publisher of the Los Angeles *Times,* who held a mortgage of $600,000 on Hearst's San Simeon estate, "goodnaturedly agreed not to foreclose." (A point of intercolossal courtesy, perhaps.) The fifty thousand shareholders came near taking over the best newspaper properties. They would

have had the right to do so if a fourth consecutive
dividend had been passed, on March 15, 1939. But
somehow Mr. Shearn got up the scratch, and the
Hearst organizations flopped into the healing shadow
of the war.

"By 1945," Crane wrote, "the Hearst papers were
making money again. Mr. Hearst was back in San
Simeon—but 165,000 acres had been sold off to get
$2,000,000 and only 75,000 acres were left." (Return
to a bobtailed farm like that must have seemed a
humiliation.) Shearn, Crane continued, was succeeded
by a triumvirate, dominated by John W. Hanes, a
former Under-Secretary of the United States Treasury,
who found that 94 Hearst organizations owed a total
of $126,000,000 even after the war-stimulated im-
provement in the publisher's affairs. "In 1945, although Gimbels department store was still unloading
Hearst art treasures, there seemed reason for hope,"
Crane wrote. "No Hearst paper had been sold since
1939. All the New York real estate had been sold, including the Ritz Tower, where Mr. Hearst lived when
here, and all the hundreds of thousands of unprofit-
able acres. . . . But by the spring of this year the
financial affairs of at least one Hearst corporation—
Consolidated, which controls the biggest newspapers—
were beginning to take another form. . . . Their operating revenue had slipped to $90,321,000. They voted
to defer the dividend to the 1,198,848 shares of Class
A stock. It is now $8.75 a share in arrears."

The *Times*'s story on the Hearst art collection made
a fitting pendant to Mr. Crane's. "In cost and total
value [cost, $40,000,000; value, estimated in 1937,
$15,000,000] Mr. Hearst's collection ranked with the
great collections of his time," this account stated. "But
the publisher, unlike his contemporaries, seemed to
have bought everything, from Egyptian mummies to a
Spanish abbey of the medieval period. . . . It cost Mr.
Hearst about $400,000 to bring the abbey here. . . .
Marked down from $50,000, it was sold for $19,000
to an anonymous buyer in 1942." In the Gimbels sales
of Hearst art, the *Times*'s story recalled, Egyptian
statuettes sold for 35,60, and 95 cents.

Lee Cooper's piece on the real estate filled in a bit of New York City history. Buildings, for a city man, acquire personal, as well as visual, associations, and their origins and ownership are as interesting as those of cattle to a farmer or ships to a Norwegian. The Ritz Tower (which never had a Ritzian quality), the Warwick (which has a good bar), and the Ziegfeld Theatre are more than abstract things, and they deserved a story to themselves in the New York newspapers. I sometimes think the reason editors forget about such matters is that most of them used to be small-town boys and are now suburban residents. "It was in cooperation with the late Arthur Brisbane, and largely under Mr. Brisbane's tutelage and influence" that Mr. Hearst invested, Cooper wrote. (Brisbane died worth $20,000,000.) "Mr. Brisbane, at one time, had felt certain a railroad bridge would be constructed across the Hudson River in the neighborhood of Fifty-seventh Street, and had made his major investments in the Fifties." Cooper didn't mention the innumerable editorials that Brisbane used to turn out for the Hearst papers extolling the future of the district in which he and the boss had invested. The other newspapers painted Brisbane only as an assistant colossus of fabulous genius. I found the real-estate relationship between the two men more diverting.

Thus the *Times*'s stories made clear that, whatever Hearst's talents as a newspaperman and an operator of newspapers, his principal contribution to American journalism—a contribution that changed the whole nature of the profession—was to demonstrate that a man without previous newspaper experience could, by using money like a heavy club, do what he wanted in the newspaper world except where comparable wealth opposed him. It was a concept as simple as a very big bankroll in a very small crap game. There were one or two fortunes of a few million dollars apiece in the newspaper field when Hearst, at the age of 23, decided to go into it, but they had been made in newspapers, by men who started with little. It had not occurred to any other mining millionaire that a man without experience but with money had a vast advantage over any editor who ever lived. Hearst went into the business as an acknowledged imitator of Joseph Pulitzer, but with enough money to hire any man he wanted. Some of the time he wasn't even selective: he hired help in platoons—the whole Sunday staff of the New York *World* at one swoop, for example. He brought $7,500,000 of his mother's money to New York with him when he came here in 1895 to buy and build up the *Journal,* and he could, quite naturally, hire more comic artists, more blood-and-thunder editorialists, more sportswriters, and more fakers of crime stories than anybody else in town. He lost money on his newspapers until they acquired vast circulation, but he put on such a show that in the end people had to buy them. It is a method open to few. The same scheme would probably have been just as successful, at the time, in the field of the conservative press. If Hearst had wanted to work that side of the street, he could have hired away from the *Herald* the foreign staff built up by James Gordon Bennett and then tripled it, beating out the *Herald,* or he could have provided such complete financial coverage that the *Times,* just beginning its climb, could not possibly have competed. But he had a predilection for the side of the street he chose.

After building his circulations, Hearst profited by practices new in journalism but old in big business: he got a rebate of $5 a ton on newsprint, for instance, because he bought so much. But when he hit a city like Chicago, where the *Tribune* was entrenched behind an even denser concentration of wealth (built up by the newspaper itself, however, over a stretch of 50 years), he took a fearful beating. Hearst wrangled rebates, but the *Tribune* owned paper mills. When he offered $500 a day in free handouts to readers—a form of lottery—the *Tribune* offered $17,000 a day. His paper never made a dent in the *Tribune,* and he quit trying after 37 years of losses. When he reached the point, in the twenties, where the store-bought empire had to support itself from its own earnings, his long retreat began.

"The question was asked on one occasion what the

losses had been, first to last, in Atlanta," a man named Jim Brown wrote in the August 18 issue of *Editor & Publisher,* which was practically a Hearst memorial. "The reply was—$21,000,000." (The Hearst organization has had no paper in Atlanta since 1939.) The prerequisite for losing $21,000,000 is not genius; it is to have $21,000,000.

It was said in some of the obituaries that Hearst had a flair for hiring good writers, but one must read page after page of his papers to find a trace of it. He certainly employed some talented men, but there has never been a time within my memory when they were not flanked by others who were hilariously inept, and the bad writers often enjoyed more esteem within the Hearst organization, and better pay, than the good. The truth seems to be that he bought talent the way he bought art—indiscriminately.

Hearst's two New York papers, in the first few days after his death, afforded a sample of what he had wound up with, as byliner after byliner approached the edge of the grave in print and threw a ceremonial fit. On Wednesday, August 15, in the *Journal,* Cholly Knickerbocker led his column with a paragraph that read, "America's Irreplaceable Loss—William Randolph Hearst has passed on but his greatness will survive eternally. No leader, president or king, has ever given so much of himself to the guidance and uplifting of his people as had The Chief. The underdog's corner was his corner, and right was his might." In the next paragraph, Cholly was back at his regular job. "Beautiful Mary Sinclair, the actress, is in Reno to divorce producer George Abbott, and, her friends say, she has her next husband already picked out," he wrote inconsolably. Dorothy Kilgallen awarded the departed full credit for promoting her career. "William Randolph Hearst gave me the space and the assignments," she wrote, "and everything I have done in other fields since then has stemmed from his long-distance faith in a very young girl, and his paper remains my first love." E. V. Durling, who writes a column called "Life with Salt on the Side," wrote, "William Randolph

Hearst was the finest, most considerate, kindliest and generous man I ever worked for. . . . Come to think of it, Mr. Hearst was probably the best friend all newspapermen ever had in the newspaper business. It was he who raised their standards of employment to a point comparable to their talents." (If he had, a number of Hearst columnists would have starved to death.) Artists were not excused from the funeral detail. Burris Jenkins, Jr., provided a dramatic drawing of the Statue of Liberty with a mourning band around her arm, marked "William Randolph Hearst." On Thursday morning, August 16, in the *Mirror,* Nick Kenny, the radio editor, produced a poem entitled "The Chief Passes," of which I shall quote only the first stanza, although the others are even more beautiful:

The Chief is gone, the man we all called Boss . . .
Colossus of an age that changed the world.
The galleons of his genius knew their course,
His fingertips around the cosmos curled.

Kenny was one of The Chief's favorite writers, and Hearst quoted the poet several times in his own occasional column, called "In the News."

That same morning, Dan Parker, the *Mirror*'s sports editor, contributed a bluff, regular-guy double column about Mr. Hearst in sports, from which I remember particularly the sentence "When racketeers invaded boxing, Mr. Hearst wouldn't let his newspapers be used to exploit the public." I suppose this referred to the time when a number of Hearst boxing writers resigned after it was disclosed that they had been receiving salaries as sub-rosa executives of Mike Jacobs's Twentieth Century Sporting Club to puff its attractions. "To say that Mr. Hearst was a great American is, to me, like saying that Ty Cobb was a great baseball player," Bill Corum wrote in the *Journal* on the afternoon of August 16, making a hook slide to get to the headstone in a tie with his colleague.

Great or not, Hearst was the man who changed the

rules of American journalism. He made it so expensive to compete that no mere working newspaperman has been able to found an important paper in this century.

A Look at
the Record

OCTOBER 14, 1961

To score a popular wow with a biography of an unhappy man, it is necessary to indicate that he was a genius. A Van Gogh or a Toulouse-Lautrec is a perfect subject, because everybody has seen art prints that certify the genius part of the yarn, and all the biographer has to do is to pour on the misery. "He was his own worst enemy" is the consecrated phrase. (Scott Fitzgerald and Edgar Allan Poe are equally foolproof; the reader accepts their credentials even if he hasn't read them.) The biographer of less widely accepted greatness must sometimes suffer from a temptation to salt his claim, and W. A. Swanberg, the latest celebrant of William Randolph Hearst, seems to have yielded to it in his book *Citizen Hearst*. It is easy to demonstrate that Hearst was his own worst enemy—and a lot of other people's—but there exists no document like "Sunflowers" or a Diners' Club card to identify him as Prometheus. In the absence of such a clue, Swanberg falls back on simple assertion. He just *says* Hearst was a genius—twice on page 356, once on page 358, and twice on page 491—without telling us what he was a genius at. Presumably it would have been at journalism, which was Hearst's business. ("In his mastery of journalistic techniques he was unrivaled." . . . "The faking of news stories and photographs was brought to a high art by the romancers of the Hearst press.") Journalistic techniques, and journalism in general, are just what he wasn't a master of, however. He not only failed to create good newspapers but failed to make money out of bad ones

—something that conspicuous mediocrities have succeeded at. And in the high art (or low practice— *ça dépend des goûts*) of news faking, the most famous of Hearst's fakes, like a considerable proportion of his art collection, were exposed before he died.

I was impelled to these reflections by reading, right after I finished *Citizen Hearst,* the intramural-victory edition of the Boston *Daily Record,* a Hearst morning tabloid, of September 30, in which it announced that it had swallowed its evening sibling, the *American,* and would appear henceforth as both of them. It is not unfair to judge the hero by the *Record* ("Let's look at the record," Hearst's next-to-worst enemy, Al Smith, used to say), because Hearst papers have changed little since his death in 1951—or, indeed, since about 1909, when the pattern hardened—and the adoption by some Hearst papers of tabloid format, in imitation of the New York *Daily News,* has never affected the nature of their content. All, like a series of neolithic potsherds, bear the imprint of the dead thumb. The Hearst heirs, in choosing between the *Record,* with a circulation of three hundred and seventy-one thousand, and the *American,* with a hundred and sixty-five thousand, elected to suppress the runt. Boston has two other morning papers—the *Globe* and the *Herald*—and there will still be three avowed evening papers in the *Christian Science Monitor* (not a true competitor), the *Evening Globe,* and the *Traveler,* the last two of which are affiliated, respectively, with the *Globe* and the *Herald.* The *American* is the second Hearst paper to go out in the past twelve months—the Detroit *Times* was put down last November.

The *Record* on its front page carried this notice:

TO OUR READERS: ◆
THE DAILY RECORD
AND
EVENING AMERICAN
WILL BE COMBINED INTO
A SINGLE EXPANDED ALL-DAY
BOSTON RECORD AMERICAN

On Monday, October 2nd, this great forward change will be made.

The Record and American have been edited and published as separate and distinct daily newspapers for many years, each winning on individual merit a commanding position in its field. All the qualities that gave readership appeal to each will now be together in one all-day newspaper to provide reading adventure and complete news coverage on a scale never before attempted.

The combined Record American will be one of the finest reader packages available. It combines into a single newspaper the columnists, features, comics—Local, National and International news coverage facilities of the two single newspapers into ONE great expanded daily publication. . . .

We are confident that the more than half a million people who have been buying the Record and American every day will find the combined expanded newspaper more interesting, more exciting and a greater value than ever before.

The rest of the front page was devoted to what the disciples of the master technician thought a hot story —and it could have been at least a funny one—about a raid on four suspected gambling rooms in the Back Bay area by United States Treasury agents, who arrested a woman and seven men they said were gamblers. They did not charge them with gambling but with not having paid for their gambling stamps. This, a point that fascinated me, was not mentioned on the first page at all, nor was it said why the Boston cops hadn't pinched the gamblers for gambling before they fell behind in their stamp payments. The headline, T-MEN RAID 4 FOR TV, stimulated curiosity. It seems that the T-men, perhaps trying to catch up with the G-men in public relations, had cooperated with a Boston documentary-television group, which had posted cameras in front of the premises to be raided. There was no explanation in the *Record* story of why this had not warned the gamblers that something outside the daily routine was about to happen. It was all as deadpan as possible, and I could only conclude that Boston must be like that.

The second page carried, in addition to the rest of the story about the raid, items on Syria, Tunisia, and a two-hundred-and-fifty-dollar holdup in Park Square. The third had a story about a stabbing, with a picture of a detective and a chemist holding a bloodstained garment, and the fourth a bit of suburban home life about the dismissal of charges against a father who had stabbed his daughter's boyfriend dead after the latter punched him in the eye. That was about it until the two-page center spread, which advertised, in two colors, the goodies that the readers were going to get in the "ONE great expanded daily publication." Here, like any faithful Hearst reader from outside Boston, I felt right at home, surrounded by familiar photographs of Bob Considine, "Famed Global Reporter"; Louella Parsons, "First Lady of Hollywood"; Dorothy Kilgallen, "Voice of Broadway"; George Sokolsky, "Dean of Political Columnists"; and Walter Winchell, "America's Best-Known Reporter"—all legacies from the Age of Genius, all making available to the provinces their unrivaled, masterly techniques of journalism. Only Arthur Brisbane was missing, but he predeceased Citizen Hearst by 15 years, mourned by the latter as "the greatest journalist of his day," which, with one reservation, he probably meant. Sokolsky is Brisbane's nearest spiritual heir, but he has never thought of anything as terrifying as the Mountain of Codfish that would overwhelm the world if Mother Nature ever permitted all codfish eggs to hatch. (The columns that Brisbane might have written on the Bomb are the world's loss. He could scare you with a fish egg.) On the editorial page, along with columns by Drew Pearson, Winchell, and Victor Riesel, there was indeed one local product, "Around Boston," devoted that day to a sterling Boston personality, Sophie Tucker. She was playing at a night club in Framingham, which advertised on page sixteen. Of the two leading editorials, one, perhaps written in Boston, began, "Diplomatic lingo never fooled anybody," and saw through a perfidious foreigner, in this case a Yugoslav. The second, headed MADE IN AMERICA, *was* identical with one that ran the same day in the New York *Journal-American* and probably in other Hearst papers. The theme of both—the treachery and ingratitude of foreigners—dates from the Hearst Golden Age.

This universal diffusion of the regimented vulgarity of Hollywood and Broadway—to the exclusion even of the vulgarity indigenous to other parts of the country—is one Hearst legacy; he did his full share to bring down the general level of culture to his own. But the system was bad for his own newspapers. The proprietor of a menagerie like the one advertised on the *Record* center spread can make money by renting individual animals, or braces or assortments of them, to outside producers for reasonable sums; this is the commercial basis of the syndicate system. But when he tries to put on a show with all his animal actors under one top, he is apt to flop. The Hearst newspapers were in difficulties as early as 1924—five years before the Wall Street crash—but not because Hearst was a bad business manager, as Swanberg proclaims, although that certainly helped them down the slope. More important, they were bad newspapers. A reporter named Burton Crane, in an illuminating analysis of Hearst's financial life that appeared in the New York *Times* in 1951, after the Citizen died, said of the 1924 position, "His properties were costing him more than they were bringing in"—and Hearst was then at the peak of his ostensible journalistic glory. He had, however, inherited $30,000,000, largely in mining equities that threw off money steadily and constantly increased in value. What would have happened to him long before 1924 without this support is problematical.

In 1951, after his death, the trade magazine *Editor & Publisher,* multiplying legends of his magnificence, reported that he had lost $21,000,000 in Atlanta before abandoning his efforts to run a newspaper there. The prerequisite for losing $21,000,000, I noted then, ten years before reading Swanberg, is not genius. It is to have $21,000,000. Hearst had 22 newspapers in 1923; creditors' committees and the prosperity of the Second World War brought him through to his death with 16. Of these, twelve and a half survive. (The San Francisco *News-Call Bulletin* is jointly owned by Hearst and Scripps-Howard.) In its latest annual report, Hearst Consolidated, the Hearst newspaper holding corporation, recorded losses for all but two or three of its papers. One on which it reported a profit was the Detroit *Times,* a ghost; the Detroit *News,* to be rid of this encumbering competition, had bought it for $10,000,000 and shut it down. After discharging the debts of the deceased, Hearst Consolidated showed a profit of $3,500,000 for the paper. I do not wish to intimate that the measure of a newspaper's success is its balance sheet, but Hearst's example, more than that of any other man, has been cited for 60 years by newspaper barroom debaters who say that "you have to give the public what it wants" and that what it wants is the worst. In these arguments, San Simeon has always appeared as the house that Hearst built out of the profits of his uncanny estimate of public taste; actually, it was a monument to the money old George Hearst made in mining.

When the young William Randolph invaded New York in 1895, his widowed mother, Mrs. Phoebe Hearst, endowed his expedition with $7,500,000—an unparalleled bankroll in the newspaper field then— which she had obtained, Swanberg says, by selling her seven-sixteenths share of the Anaconda Company. (Seven-sixteenths of the outstanding common stock of Anaconda now would be worth about a quarter of a billion dollars.) With this kind of money leverage, Hearst, like a very big gambler in a very small crap game, changed the basis of the newspaper business. In the contemptuous term of the tinhorn, he froze out the ribbon clerks—he made it impossible for the man with a small bankroll to get in. This barred the entry of all editor-founders (of whom Joseph Pulitzer remains the last successful exemplar), and no working newspaperman has founded an important American newspaper since. Marshall Field, the most recent founder of such an enterprise, is said to have poured $100,000,000 into the Chicago *Sun* before it began to repay him, having by then absorbed another paper

and changed its name to the *Sun-Times*. This is the
sort of initial capital that is hard to set aside out of a
newspaper salary. There were one or two fortunes of
a few million dollars apiece in the newspaper field
when Hearst, at the age of 23, decided to go into it,
but they had been made in newspapers by men like
Pulitzer and Scripps, who started with little. It had
not occurred to any other mining millionaire that a
man without experience but with money had a vast
advantage over any editor who ever lived. He could,
quite naturally, hire more comic artists, more blood-
and-thunder editorialists, more sportswriters, and more
fakers of crime stories than anybody else in town.
(The Hearst sportswriters, incidentally, have always
been a tower of strength, as one of them might put it.
Since they were unaffected by editorial policy, they
could afford to go merrily on their way, and, along
with the early funny cartoonists, like Herriman and
Hershfield, they gave the whole enterprise an air of
bonhomie that distracted attention from what the boss
was driving at.) Hearst lost money on his newspapers
until they acquired millions of readers, and he acquired his readers by putting on such a show, at a
time when shows were still novel, that in the end people had to buy them. It is a method open to few, like
that of the oilman who produced a play on Broadway
some years back and kept it open by buying all the
seats.

Hearst himself was always a dilettante. Swanberg
quotes a remark he made to a newspaperman: "Of
course I write my signed articles, and many more that
I do not sign. . . . I do not think it is such a trick to
write. Anybody who can think can write. It does not
take much practice to put thought into words. All you
have got to do is have some thoughts which are worth
putting into words." But, possibly because of a failing
in the second requirement, he never could write more
than a little bit, attaining a level of proficiency about
midway between Mrs. Dorothy Schiff and Bishop Fulton J. Sheen, while a specimen of his verse that Mr.
Swanberg quotes is only slightly ahead of Nick
Kenny. (It is conceivable, of course, that the unsigned

pieces were his good ones, but it is not likely.) In his
most elaborate attempted imposition on the public—
the papers forged by a Mexican named Avila, which
purported to prove that the Calles Government in
Mexico had bribed four United States senators—the
execution (what Swanberg would call the journalistic
technique) was so faulty that the documents lost credibility as soon as examined. This was dilettantism at
its worst. Hearst contented himself with saying that
they *ought* to have been true.

When I read Swanberg's record of the old genuis's
reaction to the American Newspaper Guild, I felt a
sentiment approaching peevishness. "It was true that
the moment newsmen owed allegiance to any group
other than their newspaper, the freedom of the press
was impaired," Swanberg concedes. (How about the
state, their church, if any, their family, or the Elks?
Everybody owes allegiance to more than one group.
The question is whether one allegiance precludes
others.) "Possibly Hearst's opposition to the Guild
was motivated in part by self-interest, but in it also
was the inflexible, old-fashioned journalist code he had
lived by since 1887. Newspapering, he felt, was a
high-spirited, challenging profession, not a trade. With
his own uncommon abilities, he was apt to harbor
scorn for any professional man who could not command a good salary out of his own talent and industry, without depending on the aid of a guild."

Hearst, of course, never commanded a salary anywhere except from his own corporations, where he
fixed it himself. Instead of being the famous egghead
who had never met a payroll, he was a fellow who
had never been on one. I have heard ancient newspapermen to whom he had doled out small bounties
speak of him sentimentally, like an old *sous-maîtresse*
remembering a patron who gave good tips: "Mr. Hearst
sent for me *himself,* left word for me to come over to
Martin's, bontoniest joint in town next to Delmonico's,
and there he put his hand on my shoulder and said
. . . " They remind me of a small dog, translucent
with hunger, I once met on the island of Samothrace
and to whom I gave a piece of bread. She wanted to

come to America with me, and is probably still telling the other island dogs about my munificence. Hearst enacted the kingly fantasy, but within the legal bounds of sanity—he was no Jacques Lebaudy to set out to found an Empire of the Sahara. San Simeon was real, although unlikely. And so, even as strained through Swanberg, he is a most interesting and, in the end— like everybody else—a pathetic man.

What moves me to write these few words is not esthetic protest. The own-worst-enemy, Jekyll-and-Hyde biography is a standard amusement form, like the whodunit or the Western. Sometimes it is frankly "fictionalized," and sometimes it just becomes fiction by the interjection of a running commentary on the subject's gifts, thoughts, and awful sufferings. (For example, according to Swanberg, there was once a time, late in life, when Hearst took a cut in his salary, paid by his own papers, from $500,000 to $100,000 —a blow that, to accept his biographer's assertion, "would have been fatal" to "an ordinary 75-year-old." But Hearst's "tall frame had weathered and bent under hurricanes no other man ever withstood.") What I think is perilous about any myth concerning Hearst is that it may creep into common acceptance as fact. The most dangerous myth about him is that he was a genius, or even a good newspaperman, because it might lead to the erroneous conclusion that he ran newspapers the right way, or that the way he ran them is the way to make money. The latter delusion might be the most dangerous of all.

Peg and Sock

NOVEMBER 18, 1950

Pages two and three of the *Journal-American* constitute one of my favorite areas (710 square inches) in New York journalism, at least on Tuesdays, Wednesdays, Thursdays, and Fridays. George E. Sokolsky's

brilliant column on world affairs appears on page two
Monday through Friday and Westbrook Pegler's hard-
hitting column appears on page three Tuesday through
Saturday; these descriptions are quotes from the blurbs
in blackface type that customarily follow the respective entries. (I seldom read the *Journal-American* on
Sundays, which I prefer to devote to the New York
Enquirer.) Each of the columns is accompanied by a
photograph of its dour author—brachycephalic Sokolsky frowning on page two, dolichocephalic Pegler
scowling on page three—and this gives the whole
spread an appearance of balanced ferocity. The stares
of the two writers are directed not at each other but
at some dread presence just behind the reader's right
shoulder, presumably a presidential ghost or the phan-
tom of the American Republic. "The awful truth
seems to be that the republic is dead," Pegler wrote
on October 3, confirming a diagnosis he had made
back in 1948, when he wrote that the election of Truman "means that the American Republic . . . is done
for." (I. [for Isidor] F. Stone, a columnist on the
Daily Compass, wrote last summer, "The little piano
player in the White House is improvising his country's
Götterdämmerung," and on October 4 he followed up
with, "All that made America a proud name in the
eyes of the world is being dirtied and destroyed and
degraded. The terrible thing is that I don't know that
anything can be done about it." I like to think of Peg
and Izzy, in accord at last, huddled together on the
forward thwart of the first lifeboat leaving the ship.)

It is the pages two-to-three lineup that makes the
Sokolsky–Pegler arrangement so effective. If Sokolsky
were on page four, or Pegler on page one, you
couldn't see them both at the same time, and in that
case they wouldn't strike such terror. Sokolsky's expression is a trifle out of character with the blurbs
that usually follow his column. He looks dogged rather
than brilliant—a solid, avuncular type of man with a
face nearly as wide as it is long, and his mouth set in
a straight line. He has a luxuriant crop of hair that
comes down to about the middle of his forehead, a
circumstance that perhaps explains why, on October

20, a *Journal-American* promotion man, indubitably an opportunist, like most of his kind, substituted for the conventional Sokolsky blurb one that read, "Are you getting bald? Learn how a simple injection may encourage the regrowth of hair. Read 'What Causes Baldness?' in the *American Weekly,* with Sunday's *Journal-American.*" Pegler looks hard-hitting, all right. "Westbrook Pegler pulls no punches!" the plug at the end of his piece sometimes states. His eyebrows and his mouth form parallel straight lines across his rhadamanthine mask.

Sokolsky's column has been in the *Journal-American* only since January, when the *Sun* folded, leaving him momentarily without a New York outlet. Both columnists are syndicated. For some months, Pegler, who has been in the *Journal-American* since 1944, appeared to be taking the newcomer all right. Despite their obvious inclination to combat—to judge by their pictures, either would as soon take umbrage as coffee —the two columnists, it seemed to me, a fairly faithful reader, got along fine together. Pegler's column is called "As Pegler Sees It," and Sokolsky's "These Days," often expanded to "As Sokolsky Sees: These Days." But usually they saw things the same way. They worked well as a team, with Peg shredding the Roosevelt Cerements one day while Sock disemboweled the United Nations, Sock lambasting the C.I.O. the next while Peg banged away at the Fourteenth Amendment—"put through by the Hitlerites of the North after the Civil War," he explained, "ostensibly as an emancipation measure. The true purpose was to persecute the Southern white people . . ." Then they would exchange themes. The way Sokolsky played back civil rights, for example, was: "Since when is poverty and unhappiness only for Negroes? There is plenty of poverty among white folks, North, South, and over the seas, and as for unhappiness, I am sure there is as much of it on Park Avenue as on Beale Street." The two would also toss Mrs. Roosevelt from page two to page three and back again, like the girl in an adagio act.

I was astonished, therefore, when, on October 13,

I picked up the *Journal-American,* flipped over the front page, as usual, and found out whom Peg was pulling no punches he threw at. "In the background of the word-tapestries on the World Series," Pegler's column began, "a faint pattern of political and patriotic embarrassment could be detected by the expert eye, reflecting the self-abasement of the American spirit." The expert, photo-engraved eye now seemed to be looking directly into mine, and I began to hum "Yankee Doodle" to prove my Americanism. In the second paragraph, Pegler said that Americans seemed to be spoofing the World Series more than they used to. This brought him into a position from which he could hit out in any direction. "Yet when Sokolsky tells us of the obscure wisdom of Oriental esoterics who scorn our nylons, vitamins, and bubble gum," I read, "we may draw comparisons to our own consolation. These clients of his sympathy are horribly debased, crawling on their scabby bellies through the centuries, rubbing themselves with foul corruption and propitiating serpents which fang them dead." The word "clients" made me think at first that Peg was accusing Sock of being in the employ of some particular group of Chinese, but I soon realized that I was wrong, because no such group would have scabby bellies. And I was quite sure Peg wasn't writing about the rattlesnake cults down South, because people down there *do* like bubble gum.

"They have no World Series, no Buicks or Dodges, and the sacred sewer of the Ganges is their version of the laundrymat," Peg continued, and now I got him. He was writing about yogis, the kind of people he used to say the man he calls Bubblehead Wallace associated with. Evidently, Sokolsky was also a bubblehead. A bubblehead is a contemner of bubble gum. "They think they are going to heaven, but theirs is a hell of a way to get there," Peg added, making me wonder whether he was about to tackle Sock on theological grounds, too. He didn't. He just let Sock lie there and turned raptly to Albert (Hap) Chandler, the Baseball Commissioner, who had called for 30 seconds of pre-game meditation by the World Series crowd. "Though, at Derby time in Louisville, his [Chandler's] wailing tenor can be heard in smoke-filled rooms in the sentimental strains of 'Old Kaintucky Home,' he was, for this moment, not a guru or a lama but a simple exhorter on a side-hill clearing back where he cum fum," Pegler wrote, and went on, equally beautifully, from there, winding up:

Baseball is all right. Frats are okay. So is peanut butter. Al Schacht for Mayor of New York, the people's choice if they had a choice.

To hell with the Four Freedoms, the United Nations and the Marshall Plan.

Make me a boy again just for tonight!

The piece puzzled me. I couldn't remember Sokolsky's coming out against baseball, or frats, or peanut butter, or Al Schacht, a former baseball player who now runs a restaurant in New York, and he is the last fellow I'd accuse of endorsing the Four Freedoms, the United Nations, or the Marshall Plan. I had to get out my file and read clear back to October 2 before I found what Peg was mad about. It was a thing Sock had written in favor of having religious instruction in the public schools, which he must have thought it was safe to be for, since Peg is for it, too. But the brilliant world-affairs columnist had supported it for what Peg considered a bubbleheaded reason. Sock had thought more spiritual training might help us get on with India. "Can a people who make a god of one who renounced wealth for poverty and fame for the beggar's bowl become enthusiastic about nylons and cosmetics?" he had asked. (Nothing about bubble gum, however.) That had fixed him.

After that, I read the *Journal-American* with even more attention than before. I figured Sokolsky wasn't the kind of man to pull any punches, either, and pretty soon he would throw one into Peg. Moreover, the *Journal-American* was announcing a new columnist, Fulton Lewis, Jr., whom it was going to start on page one on Monday, October 16. Pegler would be out of the paper that day, I knew, and I wondered whether the newcomer and Sokolsky planned to gang up on him. I had read elsewhere that Lewis was a hard-hitting, anti-bubblehead radio commentator. On his account, I looked at the front page first on the sixteenth.

Lewis's debut was tranquil enough. "Washington Report," his column is called. "These writings will not be what the journalistic jargon likes to refer to as 'objective' reporting," he wrote, in part.

In the first place there is no such thing—aside perhaps from the *Congressional Record*. Any columnist who purports to be producing one is either an intellectual capon or a knave.

There will be no tortuous calisthenics of trying to carry water on both shoulders, or conjuring fawning compliments as antidotes for those who may suffer political contusions as a result of factual disclosures here from day to day.

For those who want to maintain pleasant social relations for dinner conversation purposes, that's understandable. In Washington, you never know who will be seated next to you. And long ago, therefore, I adopted the simpler and more effective solution of declining the dinner parties. To me, it's easier than apostasy. Besides, the food too often is abominable. . . .

The principal satisfaction over being back in this routine is a poignant and haunting feeling that I never should have been out of it, really. [Lewis had previously explained that fifteen years ago he had been a newspaperman.] I never did grow up from being a police reporter. That's what this column is going to be.

The blurb at the end said, "Read Fulton Lewis, Jr.'s, hard-hitting column 'Washington Report,' Monday through Friday in the *Journal-American.*"

I thought Lewis had a promising turn of phrase, somewhere between Peg's and Cholly Knickerbocker's, but his photograph seemed wrong. He had had his picture taken smiling and in a dinner jacket. If he had declined a dinner, why was he dressed for it? Besides,

I had never seen a police reporter in a dinner jacket, except for a fellow named Red Gallagher, who, back around 1925, would occasionally come to work after an all-night party wearing one, but he would change his clothes before he started chasing fires. I felt, however, that a greater mistake for a hard-hitting columnist was the smile.

I turned to page two, hoping for something harsher. "Tortuous calisthenics," after all, is insipid fare for a reader used to wailing tenors crawling back where dey cum fum on scabby bellies, and Sokolsky, while no Pegler, might by now, I thought, be throwing punches. He was, but not at Pegler. NEWS ABOUT BABS LEAVES HIM COLD, the topical head over his column read. Under this, Sokolsky wrote:

During the past weeks, I have been puzzled by the amount of expensive white paper that has been consumed by the affairs of one Barbara Hutton and her fourth husband, Prince Troubetzkoy, a trivial Lithuanian whom she accuses of marrying her for her grandfather's money, which she inherited. . . . I have never seen this woman, but her pictures do not indicate she is as interesting as the Korean war, the high cost of living, the compulsory drafting [as distinguished, possibly, from the voluntary kind] of young doctors into the armed forces, or the silly correspondence, involving the President and John L. Lewis, about dog-catchers. . . . Of what significance is this unseemly dialogue between husband and wife who call press conferences to denounce each other? . . . Why would any reporter want to attend such a press conference? . . .

By george, if we are so short of things to interest us in these days of war and an election campaign, let me tell you that a fine dog I knew, named Susie, a lovely beagle and as friendly as a healthy baby, was run over by a monster of a truck and had to be put away to the tears of children who loved her.

Surely, such news is as important as that one Barbara Hutton is ready to take a fifth husband and that one Troubetzkoy objects and wants the services of his wife. Services, indeed!

I recalled having seen some mention of the Princess Troubetzkoy's troubles in the *Journal-American;* it seemed to me that Igor Cassini, the current Cholly Knickerbocker, had been giving them a pretty heavy play in his "The Smart Set" column. After reading Sokolsky and Pegler, I usually turn to "The Smart Set," for assurance that there is something left to fight for. On this particular day, it carried the head-line INSIDE STORY OF WHY BABS IS FIGHTING IGOR "The amazing inside story of the Barbara Hutton–Igor Troubetzkoy tossing of insults in the newspapers is that Babs had offered Igor $2,000,000 to get rid of him," Cholly began. "But the foolish prince let himself be advised by friends and lawyers who told him he could get more if he stood pat and that is what started the fight. Now the Hutton-tot is so mad that she has sworn she won't give Prince Igor a sou. . . . After all, he was penniless when he married Barbara and if she offered him $2,000,000 he should have grabbed it. Barbara has always been very generous to her former husbands and made more than gener-ous settlements on each of them (with the exception of Cary Grant) when she divorced them."

I could now descry a pecking order in the Hearst barnyard. Peg pecks Sock, Sock pecks Cholly, Cholly pecks Louella O. Parsons. (I remembered that when Louella, the *Journal-American*'s Hollywood author-ity, was cooing over Rita Hayworth's wedding to Ali Khan, Cholly had written a piece about a number of Occidental women who had married Orientals and died under mysterious circumstances. MARRYING A WEALTHY ORIENTAL ISN'T ALWAYS WHAT IT'S SUP-POSED TO BE, had been his chilling headline.) I have never caught Louella pecking Dorothy Kilgallen, who does a "Voice of Broadway" column midway through the same paper, but then Louella has plenty of folks to peck in Hollywood. Probably no columnist farther back in the paper than Miss Kilgallen, I thought, was worth pecking at all. Those way back on the page opposite the editorials are, in fact, only half-colum-nists, as six or eight of them share the daily space with about the same number of cartoons, the area being arranged like the berth deck in a transport. Once consigned to this Black Hole, a column carries no photograph. Fulton Lewis, Jr., was the one I couldn't yet fit into the order.

When I bought the paper the next morning, the seventeenth, I could see that somebody had wised the new boy up. He had on a lounge suit, his tie was askew (a four-in-hand, like his running mates'), and he was scowling more portentously than even Pegler, the only real difference being that Lewis was looking over the reader's *left* shoulder, which, as I could understand, was where the danger was likely to be. The column was about W. Averell Harriman, who had made a speech in Houston accusing Senator Taft of taking an isolationist stand that must have pleased the Communists. Lewis said the Military Intelligence Division of the Army had learned that on August 21, 1941, a man heard two other men say, in the Communist Party headquarters in Pittsburgh, they were "happy that W. Averell Harriman had been appointed by President Roosevelt as chairman to the commission to Moscow on war aid to Russia." (The Nazis had invaded Russia two months earlier.) "From 1943 to 1946, Mr. Harriman got along great with the Russians while he served in Moscow as U.S. Ambassador to the Soviet Union," the new hand wrote. "In his anxiety to tag Taft as a friend of the Communists [Harriman hadn't; he had said that Taft's votes served Communist purposes], he may have overlooked something that made him such a hopeful for the Reds." This might have been all right for radio, but in print it lacked invective embellishment.

This was the way Peg started on the same day, same subject: "Averell Harriman, who is as much to blame as any other individual except Roosevelt and Hopkins for the postwar ascendancy of the enemy over the United States, recently made a speech before the annual consistory of racketeers and their panoplied accomplices known as the convention of the American Federation of Labor." The roughest Lewis had got with Harriman was to call him "President Truman's super-thinker on international policies."

"Pausing briefly to justify this description of this gang of predators," Pegler digressed, "I shall quote typical excerpts from the official remarks which William Green, its president, expressed at two successive conventions of the Movie and Theatrical Employees' Union when it was under the presidency of a notorious underworld racketeer, George E. Browne, who later was forced out and sent to prison in spite of Green's official endeavors to protect him, along with Willie Bioff, the filthiest rodent of them all, who was Browne's official extortioner. Bioff started out as a brothel-keeper."

"Now let us get to Harriman," Pegler wrote 227 words later, or 318 after leaving him. "In the presence of this mob, he attacked Sen. Robert A. Taft, of Ohio, now a candidate for re-election, blaming him and the Republican Party for the ghastly plight of the United States in the Franklin D. Roosevelt memorial war in Korea. . . . Harriman's ethics and fitness for high office and public confidence are subject to consideration of the character of the mob which he addressed."

"My practice swings and windup here have taken up more wordage than I had intended they should," Pegler noted after another 300 words, mostly quoted from a speech of Senator Taft's, "but I thought I should establish the atmosphere, or stench, of the occasion which Mr. Harriman chose for his faux pas, not that I would say the atmosphere or stench was inappropriate for either his politics, his record as a statesman, or his mission."

Under all this, I came upon the blurb "In addition to Westbrook Pegler's hard-hitting column . . . read Fulton Lewis, Jr.'s, dynamic new column 'Washington Report.' " It occurred to me that the promotion department was doing Lewis no favor by inviting comparison. Sokolsky, that day, referred coyly to Mrs. Roosevelt as "the idol of Westbrook Pegler's heart." He avoided controversial subjects like nylons.

Chilly Knickerbocker, by the way, was not at all

discouraged by the Sock peck. He has continued to give masses of space to Miss Hutton's affairs, including a full column, on October 22, that began: "Exclusively Yours—There is quite a fascinating angle in the Barbara Hutton–Igor Troubetzkoy battle royal which hasn't been touched anywhere. Prince Henri de la Tour d'Auvergne, Barbara's new beau and reportedly next in line for the position of husband No. 5, for years was the romantic interest in the life of Princess Kira Troubetzkoy, a cousin of Igor, Barbara's present husband. In fact, Kira has acted as advisor to Henri in the recent commotion and has been the one to push him in his pursuit of the wealthy and beautiful Hutton-tot." Then, on November 8, Cholly took the shine off the post-election headlines with the simple announcement "Babs Hutton Has Ditched Prince Henri." He explained, "For one thing, the Hutton-tot knows that the strongest point in Igor's favor is his contention that she left him for the Frenchman."

Now let us get to Lewis. "Communists still have a key to White House security closets," the rookie, still on page one, opened up on the eighteenth, but he did not have any of the significant details, such as whether the Communists kept brothels, and I missed the practiced Peglerian vituperation. He meant well, I guess.

"If he ever does tell the story [of his part in the war] fully and truthfully, Harriman will have a good chance of getting himself tarred and feathered" was how Peg went after the ex-ambassador the next day. And in criticism of drinking parties with Russians in Moscow in 1943: "The Stork on a night out is the place to hang a bag on. American political and military missionaries dealing with the fate of mankind should have had the brains and firmness to look those bums [the Russians] dead in the eye and tell them they were up the pole."

The front page of the early editions of the *Journal-American* on Monday, the twenty-third, carried a top line saying that Lewis's "Washington Report" would be found on page four. Once a columnist starts to-

ward the rear of the *Journal-American,* it is hard for
him to make a stand. In his second week, Lewis
wrote about the waning chances of the Brannan Plan
for agricultural support (not a red-hot urban subject), the woes of persecuted lobbyists, the Taft campaign in Ohio (twice), and the coddling of Europeans
detained on Ellis Island. Of the last, he said, "The
loud and righteous wail recently from the usual clique
of professional do-gooders because some incoming
aliens were delayed at Ellis Island was in reality the
opening shot in the pinko campaign to discredit the
McCarran–Mundt–Nixon Communist-control bill and
get it off the books."

On the third Monday, "Washington Report" appeared on the editorial page, minus the portrait.
(Taking the photograph from a columnist is like
stripping the chevrons from a noncommissioned officer.) The column tarried there for only a day. The
last day of the month found "Washington Report"
halfway down the right-hand column of the page
opposite the editorials—the *Journal*'s largest colum-
nistic dormitory. It was blocked in on three sides by
"Bugs" Baer, Louis Sobol, and Henry McLemore,
with Lawrence Gould ("consulting psychologist"),
Bob Considine, and E. V. Durling only a couple of
columns away. A race chart might have said of Mr.
Lewis, "Broke fast, taken back when outrun, dropped
back steadily."

When I saw John O'Donnell's column, "Capitol
Stuff," in the *Daily News* the morning after Collazo
and Torresola tried to assassinate President Truman,
I realized how much Lewis would have had to develop to stay in real fast company. "President Truman—and his party—will most certainly benefit next
November 7th from the dramatic minutes of this
lovely Indian summer afternoon when pistols barked
on Pennsylvania Avenue and the sidewalks in front
of Blair House had blood puddles from the wounds
of attempted murderers and protecting police,"
O'Donnell wrote. "It's true, *if there's such a thing as
fate or luck in these actual or attempted deeds of
violence,* that the gods of assassination are all on the

side of the Democrats. [Italics mine.] In the history
of the republic, five attempts, including today's, have
been made on the lives of Presidents of the United
States. Three of the Presidents were Republicans;
two were Democrats. The three Republicans, Lincoln, Garfield, and McKinley, were killed. The two
Democrats, Franklin Roosevelt and Harry Truman,
escaped unwounded."

It was too much to hope that anybody in this
country, with the possible exception of Pegler himself, could match that. But in Paris, the Communist
newspaper *Humanité*, according to a dispatch in the
Times, said right out that the shooting, including the
two deaths and three woundings, was an election
trick stage-managed by the administration.

To end this critique on a happy note, I may say
that my favorite New York columnist, in a purely
literary sense, is Colonel John R. Stingo, who pro-
duces a four- or five-thousand-word department
called "Yea Verily" in the *Enquirer* every Sunday.
The *Enquirer* doesn't come out any other day, which
limits the Colonel's output. "Mr. Willis [an old acquaintance of the Colonel] frequently related how a
humorous incident he witnessed furnished the incentive for him to study the Turf just like other chaps
study Law and Medicine," Colonel Stingo wrote the
other Sunday. "His tale was about the 'thirtyish'
lady at Death Valley (Latonia) track back in '19
who had a $2 ticket on Wishing Ring, which won
and paid the longest price in the history of the Kentucky mutuels, one thousand and some odd dollars
to two, and who (the lady) hollered so darn loud
she could have been heard in the beer-gardens on
upper Vine Street over in Cincinnati. And how she
outwitted the two Johns who were with her by insisting on being paid off by check." The beer-garden
figure portrays the lady, and her insistence on a
check sketches in the Johns. "Death Valley," as a
nickname for a minor race track, conjures up a whole
milieu. Many a *Journal-American* columnist might
envy the Colonel's style.

Harold Ross—
The Impresario

It is hard for a writer to call an editor great, because it is natural for him to think of the editor as a writer manqué. It is like asking a thief to approve a fence, or a fighter to speak highly of a manager. "Fighters are sincere," a fellow with the old pug's syndrome said to me at a bar once as his head wobbled and the hand that held his shot glass shook. "Managers are pimps, they sell our blood." In the newspaper trade, confirmed reporters think confirmed editors are mediocrities who took the easy way out. These attitudes mark an excess of vanity coupled with a lack of imagination; it never occurs to a writer that anybody could have wanted to be anything else.

I say, despite occupational bias, Ross, the first editor of *The New Yorker,* was as great as anybody I ever knew, in his way. He was as great as Sam Langford, who could make any opponent lead and then belt him out, or Beatrice Lillie, who can always make me laugh, or Raymond Weeks, who taught romance philology at Columbia and lured me into the Middle Ages, or Max Fischel, who covered New York Police Headquarters for the *Evening World* and was the best head-and-legman I ever saw. The head helps the legs when it knows its way around.

Given the address of a tenement homicide, Max would go over the roofs and down while the younger men raced down to the street and then around the block and up. They would arrive to find him listening sympathetically to the widow if the police had not already locked her up, or to a neighbor if they had. People in jams liked to talk to him because he never talked to them.

Ross was as great as Max, or as a man named Flageollet, who kept a hotel with eight rooms at Feriana in Tunisia and was one of the best cooks I have known, or another named Bouillon, who had a small restaurant on the Rue Ste-Anne in Paris. (It is odd that I should have known two great cooks with comestible names.) He was as great as Eddie Arcaro, the rider, or General George Patton, or Bobby Clark and Paul McCullough, or a number of women I have known who had other talents. Ross would not have resented any of these comparisons, and the ones with Max and Patton would have flattered him particularly, because he was a newspaper and army buff.

One thing that made him a great editor was his interest in the variety of forms greatness assumes. He saw it in the entertainers he hired, as cheaply as possible so that they would work harder, to appear in his Litterographic Congress of Strange (Great) People of the World: the Greatest One-Gag Cartoonist, the Greatest Two-Gag Cartoonist, the Greatest Cartoonists Waiting for a Gag; the Greatest One-Note Male Short-Story Writer, the Greatest Half-Note In-Between Short-Story Writer, the Greatest Demi-Semi-Quaver Lady Short-Story Writer Ending in a Muted Gulp; the Greatest Woman Who Ever Married an Egyptian, the Greatest Woman Who Ever Married a Patagonian, the Greatest Woman Who Ever Married a Dravidian Pterodactyl. These latters' stories always began: "My mother-in-law could never get used to my wearing shoes," and still do, although sales territory is becoming rapidly exhausted; the only franchises still available to marry into are the Andaman Islands and Washington Heights. Ross cherished half-bad Great talents too; he knew there will never be enough good ones to go around.

E. B. White once said to me that the relation between Ross and him was like that of two railroad cars: they met only at one point. White was with Ross from the beginning of the magazine in 1925, but he admits he knew only one Ross personally and a couple of dozen others by intuition, hearsay, brag, or reputation. Ross had some raffish friends I envied him and some stuffed-shirt friends I wouldn't be seen dead with. He was equally proud and I think equally fond of all of them. He liked anybody who had a lot

of money or a good story to tell, and since these are
minerals seldom found in conjunction, he prospected
around. *The New Yorker* he made reflected this idio-
syncrasy, but not what the kids now call dichotomy.
There was no conflict; he just had more interests
than most people. I think that a number of men who
knew Ross underrated him because, coming up on
him always from one direction, they found him sometimes preoccupied with what was going on in another
ring.

It was as if a wire-walker expected a ringmaster to
be as exclusively interested in high-wire acts as he
was. Of course Ross couldn't write as well as Thurber
or Joe Mitchell, or draw as well as Steinberg. He
didn't know as much as Edmund Wilson is supposed
to, and there were at any given period of *The New
Yorker*'s existence 84 people around who knew more
about France or the East Side or where to buy a baby
bottle with an aquamarine nipple for Christmas. But
he had his own greatness—he put the show together.
Why he wanted to I don't know. What made Arcaro
a jockey?

Early in December, 1951, when Ross had been ill
since the previous April, I said to Bill Shawn, who
was doing his work and has since succeeded him, "If
I knew he was going to die, I'd put my arm around
his shoulder and say I'd always like him. But if he
recovered, he'd never forgive me." That was at a
time when the doctors had not admitted his condition was critical, but when the length of the illness
had made us all suspicious. He died about a week
later, but I think he knew that I liked him, in a way,
and I know he liked me, in a way, and that's about
as close as I ever got to him in an acquaintance of
18 years, 16 of them on *The New Yorker*.

The only letter of his I have chanced to preserve
is one I got in Reno, Nevada, in the summer of 1949.
He felt there was a great story in Reno, but did not
know just what it was. He wrote, "But of course you
are a better reporter than I am. (The hell you are!)"
He couldn't give a compliment without taking it back
in the next sentence—afraid you'd get a swelled

head, I suppose. I disappointed him with a slight report on Reno I wrote then, but I took East the seed of a much better story, which germinated until I went out to Nevada again in the fall of 1953 and reported and wrote it. He never saw it, of course.

He was a great hunch man, which is part of being a great editor. Many aspects of life entranced him imprecisely, and he knew that where there was entrancement there was a story, if he could just bring the right kind of man into its vicinity. Like a marriage broker, he could bring together a couple, writer and subject, who ought to hit it off. But sometimes not even Ross could make them go to bed together. He was also good at sensing a mismatch. Immediately after the end of the war I told him that I would like to travel in the unknown—to me—interior of this country and write about the Middle West as I would of any other strange land. "You wouldn't like it, Liebling," he said. "You wouldn't like it."

I spent the winter of 1949–50 in Chicago, and he was dead right.

Later in my Nevada summer he came to Reno with some of his Hollywood pals—Chasen and Capra and Nunnally Johnson—on a holiday. He was very happy, happier than I have seen him in any other setting. He liked the West (as distinguished from Mid-) and pretending to be a Westerner. (He had left the West when a kid, and by the time I knew him was an indefinitely urban type, though never a New York.) He got me to sit in with him at the open poker game in the Bank Club, together with the old sheepherders and railroad pensioners. There are always at least three one-armed men in that game—brakemen who fell under trains. I played a half-hour, lost $20 and got out. He stayed an hour and said he won $60. Later he went back, played until five in the morning, and returning to the Riverside Hotel, cashed a check for $500. I heard about it at breakfast from the night manager of the game room, who was just going off duty. At lunch Ross told me he had cleaned up, but I knew better.

When he was young, vaudeville was the chief national entertainment industry, and I often thought he would have made a first-class booker for variety shows. This is no faint compliment, for I adored vaudeville, which lasted well on into my own youth. So must Ross have done; he had a great affection for old comics like Joe Cook and Chasen. He put on a weekly variety bill of the printed word and the graphic gag—always well balanced and sufficiently entertaining to bring the audience back next week. He booked the best acts he could, but he knew that you couldn't get the best specialists in every spot every week. When he had no headline comic, he built the show around a dancer or even a juggler. One week he might have a cartoon that people would remember with pleasure for years. The next it might be a good profile, and the week after that the Fratellini of prose, Sullivan and Perelman, or a tear-jerking fiction turn by Dorothy Parker or O'Hara. Vaudeville, too, had its sacred moments; next to a good laugh there is nothing so nice as a sniffle.

Ross tried to polish old acts or develop new ones, but he never let his notion of what he wanted get in the way of his clear apprehension of what was to be had. In the late thirties, when all his new writers came from newspaper staffs where they had sweated through the Depression, he said to me, "Liebling, I wish I could find some young Conservative writers who could write, but there aren't any."

He was by inclination a kind of H. L. Mencken Conservative himself, but he wouldn't book a dancer who couldn't dance just because he liked the shape of her derrière. This is a higher integrity than either right-wing or left-wing editors possessed in those days. The writing in the *New Masses* was as bad, in a different way, as the writing in *Time*. (The transition, as Whittaker Chambers found out, was easy.) Ross's loyalty was to his readers. He treasured Alva Johnston, an earlier convert from the newspaper fold than we were, who wrote excellent profiles and at the same time held that stupid Presidents were best, because they let big businessmen run the country, and businessmen had brains.

Alva's only objection to Herbert Hoover was that
he was too bright. He was a hard man to satisfy; it
is a pity he did not live to see Eisenhower. Ross
relished Johnston's concurrent political opinions as
lagniappe; he wouldn't have given a hoot about them
if he hadn't esteemed Alva's technique of defining
character by a series of anecdotes on an ascending
scale of extravagance, so that the reader of the sixth
installment wolfed yarns that he would have rejected
in the first.

Nor did Ross insist on playing types of acts that had
lost their vogue. During the late twenties and very
early thirties *The New Yorker* frequently ran a type
of profile of rich and successful men that was only
superficially distinguishable from the Success Stories
in the late *American Magazine.* (The difference was
that the *New Yorker* writer might attribute to the
protagonist some supposedly charming foible like
wearing crimson ties although he had attended Prince-
ton.) The hallmark of this kind of profile was a sentence on the order of "Although Jeremy P. Goldrush
is as rich as rich, you would never think from his
plain old two-hundred dollar suits that he was more
than an ordinary weekend polo player."

After a couple of these heroes had landed in state
prisons, Ross became receptive to portraits in a less
reverent style. Although Ross loved the smell of success, he was emotionally irreverent and always enjoyed learning that a fellow he had accepted as a
monument to society was in fact a sepulcher with a
runny coat of whitewash.

He made the same good adjustment to World War
II as to the Depression. He would have preferred not
to have it, but he didn't deny it was on. That got me
a break. He sent me to France in October, 1939. I
attracted the assignment by telling McKelway how
well I could talk French. McKelway could not judge.
Besides, I was a reasonable age for the job: 35.

Ross was 47 then, and in the newspaper world
where we came out in different decades, twelve years
is a great gap. When we talked I called him "Mr.
Ross." I was never an intimate of his—just an act he

booked and learned to appreciate, though never highly enough in my opinion. I think that all the reporters of my *New Yorker* generation—Mitchell and Jack Alexander and Dick Boyer and Meyer Berger and I—had the same classical ambivalent son-to-father feeling about him. We were eager to please him and cherished his praise, but we publicly and profanely discounted his criticism. Especially we resented his familiarity with the old-timers—the Companions of the Prophet—and his indulgence for them. Our admiration for their work was not unqualified or universal. (I still think *The New Yorker*'s reporting before we got on it was pretty shoddy.)

I find it hard to admit how jealous I was one day in 1946 when Wolcott Gibbs, who was very ill, called up while Ross and I were working over proofs. Ross told him to take care of himself and said, "Don't worry about money." That was white of him, I thought, but he had never said that to me. It was a true sibling emotion. In fact, Ross thought that a healthy writer wouldn't write unless he had had to emit at least two rubber checks and was going to be evicted after the weekend. It was an unselfish conviction, a carry-over from his newspaper days. He reminded me of a showman I knew named Clifford G. Fischer—the impresarial analogy pops up constantly when I think of Ross. Fischer spoke to actors only in a loud scream, and when I asked him why, replied, in a low conversational voice he used on non-actors, "Because they are abnormal people. To abnormal people you got to talk in an abnormal voice."

Ross liked writers, but he would no more have thought of offering a writer money than of offering a horse an ice-cream soda. "Bad for them, Liebling," he would have said. But you could promote a small advance if you were in a bad jam. What continually amazed me about Ross, and convinced me of his greatness, was that he took the whole show seriously —from the fiction, which I seldom can read, to the fashion notes that I never try to. He knew no more of horse racing than a hog of heaven, but he knew

how to find and keep Audax Minor, G. F. T. Ryall,
whose tone is precisely right for *The New Yorker*.
Here again he had the instinct of a showman, who
wants the whole bill to be good, while I have that of
an educated seal, who thinks that when he plays "Oh,
say can you see" on the automobile horn, it is the
high spot of the evening. After that the crowd can go
home.

A lot has been written about Ross as an editor of
manuscript, as distinguished from Ross the editor-im-
presario. There should be different words for the two
functions in English as there are in French—*directeur*
for the boss and *rédacteur* for the fellow who works
on the copy. Ross did both, but he impressed me less
as *rédacteur* than as *directeur*. His great demand was
clarity. This is a fine and necessary quality, but you
can go just so far with it. You cannot make subtlety
or complexity clear to an extraordinarily dull reader,
but Ross in editing would make himself *advocatus
asinorum*. He would ask scores of marginal questions, including many to which he full well knew the
answers, on the off chance that unless all were pre-
explained in the text some particularly stupid woman
might pick up a *New Yorker* in a dentist's waiting
room and be puzzled. Out of the swarm of questions
there were always a few that improved the piece—
on an average, I should say, about 2¾ percent, and
none that did any harm, because you could ignore
the silliest and leave Shawn to talk him out of the
rest.

I never thought this quest for clarity naïve. It was
part of a method he had thought out for putting his
"book" across in the early days. If the silliest *New
Yorker* readers could go through a piece on a "sophisticated" subject and understand every word, they
would think themselves extremely intelligent and renew their subscriptions. But there are subjects not
susceptible of such reduction; the only way of making
clear pea soup is by omitting the peas. Ross continued his queries compulsively long after the time
when *The New Yorker* had to recruit readers. A
point had been reached when the silly ones would

pretend to understand even if they didn't. This vestigial reminder of the "book's" early hard times was exasperating, but not serious. The writer got his way in the end. Just because he was a great editor, Ross knew when to back down.

I have heard that he made a fetish of Fowler's *Modern English Usage,* a book I have never looked into. (It would be like Escoffier consulting Mrs. Beeton.) He never suggested the book to me, nor told me how to write that mythical thing, the *"New Yorker* style." What is affected as a *"New Yorker* style" by undergraduate and British contributors is, to judge from specimens I have seen, a mixture of White's style, Gibbs's and S. J. Perelman's, but as none of these three is like either of the others, the result is like a "Romance language" made up by jumbling French, Portuguese, and Romanian. It is not a satisfactory medium of communication. I don't know anybody who has written a good story for *The New Yorker* in *"New Yorker* style."

Personally, I had a tough first year on *The New Yorker,* from the summer of 1935 to the summer of 1936, because I brought to it a successful newspaper short-feature method that was not directly transferable to a magazine, especially in long pieces. It would have been like running a mile in a series of hundred-yard dashes. I rescued myself by my reporting on a profile of Father Divine. I found out more of the inner inwardness and outward outerness of that old god in a machine than anybody else had. The machine was a hundred-and-fifty-dollar Rolls-Royce acquired during the Depression when nobody else wanted a car that burned that much gas. The old newspaperman in Ross came to the top; he stopped my salary of $65 a week and gave me a drawing account of $90. I have never been out of debt to *The New Yorker* since.

And still, that isn't the whole story. It is hard to be entirely kind to Ross, and he found it hard to be entirely kind to others, as I recalled earlier on. But through five years of war I liked to know that he was behind me, unashamedly interested in what I was doing and seeing, like a kid watching a high-wire act, and that my copy would run as I wrote it. He never usurped the right to tell me what I saw, or to turn my report into a reflection of an editorial conference in Rockefeller Plaza strained through a recollection of Plattsburg in the First World War. That used to happen constantly to the collective journalists who worked for Henry R. Luce. Ross appreciated a good story, too. He seldom gave unqualified praise to a person—and who deserves it?—but he once cheered me with a note about the "unbelievably high quality" of a piece. He was a ham and understood them.

I wish I had told him once how much I liked him.

Epilogue:
Spot News
About the Leopard

The New York *Times* of April 20, 1963, carried a well-played three-column headline at the bottom center of page ten over a story that reinforced my ribs with extra rocks because it so buttressed what I have said so often. The heads were:

WIRTZ SAYS LABOR NEWS IS DISTORTED IN PRESS

BY JOSEPH A. LOFTUS

SECRETARY HITS "CATCHWORDS OF INTELLECTUAL
GUTTER" IN EDITORIALS AND ARTICLES

This followed by a fortnight or so the long stoppages of newspapers in New York and Cleveland that had provoked among their unaffected colleagues a beating of breasts and rending of garments unparalleled since the Massacre of the Innocents, inspiring new world records in standing indignation, running recrimination, duration of ululation, and the 10,000-meter howl of horror. (Publishers have never affected the stiff upper lip, and reading the sideline press during the New York and Cleveland struggles was like listening to a flock of jaybirds root for another jaybird in the hands of a cat.)

The *Times* story was datelined Washington and began:

W. Willard Wirtz, Secretary of Labor, asked newspaper editors today to take a fresh look at labor management news.

"I count it a matter of serious concern that the public receives in the press what is, in my view of it, a seriously distorted picture of American labor and labor relations,"

533

Mr. Wirtz told the American Society of Newspaper Editors . . .

"Is it . . ." he asked, "inherent in the necessities, or the rationalizations, of journalism, that every labor news story, and almost every editorial, must be cast in the polarized, loaded, semantically fraudulent catchwords of the intellectual gutter?

"I mean 'goon' and 'yellow dog contracts,' and 'scabs' and 'right to work laws' and 'labor monopoly' and 'compulsory arbitration' and 'featherbedding' and the like."

(Up to here the secretary's piece might have been a paraphrase of many of mine, or of John Macy's, who wrote the Press article in *Civilization in the United States*, the synthesis that was the young intellectual's favorite book to cite in argument in 1922. Macy wrote, "Almost invariably, the news of a strike is, if not falsified, so shaped as to be unfavorable to the workers," and the New York and Cleveland instances were particularly bad ones journalistically—except for a postscript that I hope to get around to—because it was a *newspaper* labor dispute. The situation in forty years has somewhat disimproved.)

"Is it enough excuse," asked the Secretary of Labor in this not very Leftish government, "that this is the way a lot of readers think? Or are these reader habits the product in part of writer habits of intellectual laziness, or worse?" Here I believe that as a speaker before the annual convention of the American Society of Newspaper Editors, Mr. Wirtz was being polite. Reader reactions to the newspaper anti-labor line are, as I have hinted in "Inflamed, But Cool," predominantly skeptical, but they have no alternative account put before them. There is no way of knowing what they think, and if there were, it would not excuse lying.

The presence of the Wirtz story in the *Times* pleased, although I will not say that it astonished, me. The Secretary of Labor is an important public official. He was addressing the heads of the next most important department of most newspapers, in the national Capitol. What he had to say in their august presence was not often said. It, therefore, rated space.

Mr. Nixon, I thought momentarily, had perhaps set a pattern; in his case, newspapers had printed attacks on themselves, and perhaps now it was S.O.P. I turned eagerly to each of the six other newspapers published in New York. In none could I find the Wirtz quotation. They could hardly have missed it, since he spoke before the A.S.N.E. (This was not an instance of the inadequate network of which I have otherwheres written. Indeed, there were in several papers evidences that Wirtz's presence had not gone entirely unremarked —courtesy excerpts from the duller portions of his speech.)

Since six of the seven papers in New York had ignored strictures on themselves, I concluded that the chances were six to one that if New York had been a one-ownership town, Wirtz's edition of *The Press* would never have reached the New York public at all, and I wondered how many it had reached out of town. In 1920, in a book called *Liberty and the News,* the young (30) and undented Walter Lippmann, discussing this same immunity of the press from public examination—since it was the only medium of publicity and wouldn't print any press criticism—wrote: "In a few generations it will seem ludicrous to historians that a people professing government by the will of the people should have made no serious effort to guarantee the news without which a governing opinion cannot exist. . . . And then they will recall the centuries during which the Church enjoyed immunity from criticism, and perhaps they will insist that the news structure of secular society was not seriously examined for analogous reasons."

The condition that already alarmed Lippmann and Macy in the twenties then has worsened with the diminution of diversity in the press, which was even then less uniform than now. The move toward monopoly in each city, continues, like a cataract moving across the last seeing quarter of the victim's second eye.

Since the first edition of *The Press,* in 1961, the Milwaukee *Journal* has acquired the *Sentinel* from Hearst, making of the city, eleventh in population (800,000), a one-ownership town. The fifteenth city,

New Orleans, already was one-ownership, and my favorite Mr. Newhouse, by buying the monopoly, with its already sensationally poor display of free lunch, for $42,000,000, gave some clue to what a bonanza a monopoly in a big town can be.

It is, as Roy Thomson once gratefully remarked of Scottish Television, like a license to print money. Mr. Newhouse, I hear, has already knocked the pretzels off the free lunch. He has to get that money back.

In Los Angeles, the third largest city in the country, where there were in 1961 only two ownerships, competing in both morning and evening fields, the proud exemplars of the competitive system came to an agreement, which they attempted for a clownish moment to pass off as a simultaneous spontaneous decision, each to sacrifice one ewe lamb to the ruling deity of the industry, which is Profit. This left the Chandlers alone in the morning field with the Los Angeles *Times,* and the Hearsts in the evening with something whose compound name I at the moment forget.

The Hearsts have acquired the Scripps-Howard half of the *Call-Bulletin* in San Francisco, reducing that from a two-and-a-half-ownership town to a two-ownership, with competition only in the morning—although I don't suppose this can be counted a loss, since the *Call-Bulletin* could hardly have been competing against itself even when it had two owners. (Incidentally, the notion of *old* William Randolph Hearst and old Edward W. Scripps owning a paper together would have been as hard to contemplate as the Franco-German alliance, but there isn't even a pretense of hostility among today's "rivals"—they are all selling as small beer and putting out as few peanuts as possible.) The Hearsts have also killed a paper of no account in Boston, a city which is often Exhibit A for the exception-takers because it has three competing commercial ownerships besides the *Christian Science Monitor,* and still hasn't anything first-class. My guess is that either the *Globe* or the *Herald,* freed of the stimulus of the free lunch at the competing saloon, would give still less for the reader's money.

None of these developments is epoch-making or heart-breaking. No paper of distinction was involved, although the Los Angeles *Examiner,* the Hearst foldup there, was once a great instrument of power in politics and the moving picture industry. The reason I cite them is lest the reader think that any development since the publication of the first edition of this book has tended to discredit its theme: the march to private monopoly and its inevitable, because profitable, consequences—newspapers newsless or filled with synthetic "news." This is an economic process like the displacement of oranges from "orange drink." In the intervening two years there has been, if anything, an *acceleration.*

Mr. Lippmann, in his hot youth, wrote, "No one can manage anything on pap. Neither can a people." Neither can they manage on moldy peanuts.

The most spectacular press event of the period was, without doubt, the stoppage of New York newspapers from December 8, 1962, to April 1, 1963; and the second most spectacular, the strike of Cleveland newspaper unions against the papers there that began a few days earlier and ended a few days later. The Cleveland strike, because it played so nearly day and date with the much bigger show in New York, received less national attention than it otherwise might have, but showed the same underlying emotional pattern; the issues did not appear great or hard to solve, but the hostility that they brought to the surface was amazing. (On the press, at least, it had an Oedipal character, with father-figure Louis Seltzer, the Scripps-Howard "publisher"—as used here the word means Pro-consul for a rich province—going into after-all-that-I've-done-for-you tantrums on television, which outwardly placid veterans of the staff explained to strangers: "There comes a time when you've just got to show you're a man.")

Of the New York strike, which naturally absorbed my attention, except for prizefights and book reviews, during its duration, I wrote, in part, in a piece that appeared on January 26 in *The New Yorker:* *

---

* See "Offers and Demands" in this volume.—Ed.

What disquiets me more than the possibility that newspapers *qua* newspapers will disappear is the increasing uniformity of the survivors as they wait to coalesce. The stoppage has illuminated this, just as the conjugal reaction to a stranger's interference illuminates the essential solidarity of a loving couple. The "competition" among the six New York ownerships has proved a pale and sometime thing compared to the competition of all of them against all of their employees. It seems naïve now for Bertram Powers, the leader of the striking printers, to have offered the financially weaker papers a separate peace—or separate individual peaces—when he struck the *Times* and the *News* and the *Journal* and the *World-Telegram*. The Hearsts, for example, own both the unstruck, because deemed "weak," *Mirror* and the struck, because deemed "strong," *Journal-American*. It is hard to imagine them running one of their papers while a strike is on against the other. As for the *Herald Tribune* and the *Post*, at a more competitive period in newspaper history they might have been expected to run, restoring their failing strength with the Christmas advertising revenues made available to them by the printers' generosity. They had ground not merely to hold but to make up if they were ever to get back into contention with their rivals. Their loyalty to their rivals, who are also their prospective purchasers when the pinch comes, was touching. It is all very sad, because the surest way for the seven papers to anesthetize the public to future monopoly is to make it evident that they are already alike. Even a sham battle might have improved public opinion of all seven. (Mrs. Dorothy Schiff, the publisher of the *Post,* and John Hay Whitney, the publisher of the *Tribune,* if we are to adopt *Editor & Publisher*'s point of view, might also have done their colleagues a favor by continuing to print, and so making sure that the public would not lose the habit of newspaper reading.)

As for who is to blame for the weary length that the stoppage has attained,[1] I can give no judgment beyond

---

[1] At *that* point, the twenty-sixth, only 49 days. Mrs. Schiff did bolt the other publishers and get out her paper again on March 4, Day 86. This was, according to A. H. Raskin of the *Times* in his masterly retrospective on the stoppage, "The first important power shift."

juxtaposing headlines in the *Guild Reporter,* the organ of the American Newspaper Guild, and in *Editor & Publisher:*

Guild Reporter:
N.Y. PUBLISHERS SHUNNING
COMPROMISE IN STOPPAGE

E. & P.:
PUBLISHERS ACCUSE
UNION IN STALEMATE

I have a personal hunch, too, that Amory H. Bradford, the spokesman for the Publishers' Association of New York City, and Bertram A. Powers, the printers' president, both suffer from the overcompensation that frequently afflicts boys with flossy first names, requiring them to fight so often to defend their schoolyard dignity that fighting becomes an adult habit. (For a negotiator I should always prefer somebody named Jack or Mac.) As for the issues in the strike against the four strong papers, I can only say that, as a habitual employee, I would, if offered a choice on a 6-to-5, pick-'em basis, naturally take Mr. Powers's position. . . . And the fight—because complete newspaper automation is not yet ready to be introduced—resembles those obstinate and bloody inter-trench combats of the First World War, whose declared object was to establish "dominance" over the enemy before the big push began. These invariably resulted only in heavy casualties, even when they had been preceded by long bombardments designed to weaken the nerve of the defenders. In this instance 25 years of anti-labor news, employing the semantic ammunition noted by Wirtz, had filled out the bombardment simile, but it had apparently failed of its object. "Automation," which has become a blessed word, like Mesopotamia, with employers, also proved a dud. (Anybody who refuses to believe that automation and salvation are synonymous is henceforth suspect of a new form of subversion; he might as well be against togetherness or William F. Buckley.)

I noted in the January 26 story that "the employer, in strike stories, always 'offers,' and the union 'de-

mands.' A publisher, for example, never 'demands'
that the union men agree to work for a four-bit raise;
the union never 'offers' to accept more." ("Demand,"
in English, is an arrogant word; "offer," a large, generous one.)

"The *Times,* ironically, would have covered the
strike and the stoppage more thoroughly" than the un-
engaged newspapers that described it, I wrote during
the course of my remarks, and the *Times,* when it reappeared with the *Herald Tribune, News, Mirror, Journal-American,* and *World-Telegram* on April 1—the
Post had preceded them—more than justified my estimate, publishing Raskin's retrospective story of the
struggle, which is possibly the most complete and unprejudiced story of a labor dispute ever published in
an American newspaper, and all the more remarkable
because the *Times* was a principal in the dispute.

Raskin, a veteran labor reporter who has now, except for such special occasions, retreated to the editorial rooms, started by quoting a bilateral avowal of
failure, from an official of the Publishers' Association
and from a union officer. The stoppage, both admitted,
was an uncompensated-for disaster. Raskin then set
out to recount it, but not as the agent of either party
—and here the *Times* earns the highest marks for letting him go his way. "New Yorkers, baffled by sixteen
weeks of hearing little more than that negotiations
were on or off, may find some clue to the answers in
the untold story of what went on," he began.

He then went on at great, but not excessive, length
(18 columns) to narrate the nearly endless and almost
causeless knocking together of heads that had gone on
over inconsequential issues for 114 days. Of Bertram
Powers, the president of the New York Local of the
International Typographical Union, Raskin wrote that
he was described by "one of the army of peacemakers
who got to know him well" as "honest, clean, democratic—and impossible," and of Bradford, vice-president and general manager of Raskin's own corporate
employer: "One top-level mediator said Mr. Bradford
brought an attitude of such disdain into the conference

room that the mediator often felt he ought to ask the hotel to send up more heat."

Summarizing part of Raskin, I myself wrote: "The deadline was two o'clock on the morning of December 8. A few hours before that, after four months of so-called negotiations, the publishers declared their terms —that the printer sign for a small money package and that they drop their demands on what Raskin calls 'issues more complex than the money gap . . . underlying the shutdown.' Powers presented his counter-offer at 1:45 A.M. Like an Arab with a turnip to sell, he asked for far more than he hoped to get, as he later admitted. This was a completely unrealistic confrontation, at best. Of the underlying 'issues more complex'—a common expiration date for contracts between the publishers and the unions, a 35-hour week, and limits on the introduction of automation—the printers were destined to win all three, after a costly and anguished period, during which, according to Mr. Starnes, the city forgot who it was. But in money they were destined to receive very little more than the publishers had demanded that they accept. They got a "package" valued at $12.63 a week instead of the publishers' proposal of $9.20. The magnitude of one of the underlying issues may be judged from Raskin's summary of the shorter work week: 'The printers wanted their basic work time cut from 36¼ hours a week to 35, the standard already in force for the Guild.' With a 5-day week, this means a difference of 15 minutes a day, but the printers said they would sacrifice, in return, 15 of the 30 minutes of wash-up time for which they had been receiving pay. 'The publishers resisted on the ground that there was no real assurance the printers would actually stop taking the wash-up time,' Raskin says. Time clocks in the lavatories might have averted terribly apparent astronomical disruption." *

I felt pleased that my January 26 surmise of what was going on behind the scenes, and of what the strike was really about, proved, by Raskin's story, to have

---

* See "Step by Step with Mr. Raskin" in this volume.—Ed.

been fairly accurate. But what pleased me even more about the *Times* story was that a newspaper had for once permitted a first-class reporter to have his way, without editing him on grounds of policy, editorial omniscience, or even length, which last often serves as pretext for an editor to remove all portions of a story that do not fit in with the publisher's views, while leaving intact all those that do. The play on the Wirtz story was encouraging, too.

Everybody knows what it is that one swallow doesn't make, but I am an incorrigible optimist about newspapers.

Index

Newspapers are indexed under the cities in which they are published—except for certain national and specialized newspapers, for example, the *Christian Science Monitor*.